ROMAN PEOPLE

ROMAN PEOPLE

THIRD EDITION

Robert B. Kebric

University of Louisville

Mayfield Publishing Company

Mountain View, California
London • Toronto

*In memory of Burt M. Kebric
and Florence Hamilton Kebric*

Copyright © 2001, 1997, 1993 by Mayfield Publishing Company

Library of Congress Cataloging-in-Publication Data
Kebric, Robert B.
  Roman people / Robert B. Kebric—3rd ed.
    p. cm.
  Includes bibliographical references and index.
  ISBN 0-7674-1707-0
    1. Rome—Biography. I. Title.

DG203.K43 2000
920.037—dc21   00-038011

Manufactured in the United States of America
10 9 8 7 6 5 4 3 2

Mayfield Publishing Company
1280 Villa Street
Mountain View, California 94041

Sponsoring editor, Holly J. Allen; production editor, April Wells-Hayes; manuscript editor, Barbara McGowran; design manager, Susan Breitbard; text designer, Wendy LaChance; cover designer, Amy Evans-McClure; art editor, Robin Mouat; illustrator, Martha Gilman Roach; print buyer, Danielle Javier. The text was set in 11.5/13.5 Adobe Garamond by Thompson Type and printed on 45# Chromatone Matte by the Banta Book Group.

Cover image: Lawrence Alma-Tadema. *Spring.* 1894. Oil on canvas. 70-1/4 × 31-1/2 in. By permission of the J. Paul Getty Museum.

On the half-title page: Messalina, the teenaged wife of the Emperor Claudius, holding their child, Britannicus (Louvre, Paris).

Chapter openers: The coin shown on the chapter opening pages is a silver denarius (43–42 B.C.) of Brutus, issued to commemorate Caesar's assassination. See Figure 3.7 for the reverse side. One of the most famous Roman coins, there are fewer than 60 known examples. Photograph by Karen A. Peters; courtesy of Harlan J. Berk, Ltd.

Text and illustration credits continue at the back of the book on pages 321–328, which constitute an extension of the copyright page.

 This book was printed on acid-free, recycled paper.

Preface

The Individual in History

People make up societies, comprise civilizations. We may formulate and embrace as many theories and compile as many timetables or lists of significant events as we wish to help us understand the past, but we must always return to the simple reality that people are at the foundation of our inquiries.

So often in studies of eras before our own, people have been forced into the background, assigned a role secondary to theories and events. Their humanness has been forgotten. We tend to race over their names—especially if they sound or appear foreign—to discover what happened. Who they were as individuals within the context of their own times has mostly gone unnoticed.

No "great people" theory or biographical approach to history is being argued here. There have, of course, always been the Caesars and the Constantines; they are too closely tied to the events of their times not to have been given extensive coverage. But most modern texts have developed little more than their political *personas,* and as for the less prominent individuals in ancient society, we have seldom heard of them at all. Characters of lesser note are nonetheless still important for whatever contribution they made to their society. The study of people

from many walks of life adds depth to our understanding of the ancient Romans and, ultimately, of ourselves.

Audience and Approach

Roman People should prove a useful alternative to more traditional event-and-theory books. It is another option for those who enjoy the positive response usually evoked by the biographies of Plutarch and Suetonius and who have had previous success with *Greek People,* the companion to this volume, and the few other modern works that have emphasized people.

Intended for anyone interested in ancient Roman society, *Roman People* attempts to present some ancient Romans as they were, not cardboard figures who lived in a past so distant that it seems they could never have any meaning for us today. The general historical background necessary to understand developments in antiquity is provided, but the emphasis is on people. The choice of the men and women presented here is necessarily limited. Our knowledge of the past extends only as far as our surviving sources allow. Some names will be familiar; others will be more obscure. Interestingly, many of the most memorable figures in Roman history were not Romans at all. Through war or politics—or because they resided, by force or free will, within Rome's Empire—they became indelibly linked with Rome. Several of these "Romans" are also discussed.

Some eras provide more interesting personalities than others. It can be a challenge to match the peculiar circumstances of a particular period with an individual (or individuals) who might best represent some historical or cultural aspect of that period. Because of the long history of Rome, it is especially difficult to provide a successful balance of personalities and continuity. Also, Rome *was* a political society, and discussion of prominent politicians is both inevitable and desirable. Rome provided some of the most fascinating political figures in history. Nonetheless, individuals have been included who illustrate some aspect of human activity or behavior that might have been neglected or only touched upon in more general works. The resultant cross section of people should provide a better understanding of Roman life and the "Roman personality."

Many quotations and extracts from ancient writers—sometimes the subjects themselves—have been incorporated so that the people, as much as possible, can tell their own stories. Numerous maps and illustrations, a chronological table, and a glossary and pronunciation guide also make *Roman People* a more useful book.

A Concluding Observation

When human beings began to keep track of themselves, the question they first asked was "Who am I?" and then, "What did I do?" Their own individual existence was foremost in their thoughts. In our complex and, some would say, impersonal society, the "doing" often seems to take precedence over the "being." *Roman People* tries to keep both in mind—the person *and* his or her accomplishments. It offers the lives and the world of a few people from the distant past in the hope that the gulf of years that separates us from the people of Ancient Rome will begin to diminish.

The Second Edition and Acknowledgments

I welcome the opportunity to prepare a second edition of *Roman People* because the book has been well received and has achieved a wide audience.

Inevitably, the modern publishing process and all its ramifications contributes to error, and I have attempted to correct, revise, or add to any portion of the text that needed such, remaining grateful to those who pointed out any oversight by me or the publisher. The readings at the ends of chapters have been enlarged significantly and reflect the most recent work. An expanded illustration program with many new photos further complements the book's specific content and should increase reader interest. A geographical map of Italy has been added to the map selection, and all maps have been redrawn. New material on women, the family, Roman views on multiculturalism, the Etruscans, the Roman baths, and weather at Rome has also been incorporated. The revised book should, like the new edition of *Greek People*, remain a viable resource through the turn of the century.

I reiterate my appreciation to Professors Thomas W. Africa, Erich S. Gruen, and Frank W. Walbank for reading the original draft of *Roman People*, and to the reviewers of the first edition. Thanks go as well to my previous editor, Lansing Hays; and to Bill Karlen, whose photographic work herein helps to preserve his memory. Special thanks go to users of the first edition. For the second edition, I would like to express my gratitude once again to Professor Walbank, who, as usual, is always ready and willing to spend the time to comment on and encourage a colleague's work; to the following people who reviewed the manuscript for Mayfield: Richard C. Frey, Southern Oregon State College; R. L. Hohlfelder, University of Colorado at Boulder; Timothy Long, Indiana University; C. Renaud, Carthage College; and C. A. Sneddow, University of Utah; to Dennis Korbylo for additional photographic work; to Mayfield Publishing Company for the opportunity to revise *Roman People;* to my editor, Holly Allen, who has overseen the preparation of the new edition; to April Wells-Hayes, my production editor; and, especially, to my wife, Judith Kebric, for her assistance and continued interest in my work.

I am grateful to the various authors, presses, museums, and other photo sources for their permission to use copyrighted material. Specific acknowledgments for translations and the full references for all photos, maps, and other illustrations are listed at the end of the book.

Finally, I wish to thank all the others who in some way assisted me in the preparation of *Roman People.*

The Third Edition and Acknowledgments

Recently, while the downstairs of our house was being finished, I mentioned to the carpenter, Jim Lund, that he had done such a good job that he should "sign" his work somewhere. To my surprise, he answered that he already had—

inside the casing of one of the ceiling beams he had constructed. He also said he had written the date, mentioned the weather, and left a dollar bill in it. When I asked him why he had done so, he replied that when the house was remodeled or torn down in the future (the not too-near future, I hope!), the person doing the work would know he was the one who had built it, the date, and what kind of day it was and would also have something personal of his from the time to hold. He then told me that he began the practice because when he was young, he used to accompany his father, also a carpenter, on his projects. Whenever they did remodeling jobs in older neighborhoods on houses built in the early part of the century, they would find the same kind of messages. He said he was fascinated to find the name of a carpenter like himself from the 1920s, or that on a particular date the weather had been "sunny," or a penny or nickel put there by someone now long dead. In that manner, he added with a touch of emotion, he felt a kinship with that person and that his profession was literally being passed down from generation to generation by craftspeople who had preceded him. Now he wanted to be remembered in the same way fifty or seventy-five years down the road. I told him that without really knowing it, he was enacting what history is really all about: who I am, what I did, and how I pass on information about my own time to those in the future. I can think of no more apt example to convey, simply, what history is all about than this one that just "fell into my lap." People seem to have the idea that the study of history is something separate from what they do every day—when in fact, like Jim, they are exercising the historical process with everything they do. It was with this kind of thought in mind that I originally set out to write this volume, and

I am gratified that it continues to attract new readers and keep previous ones interested. I am pleased to prepare this third edition.

I have added new sections on Roman women, including Nero's mother, Agrippina, who was murdered by her conniving son, and a birthday invitation sent from one friend to another while living a rather monotonous life on the Roman frontier in north Britain as wives of officers stationed there. Pliny's loving and thorough description of his villa, Josephus' eyewitness account of a Roman imperial military triumph, and comments about the millennium, Dionysius Exiguus, and time-reckoning complete the major text additions. I have also added new photographic material, much of it about women, and recent supplemental bibliography, which has been appended to the existing bibliographical sections.

Most of those who have assisted me in the past with the creation and production of this volume have already been mentioned in previous prefaces. I thank them again and express my appreciation. I would also like to add specific thanks to Professor Gerald E. Kadish for advice on Egyptian-related material and Professor Arthur J. Slavin and Professor Kerry E. Spiers for their input and help over the years. I mention Glenn Bugh, Virginia Technical Institute and State University; Kevin Carroll, Arizona State University; Robert L. Hohlfelder, University of Colorado at Boulder, and Myra Levin, Towson State University, as new readers for this edition and am grateful for their input. I also wish to thank Nikki Lewis and Gene Johnson for their assistance in preparing additional photographs. I remain indebted to the various authors, presses, museums, and all others who have contributed in some way to the success of this work—especially my wife, Judith.

Contents

Chapter 10

Emperors and Entertainment   276

Crowds, Cheers, and the Circus Maximus—Diocles the Charioteer

Epilogue   302

Whose Millennium Is It, Anyway?—Passing Time: "Little Dennis" (Dionysius Exiguus) Leaves a Big Impression   307

Illustrations, Maps, and Charts

Figures

Maps

Charts

Chronology

The following chronology emphasizes the major events and people discussed in this volume.

Date	Events and People

Monarchy (753–509 B.C.)

753	Traditional date Rome is founded by Romulus
753–509	Rome ruled by seven kings
6th century	Period of Etruscan domination

Republic (509–31 B.C.)

508	Horatius at the bridge (Chapter 1)
5th century	Conflict between *patricians* and *plebeians;* local wars with Latins, Aequi, Volsci, and Veii
494	*Concilium plebis* and office of tribune of the plebs established
451–449	Rome's first law code, the Law of the Twelve Tables, established

387	Gallic sack of Rome; heroics of Camillus (Chapter 1)
367	Licinio-Sextian law established that one consul elected each year be plebeian
340–338	Latin League defeated and disbanded
327–304	War with the Samnites; Appian Way built
300	Ogulnian law makes plebeians eligible for all religious offices—last barrier to their holding any office removed

287	*Lex Hortensia* makes decisions of the *concilium plebis (plebiscita)* binding on all Romans

280	Date by which Etruscans, Gauls, and Samnites had been subdued
280–275	War with Pyrrhus of Epirus, Rome's first international foe
272	Date by which Rome extends influence over all of Italy
264–241	First Punic War with Carthage over control of Sicily (which became Rome's first province)

250 ──

c. 240–c. 207	Livius Andronicus, founder of Roman literature, writing his works
237	Sardinia and Corsica occupied; made second Roman province in 227 B.C.
229	Rome established protectorate on Illyrian coast; first presence in Greek East
218–201	Second Punic War; Hannibal (Chapter 1) invades Italy
216	Roman disaster at Cannae
212–205	First Macedonian War with Philip V
213–211	Roman siege of Syracuse; Archimedes and Marcellus (Chapter 1)
202	Scipio Africanus defeats Hannibal at Zama; Carthage surrenders in 201 B.C.; Fabius Pictor composing first Roman history (in Greek)

200 ──

200–197	Second Macedonian War with Philip V
197–133	Spanish Wars
191–188	Syrian War against Antiochus III
184	Cato the Elder is censor
171–167	Third Macedonian War with Perseus; Aetolians butchered; 1000 Achaeans deported, including historian Polybius; 150,000 Epirotes sold into slavery

150 ──

149	Permanent court established to deal with extortion in provinces; death of Cato
149–146	Third Punic War; Scipio Aemilianus destroys Carthage; North Africa annexed as province
148–146	Fourth Macedonian War; Achaean League crushed, Corinth destroyed; Macedonia becomes Roman province; end of Greek autonomy
135–132	First Sicilian Slave Revolt; Eunus (Chapter 2)
133	Spanish Wars end; Roman mastery of Mediterranean world completed

---

The Late Republic (133–31 B.C.): Internal problems replace external ones; the "Roman Revolution," the gradual breakdown of the Republic and its replacement with one-man rule, takes place.

133	Tribune Tiberius Gracchus' land reform bill and his assassination
123–122	Tribunates of Gaius Gracchus; popular cause at Rome elevated to serious political movement

121	*Senatus consultum ultimum* evoked for first time; death of Gaius Gracchus; Cornelia (Chapter 2)
112–105	Jugurthine War
109–101	Wars with Cimbri and Teutones
107–100	Marius consul six times; Roman army reformed
104–100	Second Sicilian Slave War
91–88	Rome's war with Italian allies; Italians granted citizenship (89 B.C.)
88–82	Rome's first civil war
88	Consulship of Sulla; quarrels with Marius over Eastern command against Mithridates of Pontus; Sulla seizes Rome; Marius escapes
88–85	Sulla wars with Mithridates
87	Marius retakes Rome; dies in 86 B.C. during seventh consulship
82–78	Sulla dictator; reforms Rome along conservative lines; death of Sulla
75	
73–71	Spartacus' slave revolt (Chapter 2)
70	Crassus and Pompey consuls; Cicero gains prominence through prosecution of Verres for extortion
67	Pompey commissioned to clear the seas of pirates; given Eastern command in 66 B.C. to defeat Mithridates (d. 63 B.C.) and reorganize Eastern provinces
63	Cicero's consulship; Catilinarian conspiracy; Cato the Younger emerges as powerful conservative; Caesar (aedile in 65 B.C.) elected *pontifex maximus*
62	Catiline defeated and killed; Pompey returns triumphant from East; Caesar praetor
60	Caesar, Crassus, and Pompey form "First Triumvirate"
59	Caesar is consul
58–49	Caesar in Gaul; invades Britain in 55 and 54 B.C.
58–52	Civil disturbances in Rome led by Clodius and Milo
56	Triumvirs renew pact at Luca; Crassus and Pompey consuls for 55 B.C.
54	Death of Julia, Caesar's daughter and wife of Pompey; links between triumvirs weaken
53	Crassus killed at Carrhae in Mesopotamia; "Triumvirate" ends
52	Clodius killed by Milo; Pompey made sole consul to restore order; Milo exiled
51–49	Gaul annexed; attempts by Caesar's enemies to disarm him fail; negotiations break down
50	
49	Caesar crosses Rubicon; civil wars erupt; Pompey flees to Greece with army; Turia is married (Chapter 4)

48–44	Caesar is dictator
48	Pompey defeated at Pharsalus and slain in Egypt; Caesar meets Cleopatra
47–45	Caesar's victories in Pontus, Africa, and Spain; Cato's death in Africa (46 B.C.)
45	Cicero entertains Caesar in December (Chapter 3)
44	Caesar assassinated on March 15; Cleopatra flees Rome; Octavian designated Caesar's legal heir
43	Antony, Octavian, and Lepidus form "Second Triumvirate"; Cicero executed in proscriptions; death of Brutus' wife, Porcia (Chapter 3)
42	Brutus and Cassius defeated at Philippi
41–30	Cleopatra's relationship with Antony
40	Death of Antony's wife, Fulvia (Chapter 4); Pact of Brundisium; Antony and Octavian divide up Roman world; Antony marries Octavia
38 or 37	Horace's journey (Chapter 4); "Triumvirate" renewed at Tarentum (37 B.C.)
37–31	Tensions between Antony and Octavian; Antony with Cleopatra in East
34	"Donations of Alexandria"
31	Battle at Actium; Antony and Cleopatra commit suicide in 30 B.C.; Octavian seizes Egypt

The Roman Empire (31 B.C.–476 A.D.)

27 B.C.	The Principate begins; Octavian, now Augustus, made ruler of Roman world
13 B.C.	Divorce of Zois and Antipater (Chapter 9)
6 B.C.–2 A.D.	Tiberius retires to Rhodes; meets Thrasyllus (Chapter 5)
2 B.C.	Forum of Augustus with Temple of Mars dedicated; Julia banished for adulteries (Chapter 5)
4 A.D.	Augustus adopts Tiberius as heir
8 A.D.	Ovid (Chapter 10) banished by Augustus
9 A.D.	Teutoburgian Wood massacre (Chapter 6)
14 A.D.	Death of Augustus; death of Julia

The Julio-Claudian Dynasty

Tiberius (14–37 A.D.)

	Apicius active (Chapter 6)
14–31	Period of Sejanus' influence on Tiberius
19	Death of Germanicus; astrologers, Jews, and others expelled from Rome; Paulina (Chapter 5)
25	Suicide of Cremutius Cordus (Chapter 5)

26	Tiberius leaves Rome for Capri
27	Atilius' debacle at Fidenae (Chapter 6)
c. 30	Jesus crucified in Judaea
36	Death of Thrasyllus

Gaius or Caligula (37–41 A.D.)

Claudius (41–54 A.D.)

Nero (54–68 A.D.)

54–62	Seneca (Chapter 9) influences Nero; heads literary circle that includes Petronius (Chapter 5)
c. 61–113	Lifetime of Pliny the Younger; Larcius Macedo murdered by his slaves (Chapter 2); Ummidia Quadratilla and Domitius reach old age (Chapter 7)
62	Tigellinus (Chapter 10) becomes Nero's favorite; end of Seneca's influence
64	The great fire at Rome; first Christian persecution
65	Plot to overthrow Nero fails; suicides of Seneca and Petronius (d. 66 A.D.)
66–73	Jewish revolt; Vespasian in Judaea; destruction of Jerusalem (70 A.D.)
69	Year of the Four Emperors: Galba, Otho, Vitellius, and Vespasian

---

Flavian Dynasty (69–96 A.D.)

Titus (79–81 A.D.)

August 24, 79	Eruption of Mt. Vesuvius destroys Pompeii and Herculaneum; death of Pliny the Elder; Pliny the Younger eyewitness to eruption (Chapter 6)
80	Colosseum dedicated

Domitian (81–96 A.D.)

90	Cornelia's execution (Chapter 9)

Reign of the Five "Good" or "Adopted" Emperors (96–180 A.D.)

Nerva (96–98 A.D.)

97	Last recorded action by Rome's assemblies; death of Verginius Rufus (Chapter 7)

Trajan (98–117 A.D.)

100–112(?)	Tacitus composing *Histories* and *Annals*
101–106	Trajan's war against Dacians
105	Death of Spurinna (Chapter 7)
111–113	Pliny the Younger governor of Bithynia-Pontus; correspondence with Trajan about Christians (Chapter 9); Pliny dies in office
114–117	Trajan's campaign against Parthia; annexation of Armenia and Mesopotamia; Empire reaches greatest geographical limits

Hadrian (117–138 A.D.)

        Hadrian's Mausoleum, Hadrian's wall, and Hadrian's Villa built; Suetonius, Juvenal, and Appian active

122–146   Career of the charioteer Diocles (Chapter 10)

132–135   Revolt of Bar-Cochba in Judaea; defeat and dispersal of Jews

Antoninus Pius (138–161 A.D.)

144 or 145   Marcus Aurelius' letter to Fronto (Chapter 9)

150   Philoe's horoscope (Chapter 5)

Marcus Aurelius (161–180 A.D.)

Lucius Aurelius Verus (161–169 A.D.)

165–167   Plague ravages Italy and Empire; Christians persecuted

167–180   Period of Marcus' wars with Germans. Persecution at Lyons, 177 A.D.

Commodus (180–192 A.D.)

Pertinax (January 1–March 28, 193 A.D.)

Didius Julianus (March 28–June 1, 193 A.D.)

The Severan Dynasty (193–235 A.D.)

        Historians Herodian and Dio and Christian writer Tertullian active

Septimius Severus (193–211 A.D.)

Julia Domna (193–217 A.D.)

        Son of Arion writes home (Chapter 8)

194–197   Civil wars with Pescennius Niger and Clodius Albinus

198   Septimius' victory over Parthia

March 7, 203   Martyrdom of Vibia Perpetua (Chapter 9)

203   Arch of Septimius Severus dedicated

205   Death of Plautianus; suicide of Baebius Marcellinus (Chapter 8)

206–207   Bulla the bandit (Chapter 8)

208–211   Septimius' campaigns in Britain and death at York

Caracalla (211–217 A.D.)

Geta (211–212 A.D.)

212   Caracalla executes Geta; extends citizenship to all free residents within the Empire

Macrinus (217–218 A.D.)

217–235   Period of activity of Julia Maesa, Julia Soaemias, and Julia Mamaea

Elagabalus (218–222 A.D.)

Severus Alexander (222–235 A.D.)

Period of the "Barracks Emperors" (235–284 A.D.)

During this period of military anarchy, many generals were literally raised to the throne by their troops from the "barracks." There are over twenty emperors, some ruling jointly, during these fifty years, and many pretenders.

Philip I (244–249 A.D.)

247	1000th anniversary of Rome

Decius (249–251 A.D.)

249–250	First empirewide persecution of Christians
251	Goths and other barbarians begin large-scale invasions of the Empire

Aurelian (270–275 A.D.)

271–275	Aurelian Wall built around Rome; unity restored to the Empire
272	Defeat of Zenobia of Palmyra (Chapter 8); Palmyra destroyed (273 A.D.)

The Later Roman Empire

Diocletian (284–316 A.D.; abdicated 305 A.D.)

In 286 A.D., Diocletian divided rule of the Empire and appointed Maximian (286–305 A.D.) his co-ruler. Diocletian ruled the East and Maximian the West. In 293 A.D., Diocletian created the "Tetrarchy" (four-man rule) by appointing two additional junior emperors, called "Caesars," who shared the administrative duties with himself and Maximian.

301	Diocletian's edict on price and wage controls
303–311	Persecution of Christians

Galerius (305–311 A.D.)

	Galerius, Diocletian's former Caesar, raised as Eastern Emperor

Constantius (305–306 A.D.)

	Constantius, Maximian's former Caesar, raised as Western Emperor
306–337	Career of Constantine
308	Civil wars; Diocletian comes out of retirement to restore order to the Tetrarchy

Licinius (308–324 A.D.)

308	Licinius confirmed as Emperor of the West; Constantine becomes his Caesar; Galerius remains Eastern Augustus
311	Galerius issues deathbed edict ending Christian persecution; civil wars renewed
312	Constantine seizes Rome at battle of Milvian Bridge
313	Edict of Milan; Christianity becomes official religion of the Empire
315	Arch of Constantine
316	As co-emperors, Constantine rules the West and Licinius the East

324–337	Licinius executed; Constantine sole ruler of Roman Empire
325	First ecumenical council held at Nicaea
330	Capital moved to Constantinople

Julian the Apostate (361–363 A.D.)

	Julian disavows Christianity; tries to restore old Roman religion
378	Goths defeat Rome at Adrianople

Theodosius I (379–395 A.D.)

	Last great emperor of East and West; bans all non-Christian practices
410	Sack of Rome by Visigoths; first sack of city in 797 years
450	Consentius' chariot race (Chapter 10)
451	Defeat of Attila the Hun
455	Sack of Rome by Vandals
476	Final "barbarization" of the Western Empire
493–526	Reign of Theodoric the Ostrogoth; Thomas the charioteer active (Chapter 10)
527–565	Justinian is first great ruler of Byzantine Empire
1453	Constantinople falls to Turks; "Roman Empire" ends

Map 1 *Ancient Italy*

Map 2   *Geographical map of ancient Italy*

A Roman Professor

Lucius Orbilius Pupillus was born in Beneventum. . . . First he obtained a job as a menial servant for the town magistrates. Then he joined the army, was decorated, and eventually was promoted to the cavalry. When he had completed his years of service, he returned to his studies and thus fulfilled an ambition he had had since boyhood.

For a long time he lived as a teacher in his hometown, but then in his fiftieth year . . . he moved to Rome and taught there. However, he earned more fame than money. In one of his books, written when he was an old man, he complains that he is "a pauper, living in an attic." He also published a book called *My Trials and Tribulations* in which he complains about the insults and injuries done to him by negligent or ambitious parents [of students].

He had a fiery temper which he unleashed not only on his rival teachers, whom he castigated on every occasion, but also on his students. . . . Even men of rank and position did not escape his scathing sarcasm. . . .

He lived to be almost 100 years old. . . .

[Suetonius, *On Teachers* 9; trans. J. Shelton]

I

Rome, Expansion and Conquest

The Siege of Syracuse (213–211 B.C.)
Marcellus the War-Lord,
Archimedes the Weapons-Master

There can surely be nobody so petty or so apathetic in his outlook that he has no desire to discover by what means and under what system of government the Romans succeeded in . . . bringing under their rule almost the whole of the inhabited world.
(Polybius, *Histories* 1.1.5)

"Friend I have not much to say; stop and read it," begins the earnest plea on the tombstone of a Roman woman named Claudia, who lived in the second century B.C. It continues:

> This tomb, which is not fair, is for a fair woman. . . . She loved her husband in her heart. She bore two sons, one of whom she left on earth, the other beneath it. She was pleasant to talk with, and she walked with grace. She kept the house and worked in wool. That is all. You may go.
> (*Inscriptiones Latinae Liberae Rei Publicae* 973: *Inscriptiones Latinae Selectae* 8403)

In a letter sent to his mother from Egypt sometime during the period of the Roman Empire, a young soldier wrote:

> My dear mother,
> I hope this finds you well. When you receive my letter I shall be much obliged if you will send me some money. I haven't got a bit left, because I have bought a donkey-cart and spent all my money. Do send me a riding coat, some oil, and above all my monthly allowance. When I was last home you promised not to leave me penniless, and now you treat me like a dog. Father came to see me the other day and

1

left me nothing. Everybody laughs at me now, and says "His father is a soldier, his father gave him nothing." Valerius' mother sent him a pair of pants, a measure of oil, a box of food and some money. Do send me some money and don't leave me like this. Give my love to everybody at home.

Your loving son.

(Berliner Griechische Urkunden [Ägyptische Urkunden aus den Königlichen Museen zu Berlin 13.15.1])

When one thinks of Ancient Romans, the sentiments reflected above are not what first come to mind. Rome inevitably conjures up images of armies, oppression, unrivaled grandeur and spectacle. Stereotypes aside, the million or so Romans who populated the city of Rome by the Early Empire had to cope with the same kind of everyday problems faced by citizens of great capitals at any time. Still, there was no place quite like Rome:

Around [the Mediterranean] lie the continents far and wide, pouring an endless flow of goods to [Rome]. There is brought from every land and sea whatever is brought forth by the seasons and is produced by all countries, rivers, lakes, and the skills of Greeks and foreigners. So that anyone who wants to behold all these products must either journey through the whole world to see them or else come to this city. For whatever is raised or manufactured by each people is assuredly always here to overflowing. So many merchantmen arrive here with cargoes from all over, at every season, and with each return of the harvest, that the city seems like a common warehouse of the world. One can see so many cargoes from India, or, if you wish from Arabia Felix, that one may surmise that the trees there have been left permanently bare, and that those people must come here to beg for their own goods whenever they need anything. Clothing from Babylonia and the luxuries from the barbarian lands beyond

Figure 1.1   Imperial Rome in the fourth century A.D. *(reconstruction)*

arrive in much greater volume and more easily than if one had to sail from Naxos or Cythnos to Athens, transporting any of their products. Egypt, Sicily, and the civilized part of Africa are [Rome's] farms. The arrival and departure of ships never ceases, so that it is astounding that the sea—not to mention the harbor—suffices for the merchantmen. . . . and all things converge here, trade, seafaring, agriculture, metallurgy, all the skills which exist and have existed, anything that is begotten and grows. Whatever cannot be seen here belongs completely to the category of nonexistent things.

(Aelius Aristides, *To Rome* 11–13)

While all roads may have led to Rome, the noise, the bustle, the stench, and the mass of humanity that they dumped at the city's door-step made living there a struggle. As one Roman writer described it: "Rome is perched on hills and propped in valleys, its tenements hanging aloft, its roads terrible, its alleys narrow!" (Cicero, *Contra Rullum: De Lege Agraria* 2.96). Even the privileged frequently escaped to seaside villas for relief from the urban misery.

As late as the second century B.C., "Some made fun . . . of the city . . . not yet beautiful in either public or private domains" (Livy, *History of Rome* 40.4.7). Apparently, little had changed until the time of Augustus (27 B.C.–14 A.D.) when, as this glowing line from Suetonius' biography asserts, Rome's first emperor found "a city of brick and left it one of marble" (*Augustus* 28.3). Augustus must have somehow overlooked the old, dilapidated part of the city that Juvenal describes in his *Third Satire* (194–305):

> Rome is supported on pipestems, matchsticks . . . it's cheaper, so, for the landlord to shore up his ruins, patch up the old cracked walls, and notify all the tenants they can sleep secure, though the beams are in ruins above them.

Then, too, there was always the danger of fire:

> . . . I prefer to live where
> Fires and midnight panics are not quite such common events.
> By the time the smoke's got up to your third-floor apartment
> (And you still asleep) your downstairs neighbor is roaring
> For water, and shifting his bits and pieces to safety.
> If the alarm goes at ground-level, the last to fry
> Will be the attic tenant, way up among the nesting
> Pigeons, with nothing but tiles between himself and the weather.

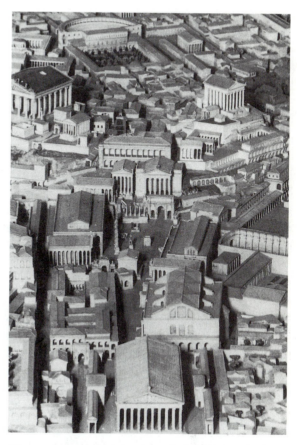

Figure 1.2 *Overview of a reconstruction of the Roman Forum at the time of the Emperor Constantine (early fourth century A.D.). In the background is the Capitoline Hill with the Temple of Jupiter (left) and the Temple of Juno (right).*

Juvenal lists insomnia, ulcers, and indigestion as other urban "advantages." As if they were not enough, there were always the congested and noisy streets:

> The wheels creak by on the narrow streets of the wards, the drivers squabble and brawl when they're stopped. . . . Traffic gets in our way, in front, around and behind us. . . . Mud is thick on my shins, I am trampled by somebody's big feet. Now what?—a soldier grinds his hobnails into my toes.

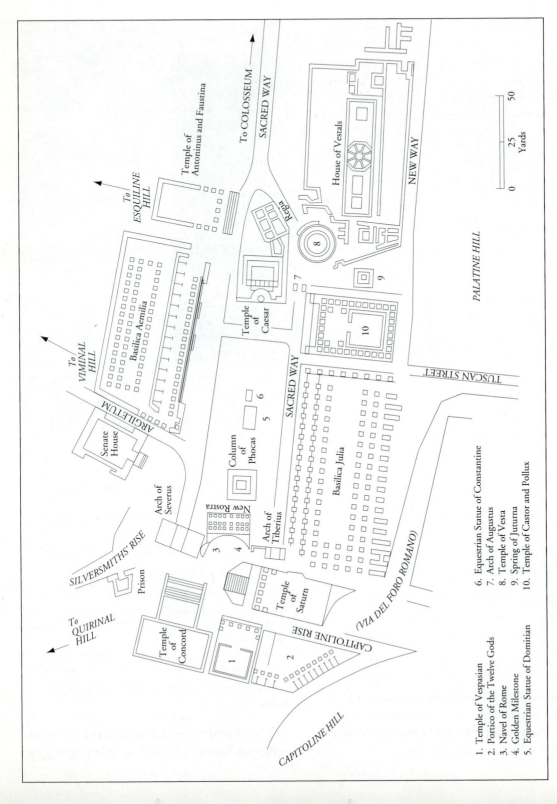

1. Temple of Vespasian
2. Portico of the Twelve Gods
3. Navel of Rome
4. Golden Milestone
5. Equestrian Statue of Domitian
6. Equestrian Statue of Constantine
7. Arch of Augustus
8. Temple of Vesta
9. Spring of Juturna
10. Temple of Castor and Pollux

Map 3   *The Roman Forum (fourth century A.D.)*

Nighttime, however, is the setting for Juvenal's most vivid impression of life in Imperial Rome:

You are a thoughtless fool, unmindful of sudden disaster,
If you don't make your will before you go out to have dinner.
There are as many deaths in the night as there are open windows
Where you pass by; if you're wise, you will pray, in your wretched devotions,
People may be content with no more than emptying slop jars.

Juvenal also warns that roof tiles can fall on your head, you may be hit by the trash that people throw out their windows—or, worst of all, you can be confronted by some drunken hoodlum who, made bolder by the dark, has nothing but contempt for your humble status:

If you try to talk back, or sneak away without speaking,
All the same thing; you're assaulted, and then put under a bail bond
For committing assault. This is a poor man's freedom
Beaten, cut up by fists, he begs and implores his assailant,
Please, for a chance to go home with a few teeth left in his mouth.

Juvenal concludes:

This is not all you must fear. Shut up your house or your store.
Bolts and padlocks and bars will never keep out all the burglars.
Or a holdup man will do you in with a switch blade.

Other Roman writers also depicted the shortcomings of Rome. The early comic playwright

Figure 1.4   This well-preserved street of buildings in Ostia (Rome's seaport) is probably a good indication of what portions of ancient Imperial Rome looked like.

Plautus (c. 254–184 B.C.) served up this impression of the Roman Forum, the nerve center of the city, in his *Curculio* (4.1). It must have made his audience nod knowingly and chuckle:

> . . . I'll fill in time by telling you where you can find any type of man you want—perverted or virtuous, honest or dishonest—where you can look to save yourselves time or trouble.
>
> If it's a perjurer you want, go straight to the law-courts! A liar and a braggart?—the temple of Venus the Purifier! Look for wealthy husbands on the loose in the Basilica. That's where you'll see clapped-out old tarts, too, and the men who haggle over them! Want to make up a bottle party? Look in the Fishmarket. At

the lower end of the Forum the real gentlemen stroll about, the ones with money; in the middle, near the Canal, you get the dandies, who just like to be seen. Above the lake, the know-all gossips congregate—malicious types who run down other people mercilessly, and really ought to hear some home truths about themselves! Below the Old Colonnade you'll find the money lenders, putting out and borrowing money on interest. Then, behind the Temple of Castor are types you'd be ill advised to trust on a brief acquaintance. In the Tuscan Quarter you get the male prostitutes, who'll turn their hands to anything—or anyone! In the Velabrum, butchers and bakers and oracle makers. And of rich husbands on the rampage, look in the house of Oppian Leucadia!

Seneca, the Stoic philosopher and advisor to the Emperor Nero, also took time to poke fun at Rome. Picturing himself as living above a public bath in a less fashionable neighborhood, he enumerates the seemingly endless problems:

> So picture to yourself the assortment of sounds which are strong enough to make me hate my very powers of hearing! When your strenuous gentleman, for example, is exercising himself by flourishing leaden weights; when he is working hard or else pretends to be working hard, I can hear him grunt; and whenever he releases his imprisoned breath, I can hear him panting in wheezy and high-pitched tones. Or perhaps I notice some lazy fellow content with a cheap rub-down, and hear the crack of the pummeling hand on his shoulder, varying in sound according as the hand is laid on flat or hollow. Then, perhaps, a professional [athlete] comes along, shouting out the score; that is the finishing touch. Add to this the arresting of an occasional roisterer or pickpocket, the racket of the man who always likes to hear his own voice in the bathroom, or the enthusiast who plunges into the swimming-tank with unconscionable

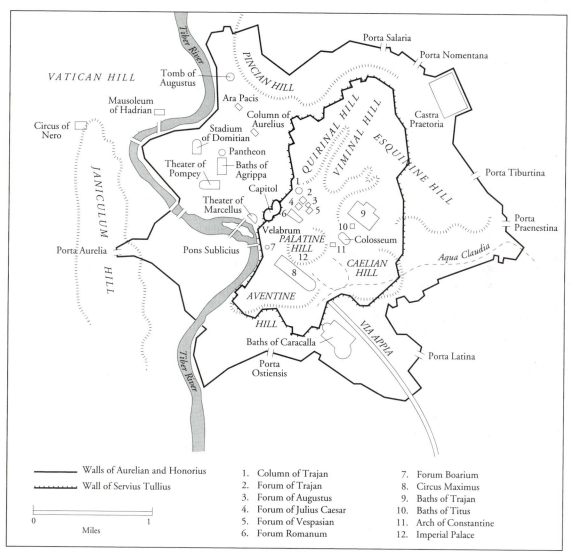

Map 4 Imperial Rome

Legend:

Walls of Aurelian and Honorius
Wall of Servius Tullius

0 — Miles — 1

1. Column of Trajan
2. Forum of Trajan
3. Forum of Augustus
4. Forum of Julius Caesar
5. Forum of Vespasian
6. Forum Romanum
7. Forum Boarium
8. Circus Maximus
9. Baths of Trajan
10. Baths of Titus
11. Arch of Constantine
12. Imperial Palace

noise and splashing. Besides all those whose voices, if nothing else, are good, imagine the hair-plucker with his penetrating, shrill voice—for purposes of advertisement—continually giving it vent and never holding his tongue except when he is plucking the armpits and making his victim yell instead. Then the cake-seller with his varied cries, the sausage-man, the confectioner, and all the vendors of food hawking their wares, each with his own distinctive intonation. . . . Among the sounds that din round me without distracting, I include passing carriages, a machinist in the same block, a saw-sharpener nearby, or some fellow who is demonstrating with little pipes and flutes at the Trickling Fountain, shouting rather than singing.

(*Epistle* 56.1–4)

Seneca's literary contemporary, Petronius, reflected the "seamy" side of city life by representing Roman "counterculture" in his racy and imaginative farce the *Satyricon*.

On the more serious side, the weather in Rome and environs could be an additional headache, as Pliny the Younger complains to a friend:

Can the weather be as bad and stormy where you are? Here we have nothing but gales and repeated floods. The Tiber has overflowed its bed and deeply flooded its lower banks, so that although it is being drained by the canal cut by the Emperor, with his usual foresight, it is filling the valleys and inundating the fields, and wherever there is level ground there is nothing to be seen but water. Then the streams, which it normally receives and carries down to the sea, are forced back as it spreads to meet them, and so it floods with their water the fields it does not reach itself. The Anio, most delightful of rivers—so much so that the houses on its banks seem to beg it not to leave them—has torn up and carried away most of the woods which shade its course. Where the banks rise high they have been undermined, so that its channel is blocked in several places with the resultant landslides; and in its efforts to regain its lost course it has wrecked buildings and forced out its way over the debris.

People who were hit by the storm on higher ground have seen the valuable furniture and fittings of wealthy homes, or else all the farm stock, yoked oxen, ploughs and ploughmen, or cattle left free to graze, and amongst them trunks of trees or beams and roofs of houses, all floating by in widespread confusion. Nor have the places where the river did not rise escaped disaster, for instead of floods they have had incessant rain, gales, and cloud-

bursts which have destroyed the walls enclosing valuable properties, rocked public buildings and brought them crashing to the ground. Many people have been maimed, crushed, and buried in such accidents, so that loss of life is added to material damage.

(*Letters* 8.17)

Such insights about Rome provide a sobering counterbalance to one-dimensional modern conceptions about the city, a city that was not without its faults but was still impressive by any standard—as this first-century A.D. description attests:

. . . the walls of Rome, embracing the seven hills, measured 13.2 miles in circumference. The city itself is divided into fourteen districts, and has 265 intersections. . . . A measurement running from the milestone set up at the head of the Roman Forum to each of the city gates—which today number thirty-seven . . . gives a total of 20.765 miles in a straight line. But the measurement of all the thoroughfares block by block, from the same milestone to the outermost edge of the buildings including the Praetorian Camp, totals a little more than sixty miles. And if one should consider in addition the height of the buildings, he would assuredly form a fitting appraisal and would admit that no city has existed in the whole world that could be compared with Rome in size.

(Pliny, *Natural History* 3.5.66–67)

The Emergence of Rome

Rome paid a high price to become a great city with an empire. The long, hard road to Mediterranean domination was set upon unconsciously. From its humble beginnings as a collection of huts along the Tiber River sometime in the eighth century B.C. (traditionally, 753 B.C.), Rome had first gone through a period of monar-

chy. Seven "kings" (initially, more like village chiefs) oversaw the growth of the fledgling community. The first was Romulus, the legendary founder and namesake of the city. Reputedly fathered by Mars and descended from the Trojan prince Aeneas, Romulus survived a harrowing basket ride down the Tiber, was rescued and nurtured by an attentive she-wolf, and killed his twin brother Remus before fulfilling his destiny by founding Rome. Others of these shadowy kings, though obscured by a nonhistorical haze, lent their names in later times to institutions whose actual origins had been forgotten. Hence, it was believed that Rome's second king, Numa, had established the state cult and given Romans their religion, while the organization of Rome's citizen-assemblies began with Servius Tullius, the fifth king of Rome.

Upon the overthrow of the monarchy in 509 B.C., indelibly remembered as the work of a patriot named Brutus, Rome became a republic for almost five centuries. A form of government that was characterized by regularly elected magistrates, the Roman Republic included three assemblies with electoral and legislative powers and the Senate, which was the guiding body of the new regime (see Chart 1, page 10).

From the beginning, Rome had to fight for its existence. The small community was initially dominated by Etruscans, a powerful, advanced people from northern Italy whose civilization still remains largely a mystery. There exist few physical remains of their society, and much of what we do know about them is based on their tombs and funerary practices (see Figures 1.6 and 1.7, page 11). They appear to be a combination of Italic and Asian elements (the area of Asia Minor, not modern Asia), and, unlike the Romans, they spoke a non-Indo-European language. They were a major land and sea power

Chart 1   Roman Republican Government (after 287 B.C.)

SENATE

Membership: about 300

Functions: finance; provincial administration and foreign policy; assignment of military commands; advisory body to magistrates; administration of public lands; on rare occasions, declarations of states of emergency (*senatus consultum ultimum*).

ASSEMBLIES

Centuriate (*comitia centuriata*)

Membership: all adult male citizens

Functions: elect censors, consuls, praetors; declarations of war and peace; ratification of treaties; appellate court for capital charges; legislative functions.

Tribal (*comitia tributa*)

Membership: all adult male citizens

Functions: elect aediles, quaestors, holders of lower offices, and members of special commissions; legislative functions (see concilium plebis).

Plebeian (*concilium plebis*)—Often identified with the Tribal Assembly

Membership: plebeians only

Functions: elect tribunes and plebeian aediles; chief legislative body by 287 B.C. Laws (*plebiscita*) passed in the plebeian assembly henceforth binding on all citizens.

OFFICERS

By the Late Republic, all officers listed below could enter the Senate.

censor ⎫
consul ⎬ *cursus honorum* (mandatory sequence of offices)
praetor ⎪
quaestor ⎭
aedile ⎫ optional offices
tribune ⎭

Functions:

censors—Highest political office in Rome. Two elected every five years from ranks of ex-consuls. Held office eighteen months. Took census; dispersed state funds; oversaw public morals.

(Annually elected officers)

consuls—The two chief civil and military officers of Rome. Presided over Senate and general assemblies; also proposed laws.

praetors (8)—Judicial officers; provincial governors; could hold military commands; also proposed laws.

quaestors (20)—Primarily financial officers.

aediles (4)—In charge of public entertainment and games, city management.

tribunes—The ten officers of the plebeians. Proposed laws and presided over the *concilium plebis*. An individual tribune could veto any piece of legislation.

Figure 1.6
Etruscan tomb. During the sixth–fifth centuries B.C., Caere (Cerveteri) was a prosperous Etruscan center, and aristocrats interred their dead in large tumuli like the one pictured here. Typically, each tumulus contained groups of chamber tombs, whose interiors were carved so as to resemble the insides of their dwellings.

Figure 1.7
Terracotta sarcophagus of a prosperous Etruscan woman, c. 150–130 B.C. Although the Etruscans had been absorbed into Roman society by this time, they remained an identifiable "minority." The practice of representing the dead reposing on their sarcophagi dates from the "glory days" of Etruscan society.

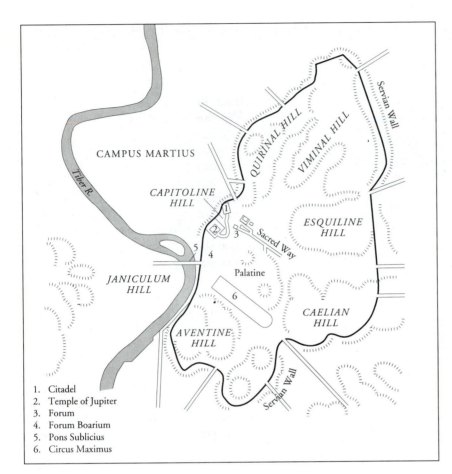

Map 5
Early Rome

1. Citadel
2. Temple of Jupiter
3. Forum
4. Forum Boarium
5. Pons Sublicius
6. Circus Maximus

before Rome became significant. Prominent Etruscan cities such as Tarquinii, Veii, and Caere were independent, and each was ruled by a king, or *lucumo;* but the twelve leading cities formed an "Etruscan League" that met at a common religious center at Volsinii and promoted cooperation among them, especially during times of war. Technologically superior, particularly in metalwork, the Etruscans provided the earliest major cultural influence upon the developing Romans, and even many Greek practices came to the Romans through the Etruscans. For example, although gladiatorial contests are most associated with Rome, they actu-

ally originated at Greek funeral games. In art, architecture, and religion—largely in practices such as augury—the Etruscan influence can be seen. Some symbols of political authority, such as the *fasces* (bound bundles of rods with axe blades projecting), which were carried upright before Roman magistrates by lictors, are Etruscan in origin; and an Etruscan king, Tarquin the Proud, was ruling Rome when the monarchy was overthrown.

The Romans not only successfully fended off subsequent Etruscan attempts to regain the city (see box, opposite) but also had conquered and absorbed them by the early third century

Horatius at the Bridge

THE EARLY HISTORY OF Rome, at least before the fourth century B.C., is an unsettled area of inquiry with problems lurking at every turn. The sack of Rome by Gauls in 387 B.C. destroyed most records up to that time, and even Roman writers frequently comment about how they are at a loss to understand this period. Names, dates, and places are difficult to reconstruct and are based mostly on traditional records, whose legitimacy can often be questioned. Nonetheless, tradition is all that we have, and even though the prominent figures who supposedly guided Rome's fortunes during these centuries may not be entirely historical and accurately portrayed, we can still learn much about the Romans through their example. Just as the Founding Fathers of America are wrapped in myth and legend—and the actual historical circumstances of their lives *are* well known—later generations of Romans looked back to their early days and built the kind of heroes they wanted from the scraps of personalities handed down to them. Eventually, Roman historians and poets stitched together an orthodox tradition of their people from the very beginning, and whether true or not, it became the Roman experience.

One of the historians most responsible for imposing unity on the early tradition of Rome was Livy, who wrote under the first Roman emperor, Augustus. Livy complained about how little one could actually know about the beginnings of Rome, yet it did not prevent him from devoting five books of his history to it! At the time Livy was composing his chronicle, Augustus was trying to restore what were perceived as the old-time values and character of Rome. It is a well-known device for politicians of any age to hark back to the "good old days," calling up time-honored images of great figures from the past to use as examples for their own programs. For the

Romans, it was Romulus, Coriolanus, Camillus, Scaevola, Cincinnatus, and, of course, Horatius Cocles (the "One-Eyed").

According to the traditional accounts, it was not long after the overthrow of Rome's monarchy in 509 B.C. that an Etruscan king named Lars Porsenna attacked the city. He probably would have succeeded in capturing it if, as the ancient record indicates, his efforts had not been thwarted by Horatius at the bridge. Livy (*History of Rome* 2.10) provides the appropriate heroic description:

> On the approach of the Etruscan army, the Romans abandoned their farmsteads and moved into the city. Garrisons were posted. In some sections the city walls seemed sufficient protection, in others the barrier of the Tiber. The most vulnerable point was the wooden bridge, and the Etruscans would have crossed it and forced an entrance into the city, had it not been for the courage of one man, Horatius Cocles—that great soldier whom the fortune of Rome gave to be her shield on that day of peril. Horatius was on guard at the bridge. . . . The enemy forces came pouring down the hill, while the Roman troops, throwing away their weapons, were behaving more like an undisciplined rabble than a fighting force. Horatius acted promptly: as his routed comrades approached the bridge, he stopped as many as he could catch and compelled them to listen to him. "By God," he cried, "can't you see that if you desert your post escape is hopeless?" . . . Urging them with all the power at his command to destroy the bridge by fire or steel or any means they could muster, he offered to hold up the Etruscan advance, so far as was possible, alone. Proudly he took his stand at the outer end of the bridge; conspicuous amongst the rout of fugitives, sword and shield

(continued)

Horatius at the Bridge (continued)

ready for action, he prepared himself for close combat, one man against an army. The advancing enemy paused in sheer astonishment at such reckless courage. . . . For a while they hung back, each waiting for his neighbor to make the first move, until shame at the unequal battle drove them to action, and with a fierce cry they hurled their spears at the solitary figure which barred their way. Horatius caught the missiles on his shield and, resolute as ever, straddled the bridge and held his ground. The Etruscans moved forward, and would have thrust him aside by the sheer weight of their numbers, but their advance was suddenly checked by the crash of the falling bridge and the simultaneous shout of triumph from the Roman soldiers who had done their work in time. The Etruscans could only stare in bewilderment as Horatius, with a prayer to Father Tiber to bless him and his sword, plunged fully armed into the water and swam, through the missiles which fell thick about him, safely to the other side where his friends were waiting to receive him.

Livy concludes his account with the observation, "It was a noble piece of work—legendary, maybe, but destined to be celebrated in story through the years to come."

Polybius, an earlier and far less dramatic historian who lived and wrote in the second century B.C., provides quite a different ending to the same story:

> Once the bridge was cut the enemy's advance was halted, whereupon Cocles threw himself into the river still wearing his armor and weapons. He deliberately sacrificed himself because he valued the safety of his country and the glory which would later attach itself to his name more than his present existence and the years of life that remained to him.
> (*Histories* 6.55)

Figure 1.8 *Bronze representation of a fifth-century* B.C. *Etruscan soldier. (British Museum)*

Whoever the real Horatius was we will never know, but his heroic example was held up to countless generations of Romans. He was what they were supposed to be. For Polybius, it was necessary that Horatius sacrifice himself in order to provide proper inspiration. For Livy a century later, one still was expected to defend his country to the best of his ability—but what good was a dead hero? He could live to fight again another day. Clearly, the traditional accounts of heroes were malleable and could be molded to fit the needs of the times.

B.C. Ultimately, the Etruscans combined with earlier Latin and Sabine elements to form the main fabric of the Roman people—a far more humble beginning than the time-honored, albeit false, Roman tradition that they were descended from the Trojans. (The Romans, it appears, were not the first—or the last—society to embrace wholeheartedly a completely erroneous idea about themselves.)

During the same period, Rome's chief local rivals succumbed after lengthy struggles, the neighboring Latin cities in Latium (the area of Italy where Rome was located) were brought under control with the defeat of the Latin League (340–338 B.C.), and successful wars were completed against the Gauls and Samnites, two of the city's most formidable and destructive enemies.

Soon after the monarchy had ended, internal disorders disrupted Rome. *Patricians,* members of the noble families who dominated the Early Republic, sparred incessantly with the city's restive commoners, who made up most of the population and were called *plebeians.* This patrician-plebeian conflict—or "Struggle of the Orders," as it is often called—eventually abated in the third century; but before it did, Rome had to learn how to juggle successfully its external military problems with social upheaval at home. The sack of the city by Gauls in 387 B.C. almost put an end to such problems altogether, but out of the ashes, Rome was rebuilt (see box, pages 16–17). The resolve among its citizens never to let such a thing happen again is a major consideration in understanding Rome's ultimate success in Italy and the Mediterranean. A growing "defensive imperialism" began to characterize Roman policy toward neighbors and foreigners; and suspicions, legitimate or not, often led Rome to embark upon preventative wars to protect itself from potential harm.

By 275 B.C., Rome had mostly subdued northern and central Italy (see Map 6, page 17). In the south, the Greeks had also fallen under Rome's control, even after calling in a formidable champion from the Hellenistic East. King Pyrrhus of Epirus, a kinsman of Alexander the Great, had arrived in Italy in 280 B.C. to defend Greek interests. Pyrrhus was Rome's first international foe, a soldier of fortune who had been involved in the wars of the Successors of Alexander, during which he had even briefly been king of Macedonia. Undoubtedly, Pyrrhus initially viewed the Romans as easy prey, but after five years without a conclusive victory, he was finally driven out. His defeat established Rome's credentials as master of Italy and a legitimate Mediterranean power. As such, Rome soon found itself involved in a war with Carthage over the island of Sicily. Carthage, located in North Africa, was the most powerful city in the western Mediterranean; and its military presence on Sicily, only a few miles from Italy, was too great a threat for Rome to ignore.

The First Punic War, or war with Carthage, erupted in 264 B.C. and lasted until 241 B.C. The twenty-three-year conflict was costly for both sides, but ultimately Rome was victorious, and Sicily became the first of its many provinces. The hatred and tensions between the two powers continued to fester, and war erupted again in 218 B.C. Hard pressed in the first war, the Romans would never face a challenge as serious as that offered by Hannibal, the leader of the Carthaginian forces in the Second Punic War (see pages 19–20).

Bent on revenge, Hannibal marched an army of about twenty-six thousand men from his base in Spain, which had become a part of the Carthaginian Empire. He moved across the Pyrenees, through southern Gaul, and over the Alps into northern Italy. After inflicting humiliating

Gauls and Geese—Camillus Saves Rome

IN 387 B.C., A FIERCE group of Gauls, or Celts, pushed their way down into Italy from north of the Po River, disastrously defeated a badly outnumbered force of Roman defenders, and sacked the city of Rome. This was remembered by Romans as perhaps the darkest day in their history, and the events surrounding the catastrophe brought forward another of Rome's great traditional heroes, Camillus.

Camillus had already distinguished himself by bringing to a close Rome's lengthy war with the nearby Etruscan city of Veii, but soon after the victory in 396 B.C. he was supposedly exiled for making off with some of the spoils. Flatterers probably invented the story later to gloss over questions about why Camillus had failed to prevent the Gauls from taking Rome. Whether true or not, the survivors who had fled Rome and taken refuge at Veii now appointed him dictator to rescue those still holding the Capitoline Hill in Rome and to drive the enemy from their homes. Before Camillus could act, Rome was almost lost when the Gauls discovered a secret way up the Capitoline. They were about to overcome the city's last defenders when they encountered the sacred geese of the goddess Juno, whose temple was on the summit. What happened next became one of the most popular Roman legends:

> While this was going on at Veii, the Citadel of Rome and the Capitol were in very great danger. For the Gauls had noticed the tracks of a man, where the messenger from Veii had got through, or perhaps had observed for themselves that the cliff near the shrine of Carmentis afforded an easy ascent. So on a starlit night they first sent forward an unarmed man to try the way; then handing up their weapons when there was a steep place, and supporting themselves by their fellows or affording support in their turn, they pulled one another up, as the ground required, and reached the summit, in

such silence that not only the sentries but even the dogs—creatures easily troubled by noises in the night—were not aroused. But they could not elude the vigilance of the geese, which, being sacred to Juno, had, notwithstanding the dearth of provisions, not been killed. This was the salvation of them all; for the geese with their gabbing and clapping of their wings woke Marcus Manlius—consul of three years before and a distinguished soldier—who, catching up his weapons and at the same time calling the rest to arms, strode past his bewildered comrades to a Gaul who had already got a foothold on the crest and dislodged him with a blow from the boss of his shield. As he slipped and fell, he overturned those who were next to him, and the others in alarm let go their weapons and grasping the rocks to which they had been clinging, were slain by Manlius. And by now the rest had come together and were assailing the invaders with javelins and stones, and presently the whole company lost their footing and were flung down headlong to destruction.

(Livy, *History of Rome* 5.47.1–6)

The implication of this story was, of course, that Juno herself, through the honking of her sacred geese, had intervened to save Rome in this most desperate hour. As the months dragged on, however, the defenders were reduced by famine to offer a bribe to the Gauls to withdraw. The tradition continues that while the gold was still being weighed out, Camillus appeared with his army and drove the Gauls out of the city and harassed them on their return north. Roman honor was thereby preserved, and Camillus became the savior and second founder of Rome.

Glowing patriotism aside, at least one Roman writer indicates that the Capitol, too, fell to the Gauls like everything else in the city. It also appears that when the Gauls left, they departed of their own choice, carrying off much plunder and, in addition, probably ransom. Their decision may have been hastened by a fever that broke out among their ranks and by recent threats upon their territory in the north. Camillus and the Romans had little to do with their ultimate withdrawal—although they probably did harass them on their way home.

To a power as great as Rome would become, such humiliation was intolerable, and later Romans preferred to believe that Camillus had been their shield in the hour of their greatest need and that Roman honor had been kept intact.

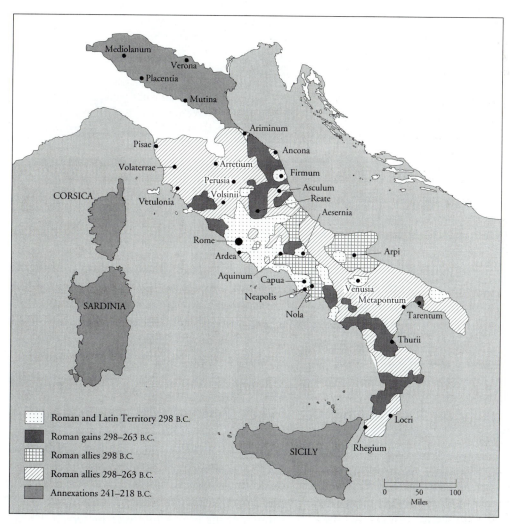

Roman and Latin Territory 298 B.C.
Roman gains 298–263 B.C.
Roman allies 298 B.C.
Roman allies 298–263 B.C.
Annexations 241–218 B.C.

Map 6   Rome's conquest of Italy

defeats on the Romans at the Trebia River in 218 B.C. and Lake Trasimene in 217 B.C., Hannibal prepared to meet the largest Roman army yet fielded against him at Cannae in southeastern Italy. There, in 216 B.C., he engineered Rome's worst defeat. Caught in a classic envelopment maneuver, as many as seventy thousand Roman troops may have perished at Cannae. The prospects looked dim as Rome entered its darkest hour since the Gallic sack of the city in the previous century.

With a Carthaginian victory appearing imminent, anti-Roman sentiment spread rapidly through hostile parts of Italy, and even some former allies expelled pro-Roman officials and declared for Hannibal. Foremost among these was the great Greek city of Syracuse in Sicily.

Syracuse and Marcellus, the "Sword of Rome"

Figure 1.9   Marcellus

Syracuse had enjoyed a long history of friendship with Rome. Hiero II, the city's tyrant, had initially sided with Carthage when the First Punic War began in 264 B.C., but he reversed his policy within a year and became a staunch Roman ally until his death forty-eight years later. The alliance proved mutually beneficial, and when the Second Punic War broke out in 218 B.C., there was no question where Syracuse's loyalty lay—as long as Hiero was alive. Even after the disaster at Cannae when it appeared Rome might be overwhelmed by Hannibal, Hiero did not flinch, but the impact of that defeat would soon have its effect.

Not everyone at Syracuse viewed Rome in the positive light Hiero did. Anti-Roman sentiments began to emerge after the old tyrant died in 215 B.C. The political maneuvering that followed his death resulted in a dramatic turn about in loyalties. Syracuse was no longer the guardian of Roman interests in Sicily but a Carthaginian ally. If Rome could not retake Syracuse, all of Sicily would probably fall into Carthaginian hands, providing Hannibal with uninterrupted reinforcements and supplies from Africa as well as Spain. Also, other Mediterranean powers who were still hesitating to commit fully to one side or the other would no longer have any reason to wait.

The Roman siege of Syracuse was placed under the direction of M. Claudius Marcellus, Rome's most capable and experienced general. Popularly known as the "Sword of Rome" because of his success against Hannibal, Marcellus had a long and distinguished military record. A veteran of the First Punic War, he served the ear-

A Worthy Opponent—Hannibal Takes His Revenge

WITHOUT QUESTION THE MOST dangerous single enemy Rome ever faced was Hannibal. During the Second Punic War, the great Carthaginian general inflicted several major defeats on the Romans, most notably at Cannae in 216 B.C., and remained sixteen years in Italy unconquered and moving at will. He was finally defeated in Africa at Zama, near Carthage, in 202 B.C. by Scipio (who would become known as "Africanus" because of his victory). The war ended the following year with Rome victorious.

Much has been made in the ancient sources of Hannibal's hatred for Rome. One of the most popular anecdotes relates to a boyhood oath he made to his father, Hamilcar Barca, the losing Carthaginian general in the First Punic War. In the years following his defeat by Rome, Hannibal had taken refuge in the East with Antiochus III, the ruler of the Hellenistic Seleucid kingdom. When Roman envoys were sent to Antiochus to arouse suspicions about his famous guest, now in his fifties, Hannibal defended his loyalty and his hatred for Rome. Cornelius Nepos (first century B.C.) writes:

> To [Antiochus'] court came envoys from Rome to sound his intentions and try by secret intrigues to arouse his suspicions of Hannibal, alleging that they had bribed him and that he had changed his sentiments. These attempts were not made in vain, and when Hannibal learned it and noticed that he was excluded from the king's more intimate councils, he went to Anti-

ochus, as soon as the opportunity offered, and after calling to mind many proofs of his loyalty and his hatred of the Romans, he added: "My father Hamilcar, when I was a small boy not more than nine years old, just as he was setting out from Carthage to Spain as commander-in-chief, offered up victims to [the god Baal]. While this ceremony was being performed, he asked me if I would like to go with him on the campaign. I eagerly accepted and began to beg him not to hesitate to take me with him. Thereupon he said: 'I will do it, provided you will give me the pledge that I ask.' With that he led me to the altar on which he had begun his sacrifice, and having dismissed all the others, he bade me lay hold of the altar and swear that I would never be a friend to the Romans. For my part, up to my present time of life, I have kept the oath which I swore to my father so faithfully, that no one ought to doubt that in the future I shall be of the same mind. Therefore, if you have any kindly intentions with regard to the Roman people, you will be wise to hide them from me; but when you prepare war, you will go counter to your own interests if you do not make me the leader in that enterprise."
> (*Hannibal* 2.2–6)

Whether the context or content of Nepos' version of the episode is accurate cannot be determined, but the idea that Hannibal was sworn by his father to hate Rome when he was a small boy does not seem unrealistic.

(continued)

liest of his five consulships (222 B.C.) fighting Gauls in the north of Italy, where he killed the Gallic chieftain, Viridomarus, in a personal duel—an incident so reminiscent of Rome's heroic past that a play was produced about it.

In the Second Punic War, Marcellus was the first Roman commander to enjoy a victory over Hannibal, defending the city of Nola (about 20 miles east of Naples) in Campania against his attack in 216 B.C. The military impact of his deed

A Worthy Opponent—Hannibal Takes His Revenge (continued)

Antiochus retained Hannibal's services and eventually went to war with Rome. However, probably worried about being overshadowed by the great general, he did not utilize Hannibal's skills to his best advantage. Antiochus was defeated by the Romans and made peace with them in 188 B.C., forcing Hannibal to flee. Eventually, with no place to run, Hannibal committed suicide in Bithynia on the Propontis in 183 (or 182) B.C. rather than fall into Roman hands.

Few men in any period were as capable as Hannibal, as even the Romans were forced to admit:

> Power to command and readiness to obey are rare associates; but in Hannibal they were perfectly united. . . . Under his leadership the men invariably showed to the best advantage both dash and confidence. Reckless in courting danger, he showed superb tactical ability once it was upon him. Indefatigable both physically and mentally, he could endure with equal ease excessive heat or excessive cold; he ate and drank not to flatter his appetites but only so much as would sustain his bodily strength. His time for waking, like his time for sleeping, was never determined by daylight or darkness: when his work was done, then, and then only, he rested, without need, moreover, of silence or a soft bed to

woo sleep to his eyes. Often he was seen lying in his cloak on the bare ground amongst the common soldiers on sentry or picket duty. His accoutrement, like the horses he rode, was always conspicuous, but not his clothes, which were like those of any other officer of his rank and standing. Mounted or unmounted he was unequalled as a fighting man, always the first to attack, the last to leave the field.

Livy, the historian who composed this admirable description, could not be overly flattering to the man who had almost destroyed his country:

> So much for his virtues—and they were great; but no less great were his faults: inhuman cruelty, a more than Punic perfidy, a total disregard of truth, honor, and religion, of the sanctity of an oath and of all that other men hold sacred. (*History of Rome* 21.4.3–10)

Both passages are largely stereotypical, for as with most great figures, the actual personality of Hannibal became lost and an image of what he was supposed to be like—created by flatterers and detractors alike—took over. For Roman children, at least, that image would never be a pleasant one, since parents made Hannibal the Roman equivalent of today's boogeyman.

---

was not as important as the effect it had on Roman morale. With Cannae and other disasters still fresh, Marcellus was able to provide the first hope that Hannibal could be defeated.

As proconsul in 215 B.C., Marcellus again thwarted Hannibal at Nola, which resulted in what Plutarch claims were the first enemy desertions to the Romans. Marcellus' efforts won him a third consulship in 214 B.C.; and after

fending off Hannibal's final attempt to take Nola, he moved to assist in the siege of Casilinum, a strategic Campanian city that had fallen into Carthaginian hands. Once that city was retaken (another encouraging victory for the Romans), Marcellus was assigned to Sicily.

In 214 B.C., Hiero's inept young grandson and successor was assassinated by pro-Romans while he was visiting the nearby city of Leon-

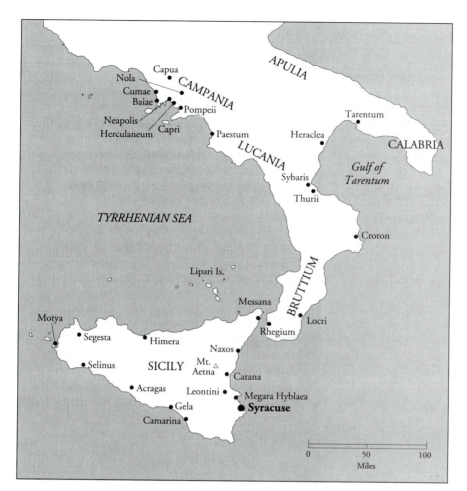

Map 7
Southern Italy and Sicily

tini. Subsequently, other members of the royal family were put to death at Syracuse, and attempts were made to realign the city with Rome. However, the violence led the Syracusans to return pro-Carthaginian leaders to power in the next elections. They also encouraged neighboring Leontini to revolt against Rome. Marcellus and his general, Appius Claudius, stormed and captured Leontini in 213 B.C., but the city's sack and the rumored atrocities associated with it resolved the Syracusans once and for all to side with Carthage. Marcellus and Appius now led a combined land and sea attack against Syracuse.

Syracuse was the greatest Greek city in the West, and only the taking of Carthage itself would have been a more difficult task. The city's defenses had long been a concern to Hiero and his predecessors, including Dionysius I, who, at the beginning of the fourth century, had concentrated on making Syracuse the most formidable military power in the Greek world. It is no surprise that Marcellus made little headway in his initial attempts to seize the city. An old man named Archimedes—who added his unique genius to the already impressive panoply of weapons, fortifications, and natural defenses that protected the city—certainly made Rome's task a more difficult one.

Archimedes of Syracuse

Traditionally, many of the weapons employed against Marcellus and the Romans at the siege of Syracuse were the work of Archimedes, the great Hellenistic Greek scientist and technological wizard. A brilliant mathematician, physicist, astronomer, engineer, mechanic, and inventor, Archimedes (c. 287–212 B.C.) was born in Syracuse. Aside from a visit to Egypt, most likely for studies at Alexandria, he appears to have remained there for the rest of his seventy-five years.

During his long career, Archimedes made numerous discoveries that would have lasting impact. Among these were his revolutionary work with gravity and leverage; his calculation of the approximate value of pi; his measurements of the sphere, the cylinder, and the cone; and the system he devised for calculating with and expressing large numbers. His pioneering work in hydrostatics produced the most enduring of the many popular stories about him. After stepping into an overfilled tub at a public bath, Archimedes suddenly realized that the water that overflowed would, if collected and measured, be equal to the volume of the body that displaced it. Since this discovery gave him the solution to a difficult problem, he supposedly got so excited that he forgot his clothes and rushed outside shouting "Eureka! Eureka!" ("I have found it!") Those observing a naked man flying past them in the street certainly must have wondered if he had not lost more than he had found!

Archimedes also constructed a celestial globe, a planetarium of sorts that Cicero saw and said depicted the movement of the sun, moon, and planets and demonstrated the occurrence of eclipses. The compound pulley is thought to be his invention, as is the water screw, although it is difficult to believe that some form of water screw had not been in operation long before his day. One source says Archimedes invented it while in Egypt, where irrigation along the Nile had been going on for millennia. Perhaps he only improved upon a device he found there and brought the idea to Europe.

The accomplishments of Archimedes continued to be embellished in the centuries after his death. Fantastic devices such as a destructive heat ray were attributed to him. While the technology for the so-called burning mirrors of Archimedes was well within his grasp, and some naive modern scholars accept the ancient tradition as valid, there never was any practical application of the idea. Sources contemporary with Archimedes are silent about it, and, as one modern critic has noted, "Had such a device existed, it would have fallen into Roman hands when Syracuse was taken, and the Romans would gladly have employed the deadly heat ray in future wars" (Africa, "Archimedes," p. 306). Even without the burning mirrors, Archimedes' engines of war were formidable. Despite his remarkable scientific and mathematical achievements, it is the legendary defense of Syracuse and his engines of destruction for which he is best remembered.

Ironically, Archimedes' weapons were devised when Syracuse was Rome's trusted ally. Supposedly, he himself cared little for such machines and had been persuaded by his kinsman, Hiero, the ruler of Syracuse, to provide the technical knowledge and skill to improve the city's defenses. Hiero's main concern at the time was protecting Syracuse from Carthage, not Rome. Plutarch provides a fitting, albeit colored, description of how Hiero prevailed upon Archimedes for his help. It includes a version of

Archimedes' fabled assertion that provided with a big enough lever and "a place to stand . . . I will move the earth":

> . . . Archimedes had written to King Hiero, his friend and relative, that with a given force it is possible to move any given weight; and it is said that, relying on the strength of his demonstration, he even boasted that if he had another earth to stand upon he could move this one. Hiero, in amazement, begged him to put his theory into practice and to show him some great mass moved by a small force. He took a three-masted ship from the royal navy which had just been drawn out of the docks with great effort and the labor of many men; and placing in this vessel many passengers and the usual cargo, he himself sat some distance away and without any great effort, but by calmly pulling with his hand the end of the pulley, dragged the ship towards him smoothly and evenly, as if it were sailing in the sea. The king marveled at this demonstration, and having understood the power of the art, convinced Archimedes to construct for him machines for all kinds of siege operations, offensive and defensive. The king never used these machines, however, since he spent most of his life in peaceful and literary pursuits.
> (*Marcellus* 14.7–9)

Plutarch's account certainly must be viewed with some skepticism. It is unlikely that Hiero would have been so completely surprised by Archimedes' mechanical skills, since he was supposedly related to him and lived with him in Syracuse for about sixty years. It also appears that Plutarch's account of Archimedes' effortlessly moving one of Hiero's ships with a compound pulley has been confused with an earlier story that has Archimedes launching a ship of gigantic proportions—the building of which he supervised—using a windlass (which, alas, he did not invent). The ship, called the *Syracusia,*

was certainly a technological marvel for the day and an appropriate project for Archimedes (whose reputation no doubt helped spawn exaggerations about the size and capabilities of the vessel: He supposedly armed it with a huge engine that could hurl a 180-pound stone or 18-foot javelin 600 feet!). Reputedly so large that it could not be safely docked at most ports, the ship was ultimately taken to Alexandria and given by Hiero to King Ptolemy of Egypt for use as a grain transport.

Plutarch intimates that Archimedes enjoyed employing his knowledge to help protect his city. The variety, the number, and the efficiency of the weapons that were deployed along the extensive walls at Syracuse demonstrate the expense and effort Archimedes exerted in maintaining and coordinating such defenses. Hiero would not have tolerated anything less than the best. Plutarch's assertion that Archimedes was really only a dabbler and that he did not view such inventions as serious work is unrealistic:

> Archimedes possessed so elevated and profound a mind and had acquired such a wealth of scientific knowledge that although these inventions gave him a reputation of an intelligence not human, but divine, he did not want to leave behind him any writings on these matters. He considered mechanics and, in general, all the arts that touched on the needs of everyday life, as base and ignoble, and devoted his zeal only to those pure speculations whose beauty and excellence are not affected by material needs—speculations which cannot be compared to any others, and in which the proof rivals the subject, the one providing grandeur and beauty, the other accuracy and a supernatural power.

Plutarch's praise of abstract over practical knowledge does echo a real sentiment in antiquity that also had social implications. Abstract thought and theoretical discussion were associated with the wellborn, while practical application was linked, contemptuously by Aristotle and others, with those who labored manually for a living. This upper-class prejudice undoubtedly did inhibit the development of some inventions that may have benefited society, but it is an attitude that is seldom, if ever, demonstrable among the scientists and inventors themselves. The high-minded Plutarch, who knew little if anything about the real character of Archimedes, assigned him a personality so esoteric that it becomes laughable:

> Thus, one cannot doubt what has been said about Archimedes, that he was always bewitched by some familiar and domestic siren so that he would forget to eat his food and neglect the care of his person, that when forcibly dragged to be bathed and to have his body anointed and perfumed he would draw geometric figures in the ashes of the fire, and that when his body was oiled he would trace diagrams on it with his finger, for he was prey to an extreme passion and was truly possessed by the Muses. (*Marcellus* 17.3–7)

It is clear how much the anecdotal tradition has come to cloud investigations into the real personality of Archimedes. We would probably be safe to conclude that, like Leonardo da Vinci's creations, Archimedes' mechanical devices were as much a regular part of his investigations as anything else.

The Siege of Syracuse

It is interesting that Archimedes, who had spent most of his life in a pro-Roman city led by his patron and relative, appears to have had so little difficulty turning these same weapons on his former benefactors. It may be that he never shared Hiero's high regard for Rome, or that he was first and foremost a patriot, whose primary concern was the safety of his city. Whatever his views, there is nothing to indicate that he did not devote himself wholeheartedly to the task of repelling Marcellus and his troops when they attacked in 213 B.C.

Polybius, our major source for the period, describes the greeting Archimedes had prepared for his Roman "friends" (*Histories* 8.3–7):

> . . . Archimedes had constructed the defenses of the city in such a way—both on the landward side and to repel any attack from the sea—that there was no need for the defenders to busy themselves with improvisations; instead they would have everything ready to hand, and could respond to any attack by the enemy with a counter-move. . . . [He] had constructed artillery which could cover a whole variety of ranges, so that while the attacking ships were still at a distance he scored so many hits with his catapults and stone-throwers that he was able to cause them severe damage and harass their approach. Then, as the distance decreased and these weapons began to carry over the enemy's heads, he resorted to smaller and smaller machines, and so demoralized the Romans that their advance was brought to a standstill. In the end Marcellus was reduced in despair to bringing up his ships secretly under cover of darkness. But when they had almost reached the shore, and were therefore too close to be struck by the catapults, Archimedes had devised yet another weapon to repel the marines, who were fighting from the decks. He had had the walls pierced with large numbers of loopholes at the height of a man, which were about a palm's breadth wide at the outer surface of the walls. Behind each of these and inside the walls were stationed archers with rows of so-called "scorpions," a small catapult which discharged iron darts, and by shooting through these embrasures they put many of the marines out of action. Through these tactics he not only foiled all the enemy's attacks, both those made

Figure 1.10
The "scorpions"
mentioned by Polybius,
"a small catapult which
discharged iron darts,"
may have been close in
design to this modern re-
construction of a Roman
"scorpion" from the mid-
first century B.C.

Figure 1.11
This is a modern recon-
struction of a mid-first-
century B.C. *Roman*
"onager," a type of cata-
pult that was in use as
early as 200 B.C. *and*
is the descendent of the
kind used at the siege
of Syracuse.

Figure 1.12
Ruins of the Fortress
of Euryalus, part of
the defensive works
of Syracuse, which
were equipped with
Archimedes' war
machines (see map
of Syracuse, page 27)

at long range and any attempt at hand-to-hand fighting, but also caused them heavy losses.

If any of Marcellus' ships did manage to get close enough to try to land marines, additional surprises awaited:

> Against these attackers the machines could discharge stones heavy enough to drive back the marines from the bows of the ships; at the same time a grappling-iron attached to a chain would be let down, and with this the man controlling the beam would clutch at the ship. As soon as the prow was securely gripped, the lever of the machine inside the wall would be pressed down. When the operator had lifted up the ship's prow in this way and made her stand on her stern, he made fast the lower parts of the machine, so that they would not move, and finally by means of a rope and pulley suddenly slackened the grappling-iron and the chain. The result was that some of the vessels heeled over and fell on their sides, and others capsized, while the majority when their

bows were let fall from a height plunged under water and filled, and thus threw all into confusion. Marcellus' operations were thus completely frustrated by these inventions of Archimedes, and when he saw that the garrison not only repulsed his attacks with heavy losses but also laughed at his efforts, he took his defeat hard. At the same time he could not refrain from making a joke against himself when he said: "Archimedes uses my ships to ladle sea-water into his wine-cups. . . ."

While Marcellus had no luck attacking from the sea, Appius apparently had no better success directing the Roman land operations against Archimedes' machines and finally had to abandon his attempts:

> While his troops were still at a distance from the walls they suffered many casualties from the mangonels and catapults. This artillery was extraordinarily effective both in volume and the velocity of its fire, as was to be expected when Hiero had provided the supplies, and

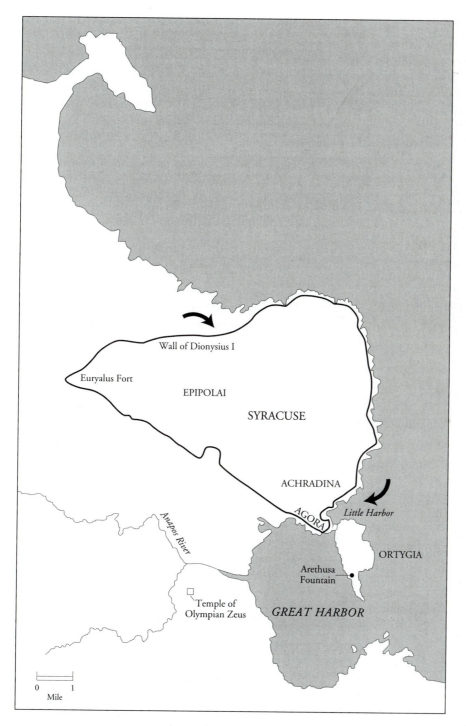

Map 8
Fortifications of Syracuse, with arrows (top) marking the probable point of Appius' land assault and (lower) Marcellus' attack by sea

Wall of Dionysius I

Euryalus Fort

EPIPOLAI

SYRACUSE

ACHRADINA

AGORA

Little Harbor

ORTYGIA

Anapos River

Arethusa Fountain

Temple of Olympian Zeus

GREAT HARBOR

0   1
Mile

Archimedes designed the various engines. Then, even when the soldiers did get close to the wall, they were so harassed by the volleys of arrows and darts which continually poured through the embrasures . . . that their advance was effectually halted. Alternatively . . . they were crushed by the stones and beams that were dropped on their heads. The defenders also killed many men by means of the iron grappling hooks let down from cranes. . . . these were used to lift up men, armor and all, and then allow them to drop. In the end [Appius] withdrew to his camp and summoned a council of the military tribunes, at which it was unanimously decided to use any other methods rather than persist in the attempt to capture Syracuse by storm. And this resolution was never reversed, for during the eight months' siege of the city which followed, although they left no stratagem or daring attempt untried, they never again ventured to mount a general assault. . . . The Romans, having brought up such numerous forces both by sea and by land, had every hope of capturing the city immediately, if only one old man out of all the Syra-

cusans could have been removed; but so long as he was present they did not dare even to attempt an attack by any method which made it possible for Archimedes to oppose them.

A Questionable Tradition?

While there can be little doubt that Archimedes did what he could to improve the weapons and machines that protected his native city, we must express skepticism about some of the devices described in the preceding passages. Might not the fearsome cranes, for example, actually be nothing more than cargo cranes called into service as makeshift weapons when the Romans attacked? If designed exclusively to lift the prows of enemy ships and stand them on end (unlikely in itself), they would have had to stand idle on the walls of Syracuse for years during peacetime; in battle, a ship would have had to sail right up to one of the hooks for it to be deployed effectively (seemingly impossible, considering Polybius' statement that Marcellus' ships only approached

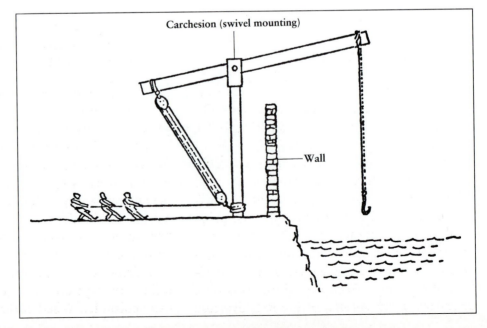

Figure 1.13
A possible reconstruction of the type of crane Polybius says Archimedes deployed for the defense of Syracuse. In reality, such "weapons" may have been nothing more than cargo cranes called into service to help repel the Roman attack.

Carchesion (swivel mounting)

Wall

the walls at night!). The cranes that supposedly picked up men in armor and dropped them are also a problem. It is hard enough to grasp a stationary prize with the pincers of a miniature crane in a modern amusement arcade. Picking off a moving man with a large crane hook would be a neat trick indeed.

Even though Polybius says that the city's defenses were so well planned that there was no need to worry about "improvisations," it still makes more sense to suggest that peacetime machinery (perhaps also designed by Archimedes) was put into operation against the Romans during the siege. If a crane were located near a spot where Romans were landing—and cargo cranes would be placed where merchant ships could most easily approach the city's shoreline to unload—obviously it could be used as a weapon. A lucky grab on one vessel, a boulder dropped on another, or a hook dangling from the walls snaring an unlucky soldier busy dodging arrows and spears may have been enough to make the Romans believe that these weapons were specifically designed by Archimedes for their destruction.

Marcellus abandoned his attempts to take the city by storm, deciding rather to blockade Syracuse and starve the population into submission. He resisted Carthaginian attempts to relieve the city, took time while Appius continued the siege to punish other anti-Roman cities in Sicily, and foiled all Syracusan attempts to break the blockade. Distracted during a festival in 212 B.C., the Syracusans became careless, and while the guards were drunk or sleeping, Marcellus led a force over the walls and captured the city's suburbs. Dogged resistance, Carthaginian interference, and a plague extended the campaign until the inner city was finally betrayed by an opportunistic Spanish mercenary who conveniently left a strategic gate unattended. Marcellus and his troops overwhelmed the remaining defenders. In late autumn of 212 B.C., Syracuse became a Roman prize, although cleanup operations did not cease until early in 211 B.C.

Archimedes' End

It was probably during the final assault on Syracuse in 212 B.C. that Archimedes perished. What actually happened to him is not known, but as might be expected, admirers contrived an end that befitted the popular concept of his life:

> Engaged in sketching a mechanical diagram, he was bending over it when a Roman came upon him and began to drag him off as a prisoner of war. Archimedes, wholly intent on his diagram and not realizing who was tugging at him, said to the man: "Away from my diagram, fellow!" Then, when the man continued to drag him along, Archimedes turned and, recognizing him for a Roman, cried out: "Quick there, one of my machines, someone!" The Roman, alarmed, slew him on the spot, a weak old man, but one whose achievements were wondrous. As soon as Marcellus learned of this, he was grieved, and together with the noblemen of the city and all the Romans gave him a splendid burial amid the tombs of his fathers. As for the murderer, he had him . . . beheaded. Dio and Diodorus record the story. (Tzetzes, *History* 2.103–149)

Other stories of his end are just as colorful —there is a strong tradition that Marcellus was greatly distressed when he learned that the great man had been killed. Not only is he supposed to have given Archimedes an appropriate burial, but he also sought out the surviving members of his family to honor them. Militarily, a living Archimedes' technological talents might have been put to good use in Rome's struggle with Hannibal (although his weapons had been designed primarily for defense), and Marcellus may have been sorry that he had missed that oportunity. Whether the Roman general's appreciation of his adversary's genius went any deeper is difficult to know. If Marcellus was so greatly upset by the loss of Archimedes, why had he not taken precautions to save him? It seems there had been opportunity to do so when representatives from Syracuse, wishing to avoid the inevitable, approached Marcellus about giving the city client-state status and placing its future in his family's hands. At that time (or during other parleys), Marcellus could have asked that Archi-medes be delivered up. Instead, he rejected all Syracusan overtures and went on to sack the city, knowing full well that any soldier could come upon Archimedes and kill him. Saving an old man who had made a fool of him and the Romans for eight months may not have been a high priority!

By exploiting the memory of the old man and his remarkable machines, Marcellus may have been trying to negate complaints in Rome about why he had taken so long to humble a stronghold of Greeks. Perhaps stories of the effectiveness of Archimedes' weapons were purposely exaggerated to mask what was, in reality, Roman incompetence.

After Syracuse: Problems for Marcellus

Marcellus preserved and brought back to Rome Archimedes' celestial globe (as well as a star globe that he placed in the Temple of Virtue). This may have been just an interesting memento for Marcellus (it is revealing that he kept it in his own house), but Cicero, writing in the first century B.C., insists that it was the only booty Marcellus had brought away from Syracuse for himself. (One of the obviously apocryphal stories concerning Archimedes' death has him in the process of bringing his globes and other instruments to

Marcellus when soldiers, thinking that his box was full of gold, attacked and killed him.) Cicero represented Marcellus as a model of self-control and restraint during the capture of Syracuse and glossed over long-standing charges of the warlord's excessiveness in the sack of the city. However, some of Marcellus' own contemporaries had apparently expressed their belief that the quantity of statuary, paintings, and other art treasures he had stripped from the fallen city and brought back to decorate Rome was offensive. It was later said, not entirely in jest, that the Romans first learned to appreciate Greek art from the massive spoils of Syracuse. Marcellus' wholesale plundering of the city does not appear to be the behavior of a man who supposedly "wept" before it was sacked. Sicilians disliked him intensely and regarded him as a person "nobody would trust except under oath." They finally persuaded Rome to replace him as commander in Sicily.

Archimedes Remembered

While Marcellus' feelings about Archimedes remain unsettled, one thing is clear: The Romans, ironically, maintained a stronger appreciation for the great master and his accomplishments than the Syracusans themselves did. This is indicated by an interesting postscript from Cicero. While in Syracuse in 75 B.C., Cicero was especially eager to visit the tomb of Archimedes. He certainly did not find the memorial he expected:

> When I was quaestor I tracked out his grave, which was unknown to the Syracusans (as they totally denied its existence), and found it enclosed all round and covered with brambles and thickets; for I remembered certain doggerel lines inscribed, as I had heard, upon his tomb, which stated that a sphere along with a cylinder had been set up on the top of his grave.

1996); M. C. Bishop and J. C. N. Coulston, *Roman Military Equipment: From the Punic Wars to the Fall of Rome* (London: Batsford, 1994); and J. Hackett, *Warfare in the Ancient World* (New York: Facts on File, 1989). On Carthage in particular, see S. Lancel, *Carthage: A History* (Cambridge, Mass.: Blackwell, 1995).

Recent General Additions

M. Le Glay, *A History of Rome* (New York: Blackwell Publishers, 1996); C. J. Smith, *Early Rome and Latium: Economy and Society c. 1000 to 500 B.C.* (New York: Oxford University Press, 1996); M. Wyke, *Projecting the Past: Ancient Rome, Cinema and History* (New York: Routledge, 1997); and S. Hornblower and A. Spawforth (eds.), *The Oxford Companion to Classical Civilization* (New York: Oxford University Press, 1998).

On women, see R. Hawley and B. Levick, *Women in Antiquity: New Assessments* (New York: Routledge, 1995); I. McAuslan and P. Walcot (eds.), *Women in Antiquity* (New York: Oxford University Press, 1996); A. Staples, *From Good Goddess to Vestal Virgins: Sex and Category in Roman Religion* (New York: Routledge, 1997); and S. Murnaghan and S. R. Joshel (eds.), *Women and Slaves in Greco-Roman Culture* (New York: Routledge, 1998).

On political, social, economic, cultural, urban, and legal issues, see W. Nippel, *Public Order in Ancient Rome* (Cambridge: Cambridge University Press, 1995); R. A. Bauman, *Crime and Punishment in Ancient Rome* (New York: Routledge, 1996); J. S. Kloppenborg and S. G. Wilson (eds.), *Voluntary Associations in the Greco-Roman World* (New York: Routledge, 1996); J. Salmon and G. Shipley (eds.), *Human Landscapes in Classical Antiquity* (New York: Routledge, 1996); G. Levi and J. Schmitt, *A History of Young People, Vol. 1: Ancient and Medieval* (Cambridge, Mass.: Harvard University Press, 1997); J. Andreau, *Banking and Business in the Roman World* (Cambridge: Cambridge University Press, 1999); H. M. Parkins (ed.), *Roman Urbanism: Beyond the Consumer City* (New York: Routledge, 1997); B. Rawson and P. Weaver, *The Roman Family in Italy:*

Status, Sentiment, Space (New York: Oxford University Press, 1997); O. F. Robinson, *The Sources of Roman Law: Problems and Methods for Ancient Historians* (New York: Routledge, 1997); D. Johnston, *Roman Law in Context* (Cambridge: Cambridge University Press, 1999); A. Sanosuosso, *Warfare and Society from Classical Greece to Republican Rome* (Boulder, Colo.: Westview Press, 1997); N. J. E. Austin and N. B. Rankov, *Exploratio: Military and Political Intelligence in the Roman World from the Second Punic War to the Battle of Adrianople* (New York: Routledge, 1998); J. Henderson, *Fighting for Rome: Poets and Caesars, History and Civil War* (Cambridge: Cambridge University Press, 1998); J. P. Hallett and M. B. Skinner (eds.), *Roman Sexualities* (Princeton, N.J.: Princeton University Press, 1997); and C. A. Williams, *Roman Homosexuality: Ideologies of Masculinity in Classical Antiquity* (New York: Oxford University Press, 1999).

On military matters, see A. K. Goldworthy, *The Roman Army at War 100 B.C.–A.D. 200* (New York: Oxford University Press, 1996); K. R. Dixon and P. Southern, *The Roman Cavalry* (New York: Routledge, 1997); P. Connolly, *Greece and Rome at War* (London: Greenhill Books, 1998); and P. B. Kern, *Ancient Siege Warfare* (Bloomington: Indiana University Press, 1999).

On religion, see M. Beard et al., *Religions of Rome,* 2 Vols. (Cambridge: Cambridge University Press, 1998).

See also J. W. Humphrey et al., *Greek and Roman Technology* (New York: Routledge, 1997); M. R. Lefkowitz, *Not Out of Africa* (New York: Basic Books, 1997); and J. G. Landels, *Music in Ancient Greece and Rome* (New York: Routledge, 1998).

2

The Republic in Transition

Internal Disorders
Eunus the Magician and the First Sicilian
Slave War (135–132 B.C.)

But of all causes of alarm the worst was the slaves—the
universal dread of having an enemy in one's own house;
no slave could be safely trusted, and to show open suspicion
was equally dangerous, as it might exacerbate hostility.
(Livy, *History of Rome* 3.16.3)

Rome won the Second Punic War in 201 B.C. and firmly established its credentials as the leading western Mediterranean power. It also prevailed in a third war with Carthage—one spawned mostly from hatred and revenge—that lasted from 149 to 146 B.C. Carthage had dwindled to less than a second-rate power, whereas Rome's strength had increased tremendously as the great Hellenistic monarchies were successfully brought into submission. The Seleucids in Syria, the Antigonids in Macedonia, and the Ptolemies in Egypt had tested Roman arms or patience and had all come up short. Greece, too, finally succumbed in 146 B.C. when the Achaean League was quashed and its leading city, Corinth, was sacked within a few months

of the destruction of Carthage. Only Spain remained rebellious, and by 133 B.C., resistance there ended also. Rome now dominated the Mediterranean world, and all had to do what Rome said.

The Problems of Success

Given the conditions, Rome's amazing success within so short a period is probably unparalleled in history. Only 131 years had passed since the Romans first set foot outside Italy, but they hardly had time to enjoy the fruits of their labors. Too much had happened too fast. The acquisition of so large a Mediterranean empire fostered new problems, and external difficulties

36

were replaced by internal ones—political, social, economic, and philosophical. Waging war is always easier than waging peace, and the strain of unsolved problems soon began to tear at the traditional fabric of the Republic.

An immediate problem directly related to the end of the wars was what to do with returning veterans. Many came home to find their small farms in ruin, themselves in debt, or their wives gone and their lands abandoned. A large number of veterans discovered that their farms had been illegally absorbed. Wealthy commoners, or *equites*—a whole new commercial class of entrepreneurs, businessmen, tax collectors, and others that sprang up to serve and profit from the Empire's needs—and Roman senators had established huge plantations (*latifundia*) to feed and supply the Roman world and meet its ever-growing demands. Other impoverished veterans had to sell their property to the great landowners and could not even remain as tenant farmers, for slave labor was cheaper and readily available.

Already faced with a large number of landless proletarians whose ranks had swollen over the years, Rome had the additional burden of having to deal with the jobless veterans. Rome was notorious for neglecting social problems and seldom acted for humanitarian reasons, but it was now confronted with the practical problem of what to do about its declining military strength. Since military service was, as a rule, based upon a property qualification and the bulk of the Roman legionaries was made up of landowners, the tens of thousands of ex-soldiers and others who had lost their farms were no longer eligible for service should emergencies arise.

In 133 B.C., Tiberius Gracchus, a tribune, was chosen to represent the interests of those in the Roman Senate who viewed land reform as the solution to the problem of military preparedness. It would also restore dignity to thousands of homeless Romans and give them a new lease on life. Tiberius himself was a blue-blooded plebeian noble. His mother, Cornelia, was the daughter of Scipio Africanus, who had ended the Second Punic War by defeating Hannibal and was a member of one of Rome's most illustrious patrician clans. His father and namesake had been censor and a leading figure in second-century B.C. Rome. His brother-in-law Scipio Aemilianus had humbled Carthage in the Third Punic War and had reduced Spain in 133 B.C. The land reform issue was one worthy of young Gracchus, who, though unable to relate fully to the plight of his fellow Romans, was not insensitive to their hardships. (Nor was he ignorant of the support thousands of appreciative voters would cast his way.)

Tiberius' bill would pool public land in Italy, apportion it to willing settlers, and provide funds to get them started. His effort was met by fierce opposition. Many of his fellow senators, owners of *latifundia* themselves (or allied with equestrian land barons), had been illegally using the public lands that Tiberius planned to redistribute. They felt threatened and let their pocketbooks rather than the public good influence their thinking. These senators did everything they could to thwart Tiberius, who, afraid that a defeat in this matter might jeopardize his political career, took the success of his land reform bill as a personal challenge.

Tiberius was finally able to push his bill through the assembly and fund it (the program would eventually settle over 70,000 people on public lands), but his unconventional methods alienated many of the ruling class—including some former supporters—who also feared his growing support among the masses. They were comforted only by the fact that Tiberius' year in the tribunate would soon be over and the protection the office afforded him (tribunes were considered sacrosanct and supposedly could not be harmed while in office) would end. Then, he could be disciplined for his anti-establishment behavior, and his land program could be dismantled. However, again rejecting conventionalism, Tiberius announced that he would seek reelection. His enemies, caught unprepared, panicked. When it became clear at the polls that he was winning a second term, Tiberius was assassinated, and several hundred of his supporters were killed in the ensuing riots.

The inability of Rome's elite to compromise in this matter and their use of violence were serious by-products of the acquisition of empire. The traditional ways of doing business were no longer applicable, for rapid change is not the handmaiden of conservative politics. Tiberius Gracchus was probably as much an "establishment" politician as any Roman aristocrat had ever been. He himself had not foreseen the impact that his maverick political machinations would have on his more firmly entrenched sena-

Cornelia—A Political Mother

CERTAINLY, ONE OF THE most remarkable women of this or any period in Roman history was Cornelia, the mother of Tiberius Gracchus. The tradition indicates that she had a decided influence on the political careers of Tiberius and her other son, Gaius, and there seems no legitimate reason to doubt it. Cornelia was the daughter of the great Scipio Africanus, conqueror of Hannibal, and the wife of Tiberius Sempronius Gracchus, censor and one of the more influential men of his day. She moved in circles that were open only to the most respected women in Rome. It is clear, however, that, while her family connections were strong, her own abilities won the admiration and confidence of important Romans. She was sought out for advice and conversation long after the deaths of her husband and sons, and later writers portrayed her as the ideal Roman matron.

It would be difficult to separate Tiberius' short and dramatic political career entirely from his mother's influence. From childhood, she had groomed him for success, and it is doubtful that Tiberius considered her any less a political ally and advisor during the stormy events of 133 B.C. Following the assassination that cut short Tiberius' promising career, Cornelia did not let her son's memory fade away. She was a major factor in fashioning his subsequent image as a martyr for the popular cause, which was gaining momentum in Rome—largely because of Tiberius' land reform program.

Her influence on her younger son Gaius— who, as tribune in 123 B.C., lionized his brother's efforts and became leader of the popular movement—must have been just as strong. When he, too, died violently in 121 B.C., Cornelia gloried in the memory of her two sons and continued to be admired for her political acumen and intelligence. She was as much a politician as any woman could be in a society that did not allow the formal participation of women in politics.

Plutarch gives the fullest account of Cornelia's life. When her husband died, leaving her, we are told, with twelve young children:

torial colleagues, who continued to embrace the time-honored formulae of the past.

Tiberius' nonconformist maneuverings did, ultimately, help spark what some of his opponents feared most—the rise of a popular cause in Rome as a viable political movement. Ten years after his death, his younger brother Gaius was tribune in 123 B.C. By that time, the only question about the popular movement was how strong it would become; and Gaius, a better politician than his brother, spearheaded the crusade. Reelected as tribune in 122 B.C., his success and growing power prompted his con-

servative enemies in the Senate to act once more. When riots broke out in 121 B.C. and the Senate declared a state of emergency (*senatus consultum ultimum*), Gaius took his own life before his foes could murder him as they had his brother. Three thousand of his followers were executed.

The deaths of Tiberius and Gaius Gracchus, two of Rome's most promising young men, the bluest-blooded of plebeian nobility, triggered the civil strife that would come to characterize the Late Republic and eventually lead to its downfall.

Cornelia took charge of the children and of the estate, and showed herself so discreet, so good a mother, and so magnanimous, that . . . when Ptolemy the king offered to share his crown with her and sought her hand in marriage, she refused him, and remained a widow. In this state she lost most of her children, but three survived; one daughter, who married Scipio the Younger, and two sons, Tiberius and Gaius. . . . These sons Cornelia reared with such scrupulous care that although confessedly no other Romans were so well endowed by nature, they were thought to owe their virtues more to education than to nature.

(*Tiberius Gracchus* 1.4–5)

Plutarch describes how Cornelia carried on her life after the deaths of Tiberius and Gaius:

. . . Cornelia is reported to have borne all her misfortunes in a noble and magnanimous spirit, and to have said of the sacred places where her sons had been slain that they were tombs worthy of the dead which occupied

them. She resided on the promontory called Misenum, and made no change in her customary way of living. She had many friends, and kept a good table that she might show hospitality, for she always had Greeks and other literary men about her, and all the reigning kings interchanged gifts with her. She was indeed very agreeable to her visitors and associates when she discoursed to them about the life and habits of her father [Scipio] Africanus, but most admirable when she spoke of her sons without grief or tears, and narrated their achievements and their fate to all inquirers as if she were speaking of men of the early days of Rome. Some were therefore led to think that old age or the greatness of her sorrows had impaired her mind and made her insensible to her misfortunes, whereas, really, such persons themselves were insensible how much help in the banishment of grief mankind derives from a noble nature and from honorable birth and rearing. . . .

(*Gaius Gracchus* 19.1–3)

Figure 2.1   A somewhat worn relief depicting a naked slave being sold at auction

Slaves in Sicily

Tiberius Gracchus' concerns about the huge *lati-fundia* were probably not restricted only to the illegal use of private and public property. The influx of tens of thousands of slaves, many of whom ended up as mistreated field hands on the same expansive plantations, was another undesirable consequence of Rome's subjugation of the Mediterranean. Most of these slaves were captives from Rome's wars in Asia, Greece, Macedonia, Africa, Spain, and Gaul, but a sizeable number were also victims of an organized, active pirate slave trade, which Roman greed and labor demands had done nothing to suppress. A dangerous situation began to emerge, especially on plantations in Sicily, where slaves were sent in wholesale lots. The island had already attracted runaway criminals, slaves, and other restive ele-

ments who joined with brigand herdsmen and shepherds to test the competency of local garrisons (usually inadequate for the task). They terrorized, robbed, and murdered travelers and residents in the more rural areas of Sicily.

Peacetime Sicily was not a major concern for Rome, involved with more pressing problems closer to home. Although many landowners in Sicily were Italian, the island was a remote, rural, largely Greek region about which most Romans knew very little. As long as the plantations were producing the necessary foodstuffs (particularly grain) for Rome and things were kept orderly, minimum attention was sufficient. Consequently, when the already dangerous slave problem became volatile in about 140 B.C., official Rome was unwilling to commit funds to put down what they considered to be just a few rebellious slaves and troublemakers.

Figure 2.2
To prevent successful escapes,
Roman slaves were often forced
to wear identifications such as
the ones pictured here.
Top: *A bronze collar (found on a*
skeleton) with the inscription: "If
captured, return me to Apronianus,
minister in the imperial palace,
at the Golden Napkin on the
Aventine, for I am a fugitive slave."
Bottom: *A bronze plaque from*
the third or fourth century A.D.
belonging to a slave named Asellus.
The inscription reads: "I am
Asellus, slave of Prejectus attached
to the ministry of markets, and
I have escaped the walls of Rome.
Capture me, for I am a fugitive
slave, and return me to Barber's
Street, near the Temple of Flora."
(Translations by A. Goldhammer)

Greedy landowners, too, preferred that Sicily not become an object of official attention, since that could lead to investigations of questionable business practices and ultimately affect their livelihoods. Rome was dependent on their knowledge of the region, their goodwill, and their support. Corrupt administrators in Sicily also took advantage of the opportunities for graft, and some of the most notorious examples of improper conduct by Roman officials during the Republic occurred there. Rome ultimately paid for turning a blind eye to affairs in Sicily.

The First Sicilian Slave War (135–132 B.C.)

The composition of Sicily's slave population changed rapidly in the years just before the First Sicilian Slave War. A large number of the recently enslaved from the East shared the same religious beliefs, language (mostly Greek), and "national" experience. There were more educated people (some of high status) in the ranks and more ex-soldiers. Since many had never experienced slavery before, they resented being overworked, cruelly treated, poorly fed, branded, chained, and quartered like animals in dingy hovels.

Close supervision of uncounted numbers of slaves who were spread all over Sicily was impossible. Brutality and the threat of more kept many in line, but there were frequent escapes. Those who fled added to the rebel population that had been plaguing Sicily for some time. Slaves were easily replaced, and Sicilian officials were more concerned with filling their pockets than with pursuing troublesome runaways. Meanwhile, Rome presumed that any servile problems were small and being taken care of by locals.

Eunus, the Slave King

Despite theories that the Slave War was a rebellion against the institution of slavery or a social revolutionary movement, it never involved all the slaves on Sicily, and it seems to have begun quite naturally for very human reasons. Sicilian landowners were notorious for committing outrages against their laborers, and it was probably sometime during 138 B.C. that the ill-treated slaves of Damophilus and his wife Megallis went to a remarkable slave named Eunus to ask if they had the gods' approval to murder their masters. Eunus had a reputation as a magician, a wonder-worker, and, most importantly, a prophet. He would become the leader of the rebellion.

Our major source for the episode is Diodorus, himself a Sicilian whose account, incomplete and mostly preserved by later writers, was composed about a century after the Slave War. Diodorus, put off by what he perceives as little more than fakery, records his initial negative impressions of Eunus, who was originally from Apamea in Syria, a major city of the Hellenistic Seleucid kingdom:

> There was a certain Syrian slave, belonging to Antigenes of Enna; he was an Apamean by birth and had an aptitude for magic and the working of wonders. He claimed to foretell the future, by divine command, through dreams, and because of his talent along these lines deceived many. Going on from there he not only gave oracles by means of dreams, but even made a pretense of having waking visions of the gods and of hearing the future from their own lips. Of his many improvisations some by chance turned out true, and since those which failed to do so were left unchallenged, while those that were fulfilled attracted attention his reputation advanced apace. Finally, through some device, while in a state of divine posses-

sion, he would produce fire and flame from his mouth, and thus rave oracularly about things to come. For he would place fire, and fuel to maintain it, in a nut—or something similar—that was pierced on both sides; then, placing it in his mouth and blowing on it, he kindled now sparks, and now a flame.
> (34/35.2.5–7)

Diodorus recounts that Eunus was owned by a man called Antigenes, who, judging from his name, was not a Roman but a Greek living in the city of Enna, which was at the geographic center of Sicily. We do not know how Eunus came to be a slave, but he appears to have been one for some time, since it is mentioned elsewhere that he had previously been the property of someone named Pytho, also from Enna. Eunus' special "skills" had obviously made him someone to whom other Eastern slaves looked for guidance and advice, and his reputation became known all over town even among the free population. Particularly amusing to local citizens was Eunus' prediction that he would someday be a king. His master, Antigenes, far from considering his slave a threat, mocked his ravings and made him a celebrity by introducing him at his dinner parties to entertain his guests with his insights into the future, a role that Eunus seems to have relished as much as anyone:

> Prior to the revolt [Eunus] used to say that the Syrian goddess appeared to him, saying that he should be king, and he repeated this, not only to others, but even to his own master. Since his claims were treated as a joke, Antigenes, taken by his hocus-pocus, would introduce Eunus . . . at his dinner parties, and cross-question him about his kingship and how he would treat each of the men present. And since he gave a full account of everything without hesitation, explaining with what moderation he would treat the masters and in sum making a colorful tale of his quackery,

Larcius Macedo—A Master Is Murdered by His Slaves

IN ANY SLAVE SYSTEM, owners fear being murdered by their slaves. This was particularly true among the Romans. The great slave revolts, like those of Eunus and Spartacus (see pages 51–55) that rocked Sicily and Italy during the last century of the Republic, made Romans even more apprehensive about their slaves—although it never occurred to them to abolish the institution. Not infrequently, the unspeakable happened to friends or acquaintances, driving home the reality of the potential dangers of keeping slaves. An anxious letter by Pliny the Younger (see Chapter 6), a Roman gentleman and prominent literary figure, gives a rare personal glimpse at the fear such incidents could cause.

Particularly interesting is Pliny's lack of sympathy for the slaves and their lot—in fact, he speaks of them more as brutish animals who deserved the punishment they got. The cruel treatment they had received from their master, a freedman himself who had risen to prominence, is given only scant note and, in Pliny's mind, appears to be no justification for what happened. This interesting assessment is made by a man who, elsewhere, shows himself to be an intelligent, sensitive, understanding individual. Pliny writes:

> This horrible affair demands more publicity than a letter—Larcius Macedo, a senator and ex-praetor, has fallen a victim to his own slaves. Admittedly he was a cruel and overbearing master, too ready to forget that his father had

been a slave, or perhaps too keenly conscious of it. He was taking a bath in his house at Formiae [in Latium] when suddenly he found himself surrounded; one slave seized him by the throat while the others struck his face and hit him in the chest and stomach and—shocking to say—in his private parts. When they thought he was dead they threw him on to the hot pavement, to make sure he was not still alive. Whether unconscious or feigning to be so, he lay there motionless, thus making them believe that he was quite dead. Only then was he carried out, as if he had fainted with the heat, and received by his slaves who had remained faithful, while his concubines ran up, screaming frantically. Roused by their cries and revived by the cooler air he opened his eyes and made some movement to show that he was alive, it being now safe to do so. The guilty slaves fled, but most of them have been arrested and a search is being made for the others. Macedo was brought back to life with difficulty, but only for a few days; at least he died with the satisfaction of having revenged himself, for he lived to see the same punishment meted out as for murder. There you see the dangers, outrages, and insults to which we are exposed. No master can feel safe because he is kind and considerate; for it is their brutality, not their reasoning capacity, which leads slaves to murder masters.
> (*Letters* 3.14)

the guests were always stirred to laughter, and some of them, picking up a nice tidbit from the table, would present it to him, adding, as they did so, that when he became king, he should remember the favor. But, as it happened, his charlatanism did in fact result in kingship, and

for the favors received in jest at the banquets he made a return of thanks in earnest.
(34/35.2.7–9)

While his master and friends viewed Eunus as little more than a court jester (an image

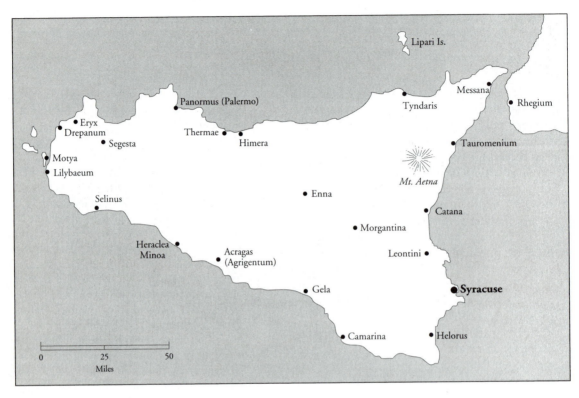

Map 9   Ancient Sicily

encouraged, no doubt, by Eunus himself), they failed to understand the impact he was having on many of his fellow slaves—especially those like him from the East who viewed his reputed powers and his identification with the "Syrian goddess" (identified by another source as "Atargatis") as legitimate within the context of their own religious practices. Consequently, he had become for many the most important leader among them, a bona fide miracle worker and prophet. It is no surprise that the disgruntled slaves of Damophilus and Megallis came to him for direction. Diodorus continues:

> Going to Eunus they asked him whether their resolve had the favor of the gods. He, resorting to his usual mummery, promised them the

favor of the gods, and soon persuaded them to act at once. Immediately, therefore, they brought together four hundred of their fellow slaves and, having armed themselves in such ways as opportunity permitted, they fell upon the city of Enna, with Eunus at their head and working his miracle of the flames of fire for their benefit.
(34/35.2.10–11)

While Diodorus indicates that the rebellion began immediately, it appears more likely that it was not until 135 B.C., three years later, that the capture of Enna actually took place. A spontaneous uprising by 400 disorganized slaves in 138 B.C. would have had little chance of success, and we would also have to accept a war of

Figure 2.3   *Household slaves preparing to serve wine to their masters*

Figure 2.4   *Slaves preparing the oven to bake bread*

at least six years (138–132 B.C.) instead of the three usually cited. It is not likely to have taken Roman armies that many years to respond successfully to the crisis. We can, however, believe that the slaves caused many disturbances and strengthened their cause between 138 and 135 B.C. No doubt there was already a slave "underground" in operation. It would have been needed in effective planning to capture the city, to identify reliable recruits, to make or steal weapons and secretly store them away (although Diodorus suggests that the slaves found their weapons as they needed them when the rebellion began), to make contacts with rebel groups in the countryside who might help, and to come up with some way to coordinate and command a diverse group of individuals. The slaves apparently aroused little suspicion while they prepared. There were always altercations between slaves and slave owners or local officials, and rumors of minor insurrections were circulating constantly. Only the slaves were prepared for what happened next.

The Rebellion Begins

Having carefully laid their plans, the 400 slaves met in a field outside Enna one midnight, probably in the early spring of 135 B.C., swore oaths, and made sacrifices. A recent eruption of Mt. Aetna on the eastern side of Sicily, undoubtedly taken as a divine sign, had strengthened their resolve. With Eunus at their head breathing his own fire into the darkness, the rebels made their way into the sleeping city. Diodorus recounts the standard kind of horrors we might expect Romans to blame on rampant slaves bent on revenge—tearing infants from their mothers' breasts and smashing them on the ground, committing outrageous acts on women while their husbands looked on. Stock charges aside, there

can be no doubt that the slaves, now joined by others in the city in a general uprising, vented years of pent-up anger against their masters.

Once the city was taken, Damophilus and his wife, whose cruelty had prompted the original conspiracy, were located and brought bound into the theater. Damophilus was allowed to defend his actions before an assembly of victorious slaves. At first, we might regard this trial as nothing but a sham, but Diodorus seems to indicate that it was a legitimate attempt on the part of the slaves to proceed in a legalistic and organized fashion. When Damophilus seemed to be winning over some of the crowd with his words, Hermias and Zeuxis—two of his former slaves who, with Eunus, had assumed leadership roles among the rebels—lost patience and slaughtered him without awaiting a formal verdict.

That the slaves had not resorted to wholesale butchery is indicated by the fact that they took special pains to protect Damophilus' daughter, who had countered her parents' cruelty by assisting the family's slaves in any way possible. She was given safe passage and escorted to relatives in eastern Sicily by the same Hermias who had killed her father. Eunus also kept his promise to those at his master's dining table who had given him food and jokingly asked him to spare them when he became king. Nevertheless, in the course of events, most citizens of Enna died, and Eunus himself personally killed his former masters Antigenes and Pytho. Since he had spared his master Antigenes' friends, the act seems mostly a symbolic one to convince the tougher slaves—not entirely impressed by his magic (Eunus was not known for his "manly courage")—of his suitability to lead them. We also hear stories of slaves cutting off the hands of captives (sometimes taking off the forearms as well). This grisly business, however, was probably for reasons more practical than revenge.

The slaves had no way of holding prisoners, so they made them useless for war. They could have just killed them.

Diodorus continues:

Thereupon Eunus was chosen king, not for his manly courage or his ability as a military leader, but solely for his marvels and his setting of the revolt in motion, and because his name ["Benevolent One"] seemed to contain a favorable omen that suggested good will towards his subjects.

Established as the rebels' supreme commander, he called an assembly and put to death all the citizenry of Enna except for those who were skilled in the manufacture of arms: these he put in chains and assigned them to this task. He gave Megallis to the maidservants to deal with as they might wish. . . . He himself murdered his own masters, Antigenes and Pytho. Having set a diadem upon his head, and arrayed himself in full royal style, he proclaimed his wife queen (she was a fellow Syrian and of the same city), and appointed to the royal council such men as seemed to be gifted with superior intelligence, among them one Achaeus . . . a man who excelled both at planning and in action. In three days Eunus had armed, as best he could, more than six thousand men, besides others in his train who had only axes and hatchets, or slings, or sickles, or fire-hardened stakes, or even kitchen spits; and he went about ravaging the countryside. Then, since he kept recruiting untold number of slaves, he ventured even to do battle with Roman generals, and on joining combat repeatedly overcame them with his superior numbers, for he now had more than ten thousand soldiers. (34/35.2.14–16)

About thirty days after Enna fell to the slaves, a rebel leader named Cleon, a Cilician, joined Eunus, who was now calling himself "Antiochus," with about five thousand more slaves. Diodorus describes his credentials:

A certain Cleon, a Cilician from the region about Taurus, who was accustomed from childhood to a life of brigandage and had become in Sicily a herder of horses, constantly waylaid travelers and perpetrated murders of all kinds. On hearing the news of Eunus' success and of the victories of the fugitives serving with him, he rose in revolt, and persuading some of the slaves near by to join him in his mad venture overran the city of Acragas and all the surrounding country. (34/35.2.43)

At first, the Romans hoped that the two groups of slaves would compete, quarrel, and eventually destroy each other; but it seems clear that there was some coordination between their activities from the start. Cleon immediately recognized the supreme authority of Antiochus-Eunus and placed himself and his men under his command.

The first levy fielded against the slaves, a Sicilian militia of 8,000, was unequal to the task. It was vastly outnumbered by a rebel army that Diodorus says numbered 20,000 and soon swelled to about 70,000. Rome was still not fully aware of what was happening in Sicily. There had never been a massive slave revolt before, and despite riots by small bands of slaves, there was no reason to expect one now. Consequently, it was some time before the full extent of the threat became known. The lack of a quick response by Rome fueled the success of the rebellion. The city of Tauromenium on the east coast fell, but not before Eunus and his men reputedly staged a mock drama just out of missile range, reenacting the original uprising and indicating what had happened to their former masters. Apparently, the slave-king also knew how to use psychology to his advantage. Catana, Morgantina, and other cities also succumbed.

However, not everything went well for the rebels. Syracuse was besieged, but lacking

Figure 2.5   Mt. Aetna in Sicily. In the foreground are the remains of the Theater at Tauromenium, a city captured by Eunus and his slave army.

supplies, the slaves had to break off, leaving the city's harbors open for Roman reinforcements. Messana and other large cities did not join the rebellion; and many slaves, particularly those who were skilled, well cared for, and unsympathetic to their "Eastern" brothers at the center of the uprising, did not participate. Nonetheless, news of the rebellion spread quickly, and slave uprisings occurred in Attica, Delos, and Asia Minor. There was even a minor disturbance in Rome itself.

Once Rome grasped the seriousness of the rebellion, one of the consuls for 134 B.C. was

dispatched to Sicily but met with little success. The next year, another consul, L. Calpurnius Piso Frugi, who would later become a historian (his lost *Annals* probably would have provided some valuable insights into the Servile War and may have been used by Diodorus), took charge. He appears to have restored sagging discipline among Roman troops, but he was unable to retake Enna from the slaves. He did, however, capture Morgantina, slaughtering thousands of its defenders and crucifying the survivors.

The consul for 132 B.C. brought the First Sicilian Slave War to a successful close. With a well-trained army of about twenty thousand, Publius Rupilius starved Tauromenium into submission. The city was finally betrayed by a defender, but not before the inhabitants were reputedly reduced to cannibalism. The surviving slaves were tortured and then thrown from the battlements. The brother of Eunus' general, Cleon, was also taken captive but committed suicide while being questioned by Rupilius. Next came Enna itself, the stronghold of the slave resistance, where Eunus and Cleon were holed up. It suffered the same fate as Tauromenium. Their cause fast becoming hopeless, Cleon attempted a feeble attack on the Romans with a small, outnumbered force. Killed in the attack, his dead body, covered with wounds, was displayed to the defenders. Finally, the city, suffering from plague and famine, was betrayed to Rupilius, who massacred any who resisted and treated the survivors to crucifixion, the customary Roman punishment for rebellious slaves. Remarkably, Eunus escaped the initial onslaught, but his capture was a foregone conclusion:

> Eunus, taking with him his bodyguards, a thousand strong, fled in unmanly fashion to a certain precipitous region. The men with him, however, aware that their dreaded fate was inevitable, inasmuch as the general, Rupilius,

was already marching against them, killed one another with the sword, by beheading. Eunus, the wonder-worker and king, who through cowardice had sought refuge in certain caves, was dragged out with four others, a cook, a baker, the man who massaged him at his bath, and a fourth, whose duty it had been to amuse him at drinking parties. Remanded to prison, where his flesh disintegrated into a mass of lice, he met such an end as befitted his knavery, and died at Morgantina.
(Diodorus 34/35.2.22–23)

Eunus' Significance

The circumstances of Eunus' end, as well as other aspects of his role in the Servile War, show him to be much more than the charlatan Diodorus paints him to be. While appearing sympathetic to the slaves' cause at times, Diodorus has no regard for their leader, describing him as unmanly, cowardly, deceptive, a faker, a quack, and a knave. Such characterizations would lead us to believe that Eunus was a man of little talent who rallied the slaves around him solely on the basis of his hocus-pocus. That does not appear to have been the case.

Rupilius was smart enough to know that the widespread respect and popularity among the slaves for Eunus would make him a martyr if he crucified him along with the others. Since there was an obvious Eastern tone to the rebellion (Eunus even referred to his followers as "Syrians"), prompting some to suggest possible messianic overtones to the movement, Rupilius may have been especially careful in dealing with Eunus—prophet, priest, and king. Romans were familiar enough with Eastern peoples, especially the Jews, to know that wizards, magicians, and miracle workers could come to be regarded as "saviors" and could rally masses of people to their side. To be sure, Eunus' fire-breathing trick, even if mostly for show, suggests some form of divine possession, something like those who walk unharmed barefooted on hot coals. If he was a fake, as Diodorus claims, then he was most certainly among the best on record. Wisely, Rupilius isolated the miracle worker, spiriting him away to prison and an eventual ignominious death.

The disease of which Diodorus says Eunus died, *phthiriasis* (consumption by lice), is noteworthy. A gruesome and painful end, it has usually been reserved by moralistic historians for hated rulers and objects of God's wrath. While most attributions of the disease cannot be substantiated and are unlikely to be true, the malady itself, long considered a fantasy by scholars, is real. Although rare, it is not caused by lice but by mites, which, under the right conditions, become accidental parasites of humans and destroy the tissue of the lower abdomen. Unknowingly, Diodorus elevated and enhanced the reputation of Eunus simply by giving him the disease, for by his time, it allegedly had caused the death of the Greek poet Alcman; Callisthenes, Alexander's historian (who, like Eunus, died a prisoner); the Macedonian king Cassander; the Roman dictator Sulla; and most interestingly, the Seleucid monarch Antiochus IV, who may have been Antiochus-Eunus' own namesake!

One of the most fascinating and revealing aspects of the rebellion was that, almost from the start, Eunus and his lieutenants went about establishing their "slave kingdom" along the lines of the great Eastern Hellenistic Seleucid monarchy in which they had formerly lived. The fact that Eunus took for himself the most common royal name among the Seleucids, Antiochus, has prompted some scholars to posit that he may have been related to the ruling family. He wore a diadem and other insignia of office, and he minted coins stamped with an abbreviation for "King Antiochus." The coins pictured Demeter, the Greek goddess of grain. She had a center of worship at Enna, and her cult obviously had great meaning for the agricultural slaves under Eunus' command. He probably identified her with his own Atargatis. Even *Eunus*, which means "Benevolent One," was probably not his real name but a title like those the Seleucid monarchs assumed—for example, Antiochus I had been called "Soter" ("Savior").

Eunus' "ministers," Hermias, Zeuxis, and Achaeus, all had the same names as ministers who had served Antiochus III, too coincidental not to suggest that the names were assumed to strengthen identity with the Seleucid kingdom. Cleon was King Antiochus-Eunus' "general"; there were a royal bodyguard and an army; and when he was caught, King Antiochus-Eunus had with him his personal butcher, baker, masseur, and court jester. All this was consistent with Seleucid court practices.

During the war, the slaves' ability to obtain food and equipment over a period of several years indicates some organization and effective chain of command. So, too, did the policy (after the initial stages of the revolt) of not ravaging the countryside, destroying crops, and killing farmhands. The evidence suggests careful consideration, intelligent planning, and foresight: Antiochus-Eunus and his chief conspirators were not mere charlatans and brigands toying with the credulity of moronic slaves.

To Antiochus-Eunus and his council, the establishment of a Seleucid kingdom in the West might have seemed a possibility—at least at the beginning of the conflict. Rome was a distant (almost absent) landlord in Sicily, always busy elsewhere. Rome's real strength was not visible, and the slaves themselves were familiar with the corruption, disorganization, and casualness that

characterized the running of the province. (One need not look far for reasons why the Second Servile War [104–100 B.C.] would also break out in Sicily and why Spartacus [see pages 51–55], who led the last and greatest of the slave rebellions [73–71 B.C.], was arranging to ferry his slave army from Italy to Sicily before his defeat.) The slaves also may have thought they could keep Rome at bay if they gained control of Sicily's crucial grain supply—although their failure to capture major coastal strongholds like Syracuse and Messana would ultimately end any hope for lasting success. Antiochus-Eunus and his followers did not know what the future might bring, but some form of administration in the present was crucial to the rebels' continued success and confidence in their leadership. The only model they knew was the Seleucid kingdom.

Interestingly, Antiochus-Eunus stopped short of the Seleucid practice of ruler worship. Whether it was dangerous for him to attempt to impose divine kingship on his rebel subjects or whether he was constrained by legitimate religious reasons cannot be known. If he actually considered himself the consort of the Syrian goddess Atargatis as some would suggest, then the question was moot—he was already viewed as the earthly manifestation of the Syrian Sun-God Hadad.

The Revolt's Impact

While the First Sicilian Slave War also included a number of free peasants who rebelled against their wealthy overlords, nothing indicates that it ever became a true social revolutionary or communist movement. The panic caused by the uprising in Sicily did have the potential to spread to the tens of thousands of landless Italian proletarians. One of the reasons Tiberius Gracchus and his faction acted when they did

Spartacus Ravages Italy

THE LAST AND MOST destructive of Rome's servile wars broke out in Italy in 73 B.C. and was led by a Thracian gladiator named Spartacus. By the time he and his slave army were defeated in 71 B.C., Spartacus had earned a place in the Roman pantheon of villains reminiscent of Hannibal's. His name became legendary, associated with what many Romans regarded as one of the greatest crises in their history.

While Spartacus' rebellion may, in scale, appear closer to a legitimate social revolutionary movement than any of the three great slave uprisings that occurred in Sicily and Italy between 135 and 71 B.C., it still lacked the essential ingredients. This was not a case of the masses rising up "against a corrupt, capitalistic Roman world." To be sure, just about every slave in Italy who wanted to join the rebellion had an opportunity to do so, as did most of the oppressed free; but most did not, and the slave armies were no more concerned about preserving the lives of the downtrodden than they were the rich. With the exception of expertly trained military leaders and the larger scope of the rebellion, the character of this revolt does not seem overly different from that of the First Sicilian Slave War. In fact, it did not even have the political and religious cohesion of Eunus' uprising, although Spartacus was associated with magical and prophetic powers through his wife. There is little to demonstrate goals or motives other than self-preservation, destruction, and revenge.

The war began when Spartacus, apparently enslaved after deserting from the Roman army, escaped with about seventy of his fellows from a gladiatorial training school in Capua. This was not far from Mt. Vesuvius, which became the rebels' initial base of operations. As the emergency grew, Rome was unprepared to meet it—mainly because after the civil wars of the 80s B.C.,

standing armies were not allowed in Italy. Consequently, it took time before Rome could field first-line troops against the slaves. Our major ancient sources for the war are Plutarch and Appian, who differ somewhat in the details and course of the rebellion. The following account, given in its entirety, is provided by Plutarch in his life of *Crassus* (8.1–11.7):

The rising of the gladiators and their devastation of Italy, which is generally known as the war of Spartacus, began as follows. A man called Lentulus Batiatus had an establishment for gladiators at Capua. Most of them were Gauls and Thracians. They had done nothing wrong, but, simply because of the cruelty of their owner, were kept in close confinement until the time came for them to engage in combat. Two hundred of them planned to escape, but their plan was betrayed and only seventy-eight, who realized this, managed to act in time and get away, armed with choppers and spits which they seized from some cookhouse. On the road they came across some wagons which were carrying arms for gladiators to another city, and they took those arms for their own use. They then occupied a strong position and elected three leaders. The first of these was Spartacus. He was a Thracian [of nomadic stock] and not only had a great spirit and great physical strength, but was, much more than one would expect from his condition, most intelligent and cultured, being more like a Greek than a Thracian. They say that when he was first taken to Rome to be sold, a snake was seen coiled round his head while he was asleep and his wife, who came from the same tribe and was a prophetess subject to possession by the frenzy of Dionysus, declared that this sign meant that he would have a great and terrible power which

(continued)

Spartacus Ravages Italy (continued)

would end in misfortune. This woman shared in his escape and was then living with him.

First, then, the gladiators repulsed those who came out against them from Capua. In this engagement they got hold of proper arms and gladly took them in exchange for their own gladiatorial equipment which they threw away, as being barbarous and dishonorable weapons to use. Then the praetor Clodius, with 3,000 soldiers, was sent out against them from Rome. He laid siege to them in a position which they took up on a hill. There was only one way up this hill, and that was a narrow and difficult one, and was closely guarded by Clodius; in every other direction there was nothing but sheer precipitous cliffs. The top of the hill, however, was covered with wild vines and from these they cut off all the branches that they needed, and then twisted them into strong ladders which were long enough to reach from the top, where they were fastened, right down the cliff face to the plain below. They all got down safely by means of these ladders except for one man who stayed at the top to deal with their arms, and he, once the rest had got down, began to drop the arms down to them, and, when he had finished his task, descended last and reached the plain in safety. The Romans knew nothing of all this, and so the gladiators were able to get round behind them and to throw them into confusion by the unexpectedness of the attack, first routing them and then capturing their camp. And now they were joined by numbers of herdsmen and shepherds of those parts, all sturdy men and fast on their feet. Some of these they armed as regular infantrymen and made use of others as scouts and light troops.

The second expedition against them was led by the praetor Publius Varinus. First they engaged and routed a force of 2,000 men under his deputy commander, Furius by name; then came the turn of Cossinius, who had been sent out with a large force to advise Varinus and to share with him the responsibility of the command. Spartacus watched his movements closely and very nearly captured him as he was bathing near Salinae. He only just managed to escape, and Spartacus immediately seized all his baggage and then pressed on hard after him and captured his camp. There was a great slaughter and Cossinius was among those who fell. Next Spartacus defeated the praetor himself in a number of engagements and finally captured his lictors and the very horse that he rode. By this time Spartacus had grown to be a great and formidable power, but he showed no signs of losing his head. He could not expect to prove superior to the whole power of Rome, and so he began to lead his army towards the Alps. His view was that they should cross the mountains and then disperse to their own homes, some to Thrace and some to Gaul. His men, however, would not listen to him. They were strong in numbers and full of confidence, and they went about Italy ravaging everything in their way.

There was now more to disturb the senate than just the shame and the disgrace of the revolt. The situation had become dangerous enough to inspire real fear, and as a result both consuls were sent out to deal with what was considered a major war and a most difficult one to fight. One of the consuls, Gellius, fell suddenly upon and entirely destroyed the German contingent of Spartacus' troops, who in their insolent self-confidence had marched off on their own and lost contact with the rest; but when Lentulus, the other consul, had surrounded the enemy with large forces, Spartacus turned to the attack, joined battle, defeated the generals of Lentulus and captured all their equipment. He then pushed on towards the Alps and was confronted by Cassius, the governor of Cisalpine Gaul, with an army of 10,000 men. In the battle that followed Cassius was defeated and, after losing many of his men, only just managed to escape with his own life.

This news roused the senate to anger. The consuls were told to return to civilian life, and Crassus was appointed to the supreme command of the war. Because of his reputation or because of their friendship with him large numbers of the nobility volunteered to serve with him. Spartacus was now bearing down on Picenum, and Crassus himself took up a position on the borders of the district with the intention of meeting the attack there. He ordered one of his subordinate commanders, Mummius, with two legions to march round by another route and instructed him to follow the enemy, but not to join battle with them or even to do any skirmishing. Mummius, however, as soon as he saw what appeared to him a good opportunity, offered battle and was defeated. Many of his men were killed and many saved their lives by throwing away their arms and running for it. Crassus gave Mummius himself a very rough reception after this. He re-armed his soldiers and made them give guarantees that in future they would preserve the arms in their possession. Then he took 500 of those who had been the first to fly and had shown themselves the greatest cowards, and, dividing them into fifty squads of ten men each, put to death one man, chosen by lot, from each squad. This was a traditional method of punishing soldiers, now revived by Crassus after having been out of use for many years. . . .

After employing this method of conversion on his men, Crassus led them against the enemy. But Spartacus slipped away from him and marched through Lucania to the sea. At the Straits he fell in with some pirate ships from Cilicia and formed the plan of landing 2,000 men in Sicily and seizing the island; he would be able, he thought, to start another revolt of slaves there, since the previous slave war had recently died down and only needed a little fuel to make it blaze out again. However, the Cilicians, after agreeing to his proposals and receiving gifts from him, failed to keep their promises and sailed off. So Spartacus marched back again from the sea and established his army in the peninsula of Rhegium. At this point Crassus came up. His observation of the place made him see what should be done, and he began to build fortifications right across the isthmus. In this way he was able at the same time to keep his own soldiers busy and to deprive the enemy of supplies. The task which he had set himself was neither easy nor inconsiderable, but he finished it and, contrary to all expectation, had it done in a very short time. A ditch, nearly forty miles long and fifteen feet wide, was carried across the neck of land from sea to sea; and above the ditch he constructed a wall which was astonishingly high and strong. At first Spartacus despised these fortifications and did not take them seriously; but soon he found himself short of plunder and, when he wanted to break out from the peninsula, he realized that he was walled in and could get no more supplies where he was. So he waited for a night when it was snowing and a wintry storm had got up, and then, after filling up a small section of the ditch with earth and timber and branches of trees, managed to get a third of his army across.

Crassus was now alarmed, thinking that Spartacus might conceive of the idea of marching directly on Rome. But he was relieved from his anxiety when he saw that, as the result of some disagreement, many of Spartacus' men

(continued)

Spartacus Ravages Italy (continued)

had left him and were encamped as an independent force by themselves near a lake in Lucania. Crassus fell upon this division of the enemy and dislodged them from their positions by the lake, but at this point Spartacus suddenly appeared and stopped their flight, so that he was prevented from following them up and slaughtering them.

Crassus now regretted that he had previously written to the senate to ask them to send for Lucullus from Thrace and Pompey from Spain. He made all the haste he could to finish the war before these generals arrived, knowing that the credit for the success would be likely to go not to himself but to the commander who appeared on the scene with reinforcements. In the first place, then, he decided to attack the enemy force under Caius Canicius and Castus, who had separated themselves from the rest and were operating on their own. With this intention he sent out 6,000 men to occupy some high ground before the enemy could do so and he told them to try to do this without being observed. They, however, though they attempted to elude observation by covering up their helmets, were seen by two women who were sacrificing for the enemy, and they would have been in danger if Crassus had not quickly brought up the rest of his forces and joined in battle. This was the most stubbornly contested battle of all. In it Crassus' troops killed 12,300 men, but he only found two of them wounded in the back. All the rest died standing in the ranks and fighting back the Romans.

After this force had been defeated, Spartacus retired to the mountains of Petelia. One of Crassus' officers called Quintus, and the quaestor Scrophas followed closely in his tracks. But when Spartacus turned on his pursuers, the Romans were entirely routed and they only just managed to drag the quaestor, who had been

Figure 2.6   Although Spartacus was the type of gladiator known as the "Thracian," who fought only with a small round shield and curved scimitar, some of his companions had been trained to fight in heavy armor and wore helmets such as the one pictured here.

wounded, into safety. This success turned out to be the undoing of Spartacus, since it filled his slaves with overconfidence. They refused any longer to avoid battle and would not even obey their officers. Instead they surrounded them with arms in their hands as soon as they began

Spartacus Ravages Italy (continued)

to march and forced them to lead them back through Lucania against the Romans. This was precisely what Crassus most wanted them to do. It had already been reported that Pompey was on his way, and in fact a number of people were already loudly proclaiming that the victory in this war belonged to him; it only remained for him to come and fight a battle, they said, and the war would be over. Crassus, therefore, was very eager to fight the decisive engagement himself and he camped close by the enemy. Here, as the men were digging a trench, the slaves came out, jumped into the trench and began to fight with those who were digging. More men from both sides kept on coming up, and Spartacus, realizing that he had no alternative, drew up his whole army in order of battle.

First, when his horse was brought to him, he drew his sword and killed it, saying that the enemy had plenty of horses which would be his if he won, and, if he lost, he would not need a horse at all. Then he made straight for Crassus himself, charging forward through the press of weapons and wounded men, and, though he did not reach Crassus, he cut down two centurions who fell on him together. Finally, when his own men had taken to flight, he himself, surrounded by enemies, still stood his ground and died fighting to the last.

---

was that they feared a full-scale revolution could erupt in Italy if something were not done to help the impoverished. It is no coincidence that the land reform issue became most heated at the exact moment the Slave War was peaking in Sicily, and Tiberius' assassination may be indirectly related to that conflict. But while Rome had long-standing, unattended social problems in both Sicily and Italy, there is no compelling evidence that the discontented or jobless cooperated or joined forces with the slave army. Nor was the Servile War a religious crusade, although common religious elements—mostly Eastern and Hellenistic—exploited by Antiochus-Eunus, played a key role in cementing the diverse peoples involved in the rebellion.

The war initially appears to have been simply an uprising led by nontraditional slaves, sparked primarily by their cruel treatment and their desire for revenge. The core of the movement was made up largely of agricultural and pastoral slaves, mostly from the East, led by intelligent men—some, it appears, once of high rank.

It is also significant that many slaves, particularly skilled ones and those treated in more humane fashion, not only did not get involved in the insurrection but also actually helped their masters defend against the rebels. Regardless of what romantics and idealists want to make of it, there was no great moral question being determined here. This was not a general slave uprising "that men might be free," nor a revolt against the institution of slavery itself, which even the slaves (some of them probably former slave owners) viewed as a fact of life.

When the Servile War was over, nothing really changed. Sicily's economy was dependent on slaves and could not run without them. Rupilius knew this and stopped the mass slaughter and crucifixions as soon as he could. Many captives were returned to their former owners because of the immediate shortage of slaves, but new slaves would soon arrive to replace the old. Things went back to the way they had been, and the Romans learned little from the experience. Future massive slave insurrections would make them pay dearly for their casual enslavement of so many tens of thousands to serve their needs cheaply.

Suggestions for Further Reading

The major ancient source for the Sicilian slave revolt and its background (and the narrative on which all modern assessments of Eunus must ultimately rest) is the incomplete and fragmented account contained in Diodorus 34/35.2. A translation may be found in Vol. 12 of the Loeb Classical Library edition of Diodorus' *History*. K. R. Bradley has published a general monograph on Roman slave rebellions, *Slavery and Rebellion in the Roman World, 140 B.C.– 70 B.C.* (Bloomington and Indianapolis: Indiana University Press, 1989). Chapter 3 is on the First Sicilian Slave War. The best single evaluation remains P. Green's "The First Sicilian Slave War," in *The Shadow of the Parthenon* (London: Maurice

Temple Smith, 1972), 193–215. See also M. I. Finley, *A History of Sicily* (noted in Chapter 1), Chapter 11; and J. Vogt, *Ancient Slavery and the Ideal of Man* (Cambridge, Mass.: Harvard University Press, 1975), Chapter 3. On Roman slavery, A. Watson's *Roman Slave Law* (Baltimore: The Johns Hopkins University Press, 1987), Bradley's *Slaves and Masters in the Roman Empire: A Study in Social Control* (New York: Oxford University Press, 1987) and (Bradley's) *Slavery and Society at Rome* (Cambridge: Cambridge University Press, 1994), and A. Kirschenbaum's *Sons, Slaves and Freedmen in Roman Commerce* (Jerusalem & CUA Washington, 1987) are other studies. On the general topic of slavery in the ancient world, see T. Wiedemann, *Greek and Roman Slavery* (Baltimore: The Johns Hopkins University Press, 1981), a sourcebook; K. Hopkins, *Conquerors and Slaves* (Cambridge: Uni-versity Press, 1978); Finley (ed.), *Slavery in Classical Antiquity* (Cambridge: Heffer, 1968); and W. L. Westermann, *The Slave Systems of Greek and Roman Antiquity* (Philadelphia: American Philosophical Society, 1955). Finley's *The Ancient Economy* (Berkeley and Los Angeles: University of California Press, 1973) also contains many references to slaves.

3

Politics and Violence in the First Century B.C.

Gambling with Rome's Future

Brutus the Assassin

I do not know what this young man wants, but everything that he wants, he wants very badly.
(Caesar speaking about Brutus, in Plutarch, *Brutus* 6.4)

The list of important people assassinated in antiquity reads like an ancient *Who's Who*. Among Romans, one tradition makes Romulus, the "founder" of Rome, an assassin's victim. During the Roman Republic, Tiberius Gracchus, Livius Drusus the Younger, Sertorius, and Pompey all had their lives cut short. Roman emperors were particularly vulnerable, and Caligula, Galba, Domitian, Commodus, Caracalla, and Aurelian were among the more notable targets. Few single acts of violence, however, have captured the attention of the world for so many centuries as has the assassination of one particular Roman—Caesar.

On the fifteenth of March, the Roman Ides, 44 B.C., Gaius Julius Caesar was cut down by a group of senatorial assassins. Although immortal-ized in literature, art, drama, and film, the ill-considered deed actually solved nothing. Caesar's death only brought about a new series of disastrous events for Rome. Marcus Junius Brutus, the leader of the plot, viewed the elimination of Caesar as a solution to personal and political problems. His efforts, while well remembered, earned him nothing more than an ignominious death at Philippi. Brutus gambled with Rome's future. In the end, he became one of the most famous losers in history. Unquestionably, his personal machinations contributed to the fall of the Republic.

The Late Republic

The hundred or so years that followed the First Sicilian Slave War and the death of Tiberius

Gracchus were among the most critical and chaotic in Rome's history. Appian, the second-century A.D. historian, looked back on the period and characterized it as follows:

> The sword was never carried into the assembly and there was no civil slaughter until Tiberius Gracchus, tribune and law-bringer, was the first to fall a victim to internal commotion; and with him many others, who were crowded together at the Capitol around the temple, were also slain. Sedition did not end with that abominable deed. Repeatedly the parties came into open conflict, often carrying daggers, and from time to time in the temples, the assemblies, or the Forum some tribune, praetor, consul, or candidate for these offices, or some person otherwise distinguished, would be slain. Unseemly violence prevailed almost constantly, together with shameful contempt for law and justice. As the evil gained in magnitude, open insurrections against the government and large warlike expeditions against their country were undertaken by exiles, criminals, or persons vying with one another for some office or military command. Factions arose repeatedly, with chiefs aspiring to sole rule, some of them refusing to disband the troops entrusted to them by the state, others even hiring forces against each other on their own account, without public authority. Whenever either side got possession of the city, the opposing side made war, ostensibly against their adversaries, but actually against their country. They assailed it like an enemy's capital: those on hand were ruthlessly and indiscriminately massacred, others suffered proscription to death, banishment, confiscation of property; some were even subjected to excruciating tortures.
> (*Civil Wars* 1, Introduction.2)

These few charged decades, strained by the intensity of divisive politics and distinguished by some of the most memorable personalities in the Western tradition, have been the object of attention for generations. The civil wars, conspiracies, and interplay of personal ambitions led to the gradual breakdown of the Republican form of government and its replacement by one-man rule. This process, popularly called by modern scholars the "Roman Revolution," had progressed to such a point that by 48 B.C. Caesar, through his defeat of Pompey and the Republicans at Pharsalus, became virtual master of Rome. His failure to complete the Revolution was dictated by factors over which he had no control.

Brutus, the "Honorable Man"

Shortly after the assassination of Caesar, Brutus received the following letter from an anxious fellow conspirator, Decimus Brutus. Caesar's death had not evoked the expected positive response among the people, and the assassins now began to fear for their lives:

> Let me tell you how we stand. Yesterday evening Hirtius was at my house. He made Antony's disposition clear—as bad and treacherous as can be. Antony says he is unable to give me my province, and that he thinks none of us is safe in Rome with the soldiers and populace in their present agitated state of mind. I expect you observe the falsehood of both contentions, the truth being, as Hirtius made evident, that he is afraid lest, if our position were enhanced even to a moderate extent, these people would have no further part to play in public affairs.
> Finding myself in so difficult a predicament, I thought it best to ask for a Free Commission for myself and the rest of our friends, so as to get a fair excuse for going away. Hirtius promised to get this agreed to, but I have no confidence that he will, in view of the gen-

eral insolence and vilification of us. And even if they give us what we ask, I think it won't be long before we are branded as public enemies or placed under interdict.

You may ask what I advise. I think we must give way to fortune, leave Italy, go to live in Rhodes or anywhere under the sun. If things go better, we shall return to Rome. If moderately, we shall live in exile. If the worst happens, we shall take any and every means to help ourselves. Perhaps one of you will wonder at this point why we should wait till the last moment instead of setting something on foot now. Because we have nowhere to base ourselves, except for Sex[tus] Pompeius and Caecilius Bassus—I imagine their hands will be strengthened when this news about Caesar gets through. It will be time enough for us to join them when we know what their power amounts to. I shall give any undertaking you and Cassius wish on your behalf. Hirtius demands that I do this.

Please let me have your reply as soon as possible. I don't doubt that Hirtius will inform me on these points before ten o'clock. Let me know where we can meet, where you wish me to come.

After Hirtius' latest talk I have thought it right to demand that we be allowed to stay in Rome with a public bodyguard. I don't suppose they will agree—we shall be putting them in a very invidious light. However, I think I ought not to refrain from demanding anything that I consider fair.

(In Cicero's *Letters to His Friends* 11.1)

So began the calamitous events that would ultimately end in the death of Brutus and his colleagues at Philippi two years later, in 42 B.C. The mythical Brutus would eventually grow to overshadow the actual man.

Over the centuries, few figures in history have been treated as variously as Brutus. His

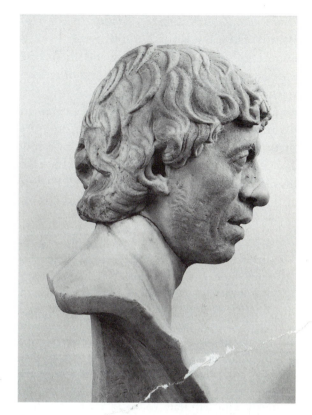

Figure 3.1   *Bust thought to represent Brutus*

person and the act he committed have been praised—or damned—according to the climate of the times. In the fourteenth century, Dante placed him with Satan on the lowest circle of the Inferno. Two hundred years later, Shakespeare had not only resurrected Brutus' spirit but also cast him as an "honorable man," driven by the purest of motivations to kill Caesar. This popular characterization has been hard to shake because of the great bard's stature in our own society. But Shakespeare was not a historian, and Brutus was not an "honorable man." One thing about Brutus *is* clear. He was not the type of individual one usually thinks of as an assassin. There certainly was some of the virtue and character of Shakespeare's Brutus in the real Brutus. He was a Roman noble, wealthy, well educated, cultured, and high-minded. At one point, Cicero, in a momentary burst of enthusiasm, described Brutus as first among the younger generation of Romans and expressed his hope that Brutus would soon become the first man in the state. Brutus was seen by many as a "coming man," who would inevitably take his place among Rome's greatest leaders. He was also a man of many disturbing contradictions, as one scholar has noted:

> Brutus' career is full of anomalies and contradictions. The man of principle engaged in usurious money-lending. The hereditary enemy of Pompey fought on his side in the civil war. The friend and protégé of Caesar conspired against him and killed him. The student became the man of action, the lover of peace a commander in war. The champion of legality and constitutionalism assumed extraordinary powers in Macedonia and Asia Minor. The man who left Italy to avoid civil war made himself the leader of a great army against his fellow-countrymen.
>
> (Clarke, *The Noblest Roman* 72)

Young Brutus, His Mother, and Caesar

Brutus was probably born in 85 B.C. His father, Marcus Junius Brutus, was executed for political reasons in 77 B.C. Consequently, Brutus grew up without a father. His mother Servilia (orphaned herself at an early age) was paramount in his life—and the man who was probably the greatest love in her life was Caesar.

The stories that make Caesar Brutus' father have no basis in fact. They attest to the malicious gossip associated with the long and intimate relationship Caesar shared with Servilia. In reality, both Caesar and Servilia would have been about fifteen at the time of Brutus' birth, and our first evidence for their love affair dates from some twenty years later. She was sending love notes to Caesar while she was married to the elderly Decimus Junius Silanus, consul in 62 B.C., by whom she had three daughters. After his death, probably in 60 B.C., she apparently preferred to be Caesar's mistress than to remarry.

Servilia was one of the most influential women of the Later Republic. One prominent scholar has assessed her power as follows:

> . . . the daughters of the great houses commanded political influence in their own right, exercising a power beyond the reach of many a senator. Of such dominating forces behind the phrases and the facade of constitutional government the most remarkable was Servilia, Cato's half-sister, Brutus' mother—and Caesar's mistress.
>
> (Syme, *The Roman Revolution*, 12)

Servilia, as the passage notes, was also the half sister of Cato the Younger. Cato was Caesar's bitterest political enemy. The two had been at odds since at least the mid-60s B.C., and their philosophical outlooks were as diametrically opposed as their personalities. For some time now, Rome's elite had been polarizing around two opposing political factions—the *optimates* and the *populares*. These were never formal parties or strict designations for politicians (and are used here mostly as convenient descriptive terms) but, rather, loosely aligned coalitions of nobles who shared a particular point of view. Cato was a leader of the *optimates* (in Latin, "the best"), conservative nobles and their followers who wished the old, traditional Republican form of government to continue and resisted any form of change. They embodied and embraced the *mos maiorum,* the "customs of their ancestors," and frequently dominated the Senate.

Figure 3.2   Caesar

On Caesar's side were the *populares,* those who had abandoned—or never subscribed to—the old ways and recognized the need for change. They believed that change could best be achieved by appealing to the common people and supporting the popular cause. Since the time of Tiberius Gracchus, many had realized that, after centuries of neglect, the wishes of the Roman masses could no longer be ignored. Ambitious politicians also recognized the benefits of exploiting their votes as a convenient avenue to political power. A struggle between the old order and the new ensued. Control of the Roman government was the ultimate objective.

The friction between the two groups had a negative effect on Rome. One civil war had already been fought in the 80s B.C.; another lay in the near future. In the meantime, Cato and his clique jealously guarded the Republic from those like Caesar, whom they considered a dangerous political heretic.

As Brutus matured, he witnessed the stormy political struggle between his mother's lover, Caesar, and his favorite uncle, Cato. Emotionally, he cannot have remained unaffected. There is no evidence to indicate just how close he and Caesar were. Certainly, Caesar was a very familiar figure in Brutus' life, and he did intercede on Brutus' behalf whenever it was opportune or necessary—either to please Servilia or because of his own affection for the young man. It must be remembered that Caesar's numerous marriages produced no male heir, a serious concern, both personally and politically, to a Roman of his stature. It would not be an overstatement to suggest that he turned some of the affection he would have had for a son to Brutus, his mistress's child.

There is tenuous evidence that Brutus was the person originally destined to marry Caesar's only child, Julia, in 60 B.C. The marriage was called off, however, when Julia was given to Pompey to seal the "First Triumvirate." This extralegal coalition that Caesar formed with Pompey and another powerful leader of the *populares,* Crassus, in 60 B.C. helped the three bully (some would say control) the Roman government. Previously, the ambitions of all three had been checked by optimate countermoves. Frustrated, they decided to pool their significant resources. Attempts to oppose them ultimately failed, and as consul in 59 B.C., Caesar made sure that the triumvirs got everything they desired—for themselves and their constituents. He also gave Servilia a magnificent pearl, worth a million and a half denarii. The gift might be construed as support for the idea that it *was* Brutus who was to marry Julia and that Caesar was trying to soothe Servilia's "disappointment" when the marriage fell through. On the other hand, the pearl may only indicate the first opportunity that the previously debt-ridden Caesar had to give his mistress a gift worthy of his love for her (he had just received millions from Cleopatra's father, Ptolemy XII, to keep him on the throne in Egypt).

If Caesar did look upon Brutus as a son, nothing indicates that Brutus returned his affection. One ancient authority says that Brutus grew to resent Caesar's affair with his mother, and there is much to suggest that he regarded Caesar as a rival for his mother's love. Intellectually, Brutus acknowledged Caesar's important role in his life, but emotionally he does not appear to have had any real feeling for him.

The Idealistic Brutus— And a Darker Side

Philosophically, Brutus could not have approved of the direction in which Caesar was taking Rome, first as one of the triumvirs (when Brutus would have been about twenty-five years old) and later as dictator. His education in Athens—where his teachers became his friends (an indication of his intellect)—had taught Brutus the Greek contempt for tyranny. In the Athenian Agora, he saw the statues of the "tyrannicides," Harmodius and Aristogiton, who were contemporaries of his own traditional ancestor, Lucius Junius Brutus. This Brutus had led the revolt in 509 B.C. that ended monarchy at Rome and supposedly sentenced his own sons to death for plotting to restore it (one variant of the story states that this left him without issue, and consequently there would have been

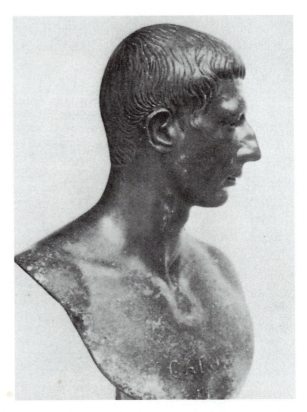

Figure 3.3   *Cato the Younger*

no one left to produce the line from which our Brutus supposedly descended!). Another of Brutus' ancestors, Servilius Ahala, had killed a man who was aspiring to tyranny in the fifth century B.C. All this was accepted Republican mythology, and it was a tradition in which Brutus and his family took great pride.

Brutus was also influenced more and more by the conservative optimate rhetoric of his uncle, Cato. He accompanied Cato to Cyprus in 58 B.C. to help him organize the island as a Roman province. Subsequently, as one of the mint masters in 54 B.C., Brutus issued coins with the images of Lucius Brutus, Ahala, and *Libertas* at a time when the future liberty of the Republic seemed in jeopardy because of the triumvirs.

Along with his lofty ideals and Republican sentiments, however, there was a darker side to Brutus, a side that seems to contradict the Brutus many admired. Brutus would ultimately accuse Caesar of being above the law, yet he placed himself above the law when he got a decree passed allowing him to charge 48 percent interest on a loan he made to a city on Cyprus. When the Senate fixed the legal interest rate at 12 percent, Brutus employed devious methods to recoup his money and even tried to obtain Cicero's help, which placed a temporary strain on their friendship. Brutus, then, was a moneylender on a large scale. His outright extortion does not conform to the traditional Roman moral code by which he supposedly guided himself—nor to the philosophical beliefs of a man who had authored a book on virtue.

Some Intriguing Choices

The "First Triumvirate" ended when Crassus was killed in the East fighting the Parthians at Carrhae in 53 B.C. The previous year, Pompey had lost his strongest link with Caesar when Julia, Caesar's daughter, died in childbirth. Caesar had been in Gaul since 58 B.C. and had become extremely wealthy and powerful militarily. Pompey, in Rome and uncertain about the future, no longer felt comfortable about his relationship with Caesar. Politically confused, he ultimately sided with the conservatives against his former colleague. Certainly, the coaxing of his old friend Cicero helped Pompey reach this decision. Cato, who disliked Pompey intensely but viewed him as his most effective weapon against Caesar, was also persuasive. The danger, real or imagined, presented by Caesar could not be ignored by the optimate leadership of the Senate. Consequently, Pompey took charge militarily of the effort to prevent Caesar

from returning successfully from Gaul. Pressed by Cato and his clique, the Roman government was headed toward a disastrous showdown.

When the Civil War finally came in 49 B.C., Brutus had an interesting choice to make. He could join Pompey—but he knew that Pompey had been responsible for executing his father for participating in an abortive popular rebellion in northern Italy in 77 B.C. Brutus hated Pompey and, as late as 52 B.C., had attacked him as an enemy of freedom. On the opposite side, he could ally himself with Caesar, the man who had contributed, not insignificantly, to his career—but Caesar was also the man who was a rival for his mother's affections. He chose Pompey.

It might appear that Brutus' choice to join Pompey was the only one possible considering his respect for Cato and support of the *optimates*. But he may not have been the political doctrinaire people thought he was. One has to wonder why, for example, with so many other marriage alliances available to him, Brutus married the daughter of Appius Claudius in 54 B.C. The union made the notorious Clodius, the most feared of the *populares* thugs, his uncle. When Caesar departed for Gaul in 58 B.C., he left Clodius, who was tribune, in Rome to look after his interests. However, Clodius proved a poor executor, for his behavior seldom coincided with his boss's wishes, and his lowbrow activities promoted political violence and chaos in Rome. He took organized hooliganism to new heights, roaming the city's streets with his gang of ruffians, thrashing opponents and innocents alike, destroying public and private property. Political (and personal) enemies, like Cicero, were his primary targets, although it appears no one was safe (he even threatened Pompey). Inevitably, his opponents countered with gangs of their own led by Milo, who was tribune in 57 B.C. When the civil violence reached its peak in 52 B.C. and Clodius was murdered, his supporters used the Senate for his funeral pyre and burned it to the ground. Clodius' sister, Clodia, whom Cicero considered utterly disreputable, was his female counterpart—and she was now Brutus' aunt! Consequently, the Republican traditionalist knowingly joined himself to a family that included the very worst of the *populares* opportunists.

Still, it can be argued that this was a good marriage connection for Brutus because Appius' *was* an old and prominent patrician family. Brutus also got along well with his father-in-law, with whom he served as quaestor in Cilicia. But even Appius seems to have had little in the way of scruples. In 51 B.C., he was brought to trial for misconduct in his province (Cicero succeeded him as governor of Cilicia and was appalled at his dishonest behavior) and for making bribes while campaigning for censor. Brutus helped defend his father-in-law, and Appius was acquitted. Family loyalties aside, we see little of the "honorable" Brutus here, since he knew that Appius *was* guilty, having personally observed some of his wrongdoings in Cilicia. Brutus probably also feared that some of his own questionable business deals (made while serving with Appius) might become public if the matter were pursued too far. He and his father-in-law, it seems, shared many of the same "ideals."

When it came to his uncle Clodius, however, Brutus showed no family loyalty whatsoever. In fact, when Clodius was murdered in 52 B.C. and his counterpart Milo was put on trial for the deed, Brutus composed a rhetorical exercise defending Milo for eliminating an enemy of the state. Obviously, he regarded political misdeeds like those of Appius (and himself) as peccadillos. However, if he felt that the state was threatened, he condoned drastic action even against a relative—a point worth remem-

Figure 3.4   Pompey

bering when considering his behavior toward Caesar, who was like a relative to him.

Brutus' marriage alliance with Appius' family placed another strain on him. One of his sisters-in-law was married to the hated Pompey's eldest son. It seems that few families in Rome were so interwoven with the principal political players of the 50s B.C. Whatever Brutus' reasons for joining the family, they could not have been accidental. Political advancement, wealth, and prestige—not ideology—seem to have been the overriding considerations behind the choice. In this respect, Brutus was no different from any other ambitious Roman.

When Brutus finally did join Pompey, he was welcomed enthusiastically by his former enemy. His presence on the Republican side was noteworthy not only because he was viewed by many as a defender of liberty and freedom but also because he had rejected Caesar in favor of the man he had previously hated and regarded as a despot. Pompey was relieved and pleased.

Having made his choice, Brutus now devoted himself to stopping Caesar.

Reconciliation with Caesar

Caesar crushed the army of Pompey at Pharsalus in 48 B.C. Pompey fled to Egypt, where, after being promised safe passage by Ptolemy XIII, he was murdered by agents of the young pharaoh (see Chapter 4). Soon after the victory, Caesar and Brutus were again closely allied. For Servilia's sake, Caesar had made sure Brutus was not injured or killed. He appears to have harbored no ill will toward Brutus, perhaps regarding Brutus' opposition in the Civil War as nothing more than a fit of misguided idealism. (Caesar also may have understood Brutus' resentment over Servilia's affection for him, since he, too, had been raised by his mother and continued to have strong ties of affection for her. Her death, while he was in Gaul, greatly disturbed him.) Caesar trusted Brutus to the extent that he made him proconsul of Cisalpine Gaul in 46 B.C., a prestigious and responsible position for one with so little experience. This was also the province from which Caesar had crossed the Rubicon River into Italy to begin the Civil War in 49 B.C. It was secure militarily, and there were symbolic implications to the appointment. There Brutus protected Caesar's interests and won the respect of the Gauls. It is clear that Caesar planned to rely on Brutus in the future.

Brutus was still holding his proconsulship when his uncle Cato was defeated by Caesar in North Africa and committed suicide. Brutus did nothing to save his uncle and, surprisingly, even made some unflattering remarks about Cato's suicide. When Caesar returned from Africa, he and Brutus toured the province and enjoyed each other's company. For the moment at least, everything indicates that Brutus attempted to please Caesar.

Brutus does not seem to have acted from any deep-seated conviction in these events. A man whose intense political feelings supposedly drove him to join his father's murderer to fight against his mother's lover does not typically embrace his enemy and accept high office from him. Nor does he turn away from an uncle who had been his role model and whose cause had been *his* cause. Roman politics are politics of convenience, and historians of Rome frequently encounter strange and apparently contradictory relationships among former enemies. But Brutus' political jockeying during this period resembles that of a confused and errant child. Perhaps his admirers saw—and still see—more in him than was actually there.

The Impact of Cato's Death

Brutus' initial reaction to Cato's suicide was rather odd. He seemed more disturbed by the method of Cato's death than the death itself. He wanted to see Cato fight to the end—not take his own life. This was a rather hypocritical view considering Brutus' own ambivalence after Pharsalus (which perhaps partly motivated his complaint about Cato). Philosophically, Brutus did not share his Stoic uncle's ideas about rational suicide, but if he had actually viewed Cato as a role model, his contempt may have been more a selfish reaction. Caesar had already demonstrated his leniency by sparing Brutus, Cicero, and many others. Brutus may have thought he would also have spared Cato had he captured him. Pompey was dead; the Republic was shaken but still intact. Caesar was not the tyrant people expected him to be. In his mind, constitutionalism had a good chance of returning—and Cato was needed in the rebuilding process. Instead,

The Man Who Came to Dinner—Cicero Entertains Caesar

WHAT FOLLOWS IS A rare insight into a few hours of Caesar's hectic life as dictator, only three months before his death. Seldom do we get as personal a glimpse into the daily "goings on" of a man such as Caesar. On the eighteenth and nineteenth of December of 45 B.C., Caesar was in Campania and visited Cicero's estate near Puteoli. After spending the night with Cicero's neighbor, Philippus, the stepfather of Octavian (Caesar's eventual heir), Caesar privately went over accounts with Balbus, one of his chief aides. Subsequently, he walked over to Cicero's nearby villa, bathed, received some news about his friend Mamurra, then had a pleasant meal with Cicero. Caesar's affable nature even caught Cicero off guard, and the gloomy Republican unexpectedly found himself having an enjoyable time. He writes to his friend Atticus about the experience:

> Strange that so onerous a guest should leave a memory not disagreeable! It was really very pleasant. But when he arrived at Philippus' place on the evening of 18 December, the house was so thronged by the soldiers that there was hardly a spare room for Caesar himself to dine in. Two thousand men, no less! I was a good deal perturbed about what would happen next day, but Cassius Barba came to the rescue and posted sentries. Camp was pitched in the open and a guard placed on the house. On the

19th Caesar stayed with Philippus until 1 o'clock admitting nobody—at accounts, I believe, with Balbus. Then he took a walk on the shore. Towards two he went to his bath. That was when he heard about Mamurra; his face did not change. After anointing he took his place at dinner. He was following a course of emetics, and so both ate and drank with uninhibited enjoyment. It was really a fine, well-appointed meal, and not only that but

> cooked and garnished well,
> good talking too—in fact a pleasant meal.

> His entourage moreover were lavishly entertained in three other dining-rooms. The humbler freedmen and slaves had all they wanted—the smarter ones I entertained in style. In a word, I showed I knew how to live. But my guest was not the kind of person to whom one says, "Do come again when you are next in the neighborhood." Once is enough. We talked of nothing serious, but a good deal on literary matters. All in all, he was pleased and enjoyed himself. He said he would spend a day at Puteoli and another at Baiae.
>
> There you are—a visit, or should I call it a billeting, which as I said was troublesome to me but not disagreeable. . . .
> (*Letters to Atticus* 13.52)

Cato took his own life. At the same time, Cato had "deserted" Brutus and left him to stand on his own. Brutus may simply have been angry that his uncle had "betrayed" him and taken the "easy way out." Brutus might also have felt some guilt for not being with Cato (Cato's natural son *was* with him). Perhaps he could have saved him—or died with him, fighting.

Ironically, Brutus *ultimately* praised his uncle's death and, at the end, emulated it. Also, within a year of Cato's suicide, Brutus divorced his wife, an action that was generally disapproved, and married Cato's daughter—his own cousin—Porcia. Porcia, now widowed, had been married to Bibulus, who was an old optimate foe of Caesar and his colleague in the con-

Figure 3.5
Cicero

sulship of 59 B.C. Porcia had one surviving son of three (also named Bibulus). While not old, she was certainly no longer young by Roman standards, and there does not appear to have been any benefit, political or otherwise, in Brutus' changing spouses. Love may have driven him to it, but there really seems to be only one explanation for his rash behavior: Brutus was beginning to identify more and more with his dead uncle, Cato. His quick marriage to Porcia appears to have been an attempt on his part to bind himself as closely as was earthly possible to his uncle—further indication of his loss when Cato died.

We also see Brutus becoming closer to Cicero than he had ever been before. Cicero had de-

cided to "retire" from politics, for good reason, as it turned out, shortly before Pharsalus. With Cato gone, he probably now came to represent for Brutus the ideals of the Republic that needed saving. Brutus recommended that Cicero eulogize Cato, producing a rather ineffective eulogy himself. During this same period, 46–45 B.C., Cicero dedicated three important philosophical works to Brutus. He seems to have found consolation in the attentions and flattery of Brutus, whose potential greatness Cicero felt had been cut short by the Civil War. Through all this, Caesar remained remarkably tolerant. His criticism of Brutus' lack of style in his eulogy of Cato may have been Caesar's subtle way of communicating to Brutus his displeasure.

Family Aggravations

While Brutus' marriage to Porcia may have provided consolation for his loss of Cato, it also caused severe family problems. Servilia had openly opposed the marriage, and she and Porcia quarreled constantly. Marriage to such a close relation profited nothing, and Servilia was very conscious of providing her son with the most advantageous marital alliance. Servilia's continued friendship with Caesar (he had allowed her to purchase confiscated estates of his enemies after the Civil War at a reduced price) was undoubtedly the greatest aggravation. Servilia must have viewed Brutus' marriage as a purposeful affront to Caesar—that could only harm Brutus' chances of advancement. And there can be no doubt of Porcia's hatred for Caesar.

Dolabella—A Concerned Son-in-Law Offers Advice to Cicero before Pharsalus

CIVIL WARS ARE A messy business, and nobody really wins when citizens of the same country struggle and die for ideas, rights, or just plain power or greed. Families are split, brother fights brother, father fights son—and once it is over, the wounds are slow to heal. As we have seen, Brutus had to choose between Caesar and Pompey when civil war erupted in 49 B.C., and countless others had to do the same. Although Cicero's relationship with Caesar had been generally cordial over the years, the two had always been political opponents; Cicero was friends with Pompey, and he had also been part of the process at Rome that had ultimately been responsible for pushing Pompey into a confrontation with Caesar. Consequently, when Caesar invaded Italy and Pompey fled to Greece with his army, Cicero had little choice but to follow him. Things were beginning to look bleak for the Republicans, and Cicero's only alternative was to retire from politics altogether—although he may not have been sure that he had that option before receiving the letter below.

Cicero's son-in-law was Dolabella, one of Caesar's officers. Dolabella was now in the difficult position of taking part in a military campaign that could result in the death of his own father-in-law. To prevent the possibility of this ever happening (and mindful of what it would do to his marriage), Dolabella sends this letter to Cicero, who is with Pompey. He urges Cicero to save himself by retiring before the final battle takes place, a battle that Dolabella naturally believes Caesar will win. The letter also shows that Cicero has been out of touch with his family for some time, and Dolabella uses the opportunity to bring him up to date. Caesar's apparent willingness to forgive Cicero is also mentioned, and this reinforces what was said previously about their relatively friendly relations with one another. The letter was written in and sent from Caesar's camp in Greece near Dyrrachium in May of 48 B.C., not long before Pompey's defeat at Pharsalus:

Dolabella to Cicero greetings.

If you are well I am glad. I myself am well and so is our Tullia [Cicero's daughter]. Terentia [Cicero's wife] has been rather out of sorts, but I know for certain that she has now recovered. Otherwise all your domestic affairs are in excellent shape.

You did me an injustice if at any time you suspected that in advising you to throw in your

Porcia must have held Caesar responsible for Cato's death, and even after he was dead, Caesar continued to blame Cato for driving him to extremes. Caesar's two *Anti-Catos* answered Cicero's (and Brutus') eulogy of Cato in the most unflattering terms. Porcia also had to endure Caesar's humiliation of her first husband Bibulus when the two were consuls. The sources indicate that Brutus revealed the plot to assassinate Cae-

sar to Porcia only after she became distraught over his secretive behavior (see box, page 70). It was probably no accident that she was one of the few outside the actual group of conspirators—and the only woman—made privy to the assassination. Even Cicero—considered too old, timid, and cautious—was not accorded that "privilege."

For a man so concerned about family—even to the end of his life—and who had written a

---

lot with Caesar and with me, or at least to retire into private life, I was thinking of party interests rather than of yours. But now, when the scales are coming down on our side, I imagine that only one thing can possibly be thought of me, namely, that I am proffering advice to you which it would be contrary to my duty as your son-in-law to withhold. On your side, my dear Cicero, you must take what follows, whether it meets with your approval or not, in the persuasion that I have thought and written it out of the most sincere loyalty and devotion to yourself.

You see Cn. Pompeius' [Pompey's] situation. Neither the glory of his name and past nor yet the kings and nations of whose dependence he used so often to boast can protect him. Even the door of an honorable retreat, which humble folk find open, is closed to him. Driven out of Italy, Spain lost, his veteran army taken prisoner, he is now to crown all blockaded in his camp, a humiliation which I fancy has never previously befallen a Roman general. Do therefore, as a man of sense, consider what he can have to hope or we to fear; so you will find it easiest to take the decision most expedient for you. One thing I beg of you; if he does manage to escape from his present dangerous position and takes refuge with his fleet, con-

sult your own best interests and at long last be your own friend rather than anybody else's. You have done enough for your party too and the form of commonwealth of which you approved. It is time now to take our stand where the commonwealth is actually in being rather than, in following after its old image, to find ourselves in a political vacuum.

Therefore, dearest Cicero, if it turns out that Pompey is driven from this area too and forced to seek yet other regions of the earth, I hope you will retire to Athens or to any peaceful community you please. If you decide to do that, please write and tell me, so that if I possibly can I may hasten to your side. Any concessions that you need from the Commander-in-Chief to safeguard your dignity you will yourself obtain with the greatest ease from so kindly a man as Caesar; but I believe that *my* petitions will carry more than negligible weight with him.

I trust to *your* honor and kindness to see that the courier I am sending you is able to return to me and brings a letter from you.
(Dolabella in Cicero, *Letters to Friends* 9.9)

A short time later, Cicero would decide to retire from politics.

An Assassin's Wife—Porcia Makes Her Point

PORCIA WAS THE DAUGHTER of Cato the Younger and the wife—and cousin—of Brutus. She was reputedly the only woman made privy to the plot to assassinate Caesar. Supposedly, if it had been up to Brutus, even she would not have known. The following passage helps preserve the image of the "honorable" Brutus—for how honorable could he have been if he had sought to involve his wife (even though she was the daughter of Cato) in such a heinous crime? It is Porcia's noting her husband's change in behavior that drives her to force the truth from Brutus. She wounds herself in the thigh to prove her mettle and worthiness of her husband's confidence. Consequently, posterity can only be sympathetic toward a couple whose love is so strong that it draws them together as allies in such a desperate plan.

Plutarch provides one version of the episode. The private dialogue spoken by Porcia to Brutus on this occasion should arouse our suspicions as to the reliability of the report. Also, it would appear that Porcia did not hold up well as the moment of the assassination approached. She became so unnerved that she fainted!

> Porcia . . . was one of Cato's daughters. She had married Brutus, who was her cousin, when she was still very young, although she was by then already a widow, and had by her first husband a little son, whose name was Bibulus. He later wrote a small book entitled *Memoirs of Brutus*. . . . Porcia, who loved her husband deeply and was not only of an affectionate nature but full of spirit and good sense, did not press her hus-

band to reveal his secrets until she had put herself to a test. She dismissed her attendants from her room, and then taking a little knife such as barbers use to cut fingernails, she gave herself a deep gash in the thigh. She lost a great quantity of blood, after which the wound became intensely painful and brought on fits of shivering and a high fever. When she was in great pain and saw that Brutus was deeply distressed for her, she said to him: "Brutus, I am Cato's daughter, and I was given to you in marriage not just to share your bed and board like a concubine, but to be a true partner in your joys and sorrows. I have no reproach to make to you, but what proof can I give you of my love, if you forbid me to share the kind of trouble that demands a loyal friend to confide in, and keep your suffering to yourself? I know that men think women's natures too weak to be entrusted with secrets, but surely a good upbringing and the company of honorable men can do much to strengthen us, and at least Porcia can claim that she is the daughter of Cato and the wife of Brutus. I did not know before this how either of these blessings could help me, but now I have put myself to the test and find that I can conquer pain." At this she showed him her wound and explained what she had done. Brutus was amazed and lifting up his hands to heaven he prayed to the gods to help him to succeed in his enterprise and show that he was a worthy husband of such a wife. Then he did all that he could to bring back his wife to health.
>
> (*Brutus* 13.2–6)

work entitled *On Duties,* which considered the duties of parents and children, Brutus must have been an uneasy peacekeeper between his mother and wife. It became more and more difficult to be the dutiful son, on the one hand,

and the loyal husband, on the other. Since Servilia and Caesar were still close after the Civil War, we must also wonder what emotional and political impact Caesar's relationship with the Egyptian queen Cleopatra (see Chapter 4), who had recently taken up residence in Rome, was having on all parties.

More Problems for Brutus

By 44 B.C., Brutus was probably viewing Caesar as the root of most of his problems. Caesar was a reminder of his own failures. Instead of dying for his cause as Cato had done, he had survived through the mercy of the same man responsible for Cato's death. Brutus now served that man, who had just made him one of the praetors for the year, and he was to be consul three years later. The contradiction of his position, at once the defender of the Republic and the servant of the man who was destroying it, was obvious to many, including Brutus himself. It was indeed ironic that Brutus' family had traditionally overthrown the last monarch of Rome in 509 B.C.; and now the man whom many accused, rightly or wrongly, of trying to reinstate it remained a major part of his—and his mother's—life. Patriotic slogans greeted Brutus wherever he went and urged him to act like his ancestor and overthrow the new "king"; the busts of the "liberators" Brutus and Ahala stared at him daily in his house; such reminders of his "heritage" cannot have failed to make an impression and encourage any action he might take.

The elimination of Caesar could have appeared to Brutus as the simplest, most logical way to end his personal anguish and to restore the Republic. Politically, it may have been Caesar's assumption of the dictatorship for life and the talk about monarchy (other honors and trappings were also elevating Caesar above the rest) that were the decisive factors in setting the plot in motion. Any hope of a return to constitutionalism now seemed lost.

Six months before he died, Caesar had revised his will. The terms of the will are specific enough so that we know Brutus was not included. Even Decimus Brutus, Brutus' kinsman and one of the assassins (it was he who would guide Caesar to his death on the Ides by convincing him to attend the Senate), was heir in the second degree. It is interesting that Caesar would provide prestigious offices for Brutus yet neglect him in his will. Perhaps by this time Caesar did not believe he could trust Brutus. Perhaps what he did for Brutus' career was only to please Servilia, who was still hopeful that Caesar would continue to regard Brutus as his "son"—and possible heir. What may be an indication of Caesar's true feelings about Brutus can be found in Plutarch (*Caesar* 62.5, *Antony* 11.3, and *Brutus* 8.1). When it was mentioned by someone that Caesar should be suspicious of those like Antony, Caesar answered, "'It is not the fat, sleek-headed men I am afraid of, but the pale, lean ones'— and here he pointed to Brutus and Cassius, the men who were to conspire against him and murder him."

We already know that, despite his philosophical posturing, Brutus was avaricious. If he had been cooperating with Caesar because he hoped ultimately to profit from the relationship, his omission from Caesar's will would have been a factor prompting him to act. Servilia could have known—either from Caesar or through other channels (she had great influence)—that her son would play little role in Rome's future and may have told Brutus as much. Caesar's primary heir was to be his grand-nephew, Octavian, but Caesar also provided that if he had a son, that son would become his primary heir. If Brutus had ever viewed Caesar as a "father," then by the terms of this will, no "son" could ever have been more betrayed. Also, since Cleopatra was claiming that she had produced a son by Caesar named Caesarion ("little Caesar"), who was at that very moment residing with her in Rome, there must have been fear that this child might somehow become Caesar's legitimate heir.

Servilia certainly would have been disappointed by all this—both for herself and her son. But it is unlikely that she was disappointed enough to want "the love of her life" killed (she did keep Caesar's gifts even after he was murdered). There were no such restraints for Brutus.

Cassius' Influence on Brutus

Brutus resolved to assassinate Caesar through forceful coaxing by others, especially his brother-in-law, Cassius. Cassius was an older, more experienced man. He had been with Crassus at Carrhae in Parthia in 53 B.C. but had escaped the disaster. Both Cassius and Brutus had studied under the same grammar teacher in their youth, had supported Pompey during the Civil War, and had been spared by Caesar. They now served Caesar, who made them both praetors in 44 B.C. They were also related by marriage. Cassius was married to Brutus' half sister, Junia Tertia. Consequently, the two chief conspirators in the assassination of Caesar were Servilia's son and son-in-law.

Cassius' wife, Junia, must also have resented Caesar. Caesar had carried on his affair with her mother Servilia while her father was still alive. While Caesar later had the opportunity to marry Servilia, he never did. Junia probably shared many of Brutus' negative feelings toward Caesar, feelings that Cassius would have encouraged. He never had any love for Caesar:

> But it was Cassius with his violent temper and his hatred of Caesar—which had its roots in personal animosity rather than in any disinterested aversion to tyranny—who inflamed Brutus' feelings and urged him on. Brutus, it is said, was opposed to the dictatorship, but

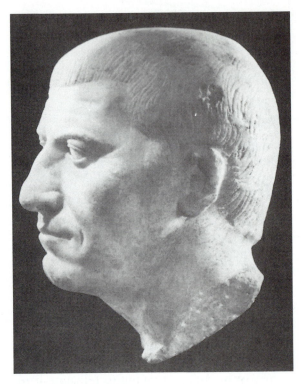

Figure 3.6   Bust thought to represent Cassius

Cassius hated the dictator, and among other grievances which he brought up against him was the matter of the removal of the lions, which Cassius had procured when he was about to take office as aedile. These animals had been left at Megara, and when the city was captured by Calenus [Caesar's officer], Caesar appropriated them for himself. They are said to have brought disaster at Megara, because when the city was on the point of being captured, the Megarians broke open the cages and unchained them, hoping that they would attack the enemy as they entered the city. But, instead of this, the lions turned against the unarmed Megarians and tore them to pieces as they ran to and fro in terror, so that even their enemies were overcome with pity at the sight.

Some people have made out that Cassius' resentment at this affair was his principal motive in organizing the conspiracy, but to say this is a travesty of the facts. From his very earliest days Cassius was inspired by a peculiar bitterness and animosity towards the whole race of those who seek to dominate their fellows, and he revealed this even as a boy, when he went to the same school as Faustus, the son of Sulla. When Faustus began to throw his weight about among the other boys and boast of his father's absolute power, Cassius jumped up and gave him a thrashing. Faustus' guardians and relatives wanted to take the matter to court, but Pompey refused to allow this, brought the two boys together, and questioned them as to what had happened. There-upon Cassius said, so the story goes, "Come on then, Faustus, you can tell Pompey, if you dare, what you said that made me so angry, and I will knock your teeth in again." . . . Such was Cassius' character.

(Plutarch, *Brutus* 8.3–9.3)

Additional reason for Cassius to move against Caesar was the rumor, promoted even by Cicero, that Servilia had allowed Caesar to have sexual relations with Junia, who was now Cassius' wife! Furthermore, although he was one of the praetors for 44 B.C., Cassius felt Caesar had purposely slighted him by awarding the senior praetorship to Brutus, a man of less experience and distinction. The fact that the day appointed for the assassination and the "salvation" of the Republic would coincide with his son's receiving the *toga virilis* (his formal entrance into manhood at age sixteen) must have been symbolically pleasing to Cassius. A number of the conspirators even accompanied the boy to the Forum before proceeding to the meeting of the Senate, where Caesar was to be killed. Alone, Cassius' rancorous personality could not attract many "defenders of liberty"; however, with Brutus—whom many considered, rightly or wrongly, the only man who could "save" Rome—in his company, Cassius had found the instrument he needed to take revenge upon Caesar.

It seems inescapable that personal motivations were as much a part of the assassination plot orchestrated by Brutus and Cassius as political ones. The fact that Brutus, who deeply resented his mother's lover, wounded Caesar in the groin (Appian says the thigh, which is close enough) is further indication of the personal nature of the attack.

The Assassination

The assassination took place at a meeting of the Senate on the Ides of March just before Caesar was to leave on a major campaign against the Parthians (see Chapter 4). The conspirators had to act fast, for he would be absent from Rome for an extended period, and there might never be another opportunity to execute their plan. The murder did not occur, as is popularly believed, in the actual Senate chamber. This session was held in the complex of buildings adjoining the Theater of Pompey (see Map 10, page 74). Ironically, here, too, was located a statue of Pompey. Plutarch offers the following account of Caesar's death:

> Indeed it is said that, just before the attack was made on him, Caesar turned his eyes towards the statue of Pompey and silently prayed for its goodwill. This was in spite of the fact that Caesar was a follower of the doctrines of Epicurus; yet the moment of crisis, so it would seem, and the very imminence of the dreadful deed made him forget his former rationalistic views and filled him with an emotion that was intuitive or divinely inspired.
> Now Antony, who was a true friend of Caesar's and also a strong man physically, was detained outside the senate house by Brutus Albinus, who deliberately engaged him in a long conversation. Caesar himself went in and

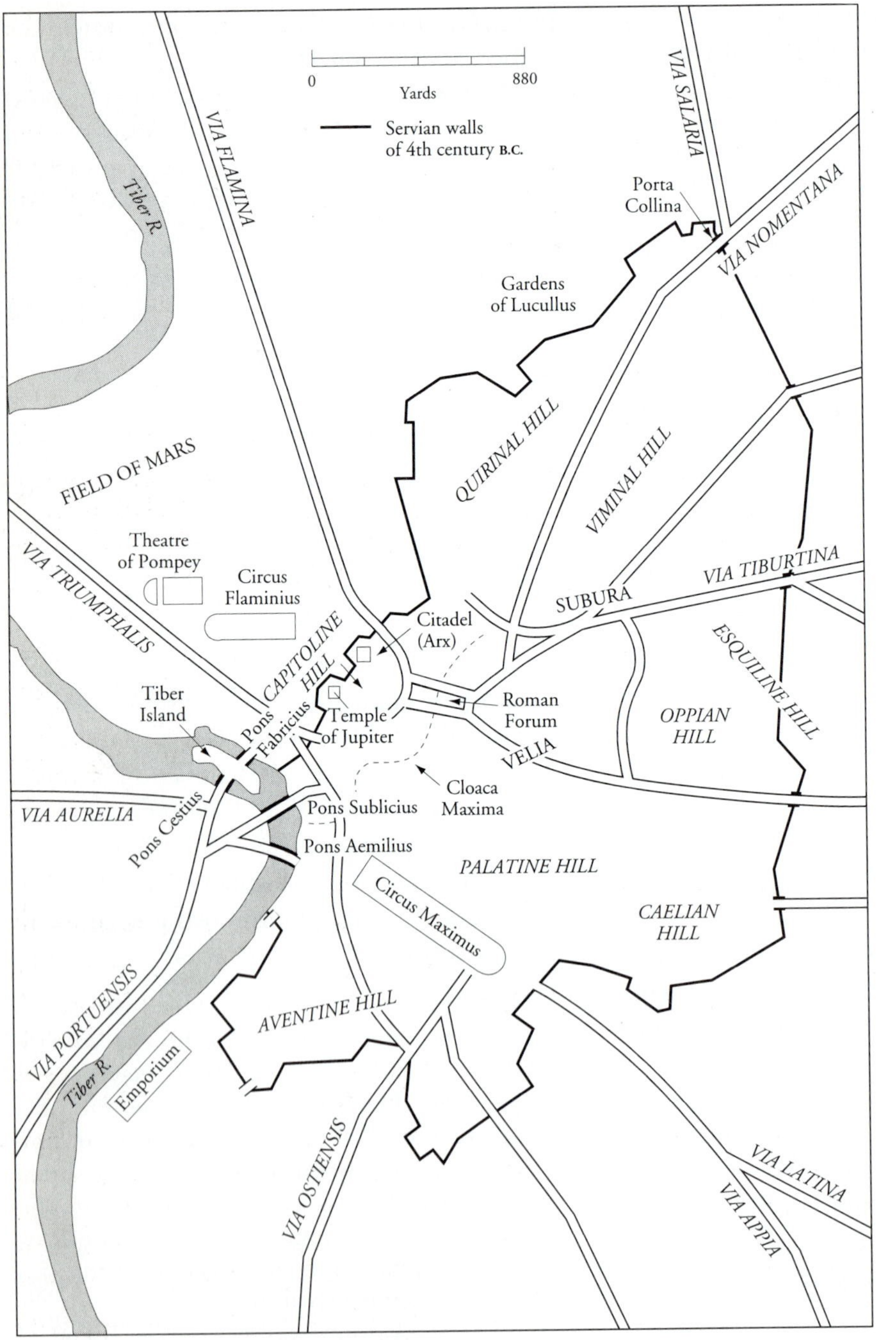

Map 10 *Rome at the time of Caesar*

the senate rose in his honor. Some of Brutus' party took their places behind his chair and others went to meet him as though they wished to support the petition being made by Tillius Cimber on behalf of his brother who was in exile. So, all joining in with him in his entreaties, they accompanied Caesar to his chair. Caesar took his seat and continued to reject their request; as they pressed him more and more urgently, he began to grow angry with them. Tillius then took hold of his toga with both hands and pulled it down from his neck. This was the signal for the attack. The first blow was struck by Casca, who wounded Caesar in the neck with his dagger. The wound was not mortal and not even a deep one, coming as it did from a man who was no doubt much disturbed in mind at the beginning of such a daring venture. Caesar, therefore, was able to turn round and grasp the knife and hold on to it. At almost the same moment the striker of the blow and he who was struck cried out together—Caesar, in Latin, "Casca, you villain, what are you doing?" while Casca called to his brother in Greek: "Help, brother."

So it began, and those who were not in the conspiracy were so horror-struck and amazed at what was being done that they were afraid to run away and afraid to come to Caesar's help; they were too afraid even to utter a word. But those who had come prepared for the murder all bared their daggers and hemmed Caesar in on every side. Whichever way he turned he met the blows of daggers and saw the cold steel aimed at his face and at his eyes. So he was driven this way and that, and like a wild beast in the toils, had to suffer from the hands of each one of them; for it had been agreed that they must all take part in this sacrifice and all flesh themselves with his blood. Because of this compact Brutus also gave him one wound in the groin. Some say that Caesar fought back against all the rest, darting this way and that to avoid the blows and crying out for help, but when he saw that Brutus had

drawn his dagger, he covered his head with his toga and sank down to the ground. Either by chance or because he was pushed there by his murderers, he fell down against the pedestal on which the statue of Pompey stood, and the pedestal was drenched with his blood, so that one might have thought that Pompey himself was presiding over this act of vengeance against his enemy, who lay there at his feet struggling convulsively under too many wounds. . . . So Caesar was done to death. . . .
(*Caesar* 66.1–67.1)

There are, of course, other descriptions of the murder. As with any assassination of a person of such prominence, details and opinions as to what exactly did happen differ—sometimes significantly. Suetonius' account (*Caesar* 82.3) includes the famous final words Caesar supposedly uttered to Brutus just before the end, "You, too, my child?" In reality, Dio (*Roman History* 44.19.5) is probably closest to the truth when he states that Caesar was unable to do or say anything before he died.

The Aftermath

There were, ultimately, about sixty senators involved in the conspiracy. Ironically, they and the rest of the Senate had recently taken an oath to defend Caesar's person. For the most part, they were an unlikely group of assassins. Reportedly, among the twenty-three wounds Caesar received, only one was fatal. It seems that the conspirators landed more blows on one another than they did on Caesar. Certainly, the greater number of assassins were tentative and uncomfortable with what they were doing. The sources indicate that Brutus, too, was anxious and could not sleep before the appointed day, although he was able to keep his composure. His wife, Porcia, did not hold up as well. She became hysterical when the time came and passed out.

Cicero, who initially hailed the act as an "almost god-like deed," would later remark that the conspirators had the "courage of men and the foresight of children" (*Letters to Brutus* 5.2.5; *Letters to Atticus* 14.21). Encased in their own little world of personal hatred and Republican sentiments, they never stopped to consider whether the majority of Romans shared their views on the necessity of eliminating Caesar. Apparently, they did not. The conspirators had little plan beyond the immediate moment. They had no military backing and must have foreseen that Caesar's soldiers would support Antony or his heir, Octavian (as they ultimately did). Also, any advantage that could have been gained in the immediate aftermath of the murder faded away through Brutus' lack of decisive action. For all the conspirators' "good intentions," they guaranteed nothing but further civil war, bloodshed, and violence.

Under Caesar, the Republic, although altered, probably would have continued. He was, comparatively speaking, a mild taskmaster. His biggest mistake was that he had let too many of his enemies live, and wishing to create an impression of security and trust, he had no bodyguard. The conspirators' biggest mistake—besides killing Caesar—was letting Mark Antony live. Against the advice of his associates, Brutus wanted Antony spared, if for no other reason than to assure his frightened colleagues in the Senate that no scheme to overthrow the government was afoot. If others were eliminated with Caesar, it would be difficult to convince anyone not party to the plot that this was not a *coup d'état*. General panic might ensue. Brutus may also have entertained some idealistic notion that Antony would realize the nobility of the act and embrace the assassins as saviors of the Republic. For his part, Antony saw things in more practical terms: Caesar was dead and he was probably next. Fearing for his life, he

Figure 3.7   *Coin issued to commemorate the assassination of Caesar. The reverse side is stamped "Ides of March" and depicts a cap of liberty and two daggers. Brutus is represented on the other side, as also seen on the coin image which begins each chapter of* Roman People.

disguised himself and fled briefly. A year later, when the cause of the conspirators was worsening, Cicero wrote Brutus, "How desperate a struggle with him [Antony] is going on at this moment you see. Obviously there would have been none, if Antony's life had not then been spared" (*To Brutus* 5.2.5).

The Conspirators in Trouble

Killing Caesar had been too easy. It reinforced the impression Caesar himself had worked to create—that he was not a tyrant but a member of a free and open society in which no one need fear for one's safety. How, then, was it justifiable to murder such a man? Many were confused, and reaction to the assassination was mixed from the beginning. Antony, finally realizing he was not in any danger, recovered. The conspirators were insisting on their respect for constitutionalism, and as consul, Antony was in position to assert himself. At first, he appeared conciliatory and reassuring.

Two days after the Ides, the Senate met and proclaimed a general amnesty. It looked as if

Figure 3.8
Remains of the Temple of the Divine Julius (center) in the Roman Forum. On or near this spot, the body of Caesar was cremated.

things would return to normal. Most of the senators indicated their goodwill toward the conspirators. As a concession to Antony and other Caesarians, it was voted that all measures enacted while Caesar was alive should be retained without alteration. However, Antony insisted on a public funeral for Caesar and the publication of his will. Despite objections from the Republicans, who saw the potential danger in such a concession, Brutus, anxious for reconciliation, supported the idea. The Senate approved it. Brutus had played directly into Antony's hands.

The public was still unsettled when it learned of the contents of Caesar's will. In it, Caesar had left a small legacy to every Roman citizen, and his gardens beyond the Tiber River were to be given to the public. At the funeral, Antony skillfully parlayed the crowd's dissatisfaction into a general reaction against the conspirators. Almost spontaneously, they piled up a funeral pyre and cremated Caesar in the Forum. Then brandishing torches, they headed toward the conspirators' houses to set them afire. Antony had turned the tide. The fears Decimus Brutus had expressed in his previously quoted letter to Brutus became a reality. The conspirators left Rome fearing for their lives, hoping that events would turn round again to their favor. They never did.

The "Second Triumvirate"

In accordance with the will, Octavian, Caesar's eighteen-year-old grandnephew, rushed to Rome to claim his inheritance—much to Antony's displeasure. The two men disliked each other intensely. As rivals, they quarreled and split the Caesarians. Cicero, hoping to "save the Republic," saw an opportunity to destroy the more experienced Antony by throwing his support behind young Octavian, whom he contemptuously referred to as "the boy." When Antony had been eliminated, it would be an easy matter, he thought, to dispose of "the boy." It would not be the first time Cicero had underestimated a rival.

After their initial disagreements—and armed conflict—Octavian and Antony found it advantageous to cooperate rather than fight. In 43 B.C., they temporarily put aside their differences and joined with another Caesarian, Lepidus, to form the "Second Triumvirate." Unlike the earlier triumvirate of Caesar, Crassus, and Pompey, this one had the effect of law. The new triumvirs controlled the Roman government. A proscription list was drawn up, and Cicero, who had injudiciously poked his nose into too many places, was among the first proscribed. Antony had not forgotten that Cicero, as consul in 63 B.C., had ordered (illegally) the execution of his stepfather for his role in the Catilinarian conspiracy, a desperate attempt by a bankrupt aristocrat named Catiline to overthrow the government. On that occasion, also, Cicero had seen himself as "Savior of the Republic" and was hailed as such by the Senate. Two decades later, however, it was Cicero's own salvation that was at stake. He had also made the mistake of writing some nasty speeches against Antony (which, reminiscent of Demosthenes' speeches against Philip of Macedonia in the fourth century B.C., were termed "Philippics"). Cicero was tracked down and executed. Antony vengefully had the great orator's head and right hand, with which he gestured, displayed on the speakers' platform (rostrum) in the Forum.

Philippi and Brutus' Death

The major business of the triumvirs was to punish the conspirators. After two years of political uncertainty about their misfortunes, the assassins met their fate. In 42 B.C., they were defeated at Philippi in Greece. First, Cassius took his own life. Then Brutus, emulating Cato, the martyr of the Republic, committed suicide. Plutarch gives this somewhat idealized description of his death:

> Then, looking quite cheerful, he shook hands with each of them [his companions], saying that he was exceedingly glad that none of his friends had been false to him. For his country's sake he blamed fortune; so far as he was concerned, he considered himself more blessed than the victors, not only yesterday and the day before, but now too, since he was leaving behind a reputation for virtue, which those who had gained power by arms or money would not do, nor could they prevent men thinking that the unjust and wicked who destroyed the just and good did not deserve to rule. Then after urgently beseeching them to save themselves he retired a certain distance in the company of two or three, including Strato, who had taught him rhetoric and remained a close friend. He placed Strato nearest himself and grasping his bare sword by the hilt with both hands he fell on it and died. There are however those who say that it was not he but Strato who, yielding to Brutus' insistence, held the sword with averted eyes while Brutus fell on it, with such force that it went through his breast and he died immediately.
> (*Brutus* 52.2–5)

Thus died the "noblest Roman of them all."

Brutus' "Evil Genius"

Plutarch had related that some time before Philippi, one night while alone in his tent, Brutus, fitful and worn by the traumatic events of the past two years, began to hallucinate. A terrifying and immense apparition appeared and spoke to him:

> [Brutus] was naturally wakeful, and by practice and self-control he had reduced his sleep

Figure 3.9
*Temple of Mars Ultor
(the "Avenger") in the
Forum of Augustus at
Rome. Octavian vowed
the building of this temple
after Brutus and the
conspirators were defeated
at Philippi in 42 B.C.
Inside, Caesar's sword
was on display as a relic.*

to the minimum. He never went to bed during the day and at night only when everybody else had retired and it was impossible to conduct business or discuss matters. On this occasion, when the war had begun and, with the conduct of the whole business in his hands, his thoughts were concentrated on the future, he would take a little sleep in the evening after eating and then devote the rest of the night to urgent matters. If he could organize the business on hand so as to dispatch it quickly, he would read a book until midnight, when the centurions and tribunes used to come and see him. When he was about to bring his army across from Asia it was the depth of night, his tent was dimly lit, and the whole camp was wrapped in silence. While he was considering something and reflecting within himself, he thought he heard someone coming in. Turning his eyes toward the entrance he saw a strange unusual figure, a monstrous and fearful form, standing in silence before him. He ventured to question it, asking "Who are you, whether man or god, and with what purpose have you come here?" The apparition answered "I am your evil genius, Brutus. And you will see me at Philippi." And Brutus unperturbed said "I shall see you."
(*Brutus* 36.3–4)

While there is a natural tendency to discard this episode as so much theater (material for Shakespeare's pen in later centuries), there is much in these lines that is consistent with Brutus' character. Brutus was under much strain. Also, his wife Porcia had died recently after an illness, and evidence suggests she committed suicide. Consequently, Porcia, like her father Cato, may have helped prepare Brutus mentally to take his own life. By this juncture, Brutus had rationalized all that had happened to him by completely engulfing himself in the idea that he was the last defender of the Republic—

a martyr awaiting his martyrdom. In a letter to Cicero, probably written in July of 43 B.C., his intentions already seemed clear:

> Your concern for me and your care for my safety, though welcome, are no novelty. It is the regular thing, almost a daily occurrence, to hear from you of words and deeds showing your loyalty and respect for my position. But I could not have been more deeply offended by what you said in that part of your letter to Octavius [Caesar's heir] about me and my friends. The way in which you thank him for his services to the Republic, the humility and subservience—

I hesitate to write this, so ashamed am I of the state into which we have fallen, but yet I must—with which you commend our safety to him—worse surely than any death—make it clear that the despotism has not been got rid of, only the despot changed. Look at your own words again and dare to deny that these appeals are those of a subject to a king. . . . I am not the sort of man who would ever be a suppliant, and I would go further than that, I would stop anyone who expected others to be his suppliants; if this is impossible, I shall keep away from those who are willing to be slaves, and shall judge Rome to be for me wherever it is possible to be

Caesar and Multiculturalism. "Scarecrows," "Lions," and "Tinmen"— A Different Kind of Oz: Vercingetorix the Gaul, Ariovistus the German, and Cassivellaunus the Briton

JULIUS CAESAR PRESENTS US with our only first-hand look at peoples on Rome's western frontier during this period. The Gauls, Germans, and Britons who lived there were far less familiar to the Romans than were the inhabitants of the eastern half of their empire—and generally viewed less favorably. Unfortunately, people tend to regard those with an unfamiliar way of life and customs in more negative terms and are usually willing to treat them with greater harshness—especially when they are seen to be uncooperative or hostile. Caesar, for example, is reported to have killed a million Gauls and captured another million. These figures are probably exaggerated, but they reflect Roman contempt for those whom they viewed as "uncivilized."

After his year as consul, Caesar took up his military command in Gaul in 58 B.C. There, he would be occupied for the remainder of the decade and gain the two things he wanted most— a military reputation and great wealth. The area

he ultimately conquered included most of modern France, Holland, Belgium, Switzerland, and Germany west of the Rhine. Caesar recorded his impressions of these years in his *Gallic Commentaries,* a kind of "report from the field" that described his campaigns and actions in dramatic, patriotic, and not unflattering terms.

What follows are partial descriptions of Caesar's encounters with leaders of the Gauls, Germans, and Britons, to whose island home he made the earliest Roman visits in 55 and 54 B.C. The first passage concerns the most formidable of his Gallic opponents, Vercingetorix, whose rebellion in 52 B.C. was the last gasp of freedom by the Gauls. Caesar, who was absent when the fighting broke out—he had returned to northern Italy because of the deteriorating political situation at Rome—describes how it began:

> The . . . Gauls . . . invented a story that Caesar was detained by the disturbances in Rome,

free, and I shall pity you and your friends when neither your age nor your distinction nor the virtue of others can diminish in you the feeling that life is sweet.

(*To Brutus* 1.16)

When Brutus was visited by his "evil genius" (said to have appeared to him again at Philippi on the eve of his death), perhaps he was, in reality, finally coming to grips with himself. What he considered his "evil genius" was that part of his being that had driven him to do so many things contrary to his philosophical nature. Whether this story about Brutus is true or only concocted by someone who knew the contradictions of his personality well, the passage may still best epitomize the essence of the historical Brutus. Philosophically, he was a man of ethics, who thought he was capable of facing his problems; in reality, he displayed unethical behavior and was incapable of dealing with the consequences of problems he had created:

> I am your evil genius, Brutus. And you will see me at Philippi. And Brutus unperturbed said "I shall see you."

---

where political strife was so acute, they said, that he could not rejoin his army. . . . They were already smarting under their subjection to Rome, and now began to plan war with greater confidence and boldness. . . .

These discussions ended with a declaration by the Carnutes [a tribe of Gauls] that they were prepared to face any danger for the common cause, and would undertake to strike the first blow. . . . When the appointed day arrived, the Carnutes . . . swooped down . . . on Cenabum, killed the Romans who had settled there . . . and plundered their property. . . . Thus . . . what happened at Cenabum at dawn was known before eight o'clock at night in the country of the Arverni, about a hundred and fifty miles away.

There, the lead given by the Carnutes was followed by Vercingetorix, a very powerful young Arvernian. . . . Assembling his retainers, Vercingetorix had no difficulty in exciting their passions, and the news of what was afoot soon brought others out in arms. An effort to restrain him was made by his uncle . . . and other chiefs, who thought the enterprise too risky, and he was expelled from the town of Gergovia. Undeterred . . . he went round the countryside raising a band of vagabonds and beggars. With these at his back he was able to win over all the Arvernians whom he approached. Calling upon them to take up arms for the freedom of Gaul, he assembled a large force and succeeded in expelling the opponents by whom . . . he had been driven out himself. He was proclaimed king . . . and sent embassies in every direction adjuring the tribes to keep faith. In a short time he had secured the support of . . . all the . . . tribes of the west coast, who unanimously elected him commander-in-chief. Armed with this power, he ordered each tribe to give hostages, to bring a specified quota of troops at once, and to manufacture a specified quantity of arms by a certain date—paying particular attention to the cavalry

(continued)

Caesar and Multiculturalism (continued)

Figure 3.10   *The Rubicon River, where the modern version of the old Roman Via Flaminia bridges it. The river formed the northern border of Italy, and above it (left in the photo) was Gaul (Cisalpine). Caesar returned from his conquest of Gaul, and, on or near this spot, he crossed the Rubicon to begin the Civil War in 49 B.C. The drama surrounding that event has prompted a more impressive visual image of the river than is warranted (note, however, the location of the actual river banks in the photo). Because Suetonius describes the bridge Caesar crossed as "little" (Caesar 31.2), the Rubicon is probably not much different in size today from what it was in antiquity.*

arm. Himself a man of boundless energy, he terrorized waverers with the rigors of an iron discipline. Serious cases of disaffection were punished by torture and death at the stake, and even for a minor fault he would cut off a man's ears or gouge out one of his eyes and send him home to serve as a warning to others of the severe chastisement meted out to offenders.

(*Conquest of Gaul* 7.1, 2, 4)

After returning to Gaul, Caesar quickly had Vercingetorix on the defensive. Ultimately, the rebellion failed, and the Gallic leader was taken prisoner. Vercingetorix was held in Rome until 46 B.C. when he was led in Caesar's Triumph and executed.

In 56 B.C., six years before his encounter with Vercingetorix, Caesar had successfully challenged the "right" of the German king, Ariovistus, to exert his influence over a portion of Gaul. What follows is Caesar's version of the king's reaction. Of particular interest is Ariovistus' statement that Caesar's enemies had already contacted

Figure 3.11 *The "Dying Gaul," a copy of a third-century* B.C. *original from Pergamum in Asia Minor, is the finest representation of a Gaul, or Celt, from the Ancient World. Romans encountered different groups of Gauls not only in Gaul itself but also in Britain, northern Italy, and Asia Minor. Caesar reputedly killed a million Gauls and captured another million during his time in Gaul.*

him about disposing of Caesar—a clear indication of how far politics could spread from Rome:

> Ariovistus had little to say in reply to these demands, but spoke at length about his own merits. He had crossed the Rhine, he said, not of his own accord but in response to the invitation of the Gauls. . . . The possessions he had in Gaul had been ceded to him by the Gauls themselves, and the hostages had been given voluntarily. . . . The large numbers of Germans he was bringing into Gaul were brought to secure his safety, not for aggression; the proof of that was that he had not come till he was asked, and had fought only in self-defense. However, he had come there before the Romans, whose armies had never before marched beyond the frontier of the Province. What did Caesar mean by invading his dominions?
>
> "This part of the country," he said, "is my province, just as the other part is yours. I could not expect you to let me make raids into your territory with impunity, and it is a gross injustice for you to interfere with me in the exercise of my lawful right. . . . I suspect that . . . your object in keeping an army in Gaul is to crush

(continued)

Caesar and Multiculturalism (continued)

me. Unless you take yourself off from this country, and your army with you, it won't be as a 'Friend' [Ariovistus had previously been designated a 'Friend' by Rome, a favored status that Caesar obviously chose to disregard] that I shall treat you. In fact, if I killed you, there are plenty of nobles and politicians in Rome who would thank me for it; I know this, because they themselves commissioned their agents to tell me so. I could make them all my grateful friends by putting an end to you. But if you will go away and leave me in undisturbed possession of Gaul I will reward you handsomely, and whenever you want a war fought, I will see the job through for you, without your lifting a finger or running any risk."

Caesar explained at some length why he could not think of abandoning his intention . . . and he could not admit that Gaul belonged to Ariovistus any more than to Rome. . . . If priority of arrival was to be the criterion, the Romans' title to rule Gaul was unimpeachable. If they were to abide by the decision of the Senate, Gaul ought to be independent, since the Senate had determined that, although conquered, it should be allowed self-government.
(*Conquest of Gaul* 1.44–45)

Unimpressed, Ariovistus decided to fight. Defeated by Caesar, he fled a broken man. He was dead by 54 B.C.

In 55 B.C., Caesar led the first Roman expedition to Britain. The invasion had little political or military impact or urgency, but it certainly attracted attention in Rome and garnered Caesar more laurels. He returned in 54 B.C. for a more extensive visit. On that occasion, he encountered resistance from a chieftain named Cassivellaunus, who would eventually come to terms. Caesar describes the scene in Britain:

As soon as the ships were hauled up and the camp strongly fortified, Caesar . . . returned to the place from which he had come. On arriving there he found that larger British forces had now been assembled from all sides by Cassivellaunus, to whom the chief command and direction of the campaign had been entrusted by common consent. Cassivellaunus' territory is separated from the maritime tribes by a river called the Thames, and lies about seventy-five miles from the sea. Previously he had been continually at war with the other tribes, but the arrival of our army frightened them into appointing him their supreme commander. . . .

On learning the enemy's plan of campaign, Caesar led his army to the Thames in order to enter Cassivellaunus' territory. The river is fordable at one point only, and even there with difficulty. At this place he found large enemy forces drawn up on the opposite bank. The bank was also fenced by sharp stakes fixed along the edge, and . . . concealed in the river-bed. He sent the cavalry across first and then at once ordered the infantry to follow. . . . The enemy was overpowered and fled from the river-bank.

Cassivellaunus had now given up all hope of fighting a pitched battle. Disbanding the greater part of his troops, he retained only some four thousand charioteers. . . . If ever our cavalry incautiously ventured too far away in plundering and devastating the country, he would send all his charioteers out of the woods . . . and deliver very formidable attacks. . . . Caesar was thus compelled to keep the cavalry in touch with the column of infantry and to let the enemy off with such devastation and burning as could be done under the protection of the legionaries—tired as they often were with marching. . . .

While these operations were proceeding . . . Cassivellaunus sent envoys to Kent ordering the four kings of that region . . . to collect all their troops and make a surprise attack on the naval camp. When these forces appeared the Romans made a sortie, in which without suffering any

Figure 3.12   *Model of the waterfront of Londinium, Roman London, and the first "London bridge." Although Caesar passed through this area during his campaigns in Britain, the Roman town was not established until after the Emperor Claudius' conquest of Britain in 43 A.D.*

loss they killed a great many of them and captured . . . a leader of noble birth. On receiving news of this action, Cassivellaunus, alarmed by so many reverses, by the devastation of his country, and above all by the defection of his allies, sent envoys to Caesar to obtain terms of surrender. . . . Accordingly he granted Cassivellaunus'

request for terms, demanding hostages, fixing an annual tribute to be paid by the Britons to the Roman government, and strictly forbidding Cassivelaunus to molest . . . the Trinovantes [a tribe of Britons protected by Caesar].
(*Conquest of Gaul* 5.11, 18–19, 22)

Suggestions for Further Reading

Information about Brutus may be found in Plutarch's lives of *Caesar, Brutus,* and *Antony;* and in Suetonius' biography of *Caesar* in *The Twelve Caesars.* There are many translations of Plutarch, and Penguin and Loeb

editions are available for both authors. Appian (*Civil Wars* 2–4), Dio (*Roman History* 44–47), Velleius Paterculus (*Roman History* 2.56–72), Florus, and Livy (*Summaries*) provide additional detail, and all are translated in Loeb Classical Library editions. Of particular interest is Cicero's correspondence with Brutus from the end of March to the end of July of 43 B.C. This can most easily be found appended to the end of Volume Two of the Penguin translation of *Cicero's Letters to His Friends* (1978). The same volume contains other letters Brutus wrote or received (13.10–14; 11.1–3, 17). Several of Cicero's dialogues also concern Brutus, particularly the *Brutus,* and he mentions him in speeches, most notably the *Philippics.* The most recent major study of Brutus is M. L. Clarke's *The Noblest Roman: Marcus Brutus and His Reputation* (Ithaca, N.Y.: Cornell University Press, 1981). This is the best place to start any survey. Also of interest is T. W. Africa's "The Mask of an Assassin: A Psycho-Historical Study of M. Junius Brutus," *Journal of Interdisciplinary History* 8 (1978): 599–626.

Additional works of interest are M. Gelzer's aging but still excellent *Caesar: Politician and States-man,* 6th ed. (Cambridge, Mass.: Harvard University Press, 1968; translated by P. Needham); Z. Yavetz's *Julius Caesar and His Public Image* (Ithaca, N.Y.: Cornell University Press, 1983); and the lively and imaginative *The Education of Julius Caesar* by A. Kahn (New York: Schocken Books, 1986). See also W. K. Lacey, *Cicero and the End of the Roman Republic* (London: Hodder & Stoughton, 1978); N. Wood, *Cicero's Social and Political Thought: An Intro-duction* (Berkeley and Los Angeles: University of California Press, 1988); and C. Habicht, *Cicero the Politician* (Baltimore: The Johns Hopkins University Press, 1990). Other useful works include L. R. Taylor, *Party Politics in the Age of Caesar* (Berkeley and Los Angeles: University of California Press [paperback], 1961); E. Gruen, *The Last Generation of the Roman Republic* (Berkeley and Los Angeles: University of California Press, 1974); R. Syme's monumental *Roman Revolution* (Oxford: Oxford Paperbacks, 1960); M. Beard and M. Crawford, *Rome in the Late Republic* (Ithaca, N.Y.: Cornell University Press, 1985); and A. W. Lintott, *Violence in Republican Rome* (Oxford: Clarendon Press, 1968). A good general survey is H. H. Scullard's *From the Gracchi to Nero,* 5th ed. (London: Methuen, 1982).

4

The End of the Republic

Antony Loses the Roman World
Cleopatra, "Queen of Kings"; Queen of Hearts

Cleopatra's own beauty . . . was not of that incomparable kind which instantly captivates the beholder.
(Plutarch, *Antony* 27.2)

The work of Brutus and his fellow conspirators altered the course of not only their own lives but also the lives of others close to Caesar—most notably, perhaps, that of Cleopatra. Since she had first met Caesar in Egypt four years earlier, the two had shared a relationship that was notorious in its own day and destined to become one of the most celebrated romances in history. Resident in Rome when her paramour was murdered, Cleopatra became an embarrassing and unwelcome guest. The twenty-five-year-old queen and her young son Caesarion, neither of whom was mentioned in Caesar's will, quietly slipped out of the city with their retinue and set sail for the friendly shores of Egypt. One chapter of her life had closed, and another would soon open.

Cleopatra's Background

When Caesar first arrived in Egypt in 48 B.C., he was pursuing Pompey, who had fled there after his defeat at Pharsalus. At that time, Caesar knew little about Cleopatra, but he had known her father, Ptolemy XII Auletes, or "Piper." Auletes owed his throne to Rome, specifically to Caesar and Pompey, through whose good graces he had ruled. During Caesar's consulship in 59 B.C., the king had guaranteed his shaky hold on Egypt by paying Caesar's and Pompey's outrageous price of 6,000 talents (a sum to be calculated in the tens of millions of dollars) to confirm him as "friend and ally" of Rome. As rich as Egypt was, the immediate payment of such a staggering sum forced Auletes to borrow the funds from a Roman financier. He had still not paid back the loan when he died in 51 B.C.

Ironically, Auletes' expensive gamble bore little fruit. The Egyptians resented the new taxes he imposed to repay his debt and viewed him as a Roman lackey whose pro-Roman policies had recently allowed Rome's annexation of Ptolemaic Cyprus. They also favored other members of the royal family over him. Eventually, they demonstrated their displeasure by driving Auletes from Egypt, and two of his daughters fought over the throne. A third daughter, Cleopatra, probably fled with Auletes to Italy, where the harried king sought help from his benefactors.

Certainly, it was not politically or economically advantageous to Caesar (now in Gaul) or Pompey—or, for that matter, to any who profited from their activities—to have Auletes cut off permanently from his resources in Egypt. Through covert activities, bribes, and additional promises of monies almost double his original contribution (he apparently agreed to let Roman opportunists ravage Egypt), Auletes gained the support he had sought. In 55 B.C., a Roman invasion of Egypt placed him back on the throne. A young cavalry commander named Mark Antony, in his mid-twenties, played a significant role in the military operations. It was probably at this time that he first saw Cleopatra, who would have been fourteen years old.

Auletes remained in power until his death several years later. Usually viewed as a marginally competent ruler (he was, after all, called the "pipe player" because of an obsession with a clarinetlike instrument), Auletes was probably as capable as anyone could be in his situation. In Egypt, much of the criticism he suffered resulted from resentment over his close ties with Rome. However, it would have been not only impractical but also dangerous for him to pur-

Figure 4.1 *Ptolemy XII Auletes, the father of Cleopatra. The prominent nose was a family trait he passed on to his daughter (see Figure 4.2).*

sue an independent policy, and a pro-Roman course was the only one possible to preserve any Egyptian autonomy. His handling of the internal and external policies that he could control show him to be a rather substantial—and decisive—figure (he even executed one of his daughters for plotting against him). Certainly, the clever, intelligent Cleopatra inherited more from her father than just a hooked nose (see Figure 4.2), a prominent family trait. She may even have been co-ruling with him when he died in 51 B.C., after which she shared the throne with her ten-year-old half brother and husband, Ptolemy XIII (the Ptolemies, like the ancient Egyptians, intermarried, and a female could not rule by herself).

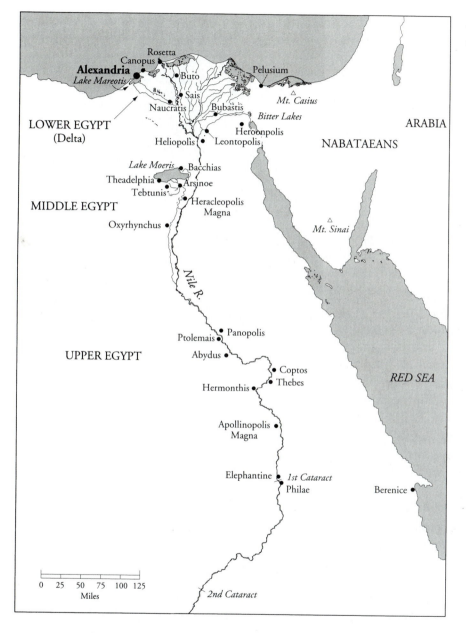

Map 11
Egypt at the time
of Cleopatra

LOWER EGYPT
(Delta)

MIDDLE EGYPT

UPPER EGYPT

Nile R.

NABATAEANS

ARABIA

Mt. Casius

Bitter Lakes

Lake Moeris

Mt. Sinai

RED SEA

1st Cataract

2nd Cataract

0　25　50　75　100　125
Miles

Rosetta
Canopus
Alexandria
Lake Mareotis
Buto
Sais
Naucratis
Bubastis
Pelusium
Heliopolis
Leontopolis
Heroonpolis
Bacchias
Theadelphia
Arsinoe
Tebtunis
Heracleopolis
Magna
Oxyrhynchus
Panopolis
Ptolemais
Abydus
Coptos
Thebes
Hermonthis
Apollinopolis
Magna
Elephantine
Philae
Berenice

Family Struggles

By the time Caesar landed in Egypt, relations between Cleopatra and her brother were at an im-
passe. A few months before, she had been driven

out of the kingdom. The same difficulties contributed to the murder of Pompey when he
sought refuge in Egypt after fleeing Pharsalus.
Young Ptolemy's advisors feared that Pompey, if
allowed to live, might try to make Egypt his base

of operations. If he did, the country would be ravaged in the ensuing struggle with Caesar. Ptolemy already had his hands full with Cleopatra, whose army was encamped near his at Pelusium on Egypt's eastern frontier. His position was by no means secure (might Pompey side with Cleopatra?). In addition, one of the lowest floods of the Nile on record practically guaranteed great internal hardship for Egypt. It was hoped that killing Pompey would eliminate a threat, place Ptolemy in good stead with Caesar, and end Caesar's immediate business in Egypt. He would depart, leaving the Egyptians to themselves. Consequently, Pompey was murdered as he was being transported to shore (while his wife and friends watched helplessly from his ship) at Pelusium. Achillas was the Egyptian who orchestrated the deed, but it was made more repugnant by the fact that Septimius, a former officer of Pompey, was the man who stabbed him.

Caesar had other ideas. He was now rid of Pompey, but always in need of funds for his war chest, he planned to exploit the riches of Egypt. When Cleopatra's father had been unable to repay his loan, Caesar had assumed responsibility for the debt. He now informed the Egyptian government that he planned to collect what was due, although he had previously reduced the amount by about half. He could have demanded more since Ptolemy had aided Pompey before Pharsalus.

Caesar also made it clear that, as Roman consul, he meant to see that the will of his "old friend" Ptolemy Auletes was carried out to the letter. That meant he was going to adjudicate the disagreement between Cleopatra and her brother. In his official capacity, he summoned Ptolemy, still with his army, to Alexandria. He also must have summoned Cleopatra, who was probably with her troops. Apparently, he did not provide her with an escort since Plutarch

Figure 4.2   *A coin (plaster cast) representing Cleopatra*

describes the following device by which she safely arrived at Caesar's feet. The story seems so absurd that it probably has some truth to it:

> Cleopatra, taking only one of her friends with her (Apollodorus the Sicilian), embarked in a small boat and landed at the palace when it was already getting dark. Since there seemed to be no other way of getting in unobserved, she stretched herself out full length inside a sleeping bag, and Apollodorus, after tying up the bag, carried it indoors to Caesar. This little trick of Cleopatra's, which showed her provocative impudence, is said to have been the first thing about her which captivated Caesar, and, as he grew to know her better, he was overcome by her charm and arranged that she and her brother should be reconciled and should share the throne of Egypt together.
>
> (*Caesar* 49.1–2)

It must have indeed been Cleopatra's charm—and also her intellect (she was conversant in eight languages)—that attracted the aging Caesar's attention, for despite modern impressions to the contrary, she was no beauty. The several existing representations show her to be average looking at best. Plutarch says:

> Her own beauty, so we are told, was not of that incomparable kind which instantly captivates the beholder. But the charm of her presence

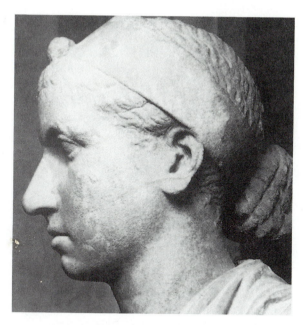

Figure 4.3 *On the basis of coin representations like the one in Figure 4.2, this female bust has been tentatively identified as Cleopatra.*

was irresistible, and there was an attraction in her person and her talk, together with a peculiar force of character which pervaded her every word and action, and laid all who associated with her under its spell. It was a delight merely to hear the sound of her voice, with which, like an instrument of many strings, she could pass from one language to another, so that in her interviews with barbarians she seldom required an interpreter, but conversed with them unaided. . . .
(*Antony* 27.2–3)

Apparently, Caesar found the ambitious twenty-one-year-old a pleasant change from her Roman female counterparts. While obviously attracted by an extraordinary woman, Caesar was no fumbling schoolboy with a runaway libido. He let Cleopatra use him only as far as he wished to be used. She was definitely a part of

his future plans for Egypt. That there was an emotional attachment (despite the thirty-year difference in their ages) between the two is undeniable, although Caesar continued to be married and to have other mistresses.

Caesar and Cleopatra

Caesar's presence in Egypt and his favoritism toward Cleopatra ultimately produced a war with her brother that literally came to the palace door in Alexandria. Severely undermanned, Caesar held out through the winter months until a relief force arrived in early spring. The final battle took place near the end of March 47 B.C. By this time, much of the Egyptian fleet had been burned in the Great Harbor (a book depository on the docks also caught fire, prompting the erroneous story that the Great Library of Alexandria had been destroyed), Ptolemy's chief advisors had been killed or had fled, and Cleopatra discovered that she was pregnant. Her defeated brother (now about fifteen) drowned in the Nile while trying to escape. Egyptian monarchs were considered divine; to drown in the Nile was a blessed death. To make sure that no stories would arise concerning young Ptolemy's resurrection, Caesar had the river dredged until the body was found.

With Egypt secure, Caesar resisted pressures from Rome to annex it as a Roman province. He undoubtedly felt that his personal ambitions were better served by keeping Cleopatra on the throne and by having ready access to Egypt's wealth. Egypt also provided an ideal refuge should he ever need one.

During his remaining time in Egypt, Caesar installed Cleopatra on the throne, married her to her twelve-year-old brother (to conform with Ptolemaic tradition and also to remind Cleopatra that she did not have free rein to do as she

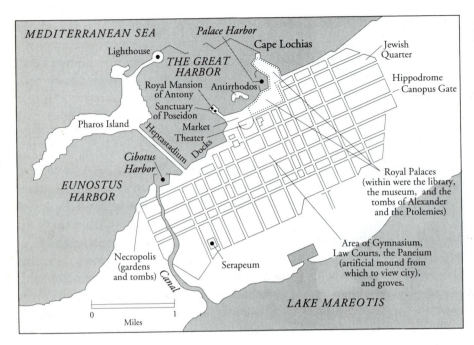

Map 12
Alexandria (the locations of the Great Library and Museum are unknown, though described as "part of the royal palaces")

pleased), and, in her company, cruised the Nile in style. This cruise, which was well attended militarily, served to strengthen and unify Cleopatra's position over all of Egypt. It also allowed Caesar to assess the country's wealth and, as tourist, to visit Egypt's fascinating sites (the pyramids at Giza were already 2,500 years old!). His lengthy stay was due in part to the political and military difficulties he encountered in Egypt, but the lure of Cleopatra kept him there longer than necessary. He departed, probably in June of 47 B.C., leaving three legions in Egypt. Not long after, Cleopatra produced a son.

A Difficult Caesarion

Cleopatra named the son she bore Ptolemy Caesar. He was popularly called Caesarion, or "little Caesar." There is no doubt of his existence. The controversy arises over his paternity—Caesar may

or may not have been the father. On the negative side, after several marriages and numerous affairs, Caesar had fathered only one child, Julia—by his first wife, Cornelia. To become a father again after thirty-six years—at age fifty-three—would have been unlikely. Some have suggested that Caesar was incapable of reproducing. His health was uneven throughout his life, and he suffered an attack of "quartan fever" not long after Julia was born. Perhaps it rendered him sterile.

Furthermore, Caesar did not mention Caesarion in his will, revised only a short time before his death. One might argue that if Caesarion had indeed been Caesar's son, he would not have been overlooked. Another argument against Caesar's paternity would seem to be the stipulation in his will (if tradition preserves the document's contents accurately) that *if* he were to have a son, that son would become his chief heir. However, in the eyes of Rome, Caesar was not legally married to Cleopatra, and any child produced by her was not legitimate. Even if Caesar had claimed paternity—and Mark Antony informed the Senate on one occasion that he did—he *could not* make Caesarion his legal heir. Consequently, we should not expect to find the boy's name mentioned in the will. A less wise Antony would later suffer the wrath of Rome by formally naming his children by Cleopatra his heirs and recognizing Caesarion as Caesar's son.

If, as it appears, Cleopatra gave birth to Caesarion soon after Caesar left Egypt, then he knew she was pregnant. If he had any doubts as to how she got that way, his actions do not show it. It is unlikely that he would have remained with her and, later, brought her and the child to Rome if he had any suspicions about Caesarion's paternity. It is also doubtful that he would have allowed Cleopatra to claim publicly that this was his son and name him after himself. Caesar may have provided for a future son in his will (even mentioning specific guardians for that son) expressly because he believed that he *had* fathered Caesarion and was still capable of fathering a "Roman" son. Either Caesarion was Caesar's son or Cleopatra, in making Caesar believe so, proved herself more clever than one of the cleverest men who has ever lived.

Cleopatra in Rome

When Caesar had successfully completed his wars in Asia Minor and Africa (where Cato died), he returned to Rome in July 46 B.C. In September, he began celebrating his victories (although judiciously ignoring his defeat of Pompey), including his earlier conquest of the Gauls. One triumphal parade commemorated the Alexandrian War, and the procession included Cleopatra's half sister, who had tried to

seize power from her. Whether Cleopatra was in Rome at this time is not known. If not (politically, it may have been wiser for her to come at a later date), she arrived soon after with her young brother-husband, a large entourage, and, although dangerously young, the infant Caesarion. It was necessary that the boy be with his "father" to stem any doubts about his paternity. The official reason for her visit was a reaffirmation of her father's treaty with Rome.

Caesar, although still married, made no secret of his regard for Cleopatra, and she was housed on his estate. When the Forum of Caesar was opened to relieve overcrowding in the main Roman Forum (to which it was adjacent), Caesar placed Cleopatra's statue next to one of Venus—from whom his family claimed descent—in the Temple of Venus located there (see Figure 4.4, page 94). This was an unprecedented honor, one more Egyptian than Roman, and certainly it would have kept tongues wagging about the queen and Caesar. It may also provide additional support for Caesar's belief that he had fathered Caesarion: Venus was mother of Caesar's family; Cleopatra, the incarnation of Isis, was mother of Caesar's son.

We have no information about Cleopatra's stay in Rome (an amazing deficiency). She undoubtedly returned to Egypt late in 46 B.C. when Caesar went to Spain to defeat the remaining Pompeians who had fled there after Pharsalus. She was back with him in Rome some months before his assassination. These remarks of Cicero (written in June 44 B.C.) probably reflect what most Romans thought of their royal guest and her attendants:

> I dislike Her Majesty. . . . The arrogance of the Queen herself when she was living on the estate across Tiber makes my blood boil to

Figure 4.4
The Forum of Caesar at Rome. The tall columns to the right are part of the Temple of Venus, in which Caesar also placed a statue of Cleopatra.

recall. So I want nothing to do with them. They must think I have no spirit, or rather that I hardly have a spleen.

(*Letters to Atticus* 15.15.2)

Parthia: A Key Piece in the Puzzle

Cleopatra's stay in Rome was not a passive one. She certainly had an influence on some of Caesar's reforms. His Julian calendar of 365 1/4 days (a month was also renamed July in Caesar's honor) and public library system had a decidedly Egyptian heritage. His political policies also would not have remained immune from the ambitious young queen's influence. Although there were strong political and "national" reasons, his decision to renew the war with Parthia was also partly based on his desire to enhance Cleopatra's image among the Romans.

Parthia was on the eastern extremity of the Roman frontier, and as Crassus had learned earlier, it was a difficult land to conquer. Crassus and much of his army had perished at Carrhae in 53 B.C. (see Chapter 3). Caesar wanted another confrontation with the Parthians, and so did the Roman people. The defeat had not been avenged, and the Parthians still possessed the army standards they had captured. Tired of the political bickering his policies evoked at Rome, Caesar undoubtedly longed for the kind of authority he had in the field, where his orders were obeyed immediately. He was fifty-six years old and not in the best of health, but what he—and Cleopatra—had to gain from the Parthian venture outweighed any risks.

To ensure success against Parthia, Caesar planned to utilize Egypt's wealth and strategic location. Cleopatra was prepared to provide whatever he needed. Caesar had just been made perpetual dictator. A successful Parthian campaign would make his military position unassailable and ensure his complete control of the East. He also hoped that, because of the key role Cleopatra would play in Parthia's defeat, Rome would willingly come to accept her and Egypt as true "friends" and "allies." With East and West unified, Egypt would have a crucial role in Rome's future—and, possibly (certainly this is what she hoped), a legal Roman union between Cleopatra and great Caesar awaited. These ideas would have been unsettling to many Romans, who saw not only dictatorship—perhaps monarchy (the Sibylline Books, it was said, predicted that only a "king" could defeat the Parthians)—replacing the Republic but also Alexandria replacing Rome. It is no accident that the conspirators decided to kill Caesar only a few days before he would leave for Parthia.

All for Naught

Had Caesar lived, the role Caesarion would have played cannot be known. What is known is that Caesar was taking his eighteen-year-old grandnephew Octavian, who only a few months before had been designated his heir, with him to Parthia. Obviously, Caesar hoped to get better acquainted with the young man and wanted him to gain military experience on the campaign. This could not have pleased Cleopatra; but Caesar knew that if something were to happen to him, only an *adult* heir, a *Roman* heir, could be his successor and have any chance of surviving. Since that heir was also a member of his legal family, it appears that Caesar had some sort of dynastic succession in mind. Whatever his plans, they all died with him on the Ides of March. Ironically, Octavian ultimately destroyed both Cleopatra and Caesarion.

Figure 4.5 Octavian

Cleopatra and Antony

When Cleopatra returned to Egypt after Caesar's death, she disposed of her young half brother and co-ruler, Ptolemy XIV, and raised Caesarion, now three years old, as her fellow monarch. She continued to insist that he was the true son and heir of Caesar. The Roman world was busy choosing sides between the "Second Triumvirate" (Antony, Octavian, and Lepidus) and Brutus and his fellow conspirators. Both the triumvirs and the conspirators coveted the wealth of Egypt.

Much of the East had already joined Brutus and Cassius, and Cassius was now demanding assistance from Egypt. Ships were sent to him, apparently independent of Cleopatra's order. It is unlikely that she would have helped the men who assassinated Caesar, and it is unclear how she would profit from such assistance (except, perhaps, forestalling an invasion of Egypt by Cassius). The conspirators would help her enemies replace her; and little needs to be said about Caesarion's future if he fell into their hands. At the same time, Cleopatra certainly could not have felt comfortable allying herself with Octavian, Caesar's acknowledged heir—but she did know Mark Antony, perhaps well.

Cleopatra had to contend with hostile elements at home, the threats and entreaties of the conspirators, and the triumvirs. The fact that she survived is a tribute to her cunning. It appears that she *was* making attempts to aid the triumvirs before the battle of Philippi. Whatever the case, the deaths of Brutus, Cassius, and their fellow conspirators necessarily meant that she would have to deal with the Caesarians—and Antony was her best hope.

The Meeting at Tarsus

Flamboyant and popular, a veteran of the battlefield, the bottle, and the bedroom, Antony was forty-two years old when he met Cleopatra at Tarsus in Cilicia in 41 B.C. Plutarch offers this description of his character:

> . . . there was a noble dignity about Antony's appearance. His beard was well grown, his forehead broad, his nose aquiline, and these features combined to give him a certain bold and masculine look, which is found in the statues and portraits of Hercules. In fact there was an ancient tradition that . . . Antony's family . . . claimed descent from . . . one of the sons of Hercules, and Antony liked to believe that his own physique lent force to the legend. He also deliberately cultivated it in his choice of dress, for whenever he was going to appear before a

Figure 4.6   Coin bearing the likeness of Antony

large number of people, he wore his tunic belted low over the hips, a large sword at his side, and a heavy cloak. And indeed it was these same "Herculean" qualities that the fastidious found so offensive—his swaggering air, his ribald talk, his fondness for carousing in public, sitting down by his men as they ate, or taking his food standing at the common mess-table—which made his own troops delight in his company and almost worship him. His weakness for the opposite sex also showed an attractive side of his character, and even won him the sympathy of many people, for he often helped others in their love-affairs and always accepted with good humor the jokes they made about his own. Besides this, his open-handed nature and the generosity with which he showered rewards upon his friends and his soldiers alike laid a splendid foundation when he first set out upon the road to power, and when he had established himself, these qualities raised his authority to still greater heights, even after he had begun to undermine it by innumerable acts of folly. (*Antony* 4.1–3)

It is clear that Antony, while capable, was no Caesar. Plutarch continues:

> His character was, in fact, essentially simple and he was slow to perceive the truth. Once he recognized that he was at fault, he was full of repentance and ready to admit his errors to those he had wronged. Whenever he had to

punish an offense or right an injustice, he acted on the grand scale, and it was generally considered that he overstepped the bounds far more often in the rewards he bestowed than in the punishments he inflicted. As for the kind of coarse and insolent banter which he liked to exchange, this carried its own remedy with it, for anyone could return his ribaldry with interest and he enjoyed being laughed at quite as much as laughing at others. And in fact it was this quality which often did him harm, for he found it impossible to believe that the real purpose of those who took liberties and cracked jokes with him was to flatter him. He never understood that some men go out of their way to adopt a frank and outspoken manner and use it like a piquant sauce to disguise the cloying taste of flattery.

(*Antony* 24.6–8)

After the battle at Philippi and Octavian's return to Italy, Antony toured the East, capitalizing on its vast resources and rekindling Caesar's ambitious plans to punish the Parthians. Egypt's role in such a campaign was as crucial now as it had been for Caesar, and a meeting with Cleopatra was essential. Antony's former closeness to Caesar must have resulted in his frequent contact with Cleopatra, and it is unlikely that he was any less immune to the charms of the captivating queen. He summoned her to Tarsus.

Anxious to clear up any doubts about her allegiance (there were charges that she had assisted the anti-Caesarians) and to renew her friendship with Antony, Cleopatra ultimately came to Tarsus. However, the queen, now twenty-eight years old, had no intention of kowtowing to Caesar's former lieutenant. She arrived in her own time and in a style that probably made Antony wonder whether he was summoning her—or vice versa. This description of the arrival of her royal barge at Tarsus, while exag-gerated, undoubtedly stems from an eyewitness account:

> . . . Cleopatra's purple-sided barge with gilded poop sailed up the Cydnus River, its rowers plying their silver oars to the music of the flute, accompanied by pipes and lyres playing all together. She herself, dressed like a painting of Venus, reclined beneath a gilded sunshade, while boys, resembling Cupids in paintings, stood fanning her from either side. Similarly, her most beautiful attendants, positioned at the rudder handle and the reefing ropes, were clad like Nereids and Graces. Marvelous scents from numerous incenses permeated the river bank. Of the spectators on shore, some accompanied her on either side from the river's mouth, while others came down from the city to view the sight.

(Plutarch, *Antony* 26.1–3)

Although already married to Fulvia (his third wife)—a politically formidable woman (see box, pages 98–99) and former spouse of Clodius, the notorious *populares* "thug" (see Chapter 3)—Antony's future was to become one with Cleopatra and Egypt. Politically and personally, the two agreed to protect each other's interests and to satisfy their mutual desires. But Antony's favoritism toward Cleopatra would cost him support in the East—and at Rome.

More Problems

When Cleopatra left Tarsus and returned to Egypt, Antony visited Syria and Judaea and continued his preparations for the war with Parthia. He then moved on to Alexandria to spend the winter. Aside from the lure of Cleopatra (she would become pregnant by him), Alexandria was also, as Caesar had seen, the best base of operations for any Eastern campaign.

Antony's decision to proceed to Egypt before settling the rest of the East proved to be

Fulvia—A Lioness among Lions

A WEALTHY NOBLEWOMAN, ANTONY'S wife Fulvia was certainly an appropriate rival for Cleopatra. Both women were extremely capable, ambitious, and strong-minded. No Roman woman had ever been as politically active as Fulvia—or was a greater political force. Fulvia had gained experience through two previous marriages, the first to the notorious Clodius. With Antony, however, she set a precedent for spouses of Roman leaders by fully involving herself in her husband's affairs. Antony's cause became her cause. She provided a daughter (Antony's stepdaughter) from her marriage to Clodius for Octavian to marry to help seal the "Second Triumvirate" (Octavian would later return her "untouched" when problems erupted with Fulvia in Italy) and went to war against Octavian to protect Antony's interests while he was in Egypt. She was also the first Roman woman ever portrayed on coins (see Figure 4.7).

The surviving tradition about Fulvia is a negative and uncomplimentary one. How closely it resembles the real person is impossible to tell. Rome was a male-dominated society, and Fulvia's political activism would have been considered an undesirable quality. Cicero disliked her husbands Clodius and Antony and also sniped at her. The poet Martial was very uncomplimentary. Since she was involved in a losing cause, it was only natural that her reputation would suffer after Octavian's victory. As the following passage from Plutarch indicates, she was regarded

Figure 4.7 *Coin representing Fulvia (with wings of victory)*

as another woman who had weakened and misguided Antony:

> At any rate, [Antony] now reformed his whole manner of living, turned his thoughts towards marriage, and chose Fulvia, the widow of Clodius the demagogue. She was a woman who took no interest in spinning or managing a household, nor could she be content to rule a husband who had no ambition for public life: her desire was to govern those who governed or to command a commander-in-chief. And in fact Cleopatra was indebted to Fulvia for teaching Antony to obey a wife's authority, for by the time he met her, he had already been quite broken in and schooled to accept the sway of women.
>
> (Plutarch, *Antony* 10.3)

unwise. Distracted, he apparently lost sight of the fact that the Parthians were a fierce, formidable enemy who had previously been responsible for one of Rome's worst defeats. The Parthians shocked Antony back to reality by invading the Roman Empire. They had no intention of waiting for him.

Antony had little time to say good-bye to Cleopatra. Departing Egypt in haste, he soon learned that the situation was worse than he thought. Some of his troops, formerly those of the anti-Caesarians Brutus and Cassius, had joined the Parthians, as did several Roman client-kings. As if this were not enough, when he

During the proscriptions that accompanied the creation of the "Second Triumvirate," Fulvia was depicted by her detractors as particularly bloodthirsty:

> As for [Q. Salvidienus] Rufus, he possessed a handsome mansion near that of Fulvia, the wife of Antony, which she had wanted to buy, but he would not sell it, and although he now offered it to her as a free gift, he was proscribed. His head was brought to Antony, who said it did not concern him and sent it to his wife. She ordered that it be fastened to the front of his own house instead of the rostra.
>
> (Appian, *Civil Wars* 4.29)

This tradition was elaborated, perhaps by apologists who wished to excuse Antony from some of the bloodletting by placing the blame on Fulvia. In this well-known passage, Fulvia is represented in Medea-like fashion, taking a ghoulish and shocking revenge on Cicero after his proscription and execution:

> And even Fulvia also caused the death of many, both to satisfy her enmity and to gain their wealth, in some cases men with whom her husband was not even acquainted; at any rate, when he saw the head of one man, he exclaimed: "I knew not this man!" When, however, the head of Cicero also was brought to them one day (he had been overtaken and slain in flight), Antony uttered many bitter reproaches against it and then ordered it to be exposed on the rostra more prominently than the rest, in order that it might be seen in the very place where Cicero had so often been heard declaiming against him, together with his right hand, just as it had been cut off. And Fulvia took the head into her hands before it was removed, and after abusing it spitefully and spitting upon it, set it on her knees, opened the mouth, and pulled out the tongue, which she pierced with the pins that she used for her hair, at the same time uttering many brutal jests.
>
> (Dio, *Roman History* 47.2–4)

Even in death, Fulvia got little respect, although Antony is depicted as having some remorse for his contribution to her demise:

> While these events were in progress the news came that Fulvia was dead. It was said that she was dispirited by Antony's reproaches and fell sick, and it was thought that she had become a willing victim of disease on account of the anger of Antony, who had left her while she was sick and had not visited her even when he was going away. The death of this turbulent woman, who had stirred up so disastrous a war on account of her jealousy of Cleopatra, seemed extremely fortunate to both of the parties who were rid of her. Nevertheless, Antony was much saddened by this event because he considered himself in some sense the cause of it.
>
> (Appian, *Civil Wars* 5.59)

arrived in Asia Minor, he was informed that his wife, Fulvia, and his brother had, without his knowledge, attempted an insurrection against Octavian in Italy. They had been soundly defeated. Fulvia fled to Greece with Antony's mother to meet her husband and explain what she had done. No doubt partially motivated by her jealousy of Cleopatra, Fulvia had tried to salvage Antony's crumbling Italian affairs while he was preoccupied in Egypt. Antony was unimpressed and now moved on to Italy, hoping to recruit fresh troops for the East but also expecting to clash with Octavian. Fulvia, already in ill health, died in Greece.

Cleopatra Alone

When Antony sailed away in early 40 B.C., Cleopatra realized that she might never see him again. What she had worked so hard to achieve for herself and Egypt was in jeopardy. More than three years passed before the two were reunited. During that time, Cleopatra gave birth to Antony's twins and must have been encouraged when Fulvia died. Nonetheless, her influence was secondary to the struggle that was taking shape between Antony and Octavian for mastery of the Roman world. Her fate, as well as Antony's, depended on the outcome.

Cleopatra must have felt a forgotten woman during this stressful period. When Antony and Octavian, following a brief confrontation at Brundisium, decided once more to put aside their differences and cooperate, the "Triumvirate" was renewed. By the Treaty of Brundisium (40 B.C.), Octavian and Antony divided up the Roman world, Antony taking the East with recruiting rights in Italy, and Octavian, the West and Illyria. To seal the pact, Antony, now a widower, married the young, beautiful sister of Octavian, Octavia.

Cleopatra was horrified by the news. The marriage to Octavia was a serious threat, for the union brought Antony closer to Octavian and the political power he desired. For the Roman world, the possibility of civil war now diminished, and the "conniving" Eastern queen was back in her place. For the moment, Cleopatra was not important to Antony, and Octavia was soon pregnant with his child.

What communication there was between Antony and Cleopatra during these years cannot be known. Cleopatra remained informed of her paramour's activities, and certainly, Antony could not have neglected her completely—if for no other reason than the upcoming Parthian campaign, in which Egypt would have a de-

ciding role. Cleopatra continued to support Antony's cause. She even gave refuge to his friend Herod. An Idumaean by birth (whose people had been forcibly converted to Judaism in the previous century), Herod had risen to high position in Judaea. When Syria and Judaea were occupied by the Parthians, Cleopatra helped Herod get to Rome, where he was made king of Judaea by Antony and Octavian in 40 B.C. This was not easy for Cleopatra, since she detested Herod, and the lands he now ruled had once been part of the Ptolemaic Empire. In the present circumstances, however, she probably thought it wise to support Herod and reemphasize her own pro-Roman posture. For his part, Antony seems to have countered any proposals in Rome that were not in Cleopatra's (or his) best interests.

Late in 39 B.C., Antony and his new wife took up residence in Athens and were soon regarded as the model couple. For the next year and a half, Antony directed the Parthian campaign from Athens, preferring to carry out the war through his generals. Perhaps he feared the political consequences of a personal military setback at this juncture. As it was, the war went well. Antony probably planned to arrive in time to inflict the crushing blow upon the Parthians himself. Conversely, Octavian had his inadequate hands full with Sextus Pompeius, the son of Pompey. Despite attempts to mollify him, Sextus was a major threat. He and his fleet continued to be a problem. Also, he was viewed by many as the last remaining symbol of Republicanism.

In the latter half of 38 B.C., Antony finally went east and enjoyed success in Asia Minor and Syria. However, difficulties and distrust between the triumvirs eventually brought him back to Tarentum in Italy in 37 B.C., where he and Octavian again worked out their differences. The "Triumvirate" was renewed again, and Antony provided ships for Octavian's war against Sextus Pompeius.

The Reluctant Tourist: Boats, Mules, and Misery— Horace Takes a Trip

THIS ACCOUNT OF A fifteen-day, rather leisurely trip from Rome to Brundisium, is one of the few we have to help us understand what traveling in Italy was like two thousand years ago. Following the Appian Way, the first of Rome's great network of roads, the poet Horace and his companions, most notably the poet Vergil and Maecenas, Octavian's chief diplomat, suffer the same problems that any modern experienced traveler encounters: bad water and food, dingy inns, undesirable folk, and physical exhaustion. Only this was the best ancient Italy had to offer!

The trip relates to negotiations taking place between Antony and Octavian in the early 30s B.C., but there is some debate as to whether it should be dated in 38 or 37 B.C. If the former date is correct, then Horace was simply part of a company traveling with Maecenas and Antony's friend Cocceius to Brundisium, where the latter two would depart for Athens to meet with Antony. However, if it took place in 37 B.C., then the party's final destination was probably Tarentum, where Antony and Octavian would agree once more to renew the "Triumvirate." This is satire, and Horace's main concern was not politics but to emphasize the negative side of the journey and make it humorous. Map 13 shows Horace's route. The town where he stays on the tenth night and will not name (probably his way of being clever) is undoubtedly his birthplace, Venusia.

Horace himself had not been immune to the political turmoil of the times. The son of a freedman, his father had provided him with the best possible education. However, while in Athens, he met Brutus and was with him at Philippi in 42 B.C. Consequently, his father's lands were confiscated, and Horace, after receiving a pardon, became a quaestor's clerk. His poetic talents were noticed by Maecenas, who, aside from his diplomatic duties, presided over Octavian's literary circle. This circle probably included Vergil, Ovid, and Propertius, and Horace would emerge as one of Rome's brightest literary stars and a good friend of the future emperor. Horace had been a member of Octavian's entourage only a few years when he wrote this piece:

I set out on my journey and left behind me the bustling city of Rome. When I reached the little town of Aricia I stopped at a small inn. My traveling companion was Heliodorus, the rhetor, by far the most learned of the Greeks. From Aricia we went to Forum Appii, which was crowded with boatmen and greedy innkeepers. Being rather lazy, we had spread this part of the trip over two days, although more energetic travelers make it in one. But the Appian Way is less tiring if you go slowly.

Because the drinking water at Forum Appii is so incredibly foul, I endured hunger pangs and waited impatiently while my traveling companions had dinner. And now night was preparing to spread her shadows over the earth and sprinkle her stars in the sky. Slaves jeered at boatmen, and boatmen chided slaves. "Put in here!" "You're taking on hundreds!" "Hey, that's enough!" By the time the fare was paid and the mule hitched, a whole hour had gone by. The damn mosquitoes and frogs in the marsh made sleep impossible, while a boatman and a passenger, both drunk from too much cheap wine, took turns serenading their absent girlfriends. Finally the passenger was exhausted and fell asleep. The lazy boatman left the mule to graze, fastening the harness traces to a rock, and then lay on his back and snored. Day was already dawning before we noticed that the boat wasn't moving an inch. So one hothead

(continued)

The Reluctant Tourist (continued)

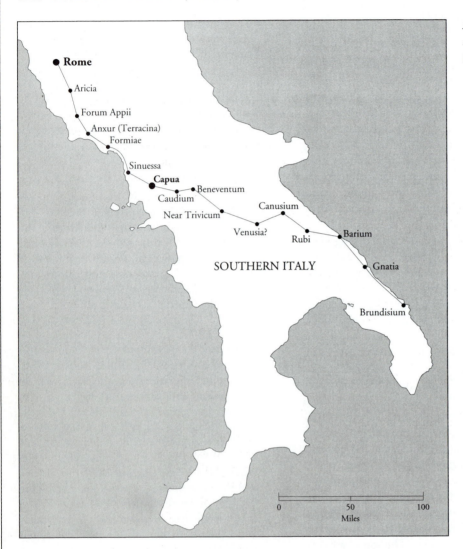

Map 13
Horace's journey
to Brundisium

Rome
Aricia
Forum Appii
Anxur (Terracina)
Formiae
Sinuessa
Capua
Beneventum
Caudium
Near Trivicum
Canusium
Venusia?
Rubi
Barium
Gnatia
Brundisium

SOUTHERN ITALY

0   50   100
Miles

jumped out of the boat and beat both the boatman and the mule on the head and loins with a willow club..Finally, about 10:00, we had just arrived at Feronia's waters.

We washed our hands and faces there and ate some breakfast. Then we crawled along for three miles, climbing steadily up to Anxur which sits atop shining, very conspicuous rocks. Maecenas, an excellent man, and Cocceius were to meet us there, both of them ambassadors, sent out on matters of great importance since they had reputations for patching up broken alliances. At

Anxur I smeared some black ointment on my sore eyes. Maecenas and Cocceius arrived and, with them, Fonteius Capito, a polished gentleman and Antony's best friend. . . . The following day, weary from our travels, we stopped at Formiae; we had dinner at Capito's and spent the night at Murena's. We were eager to see the dawn of the next day because Plotius, Varius, and Vergil met us that day at Sinuessa. The earth has not borne souls more splendid than these! And no one is more deeply attached to them than I. Oh, how many times we hugged one another and laughed with glee. As long as I'm in my right mind, there is nothing I could compare to a pleasant friend. A little house near the Campanian bridge provided shelter for the night. . . .

The next day we traveled from there to Capua. At Capua we had the mules unsaddled. Maecenas played ball, but Vergil and I took a nap because playing ball is painful if you have sore eyes or indigestion. From Capua we traveled to Caudium, where Cocceius entertained us at his well-stocked villa which is situated on a hill above the town and its inns. . . . We had a very enjoyable dinner there.

From Caudium we headed directly toward Beneventum, where the overly eager innkeeper almost burned down his whole place while roasting some scrawny thrushes on a spit. Some sparks from the fireplace fell on the floor, and the flames spread quickly through the ancient kitchen and raced upward to lick the roof. Had you been there, you would have seen hungry guests and frightened slaves grabbing the food, and everyone trying to put out the fire.

Soon after Beneventum, Apulia began to reveal her mountains, so familiar to me. They were scorched by the hot wind, and we would never have managed to crawl through them if an inn near Trivicum had not taken us in for the night. But it was filled with eye-stinging smoke because there were damp branches, leaves and all, burning in the fireplace. I very stupidly waited up half the night for a deceitful girl. When I finally fell asleep, I dreamed of Venus—and wet my bedclothes.

The next day we raced along over twenty-four miles in carriages and then spent the night in a town whose name I cannot mention in verse. But I can easily give you some clues: water, the cheapest of commodities everywhere else, is here sold, but the bread here is by far the best anywhere, and the experienced traveler usually packs a few loaves for the journey ahead. Indeed, the bread of Canusium . . . is gritty, and the town is not a jug richer in water. There Varius sadly departed, leaving his friends in tears.

When we finally reached Rubi, we were exhausted because we had covered a long distance and the trip was made even more uncomfortable by rain. The weather improved the next day, but the road was worse, right up to the walls of the fishing town of Barium. Our next stop was Gnatia . . . and finally Brundisium, the end of a long trip, and of my papyrus.
(*Satires* 1.5.1–33, 37–51, 70–97, 104)

In return, he received promises from Octavian for 20,000 troops for the Parthian campaign.

During the negotiations, Octavia was instrumental in keeping an agreeable atmosphere, since the two men's patience was wearing thin. Pregnant again, she would accompany Antony as far east as Greece before he asked her to return to Italy. This was partially for reasons of health (and the fact that Octavia was caring for all their children by previous marriages) but also because of Cleopatra, whom Antony summoned to Antioch once he was back in Syria. Apparently, he viewed his personal relationship with Octavian at an end and felt there was nothing more to be gained through his marriage to Octavia. However he envisioned the future, Cleopatra and Egypt were to be an indispensable part of it. Cleopatra wintered with him at Antioch. They would not be separated again.

Concessions Fit for a Queen

Cleopatra's price for reconciliation was a high one. Even Antony's friend Herod was forced to make concessions, as Cleopatra received Cyprus, parts of Cilicia (in Asia Minor), Syria, and adjacent lands and cities. Much of this area had previously been included in the old Ptolemaic Empire and contained vast timber resources from which to enlarge the Egyptian fleet. These "gifts" were still client-states of Rome and not Antony's to give. He was making Egypt something unique—an autonomous, allied kingdom, protected by a great Roman lord. And he obviously felt free to utilize the resources of both queen and country for his own ends. Antony had not bothered to divorce Octavia, and Cleopatra was soon pregnant with a third child. Presumably, they were married according to Egyptian custom—if not as earthly consorts, then as the gods Osiris (or Dionysus) and Isis.

Antony had never had the individual success of Caesar in battle, and the key to achieving his goals was a victory over Parthia. Alexander the Great, who, like Antony, claimed descent from Hercules, had conquered the Persian predecessors of the Parthians. Comparisons between him and Antony were unavoidable and promoted by Cleopatra. If Antony were going to convince the world that he was Octavian's superior—and the new Alexander—he had to demonstrate his abilities on the battlefield. Having prepared his political and military

groundwork, he set off for Parthia from Syria in May 36 B.C.

Disaster in Parthia: The Tide Begins to Turn

Antony's army was unquestionably one of the most splendid ever assembled. He began his campaign late in the year (winter would set in before he was ready for it), and ultimately, one problem compounded another. After enjoying success in Armenia, Antony moved into Media, where he planned to besiege the great treasure city of Phraaspa. However, as he approached the heart of the Parthian Empire, treachery, betrayal by "allies," enemy attacks, and the weather all combined to doom the enterprise. It ended in disaster. By the time Antony made it back to Syria, his losses amounted to almost thirty thousand men. At the most important moment of his life, he had failed to deliver. He was neither Alexander nor Caesar. The Parthians remained unconquered. Antony's failure undermined his position in the struggle with Octavian. Previously, he could point to his military success to counter any advances made by his inexperienced competitor. Now, the tide began to turn.

While Antony was proceeding toward his expected victory over Parthia, Octavian's inability to defeat the pesky Sextus Pompeius, the last Republican renegade, practically drove him to suicide. Cleopatra probably felt that his end was near and that she and Antony were about to win their struggle. However, Antony was soundly defeated, and Octavian's longtime friend and admiral, Agrippa, crushed Sextus in a great naval battle off the Sicilian coast in 36 B.C. His confidence restored, Octavian announced that, with this victory, he had finally brought the civil wars to a close.

Octavian had earlier divorced his wife, Scribonia, who was Sextus' aunt, because she was no longer needed. The marriage was one of political convenience, designed to bring Pompey's son and Octavian closer together. It failed to achieve its desired purpose, but Scribonia bore Octavian his only child, Julia. In 38 B.C., Octavian married the beautiful Livia, who was of an old and distinguished family. He was in love with her, but because of Livia's credentials, the union also strengthened Octavian's claim to high rank among the Romans. With the defeat of Sextus Pompeius, Octavian felt secure enough to dismiss Lepidus, the third member of the "Triumvirate." He forced him into retirement without consulting Antony. His power and prestige increasing, Octavian's capabilities were now becoming clear to Cleopatra. The danger he posed to her and her children, particularly Caesarion, was growing.

Difficult Years

When Antony returned from the disaster in Parthia, he summoned Cleopatra to meet him in Phoenicia with money and supplies. She had just given birth to their third child, another boy. After an unavoidable delay, she arrived with everything she could muster early in 35 B.C. She had pinned all her hopes on Antony, and now her future depended on how ably he could rebound from the Parthian disaster and counter the mounting successes of Octavian.

Octavian was not quite ready to challenge Antony directly. For the moment, he preferred to remain on cordial terms with him. However, he had no intention of letting his colleague recover fully. While never a great military man, Octavian was a supreme manipulator and propagandist. He knew that when the full impact of Antony's defeat became known in Rome, the lat-

ter's credibility would suffer. He also knew that most Romans found Antony's preference for Cleopatra over his sister Octavia repugnant. Negative public opinion would steadily undermine his adversary's position. Antony still had powerful friends, so there was no need to press matters—or do anything that might enhance his cause. Without risk, Octavian could place the blame for the losses in Parthia squarely on Cleopatra's shoulders and still have his jab at Antony.

As for Octavia, she remained the faithful wife, caring for her own children by Antony (she had given birth to another girl) and Fulvia's, looking after the interests of her husband and his friends. She wanted now to go to Antony during his hour of need and bring aid. Octavian, seeing the propaganda value of such a move, allowed her to go but sent only a token military force, which Antony must have regarded more as an insult than a positive gesture: At the Tarentum meeting in 37 B.C., Octavian had promised 20,000 men! Also, Octavian purposely placed Antony in an untenable position. Antony had depended upon a foreign woman for his success and had failed; now a noble Roman matron was coming to the rescue. Octavian knew that because of Cleopatra, Antony could not receive Octavia in the East. Predictably, Antony instructed her to send him the reinforcements, meager though they were, and return to Rome. He did not want to see her. Octavian had achieved what he wanted. As Plutarch notes, "[Octavia] unintentionally did great harm to Antony's reputation, since he was naturally hated for wronging such a woman" (*Antony* 54.2).

In the spring of 35 B.C., Antony and Cleopatra returned to Alexandria. They were together there (aside from campaigns) for the next three years. Antony still had plans to punish the

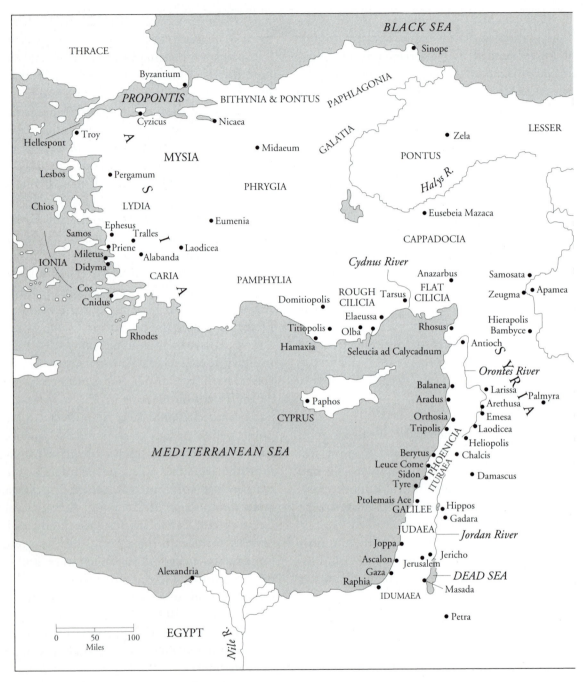

Map 14   The Eastern Empire and Parthia

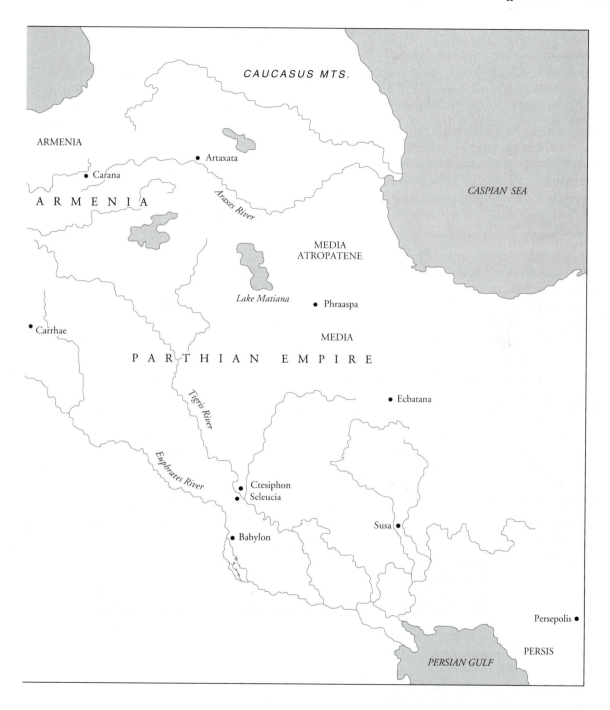

CAUCASUS MTS.

ARMENIA

Artaxata

Carana

A R M E N I A

Araxes River

CASPIAN SEA

MEDIA
ATROPATENE

Lake Matiana

Phraaspa

Carrhae

MEDIA

P A R T H I A N   E M P I R E

Ecbatana

Tigris River

Euphrates River

Ctesiphon
Seleucia

Susa

Babylon

Persepolis

PERSIS

PERSIAN GULF

Parthians, viewing his earlier defeat as merely a setback. But other problems distracted him. Cleopatra still quarreled with the Judaean monarch, Herod, and Antony had to appease Cleopatra without seriously alienating his friend. Sextus Pompeius also became a dangerous nuisance. After his defeat in Sicily by Agrippa, Sextus had fled east and enjoyed some success in Asia Minor. At first he thought to negotiate with Antony, but learning of the latter's recent defeat, he began secret talks with the Parthians. Antony could not afford more trouble. Sextus Pompeius was captured and executed by one of Antony's generals. His elimination pleased Octavian, who congratulated Antony on destroying the rebel, but Romans did not like Romans putting their own to death. Sextus was, after all, Pompey's son, and many viewed him as the last remaining hope for the Republic. There was strong feeling that Antony should have treated him differently.

During this period, it would have been advantageous for Antony to return to Rome, regroup his support, and explain away any charges made against him. Octavian was busy with a war in Illyria, so Antony could have used his rival's absence to his advantage. He still had many supporters in the Senate and in Italy. But he did not go. Perhaps his plans for a renewed Parthian campaign prevented him; perhaps Cleopatra, remembering what had happened the last time he went to Rome, did not want him to go. Whatever the reason, Antony stayed in the East.

Antony Overplays His Hand

In 34 B.C., Antony invaded Armenia as a prelude to another Parthian campaign. His chances for success had improved since the king of Media had broken his alliance with the Parthian king and promised to aid Antony. Cleopatra accompanied the expedition as far as the Euphrates River before turning back. On her way to Alexandria, she took the opportunity to survey her eastern holdings and to visit several independent cities and states, including Judaea. Her visit with Herod must have been at Antony's urging. Reportedly, their meeting was cordial (gossip-mongers, of course, described her attempts to seduce Herod, while he plotted to kill her!), but it is doubtful that their feelings and fears about each other changed.

Late in the same year, Antony returned victorious from Armenia. It was not the major victory he needed, but it improved his image. Everything that could be made of his success was made. The Armenian king, bound with golden chains, was displayed in a triumphal procession at Alexandria. The procession was not Roman in character, for it was not celebrated at Rome. It was a Hellenistic "Triumph" in a Hellenistic city. Antony was hailed as the conquering god Dionysus, returning victorious to his Isis, Cleopatra. As usual, Antony's behavior shocked and confused Romans.

At a formal and spectacular ceremony a few days later, Antony declared that Cleopatra was "Queen of Kings," that she had been wife to Caesar, now deified, and that Caesarion, declared "King of Kings," was Caesar's true son. Antony made this last pronouncement, it is said, to protect Caesar's interests; for while Octavian was Caesar's adopted son, he was usurping powers that Caesar did not mean him to have. Furthermore, Cleopatra and Caesarion (Ptolemy XV), who remained subordinate to his mother, were to rule jointly over the Ptolemaic Empire.

Antony's three children by Cleopatra were also assigned specific titles and territories to rule. Two-year-old Ptolemy Philadelphus was to receive Syria and the lands from the Hellespont to the Euphrates River; his six-year-old brother Alexander was given Armenia, Parthia, and everything east of the Euphrates to India; their sister, little Cleopatra, was to receive Cyrenaica (in Libya) and probably Crete. At the top of this imperial superstructure was Antony himself, who was playing a double role. In the Greek East, he felt comfortable and was well liked. He and Cleopatra were an irresistible couple who could restore Egypt and the Hellenistic world to its pre-Roman glory. To the Romans, Antony was triumvir, colleague of Octavian, ruler of the Roman Eastern Empire, and protector of Roman interests. Plutarch aptly notes that the Alexandrians "used to say that Antony put on his tragic mask for the Romans, but kept the comic one for them" (*Antony* 29.2).

Antony's bequests to Cleopatra and her children, the "Donations of Alexandria," were grandiose. Large portions of the territories he so generously conferred had not even been conquered—and there was no guarantee they would be. Rulers he was replacing with his children were friends and allies of Rome. Cyrenaica, for example, had been a Roman province since 67 B.C. Antony was arranging the future of states and monarchies that were not his to arrange. Certainly, he should have consulted the Senate. Even if he felt the East would be best ruled by Easterners, the ultimate question was whether Rome would accept Cleopatra and her family as rulers over a large part of their Empire. If he believed that it would, he had been in the East too long.

The East was always a source of threat to Rome's security. Sulla had returned with his legions from the East after reducing Mithridates, the rebellious king of Pontus, and thrown Rome into the calamitous civil war of the 80s B.C. More recently, when Pompey finished his settlement of the Eastern provinces in 62 B.C. and announced

that he was returning to Rome with his troops, many thought he would try to overthrow the government. Even the messianic prophecies coming out of the East, particularly Judaea, were not ignored by a superstitious society. Conservative Romans also winced at the tales they heard about Cleopatra's sexual appetite, her bewitching nature, and the extravagance of the Egyptian court. Certainly, many believed that the queen had taken the wits from Antony and that he and his Egyptian whore were preparing the masses of the Orient to march on Rome! Octavian found productive ways to channel such hysterics, and Antony was cast as someone quite villainous:

> The madness of Antony, since it could not be laid to rest by the satisfaction of his ambition, was brought to an end by his luxury and licentiousness. After the Parthian expedition he acquired a loathing for war and lived a life of ease, and a slave to his love for Cleopatra, rested in her royal arms as though all had gone well with him. The Egyptian woman demanded the Roman Empire from the drunken general as the price of her favors; and this Antony promised her, as though the Romans were more easily conquered than the Parthians. He, therefore, began to aim at sovereignty—though not for himself—and that in no secret manner; but, forgetful of his country, his name, his toga and the emblems of his office, he soon completely degenerated into the monster which he became, in feeling as well as in garb and dress. In his hand was a golden scepter, at his side a scimitar; he wore a purple robe studded with huge gems; a crown only was lacking to make him a king dallying with a queen.
> (Florus, *Roman History* 2.21.1–3)

The Gathering Storm

When Octavian returned from Illyria late in 34 B.C., he learned of Antony's arrangements for

Cleopatra and her children. At first, he said nothing, but after entering the consulship for 33 B.C., he publicly went on to the attack. Antony's "Donations" were so outrageous that Octavian no longer felt the need to be polite or compromising. He also used his own Illyrian successes to counter Antony's failure against Parthia. Both men had their adherents, and a free-for-all of charges, countercharges, smears, and accusations began to rage across the Mediterranean. However, unlike Octavian's, Antony's behavior over the past decade had been un-Roman. Ultimately, that would be his undoing. His association with Cleopatra was un-Roman, a point Vergil would later emphasize in his epic poem, the *Aeneid:* The Trojan prince, Aeneas, son of Venus and, coincidentally, ancestor of Caesar (and thereby Octavian), gave up his love for a queen in Africa so that he might fulfill his destiny and establish the Roman people in Italy. He sacrificed his personal feelings for the future of Rome. Antony had not done likewise and had also neglected Octavia, a noble Roman matron. It was un-Roman for Antony to rebuild the Ptolemaic Empire, cede territories and possessions of the Roman people, and take up residence, permanently it seemed, in a foreign capital that rivaled, or surpassed, Rome in size and splendor.

When it appeared that a confrontation with Octavian was inevitable, Antony took measures to prevent a Parthian breakthrough while he was away and, mobilizing his forces, set out for the West. Joined by Cleopatra and her fleet, Antony wintered at Ephesus in the Roman province of Asia. Meanwhile, his forces, impressive by any standard, were being assembled: 500 warships (200 were Cleopatra's), 300 merchant vessels, 30 legions (about 75,000 men), 25,000 light infantry, and 12,000 cavalry. He probably still hoped he could avoid a conflict if the Ro-

man Senate would ratify the "Donations." He also offered twice to lay down his powers as triumvir (which would expire at the end of 33 B.C., anyway) if Octavian would do the same. Nothing came of his overtures. The two sides continued to accuse each other of trying to destroy the Republic.

Early in 32 B.C., the consuls and almost three hundred senators left Rome to join Antony. This followed further attacks on their friend by Octavian, who now attended meetings of the Senate with a bodyguard. Some believed that Octavian could not win a war with Antony—or that Antony was the lesser of two evils. No longer having any reason to maintain appearances, Antony formally divorced Octavia. Cleopatra had been waiting for this moment for years, but the divorce only alienated more Romans.

Octavian produced what he claimed to be the will of Antony (which had been deposited, as was customary, with the Vestal Virgins at Rome). He announced to the Senate that it contained provisions that recognized Caesarion as Caesar's son and made heirs of Antony's children by Cleopatra. It also requested, he said, that Antony be buried in Egypt. The first two provisions could not have surprised anyone. The last was a revelation. No Roman would ever make such a request. Octavian emphasized this point, in particular, and it apparently had the desired effect. Even those senators who considered Octavian's reading of the will to be improper were outraged.

Whether this controversial material was actually in Antony's will cannot be known, but it is doubtful. Antony knew he could not legally make Cleopatra's children his heirs; he also knew that, given the situation in Rome, the document was not safe and that its contents could be revealed. Unless he were a complete fool, he never would have made such a request about his burial. Octavian probably only capitalized on the fact that the document existed.

Prelude to Actium

As Antony mobilized the East for war, the speed and scope of his preparations distressed Octavian, who was short of supplies and had to impose an unpopular tax to fill his war chest. Meanwhile, his propaganda crusade against Cleopatra continued. Her presence with Antony at his headquarters in Ephesus, for example, provided Octavian with ample material. Antony was accused of

> . . . a number of other excesses in his behavior towards Cleopatra: he had presented her with the libraries at Pergamum which contained two hundred thousand scrolls; at a banquet with a large company present he had risen from his place and anointed her feet, apparently to fulfill some compact or wager; he had allowed the Ephesians to salute Cleopatra as their sovereign in his own presence, and on many occasions, while he was seated on the tribunal administering justice to kings and tetrarchs, he would receive love-letters from her written on tablets of onyx or crystal and read them through in public; and on another occasion when Furnius, a man of great distinction and the foremost orator in Rome, was pleading a case, Cleopatra happened to pass through the Forum in her litter, whereupon Antony leaped to his feet from his tribunal, walked out of the trial, and accompanied Cleopatra on her way, hanging on to her litter.
> (Plutarch, *Antony* 58.5–6)

Such stories often had no substance, but they influenced Roman public opinion anyway.

In the view of most of Antony's Roman advisors, Cleopatra had become a political and military liability whose presence was hurting his cause. He was counseled, more than once, to send her away, but he never did. The couple moved on to the island of Samos, where they lingered and sponsored a magnificent dramatic and musical contest. The carefree atmosphere of the festival seemed to indicate that, even though the clouds of war were gathering, Antony was unconcerned—so confident was he of victory. As Plutarch records, "How will the conquerors celebrate their victories if their preparations for war are marked by festivals so costly?" (*Antony* 56.5).

In May of 32 B.C., while the army was being transported to Greece, Antony and Cleopatra arrived in Athens, where they would spend the summer. This must have been the moment Antony chose to divorce Octavia, since he did not want to confuse the Athenians about how to behave toward Cleopatra. Athens had previously been home to Antony and Octavia, and the latter was well liked among the Greeks. They were now expected to treat Cleopatra just as favorably, and the city did not disappoint. The Athenians had never entertained an Egyptian queen before, although when she was younger, Cleopatra may have taken refuge in the city with her father.

While in Athens, Antony was joined by his eldest son—and principal heir—Antyllus. Antyllus, now a teenager, was his son by Fulvia and had been raised by Octavia. He came with word about Octavia's kindness to him. His presence must have been an unpleasant reminder to Cleopatra that there were still sizable obstacles to overcome before she could attain her objectives. Antony's friends in Italy were also urging him to send her back to Egypt:

> . . . they sent one of their number named Geminius to urge Antony not to sit by and allow himself to be voted out of authority and declared an enemy of Rome. But as soon as Geminius landed in Greece, he was suspected by Cleopatra of being an agent working for Octavia, and she

arranged that he should be humiliated by being seated in the least distinguished place at the dinner table and having practical jokes played upon him. Geminius endured these insults with great patience and waited for an opportunity to speak to Antony. But when he was called upon to explain the reason for his presence, they were seated at dinner, and so Geminius answered that he would keep the rest of his message for a more sober occasion, but that he had one thing to say, sober or drunk, and this was that all would go well if Cleopatra were sent back to Egypt. Antony was furious at this reply, but Cleopatra put in, "You have done well, Geminius, to confess the truth without being put to torture." At any rate Geminius escaped a few days later and returned to Rome.

(Plutarch, *Antony* 59.1–3)

By the end of 32 B.C., Octavian had been able to deprive Antony of all the official Roman powers he had held and had received oaths of loyalty from the Italians. Antony was viewed now as a private citizen; his actions no longer had the sanction of Roman law. He was, if he continued on his current path, nothing more than a privateer who was threatening Rome's future with the forces of an oriental queen. Still, Octavian, always fearing adverse reaction, was careful never to declare war formally on Antony. When the declaration finally was made—the ceremony was carried out by Octavian himself, a member of the ancient priesthood that presided over declarations of war—it was directed at Cleopatra. To the Romans, she represented everything that they held unholy. The showdown would take place at Actium, in Greece.

Actium

Some have viewed Antony's advance to Actium as inexplicably casual and, through hindsight, criticize him for not invading Italy while he was in a position of superiority. They argue that by waiting for Octavian in Greece, Antony gave his opponent time to prepare and eventually defeat him. However, nothing indicates that Antony ever proposed to invade Italy. He had already learned how difficult that could be several years earlier when Octavian had prevented his landing at Brundisium. There was nothing to be gained by fighting a war on home soil. Antony could hardly expect his Roman supporters to be enthusiastic if Italy were going to be ravaged. Also, Octavian held Illyria, which would make any invasion of Italy by land practically impossible. Furthermore, Antony's strength was drawn from the East. If he moved too far West, his resources might be overextended. He had only recently experienced disaster in Parthia and had learned not to depend too heavily on allies. Parthia itself was still a major threat. Positioning himself between Italy and Asia was sound military strategy for any eventuality.

Antony's plan, then, was to stay in Greece and draw Octavian to him. He placed the expensive burden of moving forces across the Adriatic on his opponent. He probably thought that this formidable task, along with the fear inspired by his own huge land and sea forces, might be enough to cow Octavian, who would probably have trouble mustering the strength necessary to confront him. He waited with Cleopatra in Greece, which had already provided two victories in which he had participated—the defeat of Pompey at Pharsalus and the conspirators at Philippi. He had no reason to believe that this third confrontation, which would close the chapter begun by Caesar, would not also be successful.

Antony correctly estimated Octavian's personal military capabilities, which had improved but were still not impressive. However, he should have had more regard for Octavian's ad-

Figure 4.8 *Agrippa, architect of the victory at Actium*

miral Agrippa, who had already orchestrated a number of successes for his friend—most notably, the crucial defeat of Sextus Pompeius. It was Agrippa, probably the finest admiral Rome ever produced, who undermined Antony's position. By the time the actual battle took place at Actium, on the northwest coast of Greece, Antony was already a defeated man.

In early spring of 31 B.C., Agrippa had sailed from Italy, making sure to avoid the direct passages to Greece, and caught Antony off guard. Agrippa quickly captured a strategic coastal base, Methone, in southwest Greece, from which he disrupted Antony's supply lines from Egypt. He also raided other coastal installations. Antony was immediately placed in the dangerous situation of having no dependable

food supply, and his ships, needed to protect his bases from Agrippa's raids, were withdrawn from their primary duties. While Antony was thus occupied, Octavian crossed through Illyria into Greece with the main body of his army. He had already won the propaganda battle; he was about to win the war.

As Octavian approached Actium, Antony and Cleopatra moved there from Patrae to set up their headquarters. Octavian established his camp across from Actium on the northern side of the entrance to the Ambracian Gulf, where most of Antony's ships were anchored. He attempted a surprise attack on Antony's fleet, which failed, but it did not matter. The ubiquitous Agrippa would soon secure the coast and gain complete control of the western seas off Greece. Antony's fleet was trapped in the Gulf of Ambracia.

Antony grew desperate. He was pinned in, he lacked food and supplies, and he got no sympathy from local Greeks, who were forced to provide what little they had. Meanwhile, his enemy enjoyed uninterrupted commerce from Italy, and a local stream provided fresh water. Antony's multinational crews grew restless and became undisciplined. The summer heat, malaria, and dysentery depleted the ranks of his sailors, and desertions—some of them prominent—worked against him. Disciplinary measures failed, and Antony was unable to goad Octavian, who knew he now need do nothing but wait, into battle.

By the end of August, all of Antony's attempts to break Agrippa's blockade had failed. He was urged by his officers to settle the matter once and for all in a land engagement, where his superior military abilities and larger forces would be decisive. A sea battle would be foolhardy, considering Agrippa's experience and the condition of Antony's fleet. Some argue that Cleopatra would not have supported a land battle; the

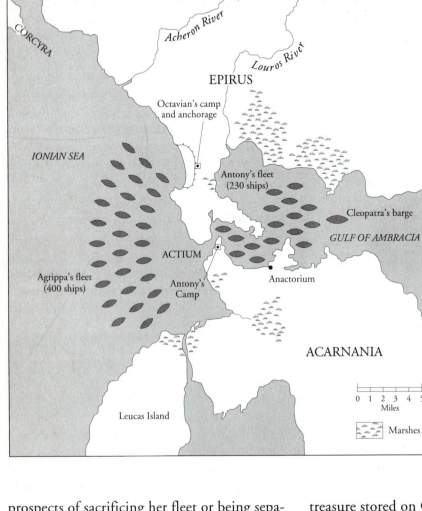

Map 15
Actium

prospects of sacrificing her fleet or being separated from Antony did not appeal to her. Ultimately, it would be entirely personal reasons that guided Antony's decision to fight at sea. However, Octavian had refused Antony's previous offers to fight on land, and there is no reason to believe that he would change tactics now. Antony, not he, was in trouble. There was no reason to jeopardize his forces. Consequently, there was really only one course of action open to Antony—and that was escape. Escape by land would be extremely difficult and would also make the safe transport of the enormous

treasure stored on Cleopatra's flagship, the *Antonias,* impossible. It would fall to Octavian. Antony *had* to take his chances with the fleet. He designed his strategy at Actium for flight—not victory. All unnecessary (or useless) ships and equipment were burned.

On September 2, 31 B.C., Antony sailed out of the Ambracian Gulf with 230 ships (Cleopatra's original fleet of 200 had been reduced to 60), not all fully manned, to challenge the 400 ships of Octavian and Agrippa. Antony had about 20,000 soldiers and 2,000 archers and slingers on board his vessels, while Octavian had almost 40,000 troops. Most of the army on both sides were spectators, watching the proceedings from the shore.

Antony's ships sailed into a half-moon formation, with Antony on the right and his senior commander, Sosius, on the left. The center, it appears, was purposely weak, for Cleopatra's treasure ship was positioned just behind it. Presumably, the object was to peel the sides of the enemy fleet away from the center, leaving room for Cleopatra to raise sail, take advantage of the afternoon winds, and make her escape. Antony and the rest of the fleet would then follow, outrunning the pursuit.

The success of Antony's plan depended on his enemy's ignorance about the sails he had placed on board his vessels. Battle-readied ships did not typically carry sails because they had to be stored on deck—an unnecessary and cumbersome burden in a sea fight. Agrippa's fleet could not pursue once Antony's ships raised their sails. However, it appears that Antony's plan was revealed to Octavian by deserters, and Agrippa organized his fleet to prevent his opponents' flight. He did not engage Antony but stood off, forcing him either to return to his anchorage or to come out and fight. Although badly outnumbered, Antony had no choice but to engage. Once more, he had played into Octavian's hands. The weak center of the battle line still offered Cleopatra the opportunity to escape, and she made a successful dash to safety.

With Cleopatra and her treasure ship out of danger, Antony now transferred to another ship, presumably a swifter craft than his flagship. He, too, got safely away, but about three-quarters of his ships were sunk or captured. Even though the fleet was lost, Antony and Cleopatra must have felt that the war could still be won. Their escape had been a victory of sorts. However, Antony soon learned that Oc-

tavian had won over most of his legions. This was probably the most serious consequence of Actium. There could be no hope of victory now.

The End Draws Near

Following Actium, Cleopatra was portrayed as the selfish oriental queen who deserted her lover and fled from battle to save herself. Antony was depicted as a man so deluded by love that he forsook his navy and army to follow after her. The battle itself was transformed into the struggle that decided the fate of the Western world, and the role of Octavian, soon to become Augustus Caesar, was glorified appropriately. Vergil gave Actium poetic immortality in the *Aeneid* (8.675–713).

While Octavian may have wanted to pursue Antony and Cleopatra immediately, he first had to restore order to the Eastern Mediterranean and consolidate his power. An even greater problem threatened security in Italy when Octavian's veterans began grumbling that they had not been rewarded for their service, forcing him to return home to make promises. It now became even more imperative for Octavian to seize the wealth of Egypt.

Meanwhile, in Egypt, Cleopatra and Antony, fighting despair, tried to put on a good face and muster the still vast resources of Egypt against Octavian. Ironically, they also held a celebration to signal the coming of age of Caesarion (Ptolemy XV) and Antony's son Antyllus (though the latter was only about fourteen). Caesarion's elevation indicated Cleopatra's determination that Ptolemaic rule in Egypt would continue and that a grown man was now ready to guide the country's fortunes as king. She would later regret the move—Caesarion was more of a threat to Octavian as an adult than he was as a minor. Cleopatra would send him to

Ethiopia, from which he was to proceed east, perhaps to India, where she might join him if Octavian seized Egypt. All attempts at escape— or recovery—ultimately failed, as the Eastern world sided with Octavian and offered no assistance to his enemies. Caesarion was captured and executed, probably after Cleopatra's death. Antony's son was also put to death. Antony's three children by Cleopatra were spared and raised by Octavia.

Octavian encountered no resistance as he began his final assault on Egypt. Syria scrambled to gain his favor, and even Antony's old friend, Herod, opened the doors to the Egyptian frontier through Judaea. Already Octavian was receiving envoys from his humbled foes— on two occasions from Cleopatra and on one from Antony—indicating their willingness to deal. Octavian took what was offered but gave no positive response to their overtures. In the process, he supposedly promised Cleopatra her safety in return for killing Antony. By late July, Octavian had entered Egypt and reached the suburbs of Alexandria. Antony prevailed in a skirmish with his cavalry, but it was nothing more than a moral victory. It was followed by promises to pay Octavian's troops to desert and a personal challenge by Antony to meet Octavian in single combat. Octavian answered by implying that Antony should commit suicide.

The Death of Antony

Out of options, Antony prepared what was left of his army and navy for a final engagement at the beginning of August. Plutarch repeats an apocryphal story that captures the eerie mood in Alexandria the night before the battle:

> That evening, so the story goes, about the
> hour of midnight, when all was hushed and a

mood of dejection and fear of its impending fate brooded over the whole city, suddenly a marvellous sound of music was heard, which seemed to come from a consort of instruments of every kind, and voices chanting in harmony, and at the same time the shouting of a crowd in which the cry of Bacchanals and the ecstatic leaping of satyrs were mingled, as if a troop of revellers were leaving the city, shouting and singing as they went. The procession seemed to follow a course through the middle of the city towards the outer gate, which led to the enemy's camp, and at this point the sounds reached their climax and then died away. Those who tried to discover a meaning for this prodigy concluded that the god Dionysus, with whom Antony claimed kinship and whom he had sought above all to imitate, was now abandoning him.
(*Antony* 75.3–4)

Dionysus must have indeed deserted Antony, for the battle never took place. Antony's fleet and cavalry left him and surrendered to Octavian. His infantry fled. Octavian marched into Alexandria the victor. The "Roman Revolution" was over. Later, after he had taken the name Augustus and become Rome's first emperor, Octavian would choose this auspicious month of victory to bear his name.

The final hours of Antony and Cleopatra have been so romantically colored that it is difficult to know exactly what happened. Apparently, when Cleopatra heard that Antony had lost, she locked herself (with her vast treasure) in the tomb that, in accordance with Egyptian practice, had been previously prepared for her. Antony mistakenly thought she had committed suicide, and after failing to convince his servant to kill him (the servant, Eros, turned the blade upon himself), he stabbed himself with a sword. Before he died, however, he was discovered by Cleopatra's secretary, Diomedes, who informed him that she was still alive and wanted him to come to her. Plutarch describes Antony's final moments:

> When he understood that Cleopatra was still alive, Antony eagerly ordered his slaves to lift him up, and they carried him in their arms to the doors of the tomb. Even then Cleopatra would not allow the doors to be opened, but she showed herself at a window and let down the cords and ropes to the ground. The slaves fastened Antony to these and the queen pulled him up with the help of her two waiting women, who were the only companions she had allowed to enter the monument with her. Those who were present say that there was never a more pitiable sight than the spectacle of Antony, covered with blood, struggling in his death agonies and stretching out his hands towards Cleopatra as he swung helplessly in the air. The task was almost beyond a woman's strength, and it was only with great difficulty that Cleopatra, clinging with both hands to the rope and with the muscles of her face distorted by the strain, was able to haul him up, while those on the ground encouraged her with their cries and shared her agony. When she had got him up and laid him upon a bed, she tore her dress and spread it over him, beat and lacerated her breasts, and smeared her face with the blood from his wounds. She called him her lord and husband and emperor, and almost forgot her own misfortunes in her pity for his. Antony calmed her lamentations and called for a cup of wine, either because he was thirsty or because he hoped it might hasten his death. When he had drunk it, he urged her to think of her own safety, if she could do this without dishonor, and told her that of all Caesar's [Octavian's] associates she would do best to put her trust in Proculeius. Last of all, he begged her not to grieve over this wretched change in his fortunes, but to count him happy for the glories he had won and to remember that he had attained the greatest fame and power of any man in the world, so that now it was no dishonor to die a Roman, conquered only by a Roman.
> (*Antony* 77.1–4)

Ironically, despite Octavian's triumph, Antony would still be represented in the new order of things. Through his daughters by Octavia, he was the grandfather of the Emperor Claudius, the great-grandfather of the Emperor Caligula, and the great-great-grandfather of the Emperor Nero.

The Death of Cleopatra

When word was brought to Octavian about Antony's death, he supposedly wept. He then ordered Proculeius—the man who, in the passage just quoted, Antony had advised Cleopatra to trust—to go to Cleopatra. He was to capture her alive and preserve the treasure she had with her. Proculeius was the brother-in-law of Octavian's chief diplomat and confidant Maecenas, the man who, among other things, had negotiated the Treaty of Brundisium in 40 B.C. Maecenas would have been proud of Proculeius on this occasion. He captured Cleopatra by having others distract her with false negotiations—the door of the tomb had a grate through which people could speak—while he secured a ladder and climbed in by the same window through which Cleopatra had received Antony's body. Octavian now had everything he desired, and the wealth of Egypt became his personal property.

Cleopatra, her strength and spirit failing, was moved to the royal palace and allowed to arrange for Antony's funeral. It is said that Octavian took great pains to look after her safety and comfort and that he planned to transport Cleopatra and her children by Antony to Rome for his triumphal parade. This is probably not true, for he had nothing to gain by keeping her alive. Bringing her to Rome could arouse public sympathy, rally supporters of Antony, insult the memory of Caesar, and cause friction with Octavia. Executing her was out of the question for many reasons. It was best that he do nothing to prevent her from taking her own life, which, considering her situation, was almost a certainty. When Octavian received her final correspondence requesting that she be buried next to Antony, he probably felt relieved, for he knew that the struggle was finally over and that his problems with Antony and Cleopatra could be buried far from Rome in the sands of Egypt.

It is not clear exactly how Cleopatra killed herself, but the most popular version, concerning an asp, is recorded by Plutarch:

> According to one account, the asp was carried in to her with the figs and lay hidden under the leaves in the basket, for Cleopatra had given orders that the snake should settle on her without her being aware of it. But when she picked up some of the figs, she caught sight of it, so the story goes, and said "So here it is," and baring her arm, she held it out to be bitten. Others say it was carefully shut up in a pitcher and that Cleopatra provoked it by pricking it with a golden spindle, until it sprang out and fastened itself upon her arm. But the real truth nobody knows, for there is another story that she carried poison about with her in a hollow comb, which she kept hidden in her hair, and yet no inflammation nor any other symptom of poison broke out on her body. And indeed the asp was never discovered inside the monument, although some marks which might have been its trail are said to have been noticed on the beach on that side where the windows of the chamber looked out towards the sea. Some people also say that two faint, barely visible punctures were found on Cleopatra's arm, and Octavius Caesar himself seems to have believed this, for when he celebrated his triumph he

had a figure of Cleopatra with the asp clinging to her carried in the procession.
> (*Antony* 86.1–3)

Cleopatra was thirty-nine years old when she died and had ruled Egypt for twenty-two years. She was the last of the Ptolemies, a line that had begun almost three centuries earlier in 322 B.C. when Ptolemy I seized the body of Alexander, later buried in Alexandria in Egypt, and declared himself king in 304 B.C. Plutarch gives a fitting conclusion—which Shakespeare admired—to the life of the famous queen, who, like Brutus, had died young and ultimately had only helped pave the way for Octavian's victory:

> The messengers rushed to the monument and found the guards still unaware that anything was amiss, but when they opened the doors, they found Cleopatra lying dead upon a golden couch dressed in her royal robes. Of her two women, Iras lay dying at her feet, while Charmian, already tottering and scarcely able to hold up her head, was arranging the crown which encircled her mistress's brow. Then one of the guards cried out angrily, "Charmian, is this well done?" and she answered "It is well done, and fitting for a princess descended of so many royal kings. . . ."
> (*Antony* 85.3–4)

Suggestions for Further Reading

Plutarch's lives of *Caesar* and *Antony* and Suetonius' *Caesar* remain pertinent for this chapter, as do other ancient writers and modern works cited in Chapter 3. Strabo's *Geography* also provides minor detail. Nicolaus of Damascus tutored Cleopatra's children and later became court historian to Herod; although his writings are lost, the Jewish historian Josephus, in his *Jewish Antiquities* and *Jewish Wars,* preserves material about Cleopatra and Antony (much of it negative) that probably derives from him. Both Strabo and Josephus are available in the Loeb Classical Library. The events described in this chapter have been discussed from Antony's perspective in

Through "Thick and Thin"—Turia, a Devoted Wife

IT IS ONLY APPROPRIATE that an account of one of the most convulsive periods in Roman (and Western) history ends with the story of a woman who lived through it all and, with her husband, experienced more than her share of the personal and political vicissitudes that accompanied the times. The inscription (which is badly damaged) cited below is the funeral eulogy of a prominent Roman matron whose name was probably Turia. If so, it was delivered by her husband Quintus Lucretius Vespillo, a Roman senator. The document is remarkable not only because it is a startlingly realistic indication of the dangers that threatened families during the civil wars but also because it reveals the couple's love for and devotion toward each other over their forty-one years of marriage.

In the eulogy, Turia is represented as the ideal Roman wife. Her husband indicates that the two were married right at the time of Caesar's invasion of Italy in 49 B.C., and that the wedding was saddened by the loss of her parents in the Civil War. Since he sided with Pompey, the husband had to flee immediately to Greece, leaving his wife and her sister to cope with the unpleasant situation—which they did, admirably. Fortunately, the husband survived Pompey's defeat at Pharsalus in 48 B.C. and, largely through Turia's efforts, was later pardoned. Nevertheless, his life was again threatened when Octavian, Antony, and Lepidus formed the "Second Triumvirate" and Lepidus proscribed him. Turia's entreaties saved him, and the couple lived into the period of peace established by Octavian after he had disposed of Antony and Cleopatra and become Rome's first emperor. Turia lived with her husband until about 8 B.C., and although they were saddened by the lack of children, the couple's life with each other appears to have been rich and fulfilling to the end:

The day before our wedding you were suddenly left an orphan when both your parents were murdered. Although I had gone to Macedonia and your sister's husband, Gaius Cluvius, had gone to the province of Africa, the murder of your parents did not remain unavenged. You carried out this act of piety with such great diligence—asking questions, making inquiries, demanding punishment—that if we had been there, we could not have done better. You and that very pious woman, your sister, share the credit for success. . . .

Rare indeed are marriages of such long duration, which are ended by death, not divorce. We had the good fortune to spend forty-one years together with no unhappiness. I wish that our long marriage had come finally to an end by *my* death, since it would have been more just for me, who was older, to yield to fate.

Why should I mention your personal virtues—your modesty, obedience, affability, and good nature, your tireless attention to wool making, your performance of religious duties without superstitious fear, your artless elegance and simplicity of dress? Why speak about your affection toward your relatives, your sense of duty toward your family (for you cared for my mother as well as you cared for your parents)? Why recall the countless other virtues which you have in common with all Roman matrons worthy of that name? The virtues I claim for you are your own special virtues; few people have possessed similar ones or been known to possess them. The history of the human race tells us how rare they are.

Together we diligently saved the whole inheritance which you received from your parents' estate. You handed it all over to me and did not worry yourself about increasing it. We shared the responsibilities so that I acted as the

(continued)

Through "Thick and Thin"—Turia, a Devoted Wife (continued)

guardian of your fortune and you undertook to serve as protector of mine. . . .

You demonstrated your generosity not only toward your very many relatives but especially in your performance of family duties. . . . For you brought up in our home young female relatives. . . . And you provided dowries for them so that they could attain a position in life worthy of your family. These arrangements which were planned by you and your sister were supported by Gaius Cluvius and me with mutual agreement; moreover, since we admired your generosity, in order that you might not reduce the size of your inheritance, we put on the market family property and provided dowries by selling our estates. I have mentioned this not to congratulate myself but in order to make known that we were compelled by a sense of honor to carry out with our own money those arrangements made by you because of your dutifulness and generosity. . . .

When my political enemies were hunting me down, you aided my escape by selling your jewelry; you gave me all the gold and pearls which you were wearing and added a small income from household funds. We deceived the guards of my enemies, and you made my time in hiding an "enriching" experience. . . .

Why should I now disclose memories locked deep in my heart, memories of secret and concealed plans? Yes, memories—how I was warned by swift messages to avoid present and imminent dangers and was therefore saved by your quick thinking; how you did not permit me to be swept away by my foolhardy boldness; how, by calm consideration, you arranged a safe place of refuge for me and enlisted as allies in your plans to save me your sister and her husband, Gaius Cluvius, even though the plans were dangerous to all of you. If I tried to touch on all your actions on my behalf, I could go on forever. For us let it suffice to say that you hid me safely.

Yet the most bitter experience of my life came later. . . . I was granted a pardon by Augustus [Octavian], but his colleague Lepidus opposed the pardon. When you threw yourself on the ground at his feet, not only did he not raise you up, but in fact he grabbed you and dragged you along as if you were a slave. You were covered with bruises, but with unflinching determination you reminded him of Augustus Caesar's edict of pardon. . . . Although you suffered insults and cruel injuries, you revealed them publicly in order to expose him as the author of my calamities. . . .

When the world was finally at peace again and order had been restored in the government, we enjoyed quiet and happy days. We longed for children, but spiteful fate begrudged them. If Fortune had allowed herself to care for us in this matter as she does others, we two would have enjoyed complete happiness. But advancing old age put an end to our hopes for children. . . . You were depressed about your infertility and grieved because I was without children. . . . You spoke of divorce and offered to give up your household to another woman, to a fertile woman. You said that you yourself would arrange for me a new wife, one worthy of our well-known love, and you assured me that you would treat the children of my new marriage as if they were your own. You would not demand the return of your inheritance; it would remain, if I wished, in my control. You would not detach or isolate yourself from me; you would simply carry out henceforth the duties and responsibilities of my sister or my mother-in-law.

I must confess that I was so angered by your suggestion that I lost my mind. I was so horrified that I could scarcely regain control of myself. How could you talk of a dissolution of our marriage before it was demanded by fate! How could you even conceive in your mind of any reason why you should, while still alive, cease to be my wife, you who remained very faithfully with me when I was in exile, indeed almost in exile from life! How could the desire or need for having children be so great that I would break faith with you! . . .

I wish that our old age had allowed our marriage to last until I, who was the elder, had passed away; it would have been fairer for you to arrange a funeral for me. . . . But by fate's decree, you finished the race of life before I did, and you left me all alone, without children, grieving and longing for you. . . . But inspired by your example I will stand up to cruel fortune, which has not stolen everything from me since it allows the memory of you to grow brighter and stronger through praise. . . .

I conclude my oration with this: you have deserved all, and I can never repay you completely. I have always considered your wishes my commands. I will continue to do for you whatever I still can.

May the Manes [protecting spirits of the dead] grant to you and protect your eternal peace, I pray.

(*Corpus Inscriptionum Latinarum* 6.1527, 31670 [*Inscriptiones Latinae Selectae* 8393])

E. G. Huzar's favorable biography *Mark Antony* (Minneapolis: University of Minnesota Press, 1978). Several works on Cleopatra appeared in the early 1970s but are of uneven quality. The most profitable is M. Grant's *Cleopatra* (New York: Simon & Schuster, 1972; rev. ed., New York: Barnes & Noble, 1992), which has been particularly useful in the present study. J. Lindsay, *Cleopatra* (New York: Coward McCann & Geoghegan, 1970), provides stimulating reading for the general enthusiast. Other studies relating to Cleopatra include J. Whitehorne's *Cleopatras* (New York: Oxford University Press, 1994), and M. Maer's *Signs of Cleopatra: History, Politics, Representation* (New York: Oxford University Press, 1993). See also D. Shotter, *The Fall of the Roman Republic* (New York: Oxford University Press, 1994). Of related interest are S. R. Pomeroy's *Women in Hellenistic Egypt from Alexander to Cleopatra* (New York: Schocken Books, 1984), and N. Lewis's *Life in Egypt Under Roman Rule* (Oxford: Clarendon Press, 1983).

Recent Additions

M. Goodman, *The Roman World 44 B.C.–A.D. 180* (New York: Routledge, 1997); R. Alston, *Soldier and Society in Roman Egypt: A Social History* (New York: Routledge, 1998); J-Y. Empereur, *Alexandria Rediscovered* (New York: George Braziller Publisher, 1998); F. Millar, *The Crowd in Rome in the Late Republic* (Ann Arbor: University of Michigan Press, 1998); J. Rowlandson (ed.), *Women and Society in Greek and Roman Egypt* (Cambridge: Cambridge University Press, 1998); L. Foreman, *Cleopatra's Palace: In Search of a Legend* (New York: Random House, 1999: A Discovery Channel Book).

5

The Early Empire

Tiberius' Troubled Reign (14–37 A.D.)
Thrasyllus the Astrologer

*Now I am aware of no people, however refined and learned or
however savage and ignorant, which does not think that signs
are given of future events, and that certain persons can recognize those signs and foretell events before they occur.*
(Cicero, On Divination 1.2)

Cato the Elder is said to have once remarked that he was always surprised that soothsayers did not break out laughing whenever they passed each other on the street. Clearly, Cato had little regard for those at Rome who claimed insight into the future. Cicero says that the poet Ennius was equally put off, condemning the whole lot of those who boasted clairvoyant powers:

> In short, I could care less for Marsian augurs, village soothsayers, astrologers at the circus, priests of Isis, or dream interpreters—they have no special skills to divine the future. They are really nothing more than a bunch of hypocrites, shameless quacks who, shiftless, mad, or destitute, presume to show others the path when they cannot find it themselves. They promise wealth then expect to be paid. Let

them take their fee from the riches they predict and give the rest to me!
(Cicero, *On Divination* 1.132)

Words such as these usually fell on deaf ears, for there were many who attached great significance to the pronouncements of soothsayers, astrologers, and other clairvoyant "professionals" and allowed them to regulate their lives. The seers themselves often became contemptuous of their clients' gullibility, as shown in a story about a man who had seen a snake wrapped around a beam in his house. Convinced of the weighty significance of the sight, the man rushed to his diviner to discover the meaning of the portent. "That was no portent," shrugged the interpreter, unimpressed, "but it would have been if the beam were wrapped round the snake. . . ."

As in any age, there were those who wanted to believe, and even wiser folk sometimes succumbed when the "readings" happened to coincide with their own aspirations. Consequently, Rome was filled with soothsayers, augurs, prophets, diviners, philosophers, wizards, sorcerers, magicians, and others, whose practices ranged from serious and officially sanctioned by the state to complete charlatanism. While some, quipped a scornful Juvenal, would "pry out the steaming lungs of a pigeon," "probe a chicken's bosom, unravel the guts of a puppy," or "even slaughter a child" to find their answers, others gained insight through the observation of birds in flight, the stars, thunder and lightning, sneezes and dreams. For affairs both public and private, no one in Rome ever suffered a setback for lack of resources to fathom the future.

Opportunities for deceit and flimflamming were great, and the government viewed many of the groups with "special knowledge" as undesirable and even subversive. Since some claimed expertise in all areas of prediction, legitimate or not, the distinctions between the various practices became blurred; and if one group fell under suspicion, they all did. Stringent restrictions could be placed upon their activities, and on a number of occasions—possibly ten between 33 B.C. and 93 A.D.—all prognosticators were expelled from the city, and some were even put to death! However, there does not seem to have been a permanent ban on them until the reign of the Christian emperors in the fourth and fifth centuries.

Among the most harassed of the groups who depended on the future for their livelihood were the astrologers, a brotherhood that Juvenal found especially despicable:

What those astrologers say appears to come
  straight from the sources

Ammon inspires, since Delphi is dumb, and a
  darkness
Falls on the human race when it comes to knowing the future . . .
Fellows like these are believed if they've been in
  some far-off prison,
Shackled hand and foot: if he hasn't a prison
  record,
Then he has no renown, but a sentence to one of
  the islands,
A narrow escape from death, procures him a
  reputation.
  (*Satire* 6.553–564)

And Cicero (*On Divination* 2.97) summed up how worthwhile he considered astrological predictions when he posed the question: "Did all the men who died at Cannae have the same horoscope?"

Despite such attacks, astrology thrived, and some astrologers moved in high circles, influencing prominent men, their predictions guiding important events. They were particularly visible during the reign of Rome's first emperor, Augustus (31 B.C.–14 A.D.), and his successor, Tiberius (14–37 A.D.), who was especially susceptible to their craft. Tiberius' friend and favorite advisor on matters of the future was Thrasyllus of Alexandria, the greatest astrologer of his day.

Octavian Becomes Augustus— The Principate Begins

Four years after Actium, Octavian walked into a Senate well disposed to his wishes and announced the restoration of the Republic. He was ready to set aside his formidable powers and become a private citizen once more. To no one's surprise, the partisan Senate "refused" to allow him to step down and gave him the quasi-divine

Figure 5.1   The Emperor Augustus

title Augustus. Octavian's powers were formalized, and Rome had given itself its first emperor.

Always the subtle manipulator, Augustus carefully selected titles for himself and his administration that were entirely inoffensive. He called himself Princeps, or First Citizen; his government was the Principate, or rule of the First Citizen. Romans already referred to their First Senator, the senior member of the Senate, as the Princeps Senatus (a position that Augustus would now also hold). Devising a title so similar to one with positive Republican associations shows the young emperor's political skill.

While the machinery of the Republic continued to crank on, in reality Rome had become a constitutional monarchy. Nothing happened without Augustus' approval. He was censor, Pontifex Maximus, and oftentimes held the consulship, which he distributed with other offices as favors to those who served his wishes. He also held the two most formidable powers of the Republic—tribunician veto and proconsular *imperium.* The former gave him control over all legislation, the latter over the army, which was sworn in loyalty to him. Citizens, too, swore their loyalty to the emperor and worshipped his spirit, or *genius,* as an act of patriotism.

Augustus' closest advisory body was an imperial council made up of the consuls, a small body of trusted senators, the faithful Agrippa, the Princeps' wife, Livia (his closest confidant over the fifty-three years they were married), and other members of the royal family. The Senate retained some prestige but had no real power. Since the Senate could influence public opinion, it was politically wise for the Princeps to create the impression that he worked in close coordination with it. The emasculated body soon became mostly a high court for treason trials.

Although born in Rome, Octavian had grown up in rural Italy and was conservative in his views. Traditional values and morals, religion, the family, and pro-Roman racial attitudes were emphasized in his reforms. Artists and writers, including Vergil, Horace, and Livy, used their skills willingly to flatter the Princeps and promote his ideals (and urge other ideals upon him). Augustus created the Praetorian Guard, an elite force of about forty-five hundred (although it may have been double that number), whose main duty was to protect the emperor (a duty that they sometimes forgot since the Praetorians would often be involved in the rise and fall of Caesars!). He also gave Rome its first permanent fire department and police force.

With peace and prosperity restored, it is no surprise that the citizen population of the Empire grew by almost a million (to 4,937,000) by the end of Augustus' long reign. After forty-one years of rule, he died in 14 A.D. shortly before his seventy-sixth birthday. The foundation of the Principate had been firmly set, and Augustus became the model for all succeeding emperors.

Tiberius Becomes Emperor

Following the death of Augustus, his family, the Julio-Claudians, continued to rule Rome. Because he and Livia had no children and his previous marriage had produced only one daughter, Julia, Augustus was ultimately forced to turn to his stepson Tiberius to succeed him (see Chart 2, page 126). Ironically, Tiberius had earlier fallen out of favor with Augustus and had been excluded from the succession, despite machinations by Livia, who worked tirelessly on her son's behalf. As the founding father of the Empire, Augustus wanted to ensure that someone of his own bloodline would sit on the throne. In the end, however, he was forced to adopt his wife's son only because he was the most suitable remaining choice—everyone else Augustus had appointed was dead! It must have appeared at the time that a nod from the emperor was guarantee of an early demise.

Augustus' first choice to succeed him was his nephew Marcellus, whom he married to his daughter, Julia. Unfortunately, the young man died in 23 B.C. Next he turned to the dependable Agrippa and shuffled the widowed Julia off to his old friend's bed to ensure that the Julian bloodline was maintained in the succession. Julia promptly obliged her father by producing five children—Gaius, Lucius, Agrippina, Julia, and Agrippa Postumus. Of these, Gaius and Lu-

Figure 5.2   Livia

cius were designated as the eventual heirs. Agrippa's death in 12 B.C. removed the second potential emperor from the scene, but Augustus could not have been too upset, since his daughter's sons were there to succeed him. In the meantime, he could play the role of adoring grandparent and supervise the boys' upbringing. However, if something were to happen to him, young Gaius and Lucius could not guide the Empire, and Tiberius was moved into the direct line of succession. Tiberius now married Julia, a move that had the unqualified approval of Livia. Julia bore Tiberius a son, who soon died, and relations between the couple deteriorated rapidly.

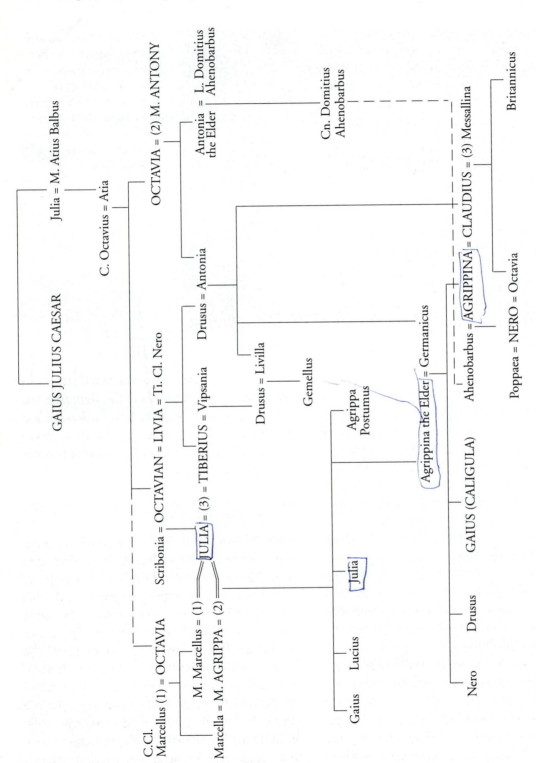

= marriage

Chart 2   Augustus (Octavian) and his family, the Julio-Claudians

Figure 5.3 Original wall painting from the remains of the so-called House of Livia, the residence of Augustus and his family on the Palatine Hill in Rome that, over the centuries, grew into a massive Imperial Palace

The marriage became a fiasco, and Augustus regretted the trust he had placed in Tiberius. As Gaius and Lucius matured, Tiberius suddenly became remarkably expendable—in many ways a nonentity. It looked as if his career were finished, but fortunately for him, both Gaius and Lucius were dead by 4 A.D. Augustus, old and disappointed, had to turn to Tiberius once more.

It is tempting to see in this unusual sequence of deaths the hand of Livia. Ancient authorities suggest her involvement in at least some of them, but there is no convincing evidence. To have arranged so many murders without arousing suspicion, Livia would have to be ranked among the cleverest manipulators of all time; and Augustus, ordinarily very perceptive, would have had to have been terribly naive not to have recognized her part in them (some say she even poisoned him!). Also, the circumstances surrounding several of the deaths in which she is supposed to have been involved

are sufficiently attested to indicate death from natural causes. Nevertheless, the outcome was certainly not displeasing to her; for having lost one of her adult sons, Drusus, on the German frontier, she now looked forward to her other son's becoming emperor of Rome.

Thrasyllus and Tiberius

Before Tiberius returned to the emperor's good graces and was made his heir, he had withdrawn to the island of Rhodes. Despite the great powers conferred upon him by Augustus, Tiberius felt unappreciated and overshadowed by Gaius and Lucius. Tired of his mother's manipulations and haunted by his disastrous marriage to Julia (who, already promiscuous, became increasingly so), he probably saw little chance of things improving. By going into voluntary exile, he may have hoped that, like Agrippa, who took an extended leave from Rome to demonstrate to an ungrateful Augustus how much he needed him (he was eventually recalled and made heir), the emperor would come to realize how much he depended upon him. If this were Tiberius' plan, it failed. All he did was further aggravate Augustus.

The years at Rhodes were disappointing ones for Tiberius, and he always remained sensitive about his experience there. Out of favor at Rome, few called upon him at his island retreat. Even locals were sometimes contemptuous of the prince—evidenced by the refusal of a celebrated scholar to change his lecture schedule to accommodate him. His own awkwardness caused others to behave awkwardly toward him, and little, if anything, was going right. Then he met the man who would change his life—Thrasyllus of Alexandria, the greatest astrologer of the day.

The sources all attest to the favored status in which Tiberius held Thrasyllus. The two were intimate friends, and there was scarcely anyone whom Tiberius trusted more. Supposedly, the astrologer had won the future emperor's confidence while on a visit to his villa on Rhodes. In his effort to discover a practitioner upon whose advice he could rely, Tiberius invited one astrologer after another to his villa, which sat perched on a cliff overlooking the sea. Apparently, the island's reserve of astrologers was dwindling rapidly when Thrasyllus first made his appearance. The historian Tacitus preserves the fullest account of the meeting:

> When seeking occult guidance Tiberius would retire to the top of his house, with a single tough, illiterate former slave as confidant. Those astrologers whose skill Tiberius had decided to test were escorted to him by this man over pathless, precipitous ground; for the house overhung a cliff. Then, on their way down, if they were suspected of unreliability or fraudulence, the ex-slave hurled them into the sea below, so that no

betrayer of the secret proceedings should survive.

> Thrasyllus, after reaching Tiberius by this steep route, had impressed him, when interrogated, by his intelligent forecasts of future events—including Tiberius' accession. Tiberius then inquired if Thrasyllus had cast his own horoscope. How did it appear for the current year and day? Thrasyllus, after measuring the positions and distances of the stars, hesitated, then showed alarm. The more he looked, the greater became his astonishment and fright. Then he cried that a critical and perhaps fatal emergency was upon him. Tiberius clasped him, commending his divination of peril and promising he would escape it. Thrasyllus was admitted among his closest friends; his pronouncements were regarded as oracular.

(*Annals* 6.21)

While Tiberius' detractors would have liked to believe that the meeting took place under such tenuous circumstances, in reality, the occasion was probably not so dramatic. Thrasyllus had come to Rhodes to further his education. The island was known as an intellectual center, and the academic atmosphere attracted Greeks and Romans from all over the Mediterranean. Thrasyllus was not only an astrologer but also a first-rate scholar, a polymath with interests in grammar, philology, Platonism, philosophy, magic, and numerology. He was already well known in intellectual circles, and Tiberius, who frequented many of the same lectures and meeting places, was probably first drawn to the brilliant Alexandrian because they shared common interests.

Eventually, Thrasyllus became friend and teacher to Tiberius, and it was in the area of astrology that he most influenced the future emperor. Through his guidance, Tiberius mastered the art himself, "his belief in astrology having persuaded him that the world was wholly ruled by fate." He became so proficient that he is sup-

posed to have predicted that Galba, one of the short-lived four emperors of the year 69 A.D., would one day rule Rome. A more cynical (and popular) story made him such an expert that he was able to discern that a certain fellow who had asked him for money in a dream was actually trying to cheat him. He supposedly had the man found and executed! Finally, after an absence of almost eight years from Rome, Augustus recalled Tiberius to Rome in 2 A.D.—just as Thrasyllus had predicted!

Tiberius and Thrasyllus at Rome

Thrasyllus accompanied Tiberius to Rome, and his royal patron made him a citizen and was undoubtedly responsible for his marriage to a foreign princess. Soon after Tiberius' return, Augustus' grandson and co-heir Lucius died. By 4 A.D., his other heir, Gaius, was also dead. His only surviving grandson, Agrippa Postumus, had been judged unsuitable for the succession. Tiberius finally emerged as Augustus' designated heir, and relations between the two men improved significantly.

Since Thrasyllus was always in the suite of Tiberius, Augustus came to know him very well and probably relied upon his pronouncements as much as Tiberius did. Publicly, the aged emperor placed restrictions upon astrologers (as Tiberius would later do) and forbade them to inquire about the death of any person. He also made it illegal to practice astrology in private. His strictures apparently had the desired effect, at least outwardly. In the future, astrologers would caution their minions:

Figure 5.4 *Despite an up-and-down relationship over the years, Tiberius served Augustus well militarily. This Roman "Sword of Tiberius" and scabbard from Mainz, Germany, c. 15 B.C., illustrates the ceding of victory to Augustus by Tiberius after successful Alpine campaigns in 16–15 B.C. The scene at the top of the scabbard shows Augustus in the pose of Jupiter receiving the statuette of victory from Tiberius. The scabbard was probably made for a senior officer to commemorate the campaign.*

You will give your answers in public and will take care to warn those who come to consult you that you are going to respond in a loud voice to everything they ask you about, so they will not ask questions that they should not and which it is forbidden to answer. Be careful to say nothing about the condition of the state or the life of the emperor, if anyone should inquire; for that is forbidden; we must not, moved by criminal curiosity, speak of the condition of the country; and he who answers questions on the destiny of the emperor would be a wretch deserving of every punishment.

(Firmicus Maternus, *Mathesis* 2.30.3–4)

Figure 5.5   Coin of Augustus (reverse) depicting his astrological sign, Capricorn

Privately (largely because of Thrasyllus), astrology was embraced wholeheartedly within the imperial circle and enjoyed unprecedented prestige. As one modern scholar has noted:

Meanwhile a new chapter in the history of astrological influence in high places began with Thrasyllus' arrival in Rome in A.D. 2. The gentlemanly acceptance, mixed with some grains of sound skepticism, which had been the aristocratic attitude during the late republic and was still adhered to by Augustus, now gave way to an unquestioning faith in the irrevocable fate of men and institutions.

(Cramer, *Astrology* 95)

As a politician, Augustus had always been aware of the dangerous effect astrology could have upon the masses, the army, and even the stability of the government. This was probably the major reason behind his destruction of 2,000 disreputable books of prophecy. Nonetheless, he utilized the tradition that his own rise to power had been predicted—as far back as his birth—and struck a coin with his astrological sign, Capricorn, on it. Although superstitious throughout his life (one tradition says he actually believed that seven birthmarks on his chest and stomach represented the Great Bear constellation), it was probably not until his final years

that he allowed astrology to significantly influence his personal and political activities.

With Thrasyllus' encouragement, Augustus came to depend more upon the craft—especially since he had experienced so many plots, intrigues, and personal tragedies, most recently, the deaths of his grandsons Gaius and Lucius. He may have thought that, through astrology, he could have foreseen all his problems, and the succession would have been simplified. Thrasyllus may even have helped convince the old autocrat that it had always been Tiberius who was destined to succeed him. Consequently, a choice that Augustus felt compelled to make may have come to be acceptable to him—it was in the stars.

Augustus, then, was not condemning astrology by his edicts, but he was trying to curb its misuse and dissuade anyone from inquiring too closely about himself, other members of the royal family, and the state. He knew his own death could not be far off, and he wanted to squelch any rumors that could lead to seditious activities. This prompted him to publish his own horoscope in 11 A.D. to dispel bogus ones circulated by enemies predicting his early demise! Since his policies regarding astrology (and other prophetic arts) coincided with Thrasyllus'

Trimalchio—A Literary Caricature of the "Neighborhood Astrologer"

PETRONIUS, WHO WAS A member of Nero's literary circle and wrote the *Satyricon,* parodied a rich freedman whom he named Trimalchio. Among the things that this excessive creature boasted was a knowledge of astrology. There were countless amateur hacks like Trimalchio in Roman society who were making astrological predictions at the drop of a hat, but our surviving sources say little about them. Although Trimalchio is a fictitious character, his behavior may not be too far removed from reality. He is probably a composite figure based on Petronius' own observations. The scene unfolds at an elaborate banquet at Trimalchio's house. The narrator of the episode, who is indulging his freeloading appetite with his fellow guests at Trimalchio's impressive table, describes what happens:

> After our applause the next course was brought in. Actually it was not as grand as we expected, but it was so novel that everyone stared. It was a deep circular tray with the twelve signs of the Zodiac arranged around the edge. Over each of them the chef had placed some appropriate dainty suggested by the subjects. Over Aries the Ram, butter beans; over Taurus the bull, a beef-steak; over the heavenly Twins, testicles and kidneys; over Cancer the Crab, a garland; over Leo the Lion, an African fig; over Virgo the Virgin, a young sow's udder; over Libra the Scales, a balance with a tart in one pan and a cake in the other; over Scorpio, a lobster; over Sagittarius the Archer, a bull's eye; over Capricorn, a horned fish; over Aquarius the Water-Carrier, a goose; over Pisces the Fishes, two mullets. In the center was a piece of grassy turf bearing a honeycomb. . . . [Trimalchio then uses the culinary Zodiac as an excuse to display his astrological talents.] "There's nothing new to me, as that there dish proves. Look now, these here heavens, as there are twelve gods living in 'em, changes into that many shapes.

First it becomes the Ram. So whoever is born under that sign has a lot of herds, a lot of wool, a hard head as well, a brassy front, and a sharp horn. Most scholars are born under this sign, and most muttonheads as well."

We applauded the wit of our astrologer and he went on:

"Then the whole heavens turns into the little old Bull. So bull-headed folk are born then, and cow-herds and those who find their own feed. Under the Heavenly Twins on the other hand—pairs-in-hand, yokes of oxen, people with big ballocks, and people who have it both ways. I was born under the Crab, so I have a lot of legs to stand on and a lot of property on land and sea, because the Crab takes both in his stride. And that's why I put nothing over him earlier, so as not to upset my horoscope. Under Leo are born greedy and domineering people. Under the Virgin, effeminates, runaways, and candidates for the chain-gang. Under the Scales butchers, perfume-sellers, and anyone who weighs things up. Under Scorpio poisoners and murderers. Under Sagittarius are born squint-eyed people who look at the vegetables and take the bacon. Under Capricorn, people in trouble who sprout horns through their worries. Under the Water-Carrier, bartenders and jugheads. Under the Fishes, fish-fryers and people who spout in public.

"So the starry sky turns round like a millstone, always bringing some trouble, and men being born or dying.

"Now as for what you see in the middle, the piece of grass and on the grass the honeycomb, I don't do anything without a reason—it's Mother Earth in the middle round like an egg, with all good things inside her like a honeycomb."

"O clever!" we all cried, raising our hands to the ceiling. . . .

(*Satyricon* 35, 39–40)

presence at court, it seems certain that the latter must have exerted a healthy influence on their adoption. Such measures would benefit Thrasyllus' own position at court and discourage the perversion of astrology by amateurs and hacks seeking to profit from its practice.

Roman emperors really did have something to fear from unchecked inquiries, as can be seen from the conspiracy of Libo Drusus during Tiberius' reign. In 16 A.D., Libo concocted a feeble plot to overthrow Tiberius. Violating Augustus' edicts, he was encouraged in his plans by consultations with astrologers, magicians, wizards, and other prognosticators. When the plot failed and Libo committed suicide, Tiberius' enemies played down any wrongdoing on Libo's part, alleging that the emperor simply wanted to destroy him. However, it is significant that Tiberius soon expelled astrologers and diviners from Rome (two were executed)—evidence that he believed they had conspired with Libo. His suspicions also prompted him to rid the city of Jews and members of other foreign religions in 19 A.D. He also destroyed the temple of the cult of Isis (see the box on the opposite page).

The Problems Begin

When Tiberius became emperor, he was a morose, sullen, unhappy man, already in his mid-fifties. His troubles began almost immediately. After deifying Augustus, he pushed his meddlesome mother, Livia, whom he viewed as responsible for many of his earlier disappointments, into an uneasy retirement. He gave a polite but mostly deaf ear to the wishes of a Senate that always viewed him as cryptic, obscure, equivocal, and guarded about his real thoughts and motives. He was blamed by many for the execution of Julia's last remaining son, Agrippa

Figure 5.6 *Germanicus*

Postumus, although it is more likely that Augustus left orders in his will to slay the youth. He did not want Postumus, who had earlier been banished to an island for his brutish behavior, to jeopardize his well-calculated plans for the succession. Tiberius may have been more directly involved in the death of Julia (or did nothing to prevent it), who starved to death while in exile shortly after her father died (see box, pages 135–136).

Because of his personality, frugality, and distaste for public spectacles, the masses loathed Tiberius, who did little to improve his public image. Popular sentiment favored the emperor's nephew Germanicus, who, while not as competent in either politics or war, was viewed as an ideal replacement for the dour emperor. Germanicus was the son of Tiberius' deceased

A "Divine" Indiscretion—The Seduction of Paulina

ONE OF THE CULTS that particularly suffered under the watchful eye of Tiberius in Rome was that of the Egyptian goddess Isis. In his *Jewish Antiquities* (18.65–88), the historian Josephus records what he says is the specific incident that led to the emperor's hostility. The story is rather incredible, and Josephus' detailed narrative deserves our skepticism if for no other reason than portions of it are too reminiscent of other contemporary popular romantic tales. Nonetheless, we cannot discount his account completely or deny that the people mentioned in it had some influence on Tiberius' actions. Josephus writes:

> There was a lady Paulina, who because of her descent from noble Romans and because of her own practice of virtue was held in high regard. She also enjoyed the prestige of wealth, had a comely appearance, and was at the age at which women are most exuberant, yet devoted her life to good conduct. She was married to Saturninus, who was fully a match for her in reputation. Decius Mundus, who ranked high among the knights of his day, was in love with her. When he saw that her character was too strong to succumb to gifts, since, even when he sent them abundantly, she scorned them, his passion was inflamed all the more, so that he actually promised to give her 200,000 Attic drachmas if he could share her bed a single time. When even this failed to shake her resolution, he, finding it intolerable not to win his suit, thought that it would be fitting to condemn himself to death by starvation and thus to put an end to the suffering that had overtaken him. And so he decided upon such a death and was actually proceeding to carry out his resolve. Mundus, however, had a freedwoman named Ida, expert in every kind of mischief, whom his father had emancipated. She had no patience with the young man's resolve to die, for it was obvious what he intended. She went to him, used argument to rouse him, and by plausibly undertaking to find a way, held out hope that he might succeed in enjoying intimate relations with Paulina. When he joyfully listened to her importunity, she informed him that she would require no more than 50,000 drachmas to secure the woman. These proposals encouraged the youth, and she received the sum for which she had asked. She did not, however, proceed by the same course as had previous agents, since she perceived that this woman would never succumb to bribes. But knowing that the lady was very much given to the worship of Isis, Ida devised the following stratagem. She had an interview with some of the priests and promised them every assurance, above all, a sum of money amounting to 25,000 drachmas payable at once and as much more after the success of the plot. She then explained the young man's passionate desire for the woman and urged them to bend every effort to secure her for him. The impact of the money was enough to sway them, and they agreed. The eldest of them hastened to Paulina's house and, on being admitted, requested a private talk with her. This being accorded, he said that he had been sent to her by the god Anubis; the god had fallen in love with her and bade her come to him. The message was what she would most have wished. Not only did she pride herself among her lady friends on receiving such an invitation from Anubis, but she told her husband of her summons to dine with and share the bed of Anubis. Her husband concurred, since he had no doubt of his wife's chastity. Go then she did to the temple. After supper, when it came time to sleep, the doors within the shrine were shut by the priest and the lamps were cleared away. Mundus, for he had been

(continued)

A "Divine" Indiscretion (continued)

concealed there beforehand, was not rebuffed when he sought intercourse with her. Indeed, it was a night-long service that she performed for him, assuming that he was the god. He departed before the priests, who had been informed of the scheme, had begun to stir. Paulina went early in the morning to her husband and described in detail the divine manifestation of Anubis, and before the ladies, her friends, she put on great airs in talking about him. Those who heard, having regard to the substance of the matter, were incredulous; and yet, on the other hand, finding it impossible not to believe her when they took into consideration her chastity and position in society, they were reduced to marvelling. Two days after the incident, Mundus put himself in her way and said: "Well, Paulina, you have indeed saved me 200,000 drachmas which you could have added to your estate, yet you have rendered to perfection the service I urged you to perform. As for your attempt to flout Mundus,

I did not concern myself about names, though I did about the pleasure to be derived from the act, so I adopted the name of Anubis as my own." With these words he departed. Then she, being now aware for the first time of his dastardly deed, rent her garment; and when she had disclosed to her husband the enormity of the scheme, she begged him not to neglect to obtain redress. He in turn brought the matter to the notice of the emperor. When Tiberius had fully informed himself by examining the priests, he crucified both them and Ida, for the hellish thing was her doing and it was she who had contrived the whole plot against the lady's honor. Moreover, he razed the temple and ordered the statue of Isis to be cast into the Tiber River. Mundus' sentence was exile, since Tiberius regarded the fact that his crime had been committed under the influence of passion as a bar to a more severe penalty. Such were the insolent acts of the priests in the temple of Isis.

brother, Drusus (d. 9 B.C.), and had married Julia's daughter by Agrippa, Agrippina the Elder. He had in him the blood of Augustus' sister, Octavia, for he was the son of Antonia, daughter of Octavia and Mark Antony (see Chart 2, page 126); and by his marriage to Agrippina, his children had the blood of both Augustus and Octavia. He was also the grandson of Livia. Augustus found this pedigree so attractive that he directed that young Germanicus would succeed Tiberius, prearranging things so that his bloodline would regain the throne in future. Feeling as it did about Tiberius, the public preferred that the transfer of power take place sooner than later, and they made the unpopular emperor feel more uncomfortable by show-

ering their affection and attention on young Germanicus and his family. It is not difficult to understand why Tiberius would feel resentful.

Things came to a head in 19 A.D. when Germanicus died suddenly while on an Eastern tour. Charges that he had been poisoned by Gnaeus Piso, Tiberius' governor of Syria, prompted a trial, but Piso committed suicide before the matter was resolved. This did nothing but fuel the suspicions of Agrippina and her friends that her husband, Germanicus, had been murdered on orders from Tiberius. However, aside from rumor, which was rampant, there is no compelling evidence to suggest that Tiberius was involved—or that Germanicus was even poisoned. The body was placed on display in the

Julia: The Star-Crossed Daughter

EVEN THRASYLLUS PROBABLY WOULD not have been able to foresee all the misfortunes Augustus' daughter, Julia, suffered during her lifetime (39 B.C.–14 A.D.). Viewed as a political pawn by her father, she was widowed twice within eleven years before entering into her disastrous marriage with Tiberius. Striking back at her disagreeable husband, her stepmother *and* mother-in-law, Livia, and her father, Julia became so promiscuous that Augustus was forced to charge her with adultery and banish her to an island in 2 B.C. She was later allowed to return to Italy, but her father never forgave her and even refused her a place in the family mausoleum. While in exile, Julia learned that her sons Gaius and Lucius had died and that two other children, Agrippa Postumus and Julia the Younger, had been banished for misconduct. She would die in the same year as Augustus, surviving him only a short while. Before starving to death, she found out that Postumus had been executed. All in all, the bad times certainly seem to have outweighed the good in Julia's life, and only figures in tragedy suffer more. Nonetheless, this passage from Macrobius attests to the charm and wit the woman once had:

> Julia was thirty-eight and had reached a time of life which, had she been sensible enough, she would have regarded as bordering on old age, but she habitually misused the kindness of her own good fortune and her father's indulgence. Nevertheless, she had a love of letters and a considerable store of learning—not hard to come by in her home—and to these qualities were added a gentle humanity and a kindly disposition, all of which won for her a high regard; although those who were aware of her faults were astonished at the contradiction which her qualities implied.
>
> Again and again her father had referred to the extravagance of her dress and the notoriety of her companions and had urged her in language at once tender and grave to show more restraint. But at the same time the sight of his many grandchildren and their likeness to their father, Agrippa, forbade him for very shame's sake to entertain any doubts about his daughter's virtue. And so he flattered himself that her high spirits, even if they gave the impression of a wanton, were in fact blameless. . . . Thus it was that he once observed, when talking among some friends, that he had two spoiled daughters to put up with—Rome and Julia.
>
> She came one day into her father's presence wearing a somewhat immodest dress. Augustus was shocked but said nothing. On the next day, to his delight, she wore a different kind of dress and greeted him with studied demureness. Although the day before he had repressed his feelings, he was now unable to contain his pleasure and said: "This dress is much more becoming in the daughter of Augustus." But Julia had an excuse ready and replied: "Yes, for today I am dressed to meet my father's eyes; yesterday it was for my husband's."
>
> Here is another well-known saying of hers. At a display of gladiators the contrast between Livia's suite and Julia's had caught the eye, for the former was attended by a number of grown-up men of distinction but the latter was seated surrounded by young people of the fast set. Her father sent Julia a letter of advice, bidding her mark the difference between the behavior of the two chief ladies of Rome, to which she wrote this neat reply: "These friends of mine will be old men too, when I am old."
>
> Her hair began to go gray at an early age, and she used secretly to pull the gray hairs out. One day her maids were surprised by the unexpected arrival of her father, who pretended not to see the gray hairs on her women's dresses and talked for some time on other matters.

(continued)

Julia: The Star-Crossed Daughter (continued)

Then, turning the conversation to the subject of age, he asked her whether she would prefer eventually to be gray or bald. She replied that for her part she would rather be gray. "Why, then," said her father, thus rebuking her deceit, "are these women of yours in such a hurry to make you bald?"

Moreover, to a serious-minded friend who was seeking to persuade her that she would be better advised to order her life to conform to her father's simple tastes she replied: "He forgets that he is Caesar, but I remember that I am Caesar's daughter."

To certain persons who knew of her infidelities and were expressing surprise at her children's likeness to her husband Agrippa, since she was so free with her favors, she said: "Passengers are never allowed on board until the hold is full. . . ."

(*Saturnalia* 2.5)

Figure 5.7   Julia

---

public square at Antioch, and even the most fervent detractors of Tiberius admit that the charge could not be legitimately substantiated by the corpse's appearance. It would appear that Germanicus died of natural causes.

One interesting point, however, deserves mention. Germanicus believed in witchcraft and magic and had a healthy interest in the stars (he had translated a very influential Greek astronomical work). Such interests suggest some relationship with Thrasyllus, who was present at court during most of Germanicus' adult life. The tradition surrounding Germanicus' death (Tacitus, *Annals* 2.69–70) includes information that the remains of human bodies, charms, curse tablets, and other magical objects designed to hasten death had been found within the floor and walls of his sickroom. If true (or even partially so), then it is clear that someone—most likely Piso (or his agents), who had quarreled with the prince—was exploiting his weakened condition to literally scare him to death. Whatever the case, the outcome was not disappointing to Tiberius. He received the news of Germanicus' death in his usual stoic manner and made his son, Drusus, his heir.

Thrasyllus' Influence at Court

Although Thrasyllus is seldom mentioned in the sources, his influence on Tiberius and his policies can be safely assumed since the emperor was still depending upon his pronouncements forty years after they had first met on Rhodes.

No other person remained so close to Tiberius for such a long time, and the longevity of the relationship was possible only because Thrasyllus never gave his friend reason to doubt his loyalty. No important action—such as the one in 26 A.D. when Tiberius moved permanently from Rome to his favorite island retreat of Capri—may be presumed completely free of Thrasyllus' influence:

> For his astrological predictions, his intimate converse with the emperor day after day, and his shrewd advice based on his own keen appraisal of men and things could not but carry great weight with Tiberius.
> (Cramer, *Astrology* 103)

The fact that Thrasyllus is mentioned so infrequently while exerting such strong influence on Tiberius is good indication that the sources for this period were not as well informed about the workings of the emperor's inner circle as they appear to be. If it had been common knowledge that a Greek scholar was Tiberius' closest advisor, we would undoubtedly have heard much more about Thrasyllus—most of it negative. Instead, the few passages relating to his role at court represent him as a sobering influence on the emperor's excesses. The real extent and meaning of their relationship—which appears so obvious—receives only scant mention.

Thrasyllus undoubtedly expected to gain from his friendship with Tiberius, and he did. As a Greek, he knew that the corridors of power were closed to him, but dependent on the goodwill of Tiberius, whose favor he continued to groom, he rose in power—informally—as few Greeks in Rome ever did. An incident involving Augustus attests to the astrologer's savvy when dealing with his imperial benefactors. Augustus had improvised two verses in Greek and questioned Thrasyllus as to the poet's identity.

Thrasyllus did not recognize the lines but, sensing the need for diplomacy, responded that the author was unknown to him but whoever he was, his poetry was very good. Augustus, amused at his friend's cleverness, burst out laughing (Suetonius, *Augustus* 98.4).

Thrasyllus' fortunes hinged on those of Tiberius. What threatened the emperor threatened him also—and one can be sure that he used astrology to help Tiberius resolve difficulties in a manner that was advantageous to them both. Working behind the scenes, Thrasyllus apparently also arranged marriages between members of his family and high-ranking Romans, intending that his descendants would continue to wield influence and power at court—or at least be secure in their newfound station. His daughter married Lucius Ennius, a Roman knight who, in 22 A.D., was accused of treason for melting down a statue of Tiberius and using it for plate. The charge seems a specious one, probably concocted to discredit Thrasyllus—a good indication that his substantial influence on Tiberius was known to at least some of the emperor's enemies. The person who lodged the charge was an expert in religious affairs and, undoubtedly, no friend of astrology and those who practiced it. Significantly, Tiberius halted the proceedings against Ennius and purposely degraded the prosecutor. The incident is small but revealing if Tiberius' swift and decisive action were taken to protect Thrasyllus' son-in-law and to prevent any further inquiry into his own close relationship with Thrasyllus.

Thrasyllus' granddaughter, Ennia Thrasylla, also made her presence felt at court. She married Naevius Sutorius Macro, who became a trusted agent of Tiberius and commander of the Praetorian Guard near the end of his reign. Macro was also a decisive influence on the young Caligula, Tiberius' eventual successor. It was said that Caligula, who is more properly known as Gaius, had an affair with Ennia.

Sejanus—The "Partner" of Tiberius' Labors

By 26 A.D., Tiberius had wearied completely of the Senate, of Rome and its people, of his irksome relatives, and of plots and intrigues. The sudden death of his son and heir, Drusus, in 23 A.D. also had been a blow from which Tiberius never fully recovered. Earlier in his life, he had escaped his problems by withdrawing to Rhodes; now he left the capital and took up residence on Capri. Capri, off the Bay of Naples, was Tiberius' favorite island retreat and one that Thrasyllus also enjoyed. From there, Tiberius, feeling secure in his isolation, guided the Roman world for almost the remainder of his life.

When Tiberius departed from Rome, he left in charge his friend L. Aelius Sejanus, a man whom he trusted as much as Thrasyllus. What Tiberius did not realize, however, was that—unlike Thrasyllus—Sejanus, the prefect of his Guard, was a false friend. He was using his position and influence with the emperor to increase his own personal power. Sejanus is viewed today mostly as a minister who rose too high. At the beginning of his career, he could not have entertained the same high aspirations that he did later, since he was not an aristocrat, the royal family was well stocked with potential successors, and he could not have foreseen what lay down the road over his sixteen years of service with Tiberius. But Sejanus was ambitious and opportunistic, and he always tried to influence events to his advantage. Agrippa, a man from a similar background and condition who would have succeeded Augustus had he not died, provided a recent model for him. As his fortunes rose, success emboldened Sejanus, so

Figure 5.8   *Remains of Tiberius' Villa Jovis on Capri*

that the throne itself, it appears, was not beyond his ambition.

How far back Sejanus' friendship with Tiberius went is unclear, but Tiberius already knew him well when he succeeded Augustus in 14 A.D. Sejanus may have been introduced to the future emperor by his father, who shared Tiberius' Greek tastes and was commander of the Praetorian Guard, a position Sejanus held jointly with him after Tiberius' accession. The blind faith Tiberius placed in Sejanus, whom he called the "partner of my labors," would be more understandable if he viewed the son as the extension of his loyal father.

Thrasyllus, who also would have known Sejanus, may even have contributed to the emperor's feeling of trust with a positive horoscope for the prefect. Certainly, Thrasyllus never would have given his blessing to the move to Capri if he thought that Sejanus would not carefully look after Tiberius' interests in Rome. He may have viewed the prefect as someone not unlike himself—lacking the credentials to rise beyond a certain station but capitalizing on whatever did come his way. Also, since many of the same people Sejanus regarded as enemies would move to destroy Thrasyllus should anything happen to Tiberius, the astrologer would not have been overly concerned if Sejanus attacked them.

While Tiberius was at Capri, Sejanus worked to strengthen his position. Treason trials were utilized by the prefect as a vehicle to eliminate his personal and political enemies and to impress the emperor with his vigilance. The frequency of these trials created a tense atmosphere in Rome. To many, it appeared as though a "reign of terror" had been unleashed, with informers and spies everywhere. Tiberius' detractors concentrate on the fact that such trials characterized a good part of his reign. He *was* a suspicious and disliked man; but the imperial system itself encouraged restlessness and dissent, and no emperor's hands were clean of bloodshed. Innocent people died under Tiberius—there was no lack of false charges and accusations—but there was never a wholesale condemnation of the accused. Tiberius himself often interceded, sometimes personally investigating the details of a case when he suspected the evidence. Certainly, Thrasyllus' horoscopes helped him determine the guilt or innocence of more than a few people. However, this period was severe enough to earn the emperor an extremely bad reputation in future histories, obscuring the more positive aspects of his reign. Hostile anecdotes abound. In one example,

someone supposedly jokingly called out to a corpse in a passing funeral procession to tell Augustus' ghost that Tiberius had not yet made good on the former emperor's promised bequest to the people. Tiberius ordered the man executed and told him that he could personally inform Augustus that he *had* carried out his wishes. In another, a fisherman wishing to present a prize mullet to the emperor made his way up the unguarded cliffs below Tiberius' villa on Capri. Tiberius was so startled by his unexpected appearance that he ordered the man's face rubbed raw with the fish. The fisherman cried out that he was glad he had not brought the crab he had caught, so Tiberius sent for the crab and rubbed his face with it also!

While Tiberius was at Capri, Sejanus' power rose steadily. Some said that it rivaled the emperor's own. Juvenal comments:

So—would you like to have been Sejanus,
   popular, courted,
Having as much as he had, appointing men to
   high office,
Giving others command of the legions, renowned
   as protector
Of that Prince who's perched on the narrow
   ledges of Capri
With his Eastern seers and fortunetellers
   around him?
    (*Satire* 10.90–94)

Sejanus had previously attempted to attach himself more closely to Tiberius in 25 A.D. when he asked to marry Livilla, the widow of the emperor's son, Drusus. Tiberius demurred, realizing, in part, that such a marriage could be construed to mean that he wished Sejanus to succeed him—especially since Sejanus would have become stepfather to young Gemellus, Tiberius' grandson and likely heir. Tiberius trusted Sejanus, but he was not ready to confer such impressive status on a man of his social

Cremutius Cordus—An Innocent Victim?

THE HISTORIAN CREMUTIUS CORDUS had Republican sentiments and was an avowed enemy of Sejanus—a position that he, unfortunately, made public once too often. A previously unheard-of charge was brought against him by friends of Sejanus: In his histories, Cremutius had praised Brutus and called Cassius the last of the Romans. His words, the prosecution alleged, implied hostility toward the imperial system and the emperor and encouraged sedition. Tacitus, no friend of emperors himself, bemoans the fate of his fellow historian, whom he considers immaculately innocent and a victim of Tiberius. He implies Tiberius' tacit approval of the charges against Cremutius by assigning him a "grim expression" as he listened to the proceedings. But Tacitus often characterized Tiberius in negative terms, and what the emperor's exact feelings were cannot be known. Tiberius did not stop the Senate from ordering the burning of Cremutius' writings, but this was after the historian, convinced that his case was hopeless, starved himself to death. His action may have convinced Tiberius that the charges had substance. Whatever the case, Tacitus represented Cremutius as acquitting himself admirably, albeit unsuccessfully, before the Senate:

> Senators, my words are blamed. My actions are not blameworthy. Nor were these words of mine aimed against the emperor or his parent, whom the law of treason protects. I am charged with praising Brutus and Cassius. Yet many have written of their deeds—always with respect. Livy, outstanding for objectivity as well as eloquence, praised Pompey so warmly that

Augustus called him 'the Pompeian.' But their friendship did not suffer. . . . Gaius Asinius Pollio gave a highly complimentary account of them. Marcus Valerius Messalla Corvinus called Cassius 'my commander.' Both lived out wealthy and honored lives. When Cicero praised Cato to the skies, the dictator Julius Caesar reacted by writing a speech against him—as in a lawsuit. Antony's letters, Brutus' speeches, contain scathing slanders against Augustus. The poems of Marcus Furius Bibaculus and Catullus—still read—are crammed with insults against the Caesars. Yet the divine Julius, the divine Augustus endured them and let them be. This could well be interpreted as wise policy, and not merely forbearance. For things unnoticed are forgotten; resentment confers status upon them.

> "I am not speaking of the Greeks. For they left license unpunished as well as freedom—or, at most, words were countered with words. But among us, too, there has always been complete, uncensored liberty to speak about those whom death has placed beyond hatred or partiality. Cassius and Brutus are not in arms at Philippi now. I am not on the platform inciting people to civil war. They died seventy years ago! They are known by their statues—even the conqueror did not remove them. And they have their place in the historian's pages. Posterity gives everyone his due honor. If I am condemned, people will remember me as well as Cassius and Brutus."

Cremutius walked out of the senate, and starved himself to death. The senate ordered his books to be burnt by the aediles.

(Annals 4.34–35)

background. Perhaps, too, Thrasyllus had not seen the marriage in Sejanus' horoscope.

Shaken momentarily, Sejanus recovered quickly and put aside his disappointment for

the time being (it appears that he ultimately obtained the engagement with Livilla that he sought). When Tiberius had left for Capri, Sejanus used the opportunity to intensify his at-

Figure 5.9 *Agrippina the Elder*

have been advised not to go by Thrasyllus. There had been numerous astrological predictions that foretold his death if he ever came back to the city. Whatever the case, encouraged by Sejanus, Tiberius soon moved against Agrippina and her sons. She and Nero were dispatched to separate islands (she was beaten and lost an eye), and Drusus was later imprisoned in the palace dungeons. They would all be dead by 33 A.D. Thrasyllus may have seen their fates in the stars; Sejanus had not that far to look!

In 31 A.D., Sejanus was at the height of his power. Ironically, he would be dead before the year was over. It was a letter to Tiberius from his sister-in-law Antonia (Agrippina's mother-in-law) that apparently led to Sejanus' undoing. Having already seen the prefect imprison two of her grandsons with their mother, Antonia now feared for the safety of the third and youngest, Caligula. The anxious grandmother communicated her concerns to Tiberius on Capri. What her letter apparently made clear was that Tiberius had been used by his minister, the man whom he had regarded for years as his most trusted servant. If, as Antonia charged, Sejanus were plotting to eliminate Caligula, then Tiberius himself could never be sure of his own safety. Also, at about the same time, Caligula's brother Nero was murdered or forced to commit suicide. It is unclear exactly who was responsible, but Tiberius later implied in his autobiography that it was Sejanus. If so, Nero's death must have convinced Tiberius of the validity of Antonia's charges.

Far from Rome and uncertain of loyalties, Tiberius quickly realized the danger in which he had placed himself by delegating so much authority to Sejanus. Whether he actually believed that Sejanus could seize the throne from him is doubtful, but as unpopular and out of touch as he was, Tiberius needed to proceed

tacks on those whom he considered obstacles to his desires. These included Germanicus' widow Agrippina and her two eldest sons, Nero and Drusus. Tiberius had never allowed Agrippina to remarry for fear of a union that could threaten his own position; suspicions, exacerbated by Sejanus, fueled his uneasy relationship with her over the years. The fact that her sons were maturing was also a concern.

While Livia was alive, Agrippina and her children remained free from harm. Nothing indicates that the old woman actively protected them—in fact, Livia detested Agrippina. But she must have provided some check (if only psychological) since Agrippina's fortunes did not change dramatically until Livia died in 29 A.D. Tiberius did not return to Rome for Livia's funeral. He did not like his mother, but he may carefully. Caligula was brought to Capri, ostensibly for his safety. However, since Tiberius did not free his mother and brother even though it was now clear they were innocent, it is unlikely that he was mainly concerned about Caligula's well-being. This seems confirmed by the fact that, in the future, Tiberius had to be dissuaded on more than one occasion from eliminating the troublesome prince.

It is more likely that Tiberius preserved Caligula largely for political reasons. In the immediacy of this critical situation, he needed him as an "ally." Caligula was the son of Germanicus and was very popular. If the people had known Sejanus was threatening his life, they would have reacted negatively. Tiberius would be the positive force; the granduncle protecting his nephew's son from the scheming prefect, who had also victimized the "unwitting" emperor. It might be made to look as if Sejanus, not Tiberius, were responsible for many of the wrongs for which the emperor was criticized (including the cruel treatment of Agrippina and Drusus). Tiberius was old, but he was no fool. He was still a match for Sejanus in the game of power politics. Also, if civil disturbances did erupt and Sejanus were killed, Tiberius' enemies might try to raise Caligula as emperor. With the young man on Capri with him, Tiberius need not be concerned about that possibility.

Ultimately, Sejanus' downfall was brought about by a cleverly disguised letter sent to the Senate by Tiberius and delivered by Macro, Thrasyllus' grandson-in-law. Macro misled Sejanus by convincing him that the letter contained the emperor's order to give him tribunician powers, something the prefect had long desired. In reality, it ordered his arrest. Caught by surprise, Sejanus was unable to protect himself. All the pent-up hostility and hatred that had been festering against him over the years burst forth. Sejanus was promptly executed, and his corpse was battered and abused. His most fervent supporters and flatterers were also rounded up and punished.

One man who was brought to trial was Marcus Terentius, and his response to the charges brought against him provides a realistic insight into the human frailty that prompted a man like himself to seek out the friendship of Sejanus:

> . . . when everyone else was untruthfully disclaiming friendship with Sejanus, a knight called Marcus Terentius bravely accepted the imputation. "In my position," he observed to the senate, "it might do me more good to deny the accusation than to admit it. And yet, whatever the results, I will confess that I was Sejanus' friend: I sought his friendship, and was glad to secure it. I had seen him as joint-commander of the Guard with his father. Then I saw him conducting the civil as well as the military administration. His kinsmen, his relations by marriage, gained office. Sejanus' ill-will meant danger and pleas for mercy. I give no examples. At my own peril only, I speak for all who took no part in his final plans. For we honored, not Sejanus of Vulsinii, but the member of the Claudian and Julian houses into which his marriage alliances had admitted him—your future son-in-law, Tiberius, your partner as consul, your representative in State affairs.
>
> "It is not for us to comment on the man whom you elevate above others, and on your reasons. The gods have given you supreme control—to us is left the glory of obeying! Besides, we only see what is before our eyes: the man to whom you have given wealth, power, the greatest potentialities for good and evil—and nobody will deny that Sejanus had these. Research into the emperor's hidden thoughts and secret designs is forbidden, hazardous, and not necessarily informative. Think, senators, not of Sejanus' last day, but of the previous sixteen years. . . . We thought it grand even if Sejanus' ex-slaves and doorkeepers knew us. You

will ask if this defense is to be valid for all, without discrimination. Certainly not. But draw a fair dividing-line! Punish plots against the State and the emperor's life. But, as regards friendship and its obligations, if we sever them at the same time as you do, Tiberius, that should excuse us as it excuses you." This courageous utterance, publicly reflecting everyone's private thoughts, proved so effective that it earned Terentius' accusers, with their criminal records, banishment and execution.

(Tacitus, *Annals* 6.8–9)

Thrasyllus' Role in Sejanus' Downfall

Because his grandson-in-law Macro played such a major role in removing Sejanus (whom he succeeded as prefect), Thrasyllus' part in the overthrow of such a dangerous foe must have been crucial. Isolated on Capri, Tiberius would have depended greatly on his old friend's guidance—a confident look into the future would have been of paramount importance. The successful conclusion of the episode could only have reaffirmed the emperor's faith in Thrasyllus. Even so, there must have been times when the astrologer wondered about his own chances of survival, and the Sejanus affair changed Tiberius for the worse. Before she committed suicide, Sejanus' former wife informed the emperor that her ex-husband had seduced his daughter-in-law Livilla and the two had poisoned his son Drusus. Lonely and despondent, Tiberius drank heavily. Those close to him could not be sure that he would continue to behave in a rational manner, but despite these personal calamities, his rule of the empire remained steady. This may have been due in part to Thrasyllus' influence, since it is clear that Tiberius continued to rely heavily on his advice.

There is a tradition that Thrasyllus took advantage of his favored position to temper some of Tiberius' more errant decisions, purposely

Figure 5.10   *Tiberius in old age*

providing him with false horoscopes. One story credits Thrasyllus with saving numerous lives by convincing the emperor that he had another ten years to live even though he knew that his aged friend would soon die. The result was that the emperor was in no hurry to prosecute or put to death a large number of the accused. Consequently, many were spared, even young Caligula, Tiberius' eventual successor.

If Thrasyllus "misguided" Tiberius at the end of his life, it seems almost certain that he had been doing the same thing for the previous forty years, nudging his friend away from decisions that may have increased his unpopularity or endangered his life. At the same time, he must have

Figure 5.11   Caligula, Tiberius' successor

law becoming more like Sejanus cannot be known. What is known is that he falsely assured Tiberius that Caligula would never become emperor. He must have been trying to protect him from Tiberius' suspicions. Both Macro and Ennia Thrasylla were staunch supporters of the young prince, and Thrasyllus, too, must have favored Caligula's succession. Ultimately, Tiberius named Caligula as co-heir with his grandson Gemellus, and it is very probable that Thrasyllus helped the emperor arrive at that decision. Fortunately, Thrasyllus never lived to see what Caligula would do to Rome—and Gemellus.

Thrasyllus died in 36 A.D., a few months before Tiberius, who expired the following year at age seventy-seven. We are told (naturally) that he predicted the exact day and hour of his death. There is every indication that Thrasyllus remained loyal to Tiberius until the end. The late tradition that, through his writings, he had tried to disassociate himself from Tiberius' cruel acts does not seem realistic—if for no other reason than Thrasyllus would not have dared to criticize Tiberius in written form. What the tradition does show is that Thrasyllus continued to be highly regarded even long after his death. His works on a variety of subjects were quoted as authoritative for centuries, and Juvenal indicates, contemptuously, that even in his day, Thrasyllus' writings were a standard for astrological inquiries:

made the emperor aware of other matters of importance and urged him to act along guidelines he recommended. This is not to say that Thrasyllus had Tiberius under his control. Tiberius made the decisions, judicious or not, but he probably did not make them without first consulting Thrasyllus. Sometimes—as in the case of Sejanus—both men were wrong.

Thrasyllus' Final Years

Thrasyllus himself had only a few years left (he was close in age to Tiberius). Since Macro was now the Praetorian prefect, Thrasyllus' own power would have increased, but what position he would have taken as he saw his grandson-in-

These are the ones your wife, like Tanaquil, truly an expert,
Goes to consult: how soon will her mother die of the jaundice?
(She asked about your last hour long ago.) And when will she bury
Her sister, her uncles? How long will her present lover survive her?
So far, she can't understand the gloomy portents of Saturn

Or beneath what star Venus reveals herself
  joyous,
Which are the losing months, and which the
  seasons for winners.
Don't forget to duck when you meet with one of
  these women
Clutching no amber beads to keep her palms
  from perspiring,
But a calendar worn till she's hardly able to
  read it.
She is an expert herself, giving, not given, advices.
If her husband goes to the wars or returns to his
  homeland,
She will not be at his side if the runes of
  Thrasyllus forbid it. . . .
    (*Satire* 6.565–576)

After Thrasyllus

The historian Tacitus (*Histories* 1.22) looked back on the reign of Tiberius with disdain and described astrologers as "a class of men who are faithless to the powerful and deceitful to the aspiring," but, as one modern critic has noted, "indeed the great majority of emperors of every century were either credulous or studiously respectful to the claims of astrology" (MacMullen, *Enemies* 139). Thrasyllus' astrologer son, Balbillus, continued the tradition his father had begun at court by advising the Emperors Claudius, Nero, and Vespasian in matters of the future. The pseudoscience, although banned,

was still so strong during the days of the Christian Roman Empire that St. Augustine complained in the *City of God* (5.1):

> Those, however, who believe that the stars, apart from the will of God, determine what we do, what goods we have, or what evils we suffer, must be thrown out of court, not only by adherents of the true religion, but also by those who choose to worship gods of any sort, false gods though they may be. For what is the effect of this belief except to persuade men not to worship or pray to any god at all? . . . Moreover, how is any room left for God to pass judgment on the deeds of men, if they are subject to astrological forces, and God is Lord both of stars and men?

One of the favorite stories that ancient critics of astrologers liked to cite concerned King Prusias of Bithynia and Hannibal. When the king, under whom the aged Carthaginian general ended his military career, prevented Hannibal from beginning battle because an augur found the entrails of a sacrificial victim unfavorable, Hannibal dryly inquired as to whether the king wished to stake his fortunes on a slice of meat or on the experience of his general. Tiberius would have smiled at such cynicism if he had heard the story, for there would have been no doubt in his mind how to respond to Hannibal. Prusias had his "slice of meat"; Tiberius had Thrasyllus.

Philoe—A Horoscope from 150 A.D.

THE BIRTH OF PHILOE. Year 10 of the lord ANTONINUS Caesar, Phamenoth 15 to 16, first hour of the night. Sun in Pisces, Jupiter and Mercury in Aries, Saturn in Cancer, Mars in Leo, Venus and Moon in Aquarius, horoscope Capricorn.
(*Select Papyri* I, no. 199)

Suggestions for Further Reading

F. H. Cramer's *Astrology in Roman Law and Politics* in the *American Philosophical Society Monographs,* No. 37 (Philadelphia: American Philosophical Society, 1954), provides the fullest treatment of Thrasyllus and is the definitive work on astrology at Rome. See too, T. Baron's "Augustus and Capricorn: Astrological Polyvalency and Imperial Rhetoric," *Journal of Roman Studies* 85 (1995): 33–51. Chapter 4 in R. MacMullen's *Enemies of the Roman Order: Treason, Unrest, and Alienation in the Empire* (Cambridge, Mass.: Harvard University Press, 1966) is also of interest on the subject. Generally, see T. Baron, *Ancient Astrology* (New York: Routledge, 1994); and G. Luck, *Arcana Mundi: Magic and the Occult in the Greek and Roman Worlds* (Baltimore: The Johns Hopkins University Press, 1985). For Tiberius, see B. M. Levick's *Tiberius the Politician* (London: Thames & Hudson, 1976), and R. Seager's *Tiberius* (Berkeley and Los Angeles: University of California Press, 1972). Also of interest for the period are M. Fox's *Roman Historical Myths: The Regal Period in Augustan Literature* (New York: Oxford University Press, 1996), and R. Syme's *The Augustan Aristocracy* (New York: Oxford University Press, 1987). The main ancient sources for Tiberius' reign and Thrasyllus' activities are Tacitus' *Annals,* Books 1–6; Suetonius' *Tiberius* in the *Twelve Caesars;* and Dio's *Roman History,* Books 57–58. Velleius Paterculus (2.94–131) is a minor source for the period, and two Jewish writers, Josephus (*Jewish Antiquities*) and Philo, are useful supplements. All are available in the Loeb Classical Library editions; Tacitus and Suetonius also appear in the Penguin Classics series as well as numerous other editions.

General Reading

On the Roman Empire, useful studies include C. Wells, *The Roman Empire,* 2nd ed. (Cambridge, Mass.: Harvard University Press, 1995); C. G. Starr, *The Roman Empire, 27 B.C.–A.D. 476: A Study in Survival* (New York: Oxford University Press, 1982); F. Millar, *The Emperor in the Roman World (31 B.C.–A.D. 337)* (London: Duckworth, 1977), and *The Roman Near East, 31 B.C.–A.D. 337* (Cambridge, Mass.: Harvard University Press, 1993); A. Garzetti, *From Tiberius to the Antonines: A History of the Roman Empire, A.D. 14–192* (London: Methuen, 1974); and E. N. Luttwak, *The Grand Strategy of the Roman Empire: From the First Century A.D. to the Third* (Baltimore: The Johns Hopkins University Press, 1979). Excellent introductory works include C. Scarre's *Chronicle of the Roman Emperors: The Reign-by-Reign Record of the Rulers of Imperial Rome* (London: Thames & Hudson, 1995), M. Grant's *The Roman Emperors: A Biographical Guide to the Rulers of Imperial Rome, 31 B.C.–A.D. 476* (New York: Scribner, 1985), and M. Bunson's *A Dictionary of the Roman Empire* (New York: Oxford University Press, 1995). Also of interest are A. Lintott, *Imperium Romanum: Politics and Administration* (New York: Routledge, 1993); R. J. A. Talbert, *The Senate of Imperial Rome* (Princeton, N.J.: Princeton University Press, 1987); P. Garnsey and R. Saller, *The Roman Empire: Economy, Society and Culture* (Berkeley and Los Angeles: University of California Press, 1987); and R. A. G. Carson, *Coins of the Roman Empire* (New York: Routledge, 1989).

On Roman frontiers, see S. L. Dyson, *The Creation of the Roman Frontier* (Princeton, N.J.: Princeton University Press, 1987); and C. R. Whittaker, *Frontiers of the Roman Empire: A Social and Economic Study* (Baltimore: The Johns Hopkins University Press, 1994). On the Roman army, see Y. Le Bohec, *The Imperial Roman Army* (London: Batsford Books, 1994); B. Campbell, *The Roman Army, 31 B.C.–A.D. 337: A Sourcebook* (New York: Routledge, 1994); R. Isaac, *The Limits of Empire: The Roman Army in the East,* rev. ed. (New York: Oxford University Press, 1993); K. Dixon and P. Southern, *Roman Cavalry from the First to the Third Century A.D.* (London: Batsford Books, 1994); and M. R. Speidel, *Riding for Caesar: The Roman Emperor's Horse Guard* (London: Batsford, 1994). Earlier studies include G. Webster, *The Roman Imperial Army,* 3rd ed. (Totowa, N.J.: Barnes & Noble, 1985); and M. Grant, *The Army of the Caesars* (New York: Evans, reprint of 1974 edition).

On the Roman games, see T. Wiedemann, *Emperors and Gladiators* (New York: Routledge, 1995); and R. Auguet, *Cruelty and Civilization: The Roman Games* (New York: Routledge, 1994). On art and literature, see M. Grant, *Art in the Roman Empire* (New York: Routledge, 1995); and G. O. Hutchinson, *Latin Literature from Seneca to Juvenal: A Critical Study* (New York: Oxford University Press, 1993).

Useful sourcebooks are provided by W. E. Kaegi, Jr., and P. White, *Rome: Late Republic and Principate* (Chicago: University of Chicago Press, 1986); D. C. Braund, *Augustus to Nero: A Sourcebook on Roman History 31 B.C.–A.D. 68* (New York: Barnes & Noble, 1985); K. Chisholm and J. Ferguson, *Rome: The Augustan Age—A Sourcebook* (New York: Oxford University Press, in association with the Open University Press, 1981); M. Reinhold, *The Golden Age of Augustus* (Toronto and Sarasota: Samuel Stevens, 1978); N. Lewis, *The Roman Principate, 27 B.C.–285 A.D.* (Toronto: Hakkert, 1974); and the works by Shelton and Lewis and Reinhold mentioned in Chapter 1.

Recent General Additions

A. Barrett, *Agrippina: Sex, Power, and Politics in the Early Empire* (New Haven: Yale University Press, 1996); J. Lendon, *Empire of Honor: The Art of Government in the Roman World* (New York: Oxford University Press, 1997); R. Alston, *Aspects of Roman History A.D. 14–117* (New York: Routledge, 1998); K. Galinsky, *Augustan Culture: An Interpretive Intro-* duction (Princeton, N.J.: Princeton University Press, 1998); R. Laurence and J. Berry, *Cultural Identity in the Roman Empire* (New York: Routledge, 1998); P. Southern, *Augustus* (New York: Routledge, 1998); D. Favro, *The Urban Image of Augustan Rome* (Cambridge: Cambridge University Press, 1998); R. Duncan-Jones, *Money and Government in the Roman Empire* (Cambridge: Cambridge University Press, 1998); S. P. Mattern, *Rome and the Enemy: Imperial Strategy in the Principate* (Berkeley and Los Angeles: University of California Press, 1999); and E. Bartman, *Portraits of Livia: Imaging the Imperial Woman in Augustan Rome* (Cambridge: Cambridge University Press, 1999).

On Roman frontiers, see H. Elton, *Frontiers of the Roman Empire* (Bloomington: Indiana University Press, 1996); A. K. Bowman, *Life and Letters on the Roman Frontier* (New York: Routledge, 1997); and D. Cherry, *Frontier and Society in Roman North Africa* (New York: Oxford University Press, 1998). On a related topic, see G. Woolf, *Becoming Roman: The Origins of Provincial Civilization in Gaul* (Cambridge: Cambridge University Press, 2000).

On Roman spectacles and entertainment, see D. G. Kyle, *Spectacles of Death in Ancient Rome* (New York: Routledge, 1998); R. C. Beacham, *Spectacle Entertainments of Early Imperial Rome* (New Haven: Yale University Press, 1999); and appropriate sections of D. S. Potter and D. J. Mattingly (eds.), *Life, Death, and Entertainment in the Roman Empire* (Ann Arbor: University of Michigan Press, 1999). The latter also contains sections on the Roman family, Roman religion, and other topics.

6

Flavian Stability—
Natural Disaster

Mt. Vesuvius Destroys Pompeii and
Herculaneum (August 24, 79 A.D.)
Pliny the Survivor

*I . . . derived some poor consolation in my mortal lot from the
belief that the whole world was dying with me and I with it.*
(Pliny the Younger, *Letters* 6.20)

Except for the traumatic final centuries that ended the Empire in the West, one does not usually associate catastrophe or disaster with Rome; but from the beginning, the Roman character was molded by adversity. Natural and military upheavals were much more a part of Roman life than the success of Rome might lead one to believe. The Gallic sack of the city in 387 B.C. could have ended Rome's existence; instead, the Romans rebuilt. Disastrous defeats like Cannae in 216 B.C. removed in an instant much of a generation.

Even during the Empire when Rome dominated the Mediterranean world, the "national tragedy" that occurred at the Teutoburgian Wood in 9 A.D., where three legions (about fifteen thousand men) were massacred by the Germans, caused grave concern and threatened Roman security. Six years later, the trauma and horror of that disaster were revived when an army commanded by Germanicus came upon the remains of its dead comrades:

Now they were near the Teutoburgian Wood, in which the remains of Varus and his three divisions were said to be lying unburied. Germanicus conceived a desire to pay his last respects to these men and their general. Every soldier with him was overcome with pity when he thought of his relations and friends and reflected on the hazards of war and of human life. . . . The scene lived up to its horrible associations. Varus' extensive first camp, with its broad extent and headquarters marked out, testified to the whole army's labors. Then a half-ruined breastwork and shallow ditch showed where the last pathetic remnant had gathered. On the open ground were whitening bones, scattered where men had fled, heaped up where they had stood and fought back. Fragments of spears and of horses' limbs lay there—also human heads, fastened to tree trunks. In groves nearby were the outlandish altars at which the Germans had massacred the Roman colonels and senior company-commanders.

Survivors of the catastrophe, who had escaped from the battle or from captivity, pointed out where the generals had fallen, and where the Eagles [Roman standards] were captured. . . . So, six years after the slaughter, a living Roman army had come to bury the dead men's bones of three whole divisions. No one knew if the remains he was burying belonged to a stranger or a comrade. But in their bitter distress, and rising fury against the enemy, they looked on them all as friends and blood-brothers.

(Tacitus, *Annals* 1.61–62)

The most famous catastrophe associated with the city of Rome during the early Empire was the great fire of 64 A.D. The fire was a major disaster, but the notoriety of Nero (54–68 A.D.), the last of the Julio-Claudian emperors, obscures the reality that fire was an everyday threat to the capital's citizens. Rome, as Juvenal had noted (see Chapter 1), was a firetrap, a tinderbox waiting for a match. Even so, the city did not receive its first permanent fire brigade until the time of Augustus (probably after the emperor's own house burned down!). One has to wonder why the service was so late in coming to such a fire-plagued city, but realistically,

a bucket-and-ladder contingent was limited in what it could do.

An insight into how large fires were handled at Rome is provided by Nero's predecessor, the Emperor Claudius (41–54 A.D.), who reportedly lodged himself for two nights in the area of an uncontrollable blaze. When official firefighters, Guards, and palace servants failed to contain the fire, Claudius called up "volunteers" from the rest of the city and, sitting with bags of coins before him, paid them for their services on the spot. Local fires probably remained the responsibility of the neighborhood. If the fire got entirely out of hand, even measures like Claudius' did no good, since there was no chance of extinguishing it. Such appears to have been the case in the conflagration of 64 A.D. The historian Tacitus describes how it spread:

Now started the most terrible and destructive fire which Rome had ever experienced. It began in the Circus, where it adjoins the Palatine and Caelian hills. Breaking out in shops selling inflammable goods, and fanned by the wind, the conflagration instantly grew and swept the whole length of the Circus. There were no walled mansions or temples, or any other obstructions, which could arrest it. First, the fire swept violently over the level spaces. Then it climbed the hills—but returned to ravage the lower ground again. It outstripped every counter-measure. The ancient city's narrow winding streets and irregular blocks encouraged its progress.

Terrified, shrieking women, helpless old and young, people intent on their own safety, people unselfishly supporting invalids or waiting for them, fugitives and lingerers alike—all heightened the confusion. When people looked back, menacing flames sprang up before them or outflanked them. When they escaped to a neighboring quarter, the fire followed—even districts believed remote proved to be involved. Finally, with no idea where or what to flee, they crowded on to the country roads, or lay in the fields. Some who had lost everything—even their food for the day—could have escaped, but preferred to die. So did others, who had failed to rescue their loved ones. Nobody dared fight the flames. Attempts to do so were prevented by menacing gangs. Torches, too, were openly thrown in, by

men crying that they acted under orders. Perhaps they had received orders. Or they may just have wanted to plunder unhampered.

Nero was at Antium. He only returned to the city when the fire was approaching the mansion he had built to link the Gardens of Maecenas to the Palatine. The flames could not be prevented from overwhelming the whole of the Palatine, including his palace. Nevertheless,

Profit over Safety—Atilius the Fight-Promoter Spawns Disaster

IN 27 A.D., a freedman and entrepreneur named Atilius constructed a makeshift amphitheater to stage a gladiatorial combat at Fidenae, a town not far from Rome. His main concern was his pocketbook, and the facility he built was apparently so flimsy that it could not withstand the pressures of the overflowing crowd. The structure collapsed, and the casualty figures seem almost too staggering: 20,000 deaths were reported, and even Tacitus, who is usually more restrained than other historians, put the number of injured and dead at 50,000. If these figures are reliable, Atilius' greed helped generate a major catastrophe—all the more tragic since it could have been so easily avoided. According to Tacitus:

> A sudden disaster which now occurred was as destructive as a major war. It began and ended in a moment. An exslave called Atilius started building an amphitheater at Fidenae for a gladiatorial show. But he neither rested its foundations on solid ground nor fastened the wooden superstructure securely. He had undertaken the project not because of great wealth or municipal ambition but for sordid profits. Lovers of such displays, starved of amusements under Tiberius, flocked in—men and women of all ages. Their numbers, swollen by the town's proximity, intensified the tragedy. The packed structure collapsed, subsiding both inwards

and outwards and precipitating or overwhelming a huge crowd of spectators and bystanders.

> Those killed at the outset of the catastrophe at least escaped torture, as far as their violent deaths permitted. More pitiable were those, mangled but not yet dead, who knew their wives and children lay there too. In daytime they could see them, and at night they heard their screams and moans. The news attracted crowds, lamenting kinsmen, brothers, and fathers. Even those whose friends and relations had gone away on other business were alarmed, for while the casualties remained unidentified uncertainty gave free range for anxieties. When the ruins began to be cleared, people rushed to embrace and kiss the corpses—and even quarreled over them, when features were unrecognizable but similarities of physique and age had caused wrong identifications.

> Fifty thousand people were mutilated or crushed to death in the disaster. The senate decreed that in future no one with a capital of less than four hundred thousand sesterces should exhibit a gladiatorial show, and no amphitheater should be constructed except on ground of proved solidity. Atilius was banished. Immediately after the catastrophe, leading Romans threw open their homes, providing medical attention and supplies all round.

(*Annals* 4.62–63)

for the relief of the homeless, fugitive masses he threw open the Field of Mars, including Agrippa's public buildings and even his own Gardens. Nero also constructed emergency accommodation for the destitute multitude. Food was brought from Ostia and neighboring towns, and the price of grain was cut. . . . By the sixth day enormous demolitions had confronted the raging flames with bare ground and open sky, and the fire was finally stamped out at the foot of the Esquiline Hill. But before the panic had subsided, or hope revived, flames broke out again in the more open regions of the city. Here there were fewer casualties; but the destruction of temples and pleasure arcades was even worse. . . . Of Rome's fourteen districts only four remained intact. Three were leveled to the ground. The other seven were reduced to a few scorched and mangled ruins. To count the mansions, blocks, and temples destroyed would be difficult. They included shrines of remote antiquity. . . . Among the losses, too, were the precious spoils of countless victories, Greek artistic masterpieces, and authentic records of old Roman genius. All the splendor of the rebuilt city did not prevent the older generation from remembering these irreplaceable objects. It was noted that the fire had started on July 19th, the day on which the . . . Gauls had captured and burnt the city.
(*Annals* 15.38–41)

It is clear that Rome was always vulnerable to such tragedies. During the reign of Tiberius—a period of twenty-three years—a fierce fire gutted structures on the Caelian Hill in 27 A.D., and ten years later, the Aventine Hill and adjacent portions of the Circus were in flames. Fire also destroyed the theater of Pompey, broke out in the Forum near the Temple of Vesta, and burned down the future emperor Claudius' house. At least three major earthquakes were recorded, the most destructive of which devastated Asia Minor:

. . . twelve famous cities in the province of Asia were overwhelmed by an earthquake. Its occurrence at night increased the surprise and destruction. Open ground—the usual refuge on such occasions—afforded no escape, because the earth parted and swallowed the fugitives. There are stories of big mountains subsiding, of flat ground rising high in the air, of conflagrations bursting out among the debris. Sardis suffered worse and attracted most sympathy. Tiberius promised it ten million sesterces and remitted all taxation by the Treasury or its imperially controlled branches for five years. Magnesia-by-Sipylus came next, in damage and compensation. Exemptions from direct taxation were also authorized for Temnus, Philadelphia, Aegeae, Apollonis, Mostene (the Macedonian Hyrcanians), Hierocaesarea, Myrina, Cyme, and Tmolus. It was decided to send a senatorial inspector to rehabilitate the sufferers.
(Tacitus, *Annals* 2.47)

Doubtless, little changed while Caligula (37–41 A.D.), Tiberius' extravagant successor, was emperor (it was said that he even prayed for disasters to strike Rome!). During Claudius' reign, Pompey's theater burned once more, earthquakes flattened houses in Rome, causing general panic (Claudius' requirement that officials call an assembly and proclaim a public holiday whenever an earthquake occurred at Rome may have been designed to save lives by getting people out of their houses and multistory apartments), and in 53 A.D., Apamea in Phrygia was devastated by an earthquake.

Of all the disasters Rome suffered, however, one was destined to be among the most memorable in Western history. On August 24, 79 A.D., Mt. Vesuvius, a volcano on the Bay of Naples, erupted. Among its victims were the city of Pompeii, a prosperous farming and commercial center of about twenty thousand inhabitants, and the nearby smaller, more affluent town of

Herculaneum. One of the survivors of the eruption was a young man named Pliny (the Younger), who was living with his mother and uncle when Vesuvius exploded. Pliny would later become a high government official under the Emperor Trajan (see Chapter 9) and one of the foremost literary figures of his day. His eyewitness account of the eruption not only constitutes one of the most incredible literary survivals from antiquity but also uniquely preserves for us the very human story of how members of a Roman family coped with disaster nineteen hundred years ago.

The Flavian Dynasty

At the time of the eruption, Titus, a member of Rome's second dynasty, the Flavians, was emperor. Nero's death in 68 A.D. had brought a disgraceful close to Julio-Claudian rule, and with no heir apparent, civil wars erupted. Generals scrambled for power, and in the year following Nero's suicide, Galba, Otho, Vitellius, and Vespasian all tested their skills in quick succession. The year 69 A.D. became known as "The Year of the Four Emperors." Much of the city of Rome had been destroyed and the Empire was in chaos when the last of these emperors, Vespasian, finally seized power and held it. With his sons Titus and Domitian, he established the Flavian Dynasty (69–96 A.D.).

Once in power, Vespasian proved a capable and efficient administrator, restoring order and returning solvency to the state. He was assisted primarily by his elder son, Titus, who had sacked Jerusalem in 70 A.D. and completed the Jewish War in which his father had been involved at the time of Nero's death. Vespasian successfully restrained disruptive elements and rebuilt portions of the capital, largely in ruins from the strife that had brought him to power. On land once occupied by Nero's Golden House, he began con-

structing the Flavian Amphitheater, or Colosseum, a 50,000-seat facility that would become the Empire's most famous gladiatorial arena. After ten successful years of rule, Vespasian died in 79 A.D., and Titus became emperor. Exactly two months later, Vesuvius exploded.

A Teenager's Brush with Death

When Mt. Vesuvius erupted, Pliny the Younger was not at Pompeii, Herculaneum, Stabiae, or any of the other sites on the Bay of Naples that were destroyed. He was at Misenum, about 20 miles across the bay from the center of the eruption. Even so, his chances of survival were not good. Some of his actions were not judicious, but what counts is that he ultimately did the right things at the right time—and lived.

Pliny recorded his impressions of the eruption in two remarkable letters (*Letters* 6.16 and 20), addressed to his friend Tacitus, greatest of the imperial historians, who had requested the information to assist him in his researches. Some twenty-six years had passed since the fateful day, but Pliny's experience was not the kind of thing one forgets. Although there may be a ragged detail here and there and a bit of self-promotion, Pliny ultimately produced a generally sober narrative—considering the circumstances. It is probably as accurate a representation of the events as we could ever hope to have. Together, the two letters provide a composite record of the activities of Pliny's family on that day.

Pliny's Account

In the summer of 79 A.D., Pliny and his mother were living at the home of her brother, Pliny the Elder, commander of the Roman fleet at Misenum on the northern promontory of the Bay of Naples (see Map 16, page 158). Young Pliny's

Figure 6.1
*The Colosseum
(Flavian Amphitheater),
built and dedicated by
Vespasian and his sons*

Eyewitness to History—Josephus Describes a Roman Triumph

AMONG THE MOST magnificent and glorious spectacles at Rome was the celebration of a military triumph. During the Republic, this was the height of a Roman general's career and eagerly desired by all ambitious aristocrats. Generally, the requirements were victory in a declared war over a foreign power and at least 5,000 enemy dead. Awarded by a popular vote requested by the Senate, the victorious commander was allowed to bring troops into the city to participate in a staggering display of arms, booty, prisoners, pageantry, and personal aggrandizement that was embraced by all of Rome. Plutarch (*Aemilius Paulus* 32–35) describes one such display in his account of the three-day triumphal procession of Aemilius Paulus in 167 B.C. for his victory over

Perseus, last of the Macedonian kings. By the time of the Empire, however, honoring individual ambition and glory in such manner was dangerous, and triumphs were reserved for the emperor and his family. What follows is an eyewitness account by the historian Josephus, who was present at the triumph the Emperor Vespasian and his son and future emperor, Titus, celebrated for their victory over the Jews in a difficult war (66–73 A.D.) that had begun under Nero and had included the sack of Jerusalem and the destruction of the Temple of 70 A.D. Josephus had been a Jewish priest and political leader who surrendered to the Romans rather than die during the war and "prophesied," correctly as it turned out, Vespasian's succession to the throne. He was

(continued)

Eyewitness to History (continued)

with Titus at the siege of Jerusalem, even calling upon the city's defenders to surrender to the Romans. Later made a Roman citizen, he was viewed as a traitor and Roman lackey by many of his fellow Jews. Josephus' account appears in his history of *The Jewish War* (7.121–157), and, while he never hesitates to flatter his imperial patrons, it does not appear that he needed to do anything more, here, than simply describe what he saw. Particularly of interest is the "detachment" Josephus displays when the precious relics of Judaism and the Temple pass by in the victory parade: (Note: refer to the Roman Forum map on page 4 and the city map on page 7 for some of the features mentioned along the triumph route.)

> Notice was given in advance of the day appointed for the victory procession, and not one person stayed at home out of the immense population of the City: everyone came out and, although there was only standing room, found a place somewhere, so that there was barely enough room left for the procession itself to pass.

> While it was still night all the soldiers had marched out under their commanders by centuries and cohorts, and had formed up not round the gates of the Upper Palace but near the Temple of Isis; for there the victorious generals had slept that night. As soon as day began to break Vespasian and Titus came out wreathed with bay and wearing the traditional purple robes and proceeded to the Octavian Walks; for there the Senate and senior magistrates and knights were awaiting their arrival. A dais had been set up in front of the colonnades, and on it placed ready for them were ivory chairs. On these they proceeded to sit; whereupon the soldiery shouted acclamations, one and all bearing full testimony to their prowess. The central figures were unarmed, in silken robes and wreathed with bay. Having received their acclamations Vespasian, though they

Figure 6.2 *Relief on the interior of the Arch of Titus in Rome depicting the triumphant Titus in his chariot after his victory in the Jewish War*

had more to say, gave the signal for silence. A complete hush fell on all and the emperor, rising from his seat and wrapping most of his head in his cloak, offered the customary prayers, Titus then doing the same. After the prayers Vespasian made a short speech to the whole gathering, dismissed the soldiers to the breakfast which it was customary for victorious generals to provide, and himself retired to the gate which took its name from the triumphal processions that always pass through it. There they first tasted food, then put on the triumphal robes and sacrificed to the gods that stand on either side of the gate, and finally resumed their triumphal advance, driving through the theaters to give the crowds a better view.

It is impossible to give a satisfactory account of the innumerable spectacles, so magnificent in every way one could think of, whether as works of art or varieties of wealth or rarities of nature; almost all the treasures that have ever come one at a time into the hands of fortune's favorites—the priceless marvels of many different peoples—were brought together on that day, showing forth the greatness of the Roman Empire. Masses of silver and gold and ivory in every shape known to the craftsman's art could be seen, not as if carried in procession but like a flowing river. There were hangings borne along, some in the rarest shades of purple, others embroidered with lifelike portraits by Babylonian artists; transparent stones, some set in golden crowns, some in other mounts, were carried past in such numbers that we could see how foolish we had been to suppose any of them rare. In the procession too were images of the Roman gods wonderful in size and of true artistic merit, every one of them made from costly materials; and animals of many kinds were led past, all decked with the proper trappings. Every item in the procession was escorted by a large group of men arrayed in garments of true purple dye interwoven with gold; those chosen

to take part in the procession itself had about them the choicest and most astonishing wealth of ornament. Furthermore, not even the host of captives went unadorned: under their elaborate and beautiful garments any disfigurement due to physical sufferings was hidden from view.

But what caused the greatest wonder was the structure of the traveling stages; indeed their immense size caused alarm through mistrust of their stability, as many of them were three or even four storeys high, while their lavish equipment was viewed with delighted surprise. Many were hung with curtains interwoven with gold, and all were framed in wrought ivory and gold. Numbers of tableaux showed the successive stages of the war most vividly portrayed. Here was to be seen a smiling countryside laid waste, there whole formations of the enemy put to the sword; men in flight and men led off to captivity; walls of enormous size thrown down by engines, great strongholds stormed, cities whose battlements were lined with defenders utterly overwhelmed, an army streaming inside the ramparts, the whole place reeking of slaughter, those unable to resist raising their hands in supplication, temples set on fire and houses torn down over the heads of their occupants, and after utter desolation and misery rivers flowing, not over tilled fields, supplying drink to men and animals, but through a countryside still blazing on every hand. Such were the agonies to which the Jews condemned themselves when they embarked on this war; and the art and marvelous craftsmanship of these constructions now revealed the incidents to those who had not seen them happen as clearly as if they had been there. Placed on each stage was the commander of a captured town just as he had been when captured. A number of ships followed.

Most of the spoils that were carried were heaped up indiscriminately, but more prominent

(continued)

Eyewitness to History (continued)

Figure 6.3   Relief on the opposite side of the interior of the Arch of Titus depicting his triumphal procession with the Menorah from the Temple at Jerusalem and other spoils

Figure 6.4   A large-scale, open-air model in modern Jerusalem depicting the city during the period of the Second Temple. It was destroyed by Titus in 70 A.D. The Temple is the high structure in the middle of the walled precinct at the back of the photo.

than all the rest were those captured in the Temple at Jerusalem—a golden table weighing several hundredweight, and a lampstand similarly made of gold but differently constructed from those we normally use. The central shaft was fixed to a base, and from it extended slender branches placed like the prongs of a trident, and with the end of each one forged into a lamp: these numbered seven, signifying the honor paid to that number by the Jews. After these was carried the Jewish Law, the last of the spoils. Next came a large group carrying images of Victory, all fashioned of ivory and gold. Behind them drove Vespasian first with Titus behind him: Domitian rode alongside, magnificently adorned himself, and with his horse a splendid sight.

The procession finished at the Temple of Jupiter Capitolinus, where they came to a halt: it was an ancient custom to wait there till news came that the commander-in-chief of the enemy was dead. This was Simon son of Gioras, who had been marching in the procession among the prisoners, and now with a noose thrown round him was bring dragged to the usual spot in the Forum while his escort knocked him about. This is the spot laid down by the law of Rome for the execution of those condemned to death for their misdeeds. When the news of his end arrived it was received with universal acclamation, and the sacrifices were begun. When the customary prayers had been offered and the omens proved favorable, the princes went back to the Palace. Some they entertained at the imperial table; for all the rest sumptuous banquets had been prepared at home. All day long the City of Rome celebrated the triumphant issue of the campaign against her enemies, the end of civil strife, and the beginning of hope for a joyous future.

father was dead (his parents seem to have been divorced), and he spent much of his adolescence at his uncle's house. His uncle, a noted antiquarian and scientist who had authored a number of important works—including a lengthy and comprehensive encyclopedia of natural history that still survives—supervised his education and general upbringing.

August 24 had apparently begun normally, although Pliny remarks that there had been earthquakes for several days previous. No one on the bay had been alarmed, for earthquakes were a frequent occurrence in the region of Campania (and still are). Pliny's uncle had been relaxing in the sun; after a cold bath and lunch, he began working on his books. It was early afternoon when Pliny's mother noticed "a cloud of unusual size and appearance" coming from the direction of Mt. Vesuvius, across the bay to the east, and called it to her brother's attention. The elder Pliny put on his shoes and climbed to a vantage point from which he could best observe the phenomenon. Pliny writes:

It was not clear at that distance from which mountain the cloud was rising (it was afterwards known to be Vesuvius); its general appearance can best be expressed as being like an umbrella pine, for it rose to a great height on a sort of trunk and then split off into branches, I imagine because it was thrust upwards by the first blast and then left unsupported as the pressure subsided, or else it was borne down by its own weight so that it spread out and gradually dispersed. Sometimes it looked white, sometimes blotched and dirty, according to the amount of soil and ashes it carried with it.

Pliny's uncle apparently still saw no reason for alarm at this point—it was his curiosity as a scholar, not any official capacity, that initially prompted him to desire a closer look. He ordered a small ship made ready and even invited his nephew to join him. Here we are provided with an insight into the serious character of the young Pliny, who refused his uncle's offer in favor of continuing his lessons. Probably few other boys his age would have made this choice, but, as it turned out, it saved his life!

What had begun as a leisurely inquiry by a curious scientist soon turned into a grave situation. As he was leaving his house, the elder Pliny finally became aware of what was really happening when he was handed a desperate message for help from a terrified woman he knew living at the foot of the mountain. He quickly ordered the fleet into action and boarded one of the vessels to personally direct the rescue operation, knowing there were many to be saved from the villas and towns along the heavily populated coast:

> He hurried to the place which everyone else was hastily leaving, steering his course straight for the danger zone. He was entirely fearless, describing each new movement and phase of the portent to be noted down exactly as he observed them. Ashes were already falling, hotter and thicker as the ships drew near, followed by bits of pumice and blackened stones, charred and cracked by the flames: then suddenly they were in shallow water, and the shore was blocked by the debris from the mountain. For a moment my uncle wondered whether to turn back, but when the helmsman advised this he refused, telling him that Fortune stood by the courageous and they must make for Pomponianus at Stabiae. He was cut off there by the breadth of the bay (for the shore gradually curves round a basin filled by the sea) so that he was not as yet in danger, though it was clear that this would come nearer as it spread. Pomponianus had therefore already put his belongings on board ship, intending to escape if the contrary wind fell. This wind was of course full in my uncle's favor, and he was able to bring his ship in. He embraced his terrified friend, cheered and encouraged him, and thinking he could calm his fears by showing his own composure, gave orders that he was to be carried to the bathroom. After his bath he lay down and dined; he was quite cheerful, or at any rate he pretended he was, which was no less courageous.

Meanwhile on Mount Vesuvius broad

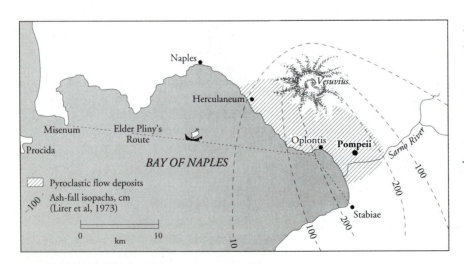

Map 16
Mt. Vesuvius and environs, August 24, 79 A.D. *The diagram reconstructs the eruption and events of August 24. Broken lines indicate direction and amount of pumice and fine-ash fall. Striping indicates pyroclastic flow.*

sheets of fire and leaping flames blazed at several points, their bright glare emphasized by the darkness of night. My uncle tried to allay the fears of his companions by repeatedly declaring that these were nothing but bonfires left by the peasants in their terror, or else empty houses on fire in the districts they had abandoned. Then he went to rest and certainly slept, for as he was a stout man his breathing was rather loud and heavy and could be heard by people coming and going outside his door.

While the elder Pliny was absent, young Pliny tried to carry on a normal routine. He continued his lessons for the remainder of the day, then bathed, dined, retired, and fell into an uncomfortable and fitful sleep. The earthquakes continued and became so violent during the night

that he and his mother sought out each other's company and comfort. They took refuge in the house's forecourt, and Pliny tried to allay his fears—and his mother's—by resuming his studies: "I don't know whether I should call this courage or folly on my part (I was only seventeen at the time) but I called for a volume of Livy and went on reading as if I had nothing else to do. I even went on with the extracts I had been making."

One of his uncle's friends, recently arrived from Spain, passed by and noticing the two, chastised them for their foolish behavior. They should flee immediately. His words had no effect, for as Pliny states—with an almost perverted sense of pride—"I remained absorbed in my book."

Pliny and his mother stayed where they were until dawn, but there was not much light

Figure 6.5 *A reconstructed provincial Roman dining room from Britain during the imperial period. Pliny the Younger would have taken his meals and relaxed in a room not unlike this one at his uncle's house at Misenum in Italy on the Bay of Naples.*

and the earth continued to tremble. Realizing that the house could collapse upon them, they finally decided to leave town, but that prompted additional problems:

> We were followed by a panic-stricken mob of people wanting to act on someone else's decision in preference to their own (a point in which fear looks like prudence), who hurried us on our way by pressing hard behind in a dense crowd. Once beyond the buildings we stopped, and there we had some extraordinary experiences which thoroughly alarmed us. The carriages we had ordered to be brought out began to run in different directions though the ground was quite level, and would not remain stationary even when wedged with stones. We also saw the sea sucked away and apparently forced back by the earthquake: at any rate it receded from the shore so that quantities of sea creatures were left stranded on dry sand. On the landward side a fearful black cloud was rent by forked and quivering bursts of flame, and parted to reveal great tongues of fire, like flashes of lightning magnified in size.

Pliny's uncle's friend from Spain had apparently remained close and now offered encouragement: "If your uncle is still alive, he will want you both to be saved: if he is dead, he would want you to survive him—why put off your escape?" Pliny and his mother were understandably reluctant to leave the area without some word about the elder Pliny's situation, so they continued to hesitate, ultimately prompting their friend to leave them and look to his own safety. Then came the most terrifying moments of the eruption:

> Soon afterwards the cloud sank down to earth and covered the sea; it had already blotted out Capri and hidden the promontory of Misenum from sight. Then my mother implored, entreated and commanded me to escape as best I could—a young man might escape, whereas she was old and slow and could die in peace as long as she had not been the cause of my death too. I refused to save myself without her, and grasping her hand forced her to quicken her pace. She gave in reluctantly, blaming herself for delaying me. Ashes were already falling, not as yet very thickly. I looked round: a dense black cloud was coming up behind us, spreading over the earth like a flood. "Let us leave the road while we can still see," I said, "or we shall be knocked down and trampled underfoot in the dark by the crowd behind." We had scarcely sat down to rest when darkness fell, not the dark of a moonless or cloudy night, but as if the lamp had been put out in a closed room. You could hear the shrieks of women, the wailing of infants, and the shouting of men; some were calling their parents, others their children or their wives, trying to recognize them by their voices. People bewailed their own fate or that of their relatives, and there were some who prayed for death in their terror of dying. Many besought the aid of the gods, but still more imagined there were no gods left, and that the universe was plunged into eternal darkness for evermore. There were people, too, who added to the real perils by inventing fictitious dangers: some reported that part of Misenum had collapsed or another part was on fire, and though their tales were false they found others to believe them. A gleam of light returned, but we took this to be a warning of the approaching flames rather than daylight. However, the flames remained some distance off; then darkness came on once more and ashes began to fall again, this time in heavy showers. We rose from time to time and shook them off, otherwise we should have been buried and crushed beneath their weight. I could boast that not a groan or cry of fear escaped me in these perils, had I not derived some poor consolation in my mortal lot from the belief that the whole world was dying with me and I with it.

At last the darkness thinned and dispersed into smoke or cloud; then there was genuine daylight, and the sun actually shone out, but yellowish as it is during an eclipse. We were terrified to see everything changed, buried deep in ashes like snowdrifts. We returned to Misenum where we attended to our physical needs as best we could, and then spent an anxious night alternating between hope and fear. Fear predominated, for the earthquakes went on, and several hysterical individuals made their own and other people's calamities seem ludicrous in comparison with their frightful predictions. But even then, in spite of the dangers we had been through and were still expecting, my mother and I had still no intention of leaving until we had news of my uncle.

Unfortunately, the news that Pliny and his mother received a few days later was not good—Pliny the Elder was dead. After he had reached his friend Pomponianus at Stabiae and calmed the household, the danger had become too great—he would have been wiser to have evacuated his friends and departed immediately. The delay cost him his life:

By this time the courtyard giving access to his [Pliny's] room was full of ashes mixed with pumice-stones, so that its level had risen, and if he had stayed in the room any longer he would never have got out. He was wakened, came out and joined Pomponianus and the rest of the household who had sat up all night. They debated whether to stay indoors or take their chance in the open, for the buildings were now shaking with violent shocks and seemed to be swaying to and fro as if they were torn from their foundations. Outside on the other hand, there was the danger of falling pumice-stones, even though these were light and porous; however, after comparing the risks they chose the latter. In my uncle's case one reason outweighed the other, but for the others it was a choice of fears. As a protection against falling objects they put pillows on their heads tied down with cloths.

Elsewhere there was daylight by this time, but they were still in darkness, blacker and denser than any ordinary night, which they relieved by lighting torches and various kinds of lamp. My uncle decided to go down to the shore and investigate on the spot the possibility of any escape by sea, but he found the waves still wild and dangerous. A sheet was spread on the ground for him to lie down, and he repeatedly asked for cold water to drink. Then the flames and smell of sulphur which gave warning of the approaching fire drove the others to take flight and roused him to stand up. He stood leaning on two slaves and then suddenly collapsed, I imagine because the dense fumes choked his breathing by blocking his windpipe which was constitutionally weak and narrow and often inflamed. When daylight returned on the 26th—two days after the last day he had seen—his body was found intact and uninjured, still fully clothed and looking more like sleep than death.

It could not have taken long for news of the disaster to reach the Emperor Titus in Rome, about 130 miles away. Naturally, Titus probably expected a full report from the elder Pliny, who was his fleet admiral and certainly the highest-ranking official on the bay. Envoys must have sought him out at Misenum, and when it was learned from young Pliny and his mother that he was among the missing, a search was probably launched immediately—but this was among the least of Titus' problems.

Only in office two months before the eruption, the emperor was faced with a monumental emergency. Thousands were homeless, there were countless dead all around the bay—many exposed and unattended—and most certainly, looters were everywhere. Titus acted quickly. Survivors were given refuge and aid and, ultimately, were resettled in nearby cities like Neapolis (Naples), which had escaped major damage. A board of former consuls was established to personally supervise the recovery of Campania. The property of those who had died in the eruption and had no heirs was pooled to

Figure 6.6
Mt. Vesuvius and
the ruins of Pompeii

establish a fund to help dig out and rebuild Pompeii and Herculaneum. The rebuilding, of course, was never done.

We know from their graffiti that, in the first few days after the eruption, people had entered buildings at Pompeii through the unburied roofs of higher structures. Most were probably former residents searching for bodies of family members and whatever valuables they could recover. Some undoubtedly were looters. Herculaneum had been so totally obliterated that similar efforts there were pointless.

Already parallels with the biblical Sodom and Gomorrah were being made by pious Christians or Jews, and many of the latter interpreted the destruction as divine retribution for Titus' sack of Jerusalem and destruction of the Temple. Of the cities of Vesuvius, only Stabiae recovered fully and went on to achieve a prosperity superior to what it had before the eruption. As for Mt. Vesuvius, the mountain has continued to be troublesome for the residents of the Bay of Naples over the centuries, its last eruption having occurred in 1944.

People of Pompeii and Herculaneum

Sextus Patulcus Felix was a baker at Herculaneum; the Vettii brothers (see Figures 6.7 and 6.8) were wealthy Pompeiian merchants; Stephanus ran a laundry; Novellia Primigenia sold her favors to men in both towns and had no shortage of admirers. Boys like Marcus, Rufus, Sabinus, Manius, Julius, and David (who, by his name, was either a Jew or Christian) were fearlessly scratching their names, as children often do, wherever it pleased them. On the outskirts of Herculaneum, the city of Hercules, lay a large villa (today referred to as the "Villa of the Papyri"), crowded with masterpieces of Greek sculpture and boasting a

Figure 6.7
House of the Vettii
brothers, Pompeii

Figure 6.8
The decorated walls of
the House of the Vettii

first-rate philosophy library, which probably belonged to descendants of Lucius Calpurnius Piso, the man who, in the previous century, had been the father-in-law of Julius Caesar.

High and low, rich and poor, slave and free, the people of Pompeii and Herculaneum formed a cross section of Roman life during the imperial period. We know literally hundreds of them by name because their lives were frozen in time. There is no moment in ancient history (or perhaps any period of history before our own) that is so perfectly preserved for us as August 24, 79 A.D. Ever since a well digger accidentally rediscovered the theater at Herculaneum in 1709, we have been able to peer intimately into a world that existed nineteen hundred years ago. People's carbonized meals are still on the table, loaves of bread are just recently torn in half, eggs are intact; scales still hold what was being weighed at the precise minute; dice wait for their owner to give them the next throw; Asellina—or one of her barmaids (Smyrna, Maria, or Aegle)—left behind petty cash, part of the day's receipts, in a drawer. Houses are replete with furnishings, wall paintings, statues, mosaics, pottery, personal effects, and utensils of every shape and kind. One residence in Herculaneum (now known as the "House of the Bicentenary") even appears to have had a small Christian chapel in it with a cross on the wall (see Figure 9.6, page 253). Our knowledge of Roman private and public life would be vastly inferior if not for the people who suffered on that day so long ago. In that respect, at least, we can perhaps look upon their misfortune in a not entirely negative light.

History of Two Cities

Both Pompeii and Herculaneum had long histories before their destruction. Over the centuries, Greeks, Etruscans, and Samnites, who

dominated Campania for the longest period, were among those who had left their stamp on the towns before they came into Roman hands after the civil wars of the 80s B.C. At the time of the eruption, forums, basilicas, theaters, public baths, and palaestrae were integral features of Pompeii and Herculaneum, and the former also had an amphitheater (see Figure 6.15, page 173).

Located 5 miles to the southwest of Vesuvius on a volcanic shelf overlooking the Sarno River, Pompeii was probably an average Italian imperial city, although the size and number of its public buildings are certainly impressive. Primarily a bustling, although not wealthy, commercial center and port, its mixed population was largely engaged in agriculture, small business, and a fishing industry. Fish sauce and wine were important exports. An inscription found on a cloth merchant's wall, *Salve Lucrum* (roughly, "Hurray for the Bucks"), demonstrates clearly that the spirit of capitalism was already alive and well. The hectic pace and noise from the shops, stalls, taverns, and apartments along Pompeii's hot, narrow streets had driven those who could afford it to villas along the coast (if they were not already residing there). It is clear from how much residents prized and decorated their gardens that they also knew how to relax.

Ten miles to the northwest on the opposite slope of Vesuvius lay the smaller town of Herculaneum with a population of about five thousand. Situated on a promontory between small rivers that flowed to the Bay of Naples, the town's walls stopped right at the shoreline. A steep drop-off to the sea (now about a third of a mile away) provided wonderful vistas for the wealthy owners of houses at the edge of the community. There was little beach area, and Herculaneum could never have developed into a major port city. Some found the town an idyllic retreat and gave it an affluent air—seen particularly in

Apicius' Guide for the Roman Gourmet

AMONG THE SHOPS THAT specialized in foodstuffs in Pompeii and Herculaneum was that of Aulus Fuferus, whose stock, when rediscovered, included preserved cereals and vegetables. His produce was obviously much more extensive, but the more perishable goods have long since disappeared. Even so, we know much about what Romans liked to eat and what they would have shopped for at neighborhood stores. Petronius' account of the banquet of Trimalchio (who is mentioned as owning property at Pompeii), described in the previous chapter, informs us about all sorts of elaborate dishes. However, Petronius was parodying a rich freedman's attempts to impress others with the sumptuousness of his table, and what was served and how it was served were made purposely extravagant. We cannot know how closely this "literary banquet" conforms to actual Roman culinary practices. A more useful—and realistic—reference on ancient food is an imperial cookbook attributed to Apicius. Among the recipes included in his *Roman Cookery* are the following:

Figure 6.9 *A reconstructed provincial kitchen from Roman Britain during the imperial period. Many of Apicius' recipes were made in facilities like this one around the Empire.*

(continued)

Apicius' Guide for the Roman Gourmet (continued)

Chicken Fronto

Brown the chicken, put in a mixture of liquamen [fish sauce] and oil to which you add a bouquet of dill, leek, savory, and green coriander; and [cook]. When it is done take it out, place on a serving-dish, sprinkle generously with defrutum, powder with pepper, and serve.
(*Cookery* 6.9.12)

Pork Fricassee with Apricots

Put in the saucepan oil, liquamen, wine, chop in dry shallot, add diced shoulder of pork cooked previously. When all this is cooked, pound pepper, cumin, dried mint, and dill. Moisten with honey, liquamen, passum, a little vinegar, and some of the cooking liquor; mix well. Add the stoned apricots. Bring to the boil, and let it boil until done. Crumble pastry to bind. Sprinkle with pepper and serve.
(4.3.6)

Lentils with Chestnuts

[Boil the lentils.] Take a new saucepan and put in the carefully cleaned chestnuts. Add water and a little cooking soda. Put on the fire to cook. [Meanwhile], put in the mortar pepper, cumin, coriander seed, mint, rue, asafoetida root, and pennyroyal; pound. Moisten with vinegar, add honey and liquamen, blend with vinegar and pour over the cooked chestnuts. Add oil, bring to the boil. When it is boiling well, stir. [Mix with the lentils.] Taste; if something is missing, add it. When you have put it in the serving-dish, add best oil.
(5.2.2)

Rose Wine

Rose wine you will make like this: Thread together rose-leaves from which the white part

Figure 6.10 *Mosaic of a servant preparing for a banquet. (Carthage, second–third century* A.D., *Louvre, Paris)*

has been removed, and steep as many as possible in wine for seven days. After seven days take the rose-leaves out of the wine, and in the same way put in other fresh rose-leaves threaded together, to rest seven days in the wine, then take them out. Repeat a third time, take out the rose-leaves, strain the wine, and, when you want to use it for drinking, add honey to make rose wine. But take care to use the best rose-leaves, when the dew has dried off them. . . .
(1.3.1)

the remains of its theater, public baths, and wide streets—but most of the people seem to have been fishermen, artisans, and craftsmen. The ubiquitous commercialism of Pompeii is missing here, although only a very little of the entire site has been excavated. While the thick, hard volcanic covering at Herculaneum has sealed the remains of the town (including victims' skeletons) and protected them from air and climate, it has proved much more difficult to remove than the pumice blanket that buried Pompeii. The forum awaits the jackhammers under tons of solidified debris. The exploration and looting in previous centuries of the still-buried theater and the impressive "Villa of the Papyri" was done through tunneling.

Voices from the Past

The two ancient cities still remain "alive" through the distant voices and thoughts of the people who, fortunately for us, had the habit of expressing themselves in literally hundreds of wall inscriptions and graffiti. Such a surprisingly complete record of Roman life is almost more than we could hope for, and nowhere is the spirited nature of these citizens (Pompeians, in this case) so well displayed as in their election campaigns.

Cicero had once commented that it was easier to get into the Roman Senate than to win a seat on Pompeii's city council. A century later, it appears that little had changed. Everyone, including women and children, became involved in election propaganda, and well over a thousand inscriptions remain from the campaign a few months before the eruption covered Pompeii. Whether this same fierce appetite for politics was typical of other Italian municipalities cannot be known, but these inscriptions tell us much about electioneering in Pompeii. The top officials, the *duoviri* and *aediles,* were elected in March, and apparently, voters felt free to make their choices known publicly. The guilds or corporations in Pompeii were especially anxious to profit from the election of a sympathetic candidate and always took an active role in campaigning:

> The goldsmiths unanimously urge the election of Gaius Cuspius Pansa as aedile. . . .

and

> The muleteers urge the election of Gaius Julius Polybius as duovir.

The fruit dealers, fullers (wool workers), wheelwrights, carpenters, plumbers, taximen, and others also stumped for their choices. Even the worshippers of the goddess Isis had a candidate who was their unanimous pick.

Individuals also kept professional sign painters busy during election time. Their political wisdom, neatly scrawled in red paint (on the sides of whitewashed buildings) with other scribblings, reflects their personal preferences:

> If upright living is considered any recommendation, Lucretius Fronto is well worthy of the office.

and

> Genialis urges the election of Bruttius Balbus as duovir. He will protect the treasury.

Sometimes there was disagreement about the credentials of a particular candidate, and his friends and foes took the battle "to the walls":

> Numerius Barcha, a fine man; I appeal to you to elect him. . . .

and

> Numerius Veius Barcha, may you rot!

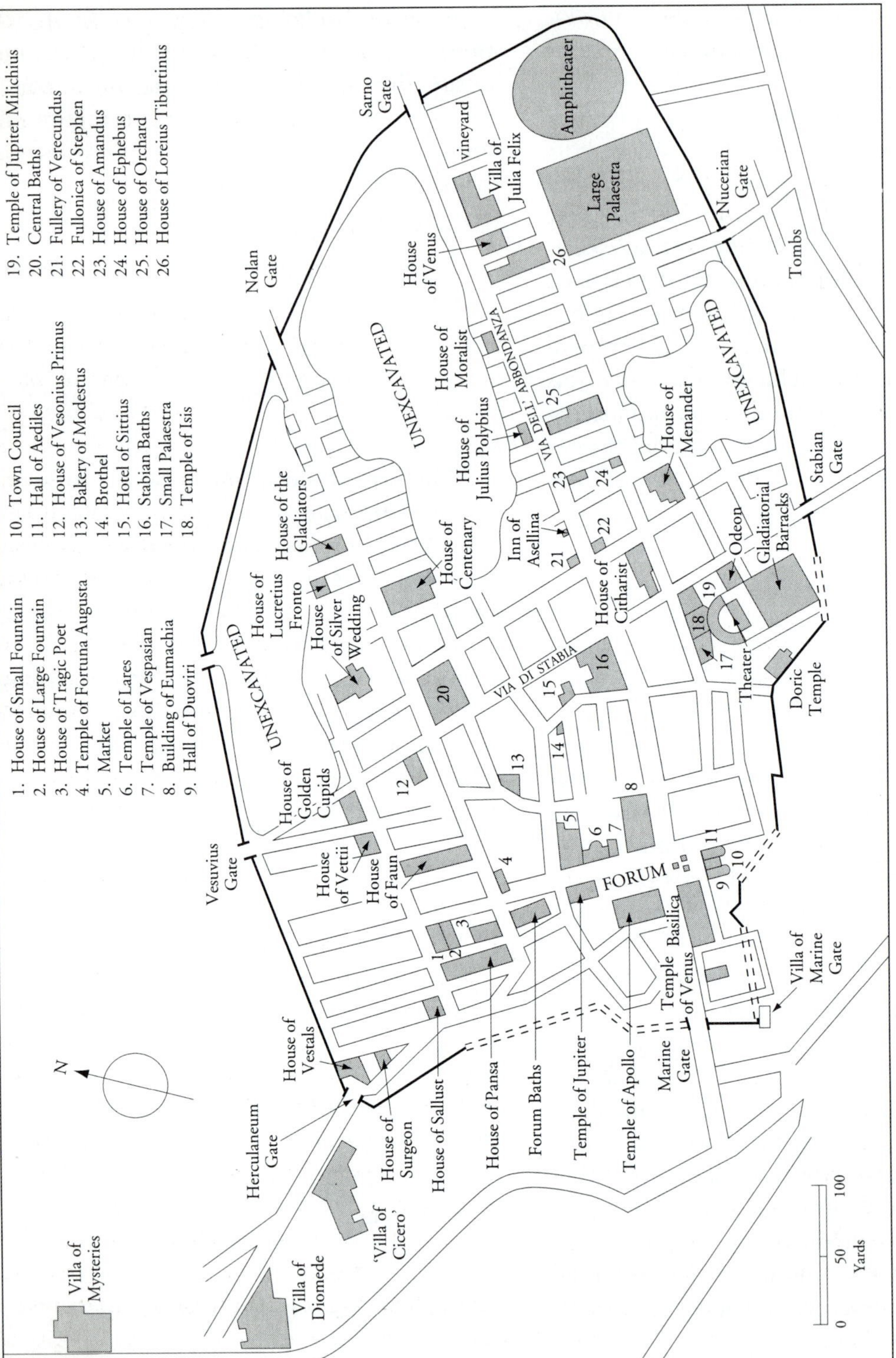
1. House of Small Fountain
2. House of Large Fountain
3. House of Tragic Poet
4. Temple of Fortuna Augusta
5. Market
6. Temple of Lares
7. Temple of Vespasian
8. Building of Eumachia
9. Hall of Duoviri
10. Town Council
11. Hall of Aediles
12. House of Vesonius Primus
13. Bakery of Modestus
14. Brothel
15. Hotel of Sittius
16. Stabian Baths
17. Small Palaestra
18. Temple of Isis
19. Temple of Jupiter Milichius
20. Central Baths
21. Fullery of Verecundus
22. Fullonica of Stephen
23. House of Amandus
24. House of Ephebus
25. House of Orchard
26. House of Loreius Tiburtinus
Villa of Mysteries
Villa of Diomede
'Villa of Cicero'
Herculaneum Gate
House of Surgeon
House of Sallust
House of Pansa
Forum Baths
Temple of Jupiter
Temple of Apollo
Marine Gate
Temple of Venus
Basilica
Villa of Marine Gate
House of Vestals
Vesuvius Gate
House of Vettii
House of Faun
House of Golden Cupids
UNEXCAVATED
FORUM
House of Lucretius Fronto
House of Silver Wedding
House of the Gladiators
House of Centenary
VIA DI STABIA
Nolan Gate
Inn of Asellina
House of Citharist
Theater
Odeon
Gladiatorial Barracks
Doric Temple
Stabian Gate
House of Julius Polybius
VIA DELL' ABBONDANZA
House of Moralist
House of Menander
House of Venus
Villa of Julia Felix
vineyard
Sarno Gate
Large Palaestra
Amphitheater
Nucerian Gate
Tombs
N
0 50 100
Yards

Map 17 Pompeii

In case someone had an idea about vandalizing another's election prose, warnings also accompanied some:

> His neighbors urge you to elect Lucius Statius Receptus duovir with judicial power; he is worthy. Aemilius Celer, a neighbor wrote this. May you take sick if you maliciously erase this!

While women were excluded from running for office, it is clear there were no restrictions placed upon their right to express their political opinions. Caprasia, most likely the proprietor of the wine shop where this inscription appears, left no doubt about where she stood:

> Caprasia along with Nymphius—her neighbors too—ask you to vote for Aulus Vettius Firmus for the aedileship; he is worthy of the office.

Another such electoral notice is sponsored by Statia and Petronia, women who recommend Marcus Casellius and Lucius Alfucius for the aedileship—"May our colony always have such citizens!"

A number of these many inscriptions must be regarded as jokes or jibes by the opposition, for otherwise, their content could hardly have had a positive effect on a candidate's campaign:

> Claudius' little girlfriend is working for his election as duovir.

or

> Vote for Lucius Popidius Sabinus; his grandmother worked hard for his last election and is pleased with the results.

Nor would many have been impressed that Florus, Fructus, and all the other "late drinkers" were supporting Marcus Cerrinius Vatia (unless this were some faddish clique of young pacesetters), especially since the same man appears to have also had the support of the "petty thieves."

Such evidence shows that politics has always been politics. The more cynical did not waste their words on transitory candidates whose promises flew to the winds but voiced their opinion of the process thus:

> I wonder, O wall, that you have not fallen in ruins from supporting the stupidities of so many scribblers.

The everyday life of Pompeii and Herculaneum is also more than adequately recaptured for us on city walls. It was apparently common practice to keep accounts, advertise, leave messages and notices, make bets, list groceries, and post personal comments and observations of all kinds on walls. Of course, if we did not have inexpensive and almost universally available writing materials, the telephone, computers, and other modern aids, we would probably be utilizing our walls more for communication (we still manage more than suits most people's tastes). Some ancient scrawlings were purposely made in public places before witnesses to give the contents a legal status if they concerned a debt, promise, or other matter of potential dispute—a tavern customer's accumulating bar tab, for example.

Although by no means conclusive, an interesting inference that may be drawn from the presence of so many signs and scribblings is that the literacy rate, even in average-size communities such as Pompeii and smaller Herculaneum, seems to have been surprisingly high. Otherwise, there would have been little point to this public and private wall "chatter."

Surviving inscriptions also provide insight into some aspects of first-century A.D. Roman life. The following brief rental advertisement, for example, indicates that real estate owners diversified, that many Romans wished to lease rather than buy, that multistory apartments were common even in smaller communities, and that slaves often handled business deals:

Figure 6.11
A street in Pompeii. Note the stone in front, which served as a crosswalk for pedestrians.

Figure 6.12
A reconstruction of a Roman street and shops. (Museum of London)

Figure 6.13
Ruins of Herculaneum

In the Arrius Pollio block owned by Gnaeus Alleius Nigidius Maius, to let from the fifteenth of next July, shops with their stalls, high-class second-story apartments, a house. Prospective lessees may apply to Primus, slave of Gnaeus Alleius Nigidius Maius.

Pompeii apparently had a very active amphitheater crowd: riots had broken out in 59 A.D. with fans from a neighboring community. Campania was an early center of gladiatorial entertainments, and the amphitheater at Pompeii was a particularly impressive one—our earliest surviving example of this type of facility. Many inscriptions relate to the activities at the arena and to individual gladiators. The following sign by Aemilius Celer, a busy man to judge from his paintbrush (see page 169), is typical and shows the casualness with which the Romans treated this business. The sign painter's postscript (it must have been a hurried job and not his best work) adds a touch of levity to an otherwise standard program:

> Twenty pairs of gladiators of Decimus Lucretius Satrius Valens, lifetime flamen of Nero Caesar, son of Augustus, and ten pairs of gladiators of Decimus Lucretius Valens, his son, will fight at Pompeii on April 8, 9, 10, 11, 12. There will be a full card of wild beast combats, and awnings [for the spectators]. Aemilius Celer [painted this sign], all alone in the moonlight.

Thieves were obviously a major problem then, as now, and a little incentive to bring evil-doers to justice might hasten any recoveries:

> A copper pot is missing from this shop. 65 sesterces reward if anybody brings it back, 20 more if he reveals the thief so we can get our property back.

Elsewhere, a tavern offers, "Pleasure says: 'You can get a drink here for an *as* [a small Roman

Figure 6.14
Bakery of
Modestus, Pompeii

money unit], a better drink for two, Falernian [a better wine] for four.'" A dissatisfied customer curses, "Innkeeper of the devil, die drowned in your own piss-wine!" A prostitute advertises, "I am yours for 2 *asses* cash." A dog mosaic decorates the floor at the entrance to a wealthy man's house. *Cave canem,* it reads: "Beware of the dog!"

The "House of the Moralist" in Pompeii is aptly named, for one has to wonder how many friends the man who had this written in his dining room was able to retain:

> The slave shall wash and dry the feet of the guests; and let him be sure to spread a linen cloth on the cushions of the couches.
>
> Don't cast lustful glances, or make eyes at another man's wife.

> Don't be coarse in your conversation.
>
> Restrain yourself from getting angry or using offensive language. If you can't, go back to your own house.

Perhaps we should not be too hard on the man, for some guests did presume too much upon their hosts. Take, for example, the lodger who left the manager the following message to greet his morning rounds:

> My host, I've wet the bed. My sins I bare.
> But why? you ask. No pot was anywhere.

Bathroom humor such as this seemed to be quite faddish, for in the latrine of the "House of the Gem" at Herculaneum, a rather stylish abode that boasted guests of the highest circles, Apollinaris, the physician of the Emperor

Figure 6.15
Amphitheater, Pompeii

Titus, left a pleasurable—but rather vulgar—remembrance of his few enjoyable minutes there:

> Apollinaris, physician of the Emperor Titus, had a good shit here!

He probably thought he was playing a great joke on his host, but let us hope he did not tarry long over his prose—his inspired graffito was etched within the month of Vesuvius' eruption.

Love, too, finds a place on the walls. Two men wage a war of egos over a girl named Iris:

> The weaver Successus loves the innkeeper's slave girl, Iris by name. She doesn't care for him, but he begs her to take pity on him. Written by his rival. So long.
> [Answer by the rival] Just because you're bursting with envy, don't pick on a handsomer man, a lady-killer and a gallant.
> [Answer by the first writer] There's nothing more to say or write. You love Iris, who doesn't care for you.

Another man has lost his love, and now he blames the love goddess herself:

> Anybody in love, come here. I want to break Venus' ribs with a club and cripple the goddess' loins. If she can pierce my tender breast, why can't I break her head with a club?

A boastful soldier named Floronius, however, does not seem to have any trouble with the ladies—at least that's what he would have us believe:

> Floronius, seconded on special duties, soldier of Legion VII, was here and the women didn't recognize him, all but a few, that is, and they succumbed on the spot.

Sexual graffiti and obscenities are also in evidence everywhere; in fact, representations of the phallus seem to decorate just about everything, from business signs to door lintels to lamp stands. Almost any place one could imagine a phallus, one (or more) is represented.

When Pompeii and Herculaneum were first rediscovered, the common depiction of, or references to, nudity, male sexual organs (some even equipped with wings), couples engaged in intercourse, hermaphrodites, homosexuality, bestiality, and Latin four-letter words offended the Judeo-Christian sensibilities of eighteenth- and nineteenth-century Europe and America. Some people are still put off today, and the impression has led to the common belief that Rome was nothing more than a decadent society, obsessed with sex and lewdness.

However, it must be remembered that Pompeii, in particular, had as its patron deity the love goddess, Venus, who condoned all acts of "love." Many such representations do not depict actual contemporary human sexual activities but portray archetypical—and for moderns, very Freudian—themes. In addition, nudity and fertility were integral parts of the evolution of ancient agricultural societies like the Romans'. A rather puritanical post-Roman Western society is largely responsible for much of the negative assessment that has been drawn from such evidence. Many of the same things can be found to some degree in our own society, although not usually expressed as openly. Nevertheless, one thing can be said for certain—the Romans surely did enjoy their sex. A few examples will suffice:

Fortunatus, you sweet little darling, you great screw, this is written by someone who knows you!

and

I like a girl with a proper mat, not depilated and shorn.
Then you can snuggle in well from the cold, as an overcoat she's worn.

And a sign by a restroom reads:

May I always and everywhere be as potent with women as I was here!

Recent Revelations About the Eruption

It has only been in the 1980s that more precise information about what happened at Pompeii and Herculaneum has been obtained. The study of the eruption of Mt. St. Helens in Washington significantly advanced the science of volcanology, and knowledge gained from that experience has been used to give us a better understanding of the eruption of Mt. Vesuvius. Also of great help was the discovery in the 1980s of the skeletal remains (a rare find for any period in Roman history) of dozens of victims—men, women, children, babies—who died at Herculaneum. This new evidence, considered with Pliny's helpful letters, allowed modern experts for the first time to form a fairly precise reconstruction of the stages of the eruption and also revealed how and when the two cities were destroyed.

Before 79 A.D., Mt. Vesuvius had been quiet for about three hundred years. Since an earthquake had violently rocked the area only seventeen years before, the earthquakes preceding the eruption certainly must have had an unsettling effect on the local population—but the residents of the area obviously had no idea about what was to happen. The earthquakes became continuous; and at about one o'clock on the afternoon of August 24, Vesuvius exploded, sending the column of pumice and ash, which Pliny's mother had noticed, about 12 miles into the sky. No lava accompanied the eruption, but a half hour after it began, windblown debris started raining down on Pompeii. The column continued spewing forth pumice and ash at the rate of almost 6 inches an hour—9 feet over seventeen hours—darkening the sky and making conditions hazardous below (rocks, baseball size and larger, were also flung from the crater). Roofs, sagging under the accumulated weight, began to collapse.

The Case of Petronia Vitalis—Vesuvius Lays Down the Law

THE ERUPTION OF MT. Vesuvius brought an impartial and abrupt end to any court cases pending at the time of the catastrophe. In Herculaneum, one lengthy legal matter still had not been resolved by August 24, 79 A.D. It had begun when a freedwoman named Petronia Vitalis sued her former master, Gaius Petronius Stephanus, over custody of her daughter, Justa. The woman had initially won her suit; but when she died, Calatoria, the widow of the now also deceased Gaius Petronius, sought the girl's return. It seems that her mother had left Justa a wealthy young lady, and Calatoria was scheming to find a legal way to get the girl's money. The various details of the complicated affair have been summarized as follows:

> Eighteen wax tablets sealed by a Roman Court reveal the following facts: shortly before or after the great earthquake, A.D. 62, a baby girl was born in the quarters of Gaius Petronius Stephanus. The child was called Justa. The mother's name was Vitalis; the father's name, if known, was not publicly acknowledged.
>
> Vitalis had been bought as a slave by Gaius Petronius, probably at the time of his wedding as a gift to his new wife. He had married a freedwoman known as Calatoria Temidis—a name evidently derived from the patrician Calatorius family of Herculaneum, to which she herself may have belonged as a slave. Gaius Petronius was a member of the lower middle class, and it was not inappropriate that he should marry a freedwoman.
>
> Nor was it inappropriate that the slave-woman Vitalis in due course should be freed, most probably by purchase of herself. Also it was necessary to pay the state a freedom tax equal to 5 percent of her assumed valuation. Vitalis assumed her master's name, and thenceforth was called Petronia Vitalis. And the girl

> Justa was accepted into the master's household and brought up "like a daughter"—though illegitimate. For a decade and more all were in accord, all harmonious and happy.
>
> But the peace dissolved at the birth of children to Gaius Petronius. Friction arose between his wife Calatoria and the freedwoman Petronia Vitalis. Arguments were unresolved, jealousies sharpened. Petronia Vitalis, as a freedwoman, could no longer be constrained to remain in her master's house; she chose to leave. She wanted a home of her own and economic independence. Apparently she was willing to work hard for what she wanted. But her master and his wife refused to relinquish Justa: a child brought up like a daughter, she was looked upon as their own. Now quite grown-up, she was intelligent and pretty, an asset to the household.
>
> Indignant at being deprived of her daughter, Petronia Vitalis brought suit against Gaius Petronius. After extensive negotiations, the case was settled with the award of Justa to her mother, provided that Gaius Petronius be reimbursed for the cost of Justa's food and upkeeping during the years of her childhood and adolescence. Petronia Vitalis, who had done very well for herself, immediately made the payment and received her daughter into her own home.
>
> This happy state of affairs for Petronia Vitalis and Justa was to be all too short, for Petronia died. And, at about the same time, so did Gaius Petronius. It seemed that this drama of little people in the town of Hercules had been played to the end. Not so. The widow of Gaius Petronius, Calatoria, brought suit to recover Justa and all the property she had inherited from her mother, on the grounds that Justa had been born while Petronia Vitalis was still a slave—hence Justa was a slave.

(continued)

The Case of Petronia Vitalis (continued)

It appears from the depositions that Petronia Vitalis had amassed considerable assets, and Calatoria was more interested in this wealth than in the girl herself. As slaves had no property rights, with the reversion of Justa to slavery all she owned would become the property of her mistress.

Justa fought back.

No substantiating documents existed for either side. Before the enormous growth of slavery in Rome, manumission had been a rather complicated process, always legally recorded. A formal statement of freedom was made before the magistrates, or the new freedman's name was recorded in the censor's register, or the master inserted a clause of emancipation in his will. But when the large majority of the population became slaves, the cumbersome rites were dropped; and a letter, or even a verbal declaration by the master in the presence of witnesses, was considered sufficient. In the freeing of the slave Vitalis, Gaius Petronius had remarked merely that the woman was no longer bound. Though he remained her patron, as was customary, no record was kept of the manumission date. Nor, if she bought herself, did Vitalis have a receipt. Thus the sole proof rested on the word of witnesses who allegedly were present at the time; and witnesses were notoriously easy to buy.

The suit was brought before the local Herculaneum magistrates, who declared that they lacked jurisdiction over the matter. The case therefore was transferred to Rome, before the tribunal of the city judge, or *praetor,* in the Forum of Augustus. Subpoenas were issued, the witnesses took the stand, and all testimony was recorded. A parade of pros and cons followed, with the declarations canceling one another. One of the witnesses against Justa was an illiterate, who claimed to have had the confidence of Gaius Petronius; but his testimony was so garbled that even with professional aid it was impossible to put his statements into grammatical, much less credible, form. His evidence, nevertheless, was admitted. The case bogged down, a morass of confusion.

Suddenly a new witness appeared—an authoritative witness who blew away the swampy miasma and cleared the air. He testified in favor of Justa. He was Telesforus, the administrator-manager-bailiff-foreman who had served Gaius Petronius for many years. He was a freedman, and though he still served Calatoria, he dared to testify against her. Moreover, he had come into Gaius Petronius' house through Calatoria, for in her girlhood he had been her tutor. His declaration was matter-of-fact and precise. He had handled the negotiations for the return of Justa to her mother, he said. It was then acknowledged that Justa had been born after the manumission of her mother. The Roman court, he said, should now make the same acknowledgement.

For all of Justa's pleas, the Roman court was not prepared to reach a rapid decision. The judge wished to take the matter "under advisement," to appraise carefully all the possible angles of the case. No decision would be possible before the end of the next year's court session . . . or the end of the year after that . . . or the year after that. The courts, after all, were so heavily burdened. . . .

The depositions in Rome had begun, as shown by the consuls in office, in the year we designate as 75, and carried over into 76. When Vesuvius erupted and buried the records of the case in 79, apparently a decision had not yet been rendered. We shall never know whether Justa was freed or reduced to slavery.

(adapted from J. Deiss, *Herculaneum: Italy's Buried Treasure* 98–100)

Figure 6.16   *The J. Paul Getty Museum in Malibu, California, is largely a reconstruction of the "Villa of the Papyri" at Herculaneum. It is the closest one can come today to visiting an actual "living" Roman villa.*

For eleven hours little changed; then, close to midnight, the towering column rising from the volcano collapsed. Life at Herculaneum ended almost immediately. Four miles from Vesuvius' mouth, Herculaneum had been jostled by earth tremors, but the winds had spared it the fiery shower that was burying its neighbor. Probably less than a foot of pumice and ash had fallen on Herculaneum's streets. People may have begun to feel that the situation was not as dangerous as it had first appeared. Some probably even decided to stay and sit it out. However, the collapse of the column unleashed a volcanic storm. The first of a number of glowing avalanches—high, superhot (over 212°F) "surge clouds" of gases and debris accompanied by slower but hotter (over 700°F) flows of volcanic matter that hugged the mountain's contours—rushed toward the town at hurricane speeds (60–190 miles per hour).

Within minutes, the searing cloud, laden with ash and fine debris, swept through Herculaneum like a furnace blast, knocking people to the ground and killing them with flying debris or suffocation. The thick pyroclastic flow followed a short time later and began the town's burial, preserving in the process (as did not occur at Pompeii) the remains of many victims and the horrifying evidence of their sudden extinction. If residents had not left during the previous hours, they never left—all who hesitated are still there.

Two additional surges and flows occurred over the next few hours. Herculaneum was buried by 5:30 A.M. Ultimately, it rested 65–100 feet below the new surface. An hour later, the ruptured mountain's fourth surge and flow hit Pompeii and extinguished whatever life remained there. By 8:30 A.M., Pliny and his mother were fleeing Misenum, but across the bay it was already over. The fifth and then the sixth and final convulsion had ended. Pompeii and Herculaneum lay dead beneath tons of volcanic debris. The contemporary poet Martial would later provide a fitting poetic epitaph:

> This is Vesuvius, green yesterday with viny shades; here the noble grape had loaded the dripping vats; these ridges Bacchus loved more than the hills of Nysa; on this mount of late the Satyrs set afoot their dances; this [Pompeii]

"Home Sweet Home"—Pliny Describes His Villa

ALTHOUGH THE REMAINS OF Pompeii, Herculaneum, and Stabiae give us a good idea about what Roman villas looked like (as does the beautiful Getty Museum reconstruction shown in Figure 6.16), there is nothing like a personal contemporary description to help us breathe life back into the empty shells of the once-proud edifices. We may turn once more to Pliny the Younger, who, after surviving the eruption of Mt. Vesuvius, became successful and had a villa of his own (excavated in the 1980s) on the seashore near Rome. Pliny would live only another thirty-four years (d. 113 A.D.) after his experience with Vesuvius, so this description of his villa is contemporary enough to give us a fair idea of what life had been like in some of the villas destroyed in the 79 A.D. catastrophe. It is clear that Pliny is not only proud of his house and its grounds but also of the "harmony" of the place, which makes him feel particularly at home. Especially interesting is his continual reference to how the villa and its rooms relate so purposefully to the daily positions of the sun. Pliny's villa (see Figures 6.17a and b and 6.18) strikes us as sumptous and is surpassed in size only by the grandest modern mansions, but by Roman standards he was not an especially wealthy or powerful man. Consequently, his impressive acreage was probably even within the realm of those whom we term "affluent" today. Pliny's description is not just a floor plan—it contains so many other details of interest about Roman personal life that we cite that entire passage here (*Letters* 2.17):

> You are surprised that I am so fond of my Laurentine villa—but you will cease to be surprised once you know about its charm, the convenience of its location, and the extent of its ocean frontage. It is only seventeen miles from Rome, and therefore you can carry out a full day of business in the city, and still be here before sunset. And it is accessible by more than one road because both the Laurentine and Ostian highways come this way, although you must turn off the Laurentine highway at milestone 14, and off the Ostian highway at milestone 11. From either direction, each access road has a sandy stretch part of the way, and is therefore a little difficult and slow for a team pulling a carriage, but fast and easy on horseback. The scenery varies from one spot to the next; sometimes the road narrows, with forests on both sides, sometimes it opens up and widens through very broad meadows where many flocks of sheep and many herds of horses and cattle, which have been driven down from their mountain pastures by the winter, grow fat on the grass and the warmth of spring.

was the haunt of Venus, more pleasant to her than Lacedaemon; this spot [Herculaneum] was made glorious by the name of Hercules. All lies drowned in fire and melancholy ash; even the High Gods could have wished this had not been permitted them.
(*Epigrams* 4.44)

Not long before the eruption, a troubled lover had unknowingly inscribed on a Pompei-ian wall a poem that seems almost prophetic in hindsight:

Nothing can last in unending time.
When the sun has shone brightly, it returns to
   the sea;
The moon wanes which just now was full.
So the savagery of love's passions often ends
   up as a gentle breeze.

The villa is roomy enough for my needs, and its maintenance is not expensive. At the front of the villa is an atrium [reception area] which is modest but not shabby. Then there are two porticoes, both of which curve round to produce a shape similar to the letter *D* and which together enclose a small but pleasant courtyard. These porticoes create a splendid retreat from stormy weather, because their walkways are protected by windows [the Romans used glass or sheets of mica, or even wooden shutters in less expensive dwellings such as apartments] and, even better, by the overhang of the roof.

Facing the middle of this area is an inner courtyard and then a rather pretty dining room which fronts on the sea and is gently washed by a few weak waves, remnants of a storm far from shore where the southeast wind has ruffled the sea. This room has folding doors or windows as large as doors on every side, and therefore provides, from the sides and from the front, three views of the sea. From the front of the room, you can turn and look back at the inner court-yard, the portico, the little courtyard, the other portico, then the atrium, the forests beyond, and even the distant mountains.

To the left of the dining room, but set back somewhat from the sea, is a large cubiculum [a *cubiculum,* often rendered as "bedroom," can refer (usually with a defining word) to a room of any description], and then, beside it, an-other smaller one with two windows, one to catch the rays of the rising sun, the other the rays of the setting sun. This second window looks over the sea, but from a distance, and therefore offers a nice but not dramatic view. The angular area formed by the projection of the dining room beyond the cubiculum traps and intensifies the brightest light. This area serves as a winter sunning place and also as an exercise enclosure for my household. No winds blow here except those which bring the rain clouds with them, and after the weather has passed, it can still be used.

Connected to this area of the villa is a cu-biculum whose wall is curved like an apse; be-cause of all its windows, it is able to trace the daily movement of the sun. Built into the wall of this room is a cupboard, or bookcase, which contains books which should be not just read but studied. A heating corridor connects this room with a bedroom. The heating corridor has a hollow floor and hollow walls; from the floor and the walls it receives air warmed to a healthy temperature, and then distributes and supplies this air in all directions.

(continued)

"Home Sweet Home" (continued)

Figure 6.17a
A model of Pliny's villa (some of the roofing has been left open to allow an inside view of the rooms). Based entirely on Pliny's description, subsequent excavations in the 1980s have revealed some differences between it and the actual site.

The remaining rooms on this side of the villa are reserved for the use of slaves and freedmen, although most of them are elegant enough to accommodate guests.

On the other side of the villa is a very elegant cubiculum; then there is a room—either a large cubiculum or an unpretentious banquet room—which is brightened by a great deal of sunlight and a very extensive sea view. Behind this room is a cubiculum, with an antechamber, which is suitable both for summer use, because of its high ceiling, and for winter use, because it is protected and sheltered from all the winds. Another antechamber and cubiculum are connected to this one by a common wall.

Next comes the broad and spacious cold room of the baths. It contains two bathing tubs which project outward, from opposite walls, with curved rims; they are quite large, especially considering how close the sea is. Nearby are the room for applying bath oil, the furnace

room, a corridor, and then two small rooms which are more tasteful than sumptuous. Adjacent to these is a marvelous warm pool from which swimmers look out over the sea. Not far away is the ball court which receives the very warm afternoon sun.

At this point there rises up a tower. On its ground floor are two rooms, and, in the tower itself, there are another two rooms as well as a banquet room which looks out over the very broad expanse of the sea, the very long stretch of coastline, and the very delightful villas of my neighbors. There is, moreover, a second tower with a cubiculum which is lit by both the rising and the setting sun. Behind this are situated a wine storeroom and a grain storage room. Beneath this room is a dining room in which you can hear only a faint and subdued echo of the crash and roar of a stormy sea.

This dining room looks out over a garden and promenade. The promenade, which encir-

Figure 6.17b   Another view of Pliny's villa. (Ashmolean Museum, Oxford)

cles the garden, has a border of evergreen shrubs, or rosemary where there are no evergreen shrubs, since the shrubs flourish in places sheltered by buildings, but wither under an open sky, an open wind, and the spray of the sea, however far away. Adjacent to the promenade, and within the garden area it encloses, is a small, shady vineyard, whose soil is spongy and soft even to bare feet. Mulberry and fig trees grow luxuriantly in the garden because the soil is especially suitable for these two, although rather unsuitable for other types of trees. There is a dining area here which is, of course, some distance from the sea, but which enjoys a view of the garden that is not at all inferior to a view of the sea. Bordering the rear of the dining area are two small apartments whose windows overlook the vestibulum [small entrance hall or lobby] of the villa and another garden, a lush herb garden.

From this point there extends a cryptoporticus [covered walkway] which is almost as long as a cryptoporticus of a public building. It has windows on both sides, although more of them on the side facing the sea; on the garden side there is only one window for every two in the opposite wall. When the sky is clear and the air still, all these windows are left open; but when a breeze is flowing from either direction, only those windows on the side where the wind is not flowing can be kept open without danger.

In front of the cryptoporticus is a terrace fragrant with violets; the warmth of this terrace area is increased by the reflection of the sun pouring down on the cryptoporticus, which checks and wards off the north wind at the same time as it absorbs the sun's warmth; it is therefore as warm in front of the cryptoporticus as it is cool in the back. It offers a similar barrier to the southwest wind, and breaks the force of or brings to a standstill winds from any direction. This is the special attraction of this part of the villa in winter, an attraction even greater in the summer; before noon the shade from the cryptoporticus keeps the terrace cool; after noon, it keeps cool the nearest part of the promenade and garden. As the days grow longer or shorter, the cryptoporticus casts a shorter or longer shadow in one place or the other. But the cryptoporticus itself is least sunny when the sun burns brightest and stands

(continued)

"Home Sweet Home" (continued)

directly over its roof. In addition, when the windows are open, westerly winds enter and circulate through, and the air of the cryptoporticus never seems heavy, stale, or stagnant.

At the end of the terrace and the cryptoporticus is a garden apartment, my real favorite; I had it constructed myself. It contains a sun room, one side of which looks over the terrace; another side looks over the sea, and both sides receive sunlight. In this apartment is a cubiculum which has a view of the cryptoporticus from its folding doors, and a view of the sea from its window. Across from the center wall is a very elegant recessed alcove which can be connected or separated from the cubiculum by opening or closing the curtains and glass doors. It contains a couch and two chairs. Below is the sea, behind are villas, in front is the forest. From its three windows you can see these three views either separately or in one sweeping panorama.

Adjacent to this alcove is a bedroom for sleeping or taking naps. Neither the voices of young slaves, nor the murmur of the sea, nor the gusty winds of storms, nor the flash of lightning, nor even the daylight penetrate this room unless the windows are open. The explanation for this deep and very secluded peacefulness is as follows: a corridor lies between and separates the wall of the bedroom and the wall of the garden, and this intervening empty space absorbs every sound. Attached to the bedroom is a heating or furnace room which, by means of a small glass window, gives off or retains, as the situation demands, the heat radiating from its hollow floor. Next a small room with an antechamber stretches out toward the sun; it holds until the afternoon the warm rays of the rising sun, which it catches at an angle. When I retire to this apartment, I feel far away even from my own villa; and I take particular pleasure in it during the Saturnalia [a festive, yearly celebration of the god Saturn on December 17] when the other parts of the house resound with the merry making and holi- day cheer of this season; for here I don't disturb the festivities of my household, and they don't disturb my studies.

Running water is the one thing missing amid all these amenities and charms, but there are wells—or rather springs, for the water flows up to the surface. And this part of the coastline is quite remarkable in nature; wherever you dig you hit water, ready to gush up. And the water is pure and not even a little brackish despite its proximity to the sea. The neighboring forests offer an abundant supply of wood. And the town of Ostia [the port of Rome] stocks all other necessities. Indeed even the nearby village, which is separated from my villa by just one villa, has resources adequate for the moderate man. It has three public baths, which are very handy if by chance a sudden arrival or a rather brief stay make it inconvenient to heat up the baths at the villa.

The roofs of other villas, some clustered together, some rather isolated, decorate the shoreline with a very pleasing diversity and create an impression of a series of cities, whether you view them from the sea or from the shore. Sometimes a long period of fair weather makes the beach dry and soft, but, more often, frequent and pounding waves make it wet and hard. The sea does not, it is true, abound in expensive types of fish, yet it does supply sole and excellent lobsters or prawns. And agricultural products are also abundant along the coast, milk in particular, because cattle gather here from their pastures whenever they want water or shade.

Don't you agree, then, that I have good reason to visit, live in, and love my country retreat? You are too much a "city slicker" if you do not yearn for it. I wish you did! I could then add the very great pleasure of your company to the many fine attractions of my little villa.

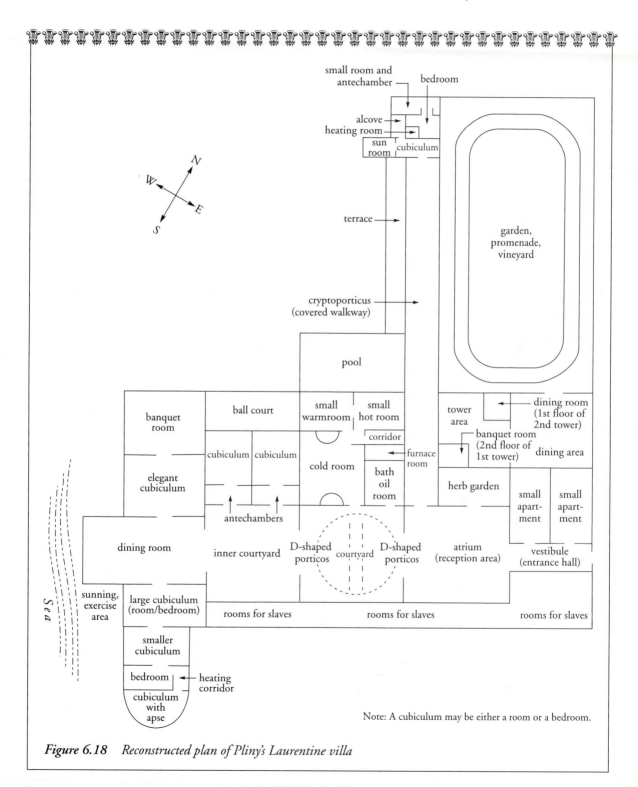

Figure 6.18 *Reconstructed plan of Pliny's Laurentine villa*

Suggestions for Further Reading

Books on Pompeii and Herculaneum abound. Most, however, were printed before the 1980s and do not include recent important revelations. Two of the best starting places, therefore, are R. Gore, "The Dead Do Tell Tales at Vesuvius," *National Geographic* 165, No. 5 (May 1984): 557–613; and J. J. Deiss, *Herculaneum: Italy's Buried Treasure,* rev. ed. (New York: Harper & Row, 1985). M. Grant's well-illustrated survey, *Cities of Vesuvius: Pompeii and Herculaneum* (New York: Macmillan, 1971), remains a useful introduction. He also includes more recent information about Pompeii and Herculaneum in his *The Visible Past: Recent Archaeological Discoveries of Greek and Roman History* (New York: Scribner, 1990). *Pompeii A.D. 79* (Boston: Macmillan, 1978), a well-crafted volume published in conjunction with the Pompeii exhibition that toured in the late 1970s, is also of value. R. Laurence's *Roman Pompeii: Space and Society* (New York: Routledge, 1994) complements Q. M. Jongman's *The Economy and Society of Pompeii* (Amsterdam: J. C. Gieban, and Philadelphia: John Benjamins, 1988), and L. Richardson's *Pompeii: An Architectural History* (Baltimore: The Johns Hopkins University Press, 1988). T. Kraus and L. von Matt, *Pompeii and Herculaneum: The Living Cities of the Dead* (New York: Harry N. Abrams, 1975); A. De Franciscis, *The Buried Cities: Pompeii and Herculaneum* (London: Orbis, 1978); and W. E. Jashemski, *The Gardens of Pompeii, Herculaneum and the Villas Destroyed by Vesuvius* (New Rochelle, N.Y.: Caratzas, 1979; now with Vol. 2) are among other better publications. An entertaining, but still instructive, approach to life in the two cities can be found in J. Lindsay's *The Writing on the Wall* (London: Frederick Muller, 1960). The National Geographic Society has also published *The Adventure of Archaeology* (1985) and *People and Places of the Past* (1983), which contain small sections on the topic. Of related interest is E. Gowers' *The Loaded Table: Representations of Food in Roman Literature* (New York: Oxford University Press, 1993). Numerous guidebooks and pamphlets may be obtained by visiting (or writing to) the actual sites. The Getty Museum in Malibu, California, has available a small booklet entitled *Herculaneum to Malibu* for those who wish more information about this fascinating re-creation of the Villa of the Papyri. Pliny the Younger is, of course, our main ancient source for the eruption, although Dio also included information about it in his *Roman History* (66.22. 4–23.5). Most inscriptions cited in this chapter can be found translated in Lewis and Reinhold, *Roman Civilization,* Vol. 2, and Shelton, *As the Romans Did,* both cited in Chapter 1. Inscriptional material is catalogued primarily in *Corpus Inscriptionum Latinarum* (4, 10) and *Inscriptiones Latinae Selectae.*

Recent Additions

A. Wallace-Hadrill, *Houses and Society in Pompeii and Herculaneum* (Princeton, N.J.: Princeton University Press, 1994); and P. Zanker, *Pompeii: Public and Private Life* (Cambridge, Mass.: Harvard University Press, 1998).

Recent General Additions

A. Dalby and S. Grainger, *The Classical Cookbook* (New York: Oxford University Press, 1996); A. G. McKay, *Houses, Villas, and Palaces in the Roman World* (Baltimore: The Johns Hopkins University Press, 1998); J. T. Smith, *Roman Villas: A Study in Social Structure* (New York: Routledge, 1998); P. Garnsey, *Food and Society in Classical Antiquity* (Cambridge: Cambridge University Press, 1999); and B. Levick, *Vespasian* (New York: Routledge, 1999).

7

The Golden Age
of Empire

Growing Old in the Second Century A.D.
Spurinna, an Aged Roman

*It is our duty to give up our youth and manhood
to our country, but our last years are our own.*
(Pliny the Younger, *Letters* 4.23)

"If a man were called to fix the period in the history of the world during which the condition of the human race was most happy and prosperous," wrote Edward Gibbon in his *Decline and Fall of the Roman Empire* in 1776, "he would without hesitation name that which elapsed from the death of Domitian to the accession of Commodus." Such hyperbole in a historian of Gibbon's stature might be surprising, but from his perch atop the eighteenth-century Enlightenment, what had transpired within the eighty-four-year period from 96 to 180 A.D. seemed to him an ideal mixture of power and virtue, wisdom and strength, a "Golden Age" that had no equal before or since:

> The vast extent of the Roman empire was governed by absolute power under the guidance of virtue and wisdom. The armies were restrained by the firm but gentle hand of four successive emperors, whose characters and authority commanded involuntary respect. The forms of the civil administration were carefully preserved by Nerva, Trajan, Hadrian, and the Antonines, who delighted in the image of liberty and were pleased with considering themselves as the accountable ministers of the laws. . . . The labors of these monarchs were overpaid by the immense reward that inseparably waited on their success, by the honest pride of virtue, and by the exquisite delight of beholding the general happiness of which they were the authors. (1.78)

Gibbon's glowing appraisal of this period is, of course, naively overenthusiastic, for it was not an epoch without its problems; but through

Figure 7.1 During the "Golden Age," the Roman army, too, reached its height of proficiency. Under Trajan (98–117 A.D.), there were 30 legions, numbering about 160,000 men, and a total of about 400,000 men under arms. Pictured above is a reconstruction of a Roman legionary as he would have appeared in the latter half of the first century A.D.

jan (98–117 A.D.) and Hadrian (117–138 A.D.), was perpetuated by Antoninus Pius (138–161 A.D.), and gradually began to unravel under the latter's highly able but much overwrought successor, Marcus Aurelius (161–180 A.D.).

The beginning of this Golden Age coincided with the "golden years" of an old and distinguished Roman aristocrat named Titus Vestricius Spurinna, one of the Empire's most venerable and admired senior citizens. He died in his late seventies in 105 A.D. To the end, Spurinna remained an active and contributing member of Roman society, and he provides a revealing and rare insight into the lifestyle and habits of an upper-class elderly Roman gentleman.

Growing Old in Rome

While it is popularly believed that not many people in antiquity lived to an old age, there is ample evidence to demonstrate otherwise. Four of the five emperors mentioned above lived past 60, considered the threshold of old age in Ancient Rome. One of the four, Antoninus Pius, lived into his 70s. Augustus died at 75, while his wife, Livia, lived to be 86 (Scribonia, Augustus' first wife, also must have been at least in her 70s). Livia's son Tiberius was 77 when he expired, and Claudius was poisoned when he was 63. His mother, Antonia, also lived into her 60s. Seneca was probably over 65 when he committed suicide; Cicero had reached 63 before he was put to death. That was nothing compared to his first wife, Terentia, who lived to extreme old age—reputedly 103. Marius, the man who held more consulships than anyone else during the Republic, died at 70. Cato the Elder was 84.

This is only a small list of famous Romans who lived past sixty. A review of literary and inscriptional remains will produce hundreds more. Admittedly, this is a small number of individu-

much of its existence, this was a prosperous era, at times perhaps even deserving the designation "Golden Age." When Titus died unexpectedly in 81 A.D. and his brother Domitian was assassinated fifteen years later, the Flavian Dynasty ended. Rome then *was* ruled by several capable men, some with outstanding ability. The new age began tenuously with the brief and hectic reign of the elderly Nerva (96–98 A.D.), who was pushed to the front in the chaotic aftermath of Domitian's death. It reached maturity with Tra-

Figure 7.2
Busts (left to right)
of the Emperors Titus
(79–81 A.D.), Domitian
(81–96 A.D.), and
Trajan (98–117 A.D.)

als for a thousand-year period, but our resources are so meager that we know only a fraction of 1 percent of the population by name during these ten centuries. It is reasonable to suggest that if so many prominent Romans lived past sixty—and a good many of them did not die from old age—then there must have been countless other men and women about whom we know nothing who also reached advanced age. That number would obviously have been much smaller, proportionally, than it is today.

While we do not know how many people lived past sixty, we do have some idea of how long Romans thought a person could possibly live. The most revealing indication is provided by the interval of years between Secular Games at Rome. These games—a combination of thanksgiving to the gods and prayers that Rome and its people would continue to enjoy divine favor—marked the passing of a 110-year period, or *saeculum,*

considered the fullest extent of a human life. Secular Games had come to represent the end of one era and the beginning of a new one. The priests in charge needed (for total purification) to make sure that anyone who had witnessed the previous games would not be alive at the next. Hence, when heralds "travelled throughout Rome and Italy," they could rightfully summon "all the people to come and attend games the likes of which they had never seen before and would not see again" (Herodian, *History* 3.8.10).

Practices such as child exposure and slavery, continual warfare, plagues, and generally poor living conditions contributed to a lower median age for Romans than might be indicated by the examples given above. Nevertheless, about one-fifth of the population in the Late Roman Empire survived to age fifty-five, a remarkable statistic since Western life spans did not increase significantly until the eighteenth century.

Figure 7.3 *The Stoic philosopher Chrysippus of Soli (c. 280–207 B.C), a favorite among Romans, shown in old age*

Roman Views about Aging

More revealing than any statistic is what the Romans themselves thought about the prospects of living to an advanced age. Cicero's well-known and uplifting philosophical treatise *On Old Age (De Senectute),* while overenthusiastic, at least provides a convenient starting place. Cicero was sixty-two and in good health when he composed the essay—a sort of therapy as he prepared for his own advancing years. The mouthpiece through which Cicero chose to express his views, Cato the Elder, is of great interest because he was a man who had already lived the kind of old age Cicero envisioned for himself. Cato was one of the most remarkable fig-

ures from the great days of the Republic. He had been a successful military commander and a senator, and he had held the highest offices Rome had to offer. Moreover, he had remained active and productive—not only in politics but also in literature and farming—until his death at eighty-four in 149 B.C. Cicero hoped that Cato's example would "lighten the burden impending or at any rate advancing on us," because, as he imagined it, Cato's old age had brought nothing but wisdom, patience, veneration, influence, and satisfaction.

Cicero's idealization of old age was undoubtedly a comfort for many, and it did have a definite impact on contemporary views about aging. The Roman attitude about retirement and growing old—at least among the upper class—generally appears to have been positive. However, it is also clear that tracts like Cicero's could not hide the negative aspects of growing old for rich and poor alike. That side of the issue was often left to the pens of satirists such as Lucian (who lived in the Eastern Roman Empire in the second century A.D.) and Juvenal.

In a satire entitled "A Voyage to the Underworld" (5–6), Lucian, through his characters Clotho, the Fate who spun the threads of life, Hermes (Mercury among the Romans), the god who escorted the souls of the dead to the Underworld, and Charon, the Ferryman, probably reflected more accurately how cynically most people viewed the elderly. Hermes has recently arrived in the Underworld with an assortment of souls and is helping Clotho and Charon sort them out for transportation across the River Styx:

HERMES: Clotho, do you want the unlamented next?

CLOTHO: The unlamented? Oh, you mean the aged. Yes. After all, why should I bother asking questions about a lot of ancient history? Every-

Figure 7.4   A mosaic of an aging playwright (or actor) sitting with his troupe

body over sixty, on board! What's the matter? They're so old they're deaf and don't hear me. You'll probably have to carry them aboard too.

HERMES: Here you are. Three hundred and ninety-eight, all soft and juicy and picked at a ripe old age.

CHARON: No, sir, they're a bunch of dried-up raisins.

Juvenal, also writing in the second century A.D., provides a much fuller negative assessment of the elderly in this extended passage:

"Grant us a long life, Jupiter, O grant us many years!"

In the bloom of youth it's this which, pale with anxiety,
You pray for, and this alone. Yet how grisly, how unrelenting
Are longevity's ills! Look first at your face, you'll see an ugly
And shapeless caricature of its former self: your skin
Has become a scaly hide, you're all chapfallen, the wrinkles
Scored down your cheeks now make you resemble nothing so much
As some elderly female baboon in darkest Africa.
Young men are all individuals: A will have better looks

Or brains than B, while B will beat A on muscle;
But old men all look alike, all share the same bald
    pate,
Their noses all drip like an infant's, their voices
    tremble
As much as their limbs, they mumble their bread
    with toothless
Gums. It's a wretched life for them, they become
    a burden
To their wives, their children, themselves, so
    loathsome a sight
That it turns the stomach of even the toughest
    legacy-hunter.
Their taste-buds are just about useless, they get
    little pleasure
From food or wine, it's years since they had any
    sex—
Or if they try, it's hopeless: though they labor all
    night long
At that limp and shriveled object, limp it
    remains.
What can the future hold for these impotent
    dodderers?
Nothing very exciting. Sex is a pretty dead loss—
The old tag's true—when desire outruns
    performance.
      Other senses deteriorate: take hearing, for
    instance.
How can the deaf appreciate music? The standard
Of the performance eludes them: a top-line soloist,
Massed choirs in their golden robes, all mean less
    than nothing.
What does it matter to *them* where they sit in the
    concert-hall
When a brass band blowing its guts out is barely
    audible?
The slave who announces the time, or a visitor,
    must bawl
At the top of his lungs before they take in the
    message.
The blood runs thin with age, too: now nothing
    but fever
Can warm that frigid hulk, while diseases
    of every type

Assault it by battalions. . . . One has an
    arthritic hip, another sciatica,
Lumbago plagues a third, while the totally
    sightless
Envy the one-eyed. Here's a fellow whose jaws
    would open
Wide, once long ago, at the prospect of dinner—
    but now
Those leaden lips must mumble the tidbits another
    hand
Feeds to him; when he gapes today, he's like a baby
Swallow that sees its mother approaching, her
    beak
Well-crammed with grubs. But worse than all
    bodily ills
Is the senescent mind. Men forget what their own
    servants
Are called, they can't recognize yesterday's host at
    dinner,
Or, finally, the children they begot and
    brought up. A heartless
Codicil to the will disinherits their flesh and blood,
And the whole estate is entailed to some whore,
    whose expert mouth
—After years in that narrow archway—earns
    her a rich reward.
If he keeps his wits intact, though, a further
    ordeal awaits
The old man: he'll have to bury his sons, he'll
    witness
His dear wife's end, and his brother's, he'll see the
    urns
Filled with his sisters' ashes. Such are the
    penalties
If you live to a ripe old age—perpetual grief,
Black mourning, a world of sorrow, ever-
    recurrent
Family bereavements to haunt your declining
    years.
(*Satire* 10.188–247)

Two points of view on aging during Roman
times: Cicero's and those of Juvenal and Lucian.
Certainly, everybody wished for the former to be

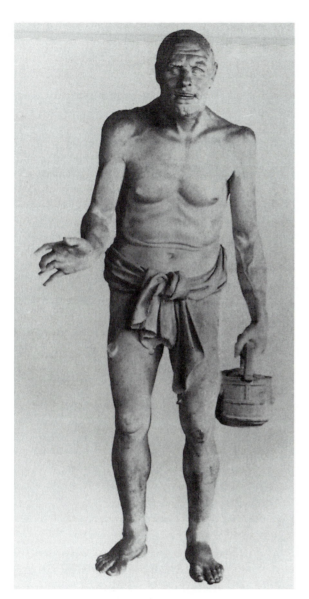

Figure 7.5 *An old fisherman with his basket of fish*

process, but along with it, one must also have the health, the substance, the companionship, the respect, and the activity that continue to make life worth living. These things were often not within the reach of the elderly in antiquity, and they had to make it through old age as well as they could.

The "Productive" Elderly at Rome

Judging from the arduous tasks they were asked to perform, it would appear that, on average, the elderly at Rome were more active and in better condition than many senior citizens are today. Just the rigors of living to old age were one reason, but perhaps just as important were more positive societal attitudes about what healthy people over sixty were capable of doing. Until very recently, modern society felt almost compelled to intervene and complicate the aging process. As people grew older, they were made to feel more obsolete, although in fact they may not have been. Even before reaching what was generally considered "old age," they had been given the impression that they were losing ground, were not as effective, that age equaled loss of productiveness. The emphasis was on youth, and there was an almost built-in obligation that the old should step aside to make room for the young—in the workplace and elsewhere. Much of this stigma still remains.

There were some societal pressures on the aged at Rome, too, but they were hardly the equivalent of today's—and they usually applied only to a small segment of society. During the Empire, for instance, Roman law exempted an upper-class gentleman of sixty from most responsibilities to the state. This did not mean that one *had* to retire at this age, but Pliny the Younger indicates it was considered unseemly if a person continued to actively pursue a full-time career:

right but, realistically, most probably found the latter to be closer representations of what old age was actually like. A positive philosophical outlook such as Cicero's certainly eases the aging

Verginius Rufus Suffers a Fall

OF THE VARIOUS PROBLEMS accompanying old age, those related to physical health are certainly the most debilitating. The body begins to deteriorate, coordination suffers, reflexes are slowed, bones can become brittle. Some aged individuals are able to avoid serious physical catastrophe; others are not so lucky, and the difficulties of aging bring misery to them and those around them. Verginius Rufus, a celebrated Roman aristocrat who had once been offered the throne, suffered a minor fall when he was eighty-three and in otherwise good health. It is particularly tragic that an accident so minor made the end of Verginius' life so miserable. In 97 A.D., during Nerva's reign, Pliny the Younger praised the great old man, his personal friend, and described the final painful days:

> It is some years since Rome has had such a splendid sight to remember as the public funeral of Verginius Rufus, one of our greatest and most distinguished citizens whom we can also count a fortunate one. For thirty years after his hour of glory he lived on to read about himself in history and verse, so that he was a living witness of his fame to come. He was three times consul, and thus attained the highest distinction short of the imperial power itself; for

this he had refused. His virtues had been suspected and resented by certain of the Emperors, but he had escaped arrest and lived to see a truly good and friendly ruler safely established; so that he might have been spared for the honor of a public funeral we have just seen. He had reached the age of eighty-three, living in close retirement and deeply respected by us all, and his health was good, apart from a trembling of the hands, not enough to trouble him. Only death when it came was slow and painful, though we can only admire the way he faced it. He was rehearsing the delivery of his address of thanks to the Emperor for his election to his third consulship, when he had occasion to take up a heavy book, the weight of which made it fall out of his hands, as he was an old man and standing at the time. He bent down to pick it up, and lost his footing on the slippery polished floor, so that he fell and fractured his thigh. This was badly set, and because of his age it never mended properly. . . . He died too when full of years and rich in honors, even those which he refused; and it is left to us to seek him and feel his loss as a figure from a past age.
> (*Letters* 2.1)

A well-ordered life, especially where the old are concerned, gives me the same pleasure as the fixed course of the planets. A certain amount of irregularity and excitement is not unsuitable for the young, but their elders should lead a quiet and orderly existence; their time of public activity is over, and ambition only brings them into disrepute.
(*Letters* 3.1)

There were other limited restrictions (such as Tiberius' edict that no one over sixty should

reproduce), but generally, age guidelines in antiquity were designed to free individuals from obligatory or expected service—not to force them out of a job or proclaim their uselessness. Ancient Rome was, of course, not an industrialized society. The majority of people were farmers, and there was no organized work force as we understand it. Many jobs were done by slaves. Old people were not forced to step aside for the young because the young were not as numerous as they are today; skilled labor con-

Ummidia Quadratilla—An Excessive Grandmother's Affection

UMMIDIA QUADRATILLA WAS NOT what some might call the typical grandmother. She engaged in activities that were not considered appropriate for a woman of her advanced age and standing—mostly, it appears, because of boredom. However, while she had chosen to pursue her questionable life-style and accept public criticism for it, she did not want her grandson, who lived with her, to follow in her footsteps. She was particularly careful not to expose him to her excesses. For this, she earned the praise of Pliny the Younger, a friend of the young Quadratus, when she finally died:

> Ummidia Quadratilla is dead, having almost attained the age of seventy-nine and kept her powers unimpaired up to her last illness, along with a sound constitution and sturdy physique which are rare in a woman. She died leaving an excellent will; her grandson inherits two-thirds of the estate, and her granddaughter the remaining third. I scarcely know the latter, but the grandson is a close friend of mine. He is a remarkable young man who inspires a sort of family affection amongst people in no way related to him. In the first place, though conspicuous for his good looks, he spent his youth and early manhood untouched by scandal; then he married before he was twenty-four and would have been a father had his prayers been granted. He lived in his grandmother's house, but managed to combine personal austerity with deference to her sybaritic tastes. She kept a troupe of mimic actors whom she treated with an indulgence unsuitable in a lady of her high position, but Quadratus never watched their performances either in the theater or at home, nor did she insist on it. Once when she was asking me to supervise her grandson's education she told me that as a woman, with all a woman's idle hours to fill, she was in the habit of amusing herself playing draughts or watching her mimes, but before she did either she always told Quadratus to go away and work: which, I thought, showed her respect for his youth as much as her affection.

> This incident will surprise you as it did me. The last Sacerdotal Games were opened by a performance of mime, and as we left the theater together Quadratus said to me: "Do you realize that today was the first time I have seen any of my grandmother's dancers?" So said her grandson; but meanwhile people who were nothing to Quadratilla were running to the theater to pay their respects to her—though "respect" is hardly the word to use for their fawning attentions—jumping up and clapping to show their admiration, and then copying every gesture of their mistress with snatches of song. Today there is only a tiny bequest as a gratuity for their hired applause, which they will receive from the heir who never watched them perform. . . . It is a joy to witness the family affection shown by the deceased and the honor due to an excellent young man.
> (*Letters* 7.24)

tinued to be exploited as long as possible. Only the wealthy could think about retirement, and most people worked until they dropped. Jobs were more important than efficiency of production. A case in point is the Emperor Vespasian's reply to an engineer who informed him that he had a machine that could do the work assigned to a force of manual laborers. Vespasian replied that the job might get done faster with the machine, but then all the men employed on the project would be out of work (Suetonius, *Vespasian* 18.1).

Old Domitius Gets the "Last Laugh"

IN HIS OLD AGE, Domitius Tullus had engaged in many unsavory practices and, encouraged by legacy hunters, apparently had no regard for his family while he lived. His wife, widowed and with children of her own, had married him when he was already a crippled old man. She had been criticized for taking an elderly—and rich—invalid for a husband, but she dedicated herself to his care and turned that criticism into praise. Domitius left a will that was totally uncharacteristic of his life. He rewarded his wife amply and remembered favorably other members of his family. Since he disappointed the legacy hunters and gossip-mongers of Rome, they branded him a hypocrite and whined about his fickleness and ingratitude. Pliny the Younger praised the old man for turning the tables on all the sycophants and flatterers who expected to benefit by his demise and for finally behaving in a decent manner toward his family—albeit at his death:

> There is certainly no truth in the popular belief that a man's will is a mirror of his character, for Domitius Tullus has proved himself to be much better in death than life. Although he had encouraged legacy hunters, he left as heiress the daughter he shared with his brother (he had adopted his brother's child). He also left a great many welcome legacies to his grandsons and to his great-granddaughter; in fact the whole will is ample proof of his affections for his family, and so all the more unexpected.
>
> Consequently the city is full of conflicting opinions; some accuse him of hypocrisy, ingratitude and fickleness, and in attacking him betray themselves by their own disgraceful admissions, for they complain about a man who was a father, grandfather, and great-grandfather

as if he were childless. Others applaud him for the very reason that he has disappointed the shameless expectations of men whose frustration in this way accords with the spirit of the times. They also say that Tullus was not free to leave any other will, for he did not bequeath his wealth to his daughter so much as restore what he had acquired through her. . . .

> So this will is all the more creditable for being dictated by family affection, honesty, and feelings of shame; and in it Tullus acknowledges his obligations to all his relatives in return for their services to him, as he does to the excellent wife who had borne with him so long. She has inherited his beautiful country houses and a large sum of money, and deserved all the more from her husband for having been so severely criticized for marrying him. It was thought most unsuitable that a woman of her high birth and blameless character, who was no longer young, had borne children in the past and long been widowed, should marry a wealthy old man and a hopeless invalid, whom even a wife who had known him when young and healthy might have found an object of disgust. Crippled and deformed in every limb, he could only enjoy his vast wealth by contemplating it and could not even turn in bed without assistance. He also had to have his teeth cleaned and brushed for him—a squalid and pitiful detail—and when complaining about the humiliations of his infirmity was often heard to say that every day he licked the fingers of his slaves. Yet he went on living, and kept his will to live, helped chiefly by his wife, whose devoted care turned the former criticism of her marriage into a tribute of admiration.

(*Letters* 8.18)

Figure 7.6   An elderly Roman woman

Roman society was neither affluent nor comfortable enough for people to be wasted as resources. The aged did suffer the usual jokes and jibes and disrespect—there are enough examples from Roman literature to testify to that—but those who were capable did not have to feel obsolete. There was always something for them to do for the family or business. Since the reading population was much smaller in ancient times and books were expensive and not in general public circulation, older people were also viewed as repositories of knowledge and wisdom and held a role that is now foreign to industrial-

ized society. There did, however, remain the problem of what to do with aged people who could no longer look after themselves. To be sure, some died unattended—a fearful prospect for religious as well as practical concerns. Most were looked after by their families (often obliged to by law)—a prime reason for having children. We also know of some forms of ancient "welfare programs" that aided the old as well as the general poor. In Rome, there were always the grain doles and public banquets. Old women were, of course, more vulnerable than men since Roman society was male-oriented. Nonetheless, it is clear that society took measures to ensure that elderly women were looked after. Part of the reason for a dowry was to ensure some support for a widow in her later years.

The Military as Specific Example

Senior citizens who were fit and wished to remain active continued to do so, and no task seems to have been completely outside their capabilities. There is no better example to attest to this fact, at least for old men, than the Roman military, for there are numerous examples to show that their participation in battle was common—if not normal. General Douglas MacArthur's "Old Soldiers Never Die . . ." speech would have been even more apropos in ancient times. During most of the Roman Republic, forty-six was the oldest age at which one might be called up, but there were many soldiers who continued to serve well past the upper limit for induction. It was not unusual during the Roman Empire to find centurions, the mainstays of the legions on the battlefield, in their fifties and sixties. In fact, there is indication that senior centurions were typically sixty years of age (e.g., Juvenal, *Satire* 14.193). Petronius Fortunatus is one centurion whose career

An Anonymous Ghost

EVERYONE LOVES A GOOD ghost story, and the Romans were no exception. The humorous side of their belief in spirits is portrayed in works such as Plautus' *The Haunted House,* but there was also a serious side. A large segment of the population, including many highly educated Romans, accepted the existence of ghosts. Older people, in particular, were concerned that their bodies might not be properly attended at their death, a scary prospect since it was thought that without last rites their spirits would wander aimlessly without peace for all eternity. Pliny the Younger was one of the most literate men of his day, yet it is clear that he was deeply disturbed by the question of ghosts. In a letter to a friend, he attempts to consider that question rationally but is unable to resolve it. In the process, he tells this story about a philosopher named Athenodorus (who, as will be seen, was a man with an unusually high threshold for excitement) and the ghost of an unknown old man:

> Now consider whether the following story, which I will tell just as it was told to me, is not . . . remarkable and . . . terrifying. In Athens there was a large and spacious mansion with the bad reputation of being dangerous to its occupants. At dead of night the clanking of iron and, if you listened carefully, the rattle of chains could be heard, some way off at first, and then close at hand. Then there appeared the specter of an old man, emaciated and filthy, with a long flowing beard and hair on end, wearing fetters on his legs and shaking the chains on his wrists. The wretched occupants would spend fearful nights awake in terror; lack of sleep led to illness and then death as their dread increased, for even during the day, when the apparition had vanished, the memory of it was in their mind's eye, so that their terror remained after the cause of it had gone. The house was therefore deserted, condemned to stand empty and wholly abandoned to the specter; but it was advertised as being to let or for sale in case someone was found who knew nothing of its evil reputation.
>
> The philosopher Athenodorus came to Athens and read the notice. His suspicions were aroused when he heard the low price, and the whole story came out on inquiry; but he was nonetheless, in fact all the more, eager to rent the house. When darkness fell he gave orders that a couch was to be made up for him in the front part of the house, and asked for his notebooks, pen and a lamp. He sent all his servants to the inner rooms, and concentrated his thoughts, eyes and hand on his writing, so that his mind would be occupied and not conjure up the phantom he had heard about nor other imaginary fears. At first there was nothing but the general silence of night; then came the clanking of iron and dragging of chains. He did not look up nor stop writing, but steeled his mind to shut out the sounds. Then the noise grew louder, came nearer, was heard in the doorway, and then inside the room. He looked round, saw and recognized the ghost described to him. It stood and beckoned, as if summoning him. Athenodorus in his turn signed to it to wait a little, and again bent over his notes and pen, while it stood rattling its chains over his head as he wrote. He looked round again and saw it beckoning as before, so without further delay he picked up his lamp and followed. It moved slowly, as if weighed down with chains, and when it turned off into the courtyard of the house it suddenly vanished, leaving him alone. He then picked some plants and leaves and marked the spot. The following day he approached the magistrates, and advised them to give orders for the place to be dug up. There they found bones, twisted round with chains, which were left bare and corroded by the fetters when time and the action of the soil had rotted away the body. The bones were collected and given a public burial, and after the shades had been duly laid to rest the house saw them no more.
>
> (*Letters* 7.27)

is well documented. He was at least sixty-three when he ended his forty-six-year military career. Camp prefects, former chief centurions who supervised the operation of Roman fortresses and were third in command of a Roman legion, usually held the office late in life. For a man such as M. Aurelius Alexander, who died while still holding the position at seventy-two, this was the peak of his career.

Many old soldiers served in the legions—sometimes willingly, sometimes not. During the mutinies in Pannonia and Germany in 14 A.D., for example, some of the veterans had served thirty years and more, were white-haired, and were deformed by age (Tacitus, *Annals* 1.17–18). They were long overdue for discharge and the accompanying benefits, but the state simply disregarded them for economic reasons. Nevertheless, they continued to perform their military duties and functions. Many elderly veterans voluntarily stayed in the army if no one forced them out because they thought they were better off there.

We also have numerous examples of emperors, kings, and generals who engaged in combat in their senior years. Rome's ally King Attalus I of Pergamum was still involved in the Second Macedonian War when he was seventy-two; Rome's most formidable enemy, Hannibal, was militarily active until his mid-sixties, as was the elderly consul Marius, who died at seventy. The Emperor Galba was seventy-two years old when he was killed defending his throne from Otho in 69 A.D. Trajan was campaigning in the East when he was felled by a stroke in his sixties. Septimius Severus was sixty-five and directing operations against the Scots when he died at York in England in 211 A.D. Consequently, there must always have been many men over sixty serving in Roman armies. Obviously, they would not have been allowed active roles unless they were capable of fulfilling them, and actual experi-

ence—not theoretical discussion—proved that they could get the job done. Those who could still fight took their place alongside members of their own age group and, of course, were not expected to bear the brunt of an attack—that was left to younger men. Others were successful in performing whatever tasks were assigned to them: giving advice, encouraging their compatriots, guarding supplies, or planning attacks. The Romans, it appears, could not be as dogmatic as we are about assigning particular tasks to particular age groups. Everyone who could contribute did contribute—it was their duty.

We might also mention the charioteers, although small in number, who were still racing in the Great Circus when they were "senior citizens." Few professions, if any, have ever depended so much on reflex, skill, and strength, and the fact that these men could continue to compete attests to their abilities—even in old age (see Chapter 10).

Spurinna's Old Age

Born about 25 A.D. during Tiberius' reign, Titus Vestricius Spurinna lived under and served twelve emperors. He was already a man of distinction in 69 A.D., the "Year of the Four Emperors," when, in his forties, he supported the Emperor Otho in his losing cause to retain the throne. Spurinna successfully defended the city of Placentia, but his efforts could not prevent Vitellius' ultimate victory over Otho, who killed himself rather than fall into his enemy's hands. Spurinna survived Vitellius' short reign and won favor with the Flavians. He held the consulship under Vespasian.

During the rule of Vespasian's second son, Domitian, Spurinna reached retirement age, although he does not appear to have been inactive. Nerva would later honor him with a triumphal statue for his military successes in Germany.

It is not clear exactly when he campaigned in Germany, but it could not have been too many years earlier or the statue—and the honor—would not have had much meaning.

During the latter years of Domitian's reign, Spurinna, as well as many other successful and respected individuals, had reason to fear the erratic emperor. When Domitian was assassinated and Nerva was elevated by the Senate, the new emperor viewed Spurinna as a valuable ally. In addition to the triumphal statue mentioned above, Nerva awarded him a second consulship. Some have viewed this appointment as mostly decorative, but the emperor himself was in his late sixties. He could not very well confer a "decorative" consulship on Spurinna without also implying a "decorative" reign for himself. Nerva wanted to return Rome to the "good old days" before Domitian's oppression. He appointed reputable men associated with those times—men like Spurinna, who were of his generation and with whom he felt most comfortable. Nerva flattered Spurinna further by raising a statue for his son (at the same time that Spurinna's triumphal statue was erected), who had died while his father was in Germany.

Spurinna must have foreseen the troubles brewing for Nerva, the least effective of the "Golden Age" emperors. As a senator, Nerva had no support from the military, without whose blessing he could not survive. He was forced to adopt as his heir the army's favorite general, Trajan, who in 98 A.D. succeeded Nerva after a rule of only two years.

Spurinna lived seven years into the reign of Trajan, who was a Spaniard and Rome's first non-Italian emperor. A rarity among rulers, Trajan had the enthusiastic support of both the army and the Senate and was more than a match for most of the civil and military problems he encountered during his nineteen-year administra-

Figure 7.7 *A coin representing the Emperor Nerva (96–98 A.D.), issued when he was about sixty-six years old*

tion. He also expanded the geographical limits of the Empire, and Rome would never again control as much territory as it did under Trajan (see Map 18 and box on pages 200–201.)

Trajan was not one to neglect influential senior statesmen who could assist him, and he, like Nerva, turned to Spurinna as an advisor. As a sign of his respect and admiration, he made Spurinna consul for the third (and last) time. It was during the reign of Trajan that Pliny the Younger spent a few days with Spurinna and recorded his impression of his old friend's activities. Through Pliny, we learn how this aged Roman aristocrat utilized his time. Spurinna lived his golden years in a manner as well ordered as was his previous life. For him, the old age Cicero had envisioned was a reality. He is seventy-seven at the time we are introduced to him, and he certainly bears no resemblance to most people's idea of an old man: Sight and hearing are unimpaired; he is active, agile, energetic. There appears to be nothing he is not capable of doing, and he provides a model for people of all ages. It is clear that there were others like him, since we are informed about Roman "retirement communities" at the foot of the Apennine Mountains in the mild climate of Tuscany and at Lake Como in northern Italy during the

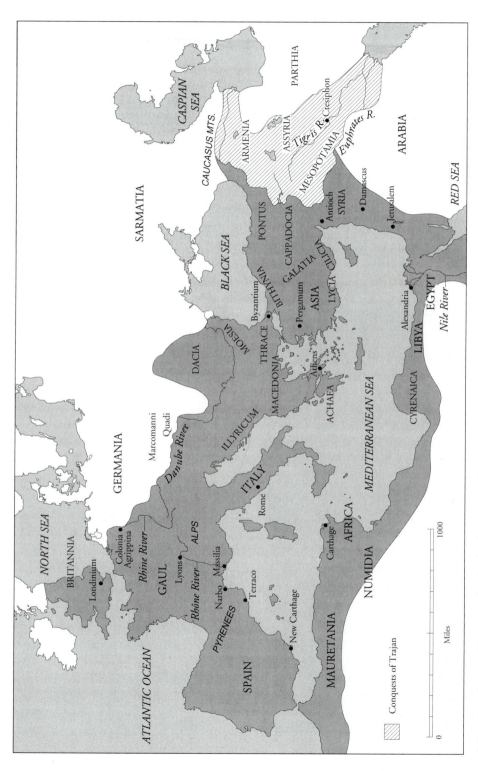

Map 18   Roman Empire at the death of Trajan (117 A.D.)

A Frontier Birthday in Roman Britain—Claudia Severa Sends an Invitation to Her Friend

SOMETIMES WE FORGET JUST how big the Roman Empire was. At its largest extent under the Emperor Trajan (98–117 A.D.), it stretched, in modern terms, from Scotland into Iran. Such extensive borders had to be protected, and we usually have little opportunity to gain insight into the personal lives of the men who staffed Rome's frontier outposts—and even less so their women. Thus, the following letter, penned on a thin wooden tablet and discovered at Vindolanda, a Roman fort in Northern England, is a welcome find—a birthday invitation sent about 100 A.D. by a woman named Claudia Severa, the wife of a man we presume to be an officer at another fort in northern Britain. The recipient was Sulpicia Lepidina, wife of Flavius Cerealis, a unit commander at Vindolanda (Chesterholm in Northumbria). Britain had been annexed by the Romans after the Em-

Figure 7.8   A model of the fort at Housesteads along Hadrian's Wall in Roman Britain. Such frontier outposts were home to many officer's wives, such as Claudia Severa and Sulpicia Lepidina. (British Museum)

Figure 7.9   This is the actual letter sent by Claudia Severa to Sulpicia Lepidina. The personal postscript in the lower right-hand corner, if penned by Claudia herself, would be the earliest existing example of Latin written by a woman. (British Museum)

Figure 7.10   *Claudia Severa and Sulpicia Lepidina probably would have been familiar with this kind of household scene (reconstructed) in Roman Britain. (Museum of London)*

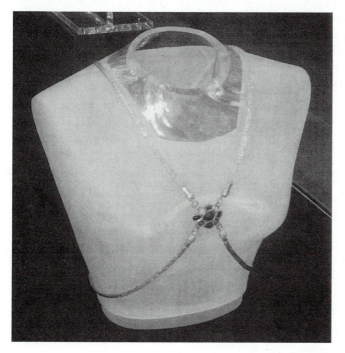

Figure 7.11   *This elegant gold body chain was probably worn by a woman who lived in Roman Britain. On the backside is a clasp containing a gold coin of the Emperor Gratian (367–383 A.D.). The piece is from the Hoxne Treasure found in England. (British Museum)*

(continued)

A Frontier Birthday in Roman Britain (continued)

peror Claudius' invasion in 43 A.D., and, at the time the letter was written, Vindolanda, where Sulpicia Lepidina lived, was one of several forts (later to be part of Hadrian's Wall) along the Stanegate road on the north British frontier.

Only officers were allowed to marry, a situation which isolated wives who accompanied their husbands to their assignments. There was little opportunity to visit friends or relatives, and local women were unsuitable companions. The birthday invitation must have been a pleasant excuse for both Severa and Lepidina to relieve what had to have been a rather boring existence (Severa addresses her friend as "sister"). Just how tenuous life was in this region is evidenced by the Romans' temporary abandonment in or around 100/5 A.D. (soon after this letter was written) of southern Scotland and the demolishing or burning of a number of forts—either because of enemy pressure or an imperial decision to withdraw further back into England. This and other letters found at Vindolanda also indicate that Roman Britain's Post system was already an efficient one. The letter reads:

Claudia Severa to her Lepidina Greetings.

On the 3rd day before the Ides of September [Sept. 11], sister, for the day of the celebration of my birthday, I give you a warm invitation to make sure that you come to us, to make the day more enjoyable for me by your arrival, if you come. Give my greetings to your Cerialis. My Aelius and my little son send you [?] their greeting.

This part of the letter appears to have been dictated because of the professional appearance of the script, but in the lower corner a "clumsier" personal postscript is added, presumably by Severa herself. If so, Severa has provided the earliest example of Latin known to have been written by a woman:

I shall expect you sister. Farewell sister, my dearest soul, as I hope to prosper, and hail.
(Vindolanda, inv. no 85/57 [Bowman and Thomas 1987, no. 5])

A Golden Wedding Anniversary—Python and Epicydilla

IT IS ONLY FITTING that a chapter concerning things "golden" should include a funerary inscription from the first century A.D. witnessing the golden wedding anniversary of a couple from the Greek island of Thasos in the Eastern Roman Empire:

Python son of Hicesius set up this common memorial to himself and to his wife Epicydilla

daughter of Epicydes. He was married at eighteen and she at fifteen, and for fifty years of life together they shared agreement unbroken and were . . . happy among the living and blessed among the dead.
(H. W. Pleket, *Epigraphica II: Texts on the Social History of the Greek World*, no. 10 [Leiden, 1969])

Figure 7.12
*The Lake Como area
in northern Italy, a
favorite retreat for
Rome's elderly rich*

summer season. Spurinna adheres to a daily routine, which, presumably, is largely responsible for his excellent condition:

> Every morning he stays in bed for an hour after dawn, then calls for his shoes and takes a three-mile walk to exercise mind and body. If he has friends with him he carries on a serious conversation, if he is alone a book is read aloud, and this is sometimes done when there are friends present, so long as they do not object. Then he sits down, the book is continued, or preferably the conversation; after which he goes out in his carriage accompanied by his wife (a model to her sex) or one of his friends. . . . After a drive of seven miles he will walk another mile, then sit again or retire to his room and his writing, for he composes lyric verses in both Greek and Latin with considerable success; they are remarkable for their wit, grace, and delicacy, and their charm is enhanced by the propriety of their

author. When summoned to his bath (in mid-afternoon in winter and an hour earlier in summer) he first removes his clothes and takes a walk in the sunshine if there is no wind, and then throws a ball briskly for some time, this being another form of exercise whereby he keeps old age at bay. After his bath he lies down for a short rest before dinner, and listens while something light and soothing is read aloud. Meanwhile his friends are quite free to do the same as he does or not, as they prefer. Dinner is brought on in dishes of antique solid silver, a simple meal but well served; he also has Corinthian bronze for general use, which he admires though not with a collectors' passion. Between the courses there is often a performance of comedy, so that the pleasures of the table have a seasoning of letters, and the meal is prolonged into the night, even in summer, without anyone finding it too long amid such pleasant company.
(Pliny, *Letters* 3.1)

The Roman Baths—Lucian Takes a Dip

ONE THING PLINY MAKES clear in his discussion of Spurinna's daily routine is his love of bathing. Everybody at Rome, not just the elderly, loved bathing and the bathing scene. Every house or villa of any consequence had a bath or baths; there were neighborhood baths, some rather "seedy," as Seneca describes in humorous fashion in Chapter 1; and there were massive bathing complexes, one of which, the Baths of Diocletian (fourth century A.D.) in Rome, comprised an area of over a million square feet. It could accommodate two thousand bathers, who utilized the great swimming pool, as well as smaller hot, warm, and cold baths. At such facilities, Romans could also have rubdowns and saunas; they could exercise, socialize, conduct business, and do a number of other things—not all of them always savory.

Below, Lucian, previously quoted in this chapter, provides one of the most detailed surviving descriptions of a Roman bath, which, along with the impressive physical remains of baths at Rome, Pompeii, and especially those at

Figure 7.13 Remains of the "Great Pool" of the Roman baths at Bath, England. This and other existing facilities here provide us with the finest extant example of a complete Roman bathing complex.

Figure 7.14
The "Tepid" or lukewarm, pool at Bath to the east of the "Great Pool"

Figure 7.15
Semicircular warm-water bath, probably for curative treatments, at Bath, east of the "Great Pool" and adjacent to the "Tepid" pool

(continued)

The Roman Baths (continued)

Bath in England, help us reconstruct the bathing atmosphere. Lucian writes (*The Baths*, 5–8):

> The entranceway is lofty and has a wide flight of steps which are low rather than steep, for the convenience of people walking up them. You enter into a very spacious hall which provides a large waiting area for slaves and attendants. To the left of this hall are rooms designed for relaxation, and therefore particularly well suited to a bath building—elegant, well-lit, and private rooms. Next to these is a meeting room larger than one normally finds in a bath building, but necessary for reception of the wealthy. Beyond this room are two spacious locker rooms and, between them, a lofty and brightly lit hall which contains three cold-water swimming pools. It is decorated with slabs of Laconian marble and with two white marble statues. . . .
>
> Upon leaving this hall, you enter into a large room which is long, rounded at each end, and slightly warm, rather than being confronted suddenly with intense heat. Beyond this room and to the right is a very bright room which is quite suitably arranged for rub-downs with oil. At each end it has an entryway decorated with Phrygian marble to provide access for those coming in from the exercise area. And then near this room is another large room, the most beautiful of all rooms, very well designed for standing about or sitting down, for whiling away time without fear of reproach, or for occupying your time most profitably. It, too, gleams from top to bottom with Phrygian marble.
>
> Next you enter a passageway heated with hot air and faced with Numidian marble. It leads into a very beautiful room which is filled with bright light and resplendent with purple. This room contains three hot tubs. Once you have bathed, you don't need to go back again through the same rooms. Instead, you can go immediately through a small, slightly warm room to a cold room.

Figure 7.16
The "Frigidarium," or cold bath, at Bath, in the complex west of the "Great Pool"

Every room has a great deal of sunlight coming in. In addition, the height of each room is of good proportion, and the width corresponds well with the length. . . . The cold room lies in the north part of the building, but the rooms that need a lot of heat are situated in the south, east, and west. . . .

The building also has two privies and many entrances and exits, and provides two devices for telling time—a loud water clock and a sundial.

Figure 7.17 Model of the Roman bath complex at Lutetia, later called Parisii (Paris, France; Musée de Cluny)

Spurinna lived about two more years after Pliny's visit. He had seen the best and the worst the Empire had to offer and survived it all. Certainly, few Romans could have had a fuller life from beginning to end:

> This is the right way to grow old for a man who has held the highest civil offices, commanded armies, and devoted himself entirely to the service of the State as long as it was proper for him to do so.
>
> (Pliny, *Letters* 4.23)

Suggestions for Further Reading

The subject of old age in Rome is only beginning to receive adequate attention, and much of the discussion is specialized and in foreign languages. There are no recent monographs in English, and L. Berelson's "Old Age in Ancient Rome" (Ph.D. dissertation, University of Virginia, 1934) is in need of revision. The interested reader is left with several possibilities. Simone de Beauvoir's *The Coming of Age* (New York: Putnam, 1972): 95–126, collects many pertinent passages on aging from ancient writers, but her treatment suffers because of her inadequate grasp of the sources. M. I. Finley has provided the best introductory article on the subject with "The Elderly in Classical Antiquity," *Ageing and Society* 4 (1984): 391–408. A collection of essays (and comments) has been published by T. M. Falkner and J. de Luce in *Old Age in Greek and Latin Literature* (Albany: SUNY Press, 1989). Other useful articles are M. S. Haynes's "The Supposedly Golden Age for the Aged in Ancient Rome (A Study of Literary Concept of Old Age)," *Gerontologist* 3 (1963): 26–35; and Robert B. Kebric's "Aging in Pliny's Letters: A View from the Second Century A.D.," *Gerontologist* 23 (1983): 538–545, and "Old Age, the Ancient Military, and Alexander's Army: Positive Examples for a Graying America," *Gerontologist* 28 (1988): 298–302. Among ancient sources, Cicero's *On Old Age (De Senectute)* is, of course, the most famous piece, but the *Letters* of Pliny the Younger contain more realistic references to old people. The Penguin and Loeb Classical Library editions of both provide easy access.

Recent General Additions

J. Bennett, *Trajan: Optimus Princeps* (New York: Routledge, 1997); A. R. Birley, *Hadrian: The Restless Emperor* (New York: Routledge, 1997); J. E. Packer, *The Forum of Trajan in Rome: A Study of the Monuments,* 3 Vols. (Berkeley and Los Angeles: University of California Press, 1997); P. Southern, *Domitian: Tragic Tyrant* (Bloomington: Indiana University Press, 1997); and G. G. Fagan, *Bathing in Public in the Roman World* (Ann Arbor: University of Michigan Press, 1999).

8

Empire and Army

Septimius and the Severan Dynasty
(193–235 A.D.)
Julia Domna, the Syrian Empress

Where the emperor is, there is Rome.
(Herodian, *History*, 1.6.5)

By the end of Marcus Aurelius' rule in 180 A.D., the general prosperity and success enjoyed during the reigns of Trajan, Hadrian, and Antoninus Pius were over. Barbarians, plagues, and other maladies were infecting the Empire, and the subsequent destructive rule of Marcus' brutish son Commodus only exacerbated the difficulties. With his assassination late in 192 A.D., the Empire was on the verge of collapse.

In the civil wars that followed, Septimius Severus, Rome's first African emperor, restored order and established a military dynasty. At his side was his Syrian wife, Julia Domna. During the reigns of her husband and their son, Caracalla, she achieved a status and influence that were unrivaled by any previous imperial woman. Julia's example was not lost on her sister and

nieces, who, after her death, ruled the Empire behind their weak male children. Seldom has there been a period in history where women wielded such power.

The Background of Julia Domna

Julia Domna was from Emesa, a city in southern Syria, where she was born probably in the 160s A.D. She first met Septimius Severus when he was stationed in Syria from 180 to 182 A.D. Her father, Julius Bassianus, was high priest of the god Elagabal, whose cult was centered at Emesa. Septimius appears to have become quite well acquainted with Bassianus, an important man whose goodwill any Roman commander would have sought. Julia Domna and her sister,

209

Julia Maesa (Domna and Maesa were both Semitic names), were also devotees of Elagabal, literally the "god of the mountain." In the Eastern Roman world, he had come to be identified with the Sun-God—"the ancestral Sun-God Elagabal"—and was worshipped at Emesa in the form of a conical black stone.

Septimius was already married to a fellow African at the time he met Julia Domna. He grew to know Bassianus and his daughters well enough to learn that Domna's horoscope foretold she would one day marry a king. Such a story is not unlikely since any astrologer would realize that the daughter of the high priest of Elagabal at Emesa would marry well—perhaps even a king; and Bassianus himself may have "obtained" the propitious horoscope for his daughter as a convenient way of attracting the best possible suitors. Horoscopes aside, Julia Domna would have made an impressive mate for any man.

Considering Septimius' ambitions and interest in astrology, Julia's horoscope was not lost on him (Bassianus would have made sure of that). An extremely superstitious man, he believed through dreams and other signs that he was destined to become emperor of Rome. In fact, Julia and her horoscope made so great an impression on him that when his wife died several years later while he was governing Gaul, Septimius dispatched a letter to Syria almost immediately with a proposal of marriage. Julia accepted and traveled to Gaul, where she and Septimius were married at Lugdunum (Lyons) in the summer of 187 A.D. They probably communicated at first in Greek, although considering her position, Domna must already have known some Latin. Naturally, with Julia's horoscope now linked to his, Septimius' dreams that he would one day be emperor increased accordingly. In reality, he had less than six years to wait.

Before Julia—Septimius' Early Career

The small but physically powerful general who would become Rome's twenty-first emperor in 193 A.D. had a different background from any of his predecessors. Since Trajan's reign, Romans had become used to provincials on the throne, but Septimius was the first to come from Africa. Although fully Romanized, he was, like Julia, from a part of the world that was still quite alien and mysterious to Europe and Italy. As a Semite, the fact that he could become emperor at all is indication of just how much the Empire had changed.

Born and reared in Leptis (Lepcis) Magna, a great old city in Tripolitania in Roman Africa, Septimius came from a family that was among the city's most prominent and wealthy. His grandfather had been the leading citizen, and although his father Geta (a rare name originally applied to slaves) was rather obscure, other members of his family were Roman senators. His city, Leptis Magna, had a long history and was, like Hannibal's Carthage, founded by Phoenicians. While long treated as part of Roman Africa and as an ally, Leptis Magna had only recently been granted the rank of colony (*colonia*) by Trajan and all its people made Roman citizens. It shed its Punic cloak and took on all the outward features of a major imperial city; underneath, Punic tradition, culture, and language remained very much alive. Septimius himself spoke and undoubtedly read Punic, and his Latin and Greek may have been tinged with a slight African accent (according to one story, his sister visited Rome while he was emperor and so embarrassed him because of her inability to speak Latin that he sent her back to Africa). Before he left for Rome at seventeen to complete his studies and enter upon an official

Figure 8.1   Julia Domna

career, he was, like many of his fellow citizens, still largely a Punic African in a Roman toga.

Septimius' early career corresponded with the reigns of Marcus Aurelius and Commodus. He was granted senatorial rank soon after his arrival in Rome, but he did not enter the Senate until he came of age and held the quaestorship in 169 A.D. Minor officialdom took him to Sardinia, Africa, and Spain, and his contacts with important Romans grew with his duties. The energy, the administrative abilities, and the quiet originality that characterized his reign as emperor were already at work. Astrology, dreams, and omens continued to indicate to him his im-

perial future. Much of this tradition is, of course, apocryphal and propagandistic, but it cannot be denied that for someone like Severus, the absolute confidence he placed in the validity of such signs was a driving force in his success.

That Septimius took himself and his rising authority seriously is indicated by a story about his return to his hometown while serving as legate to the proconsul of Africa (who was his kinsman) in 174 A.D. While he was proceeding on foot in his official capacity, an old plebeian friend could not restrain himself and rushed up and hugged him. Septimius had the man beaten and issued a proclamation that no plebeian was to embrace a legate of the Roman people in such an undignified manner.

In 180 A.D., Septimius, now thirty-five, went east to Syria to serve as one of three legionary commanders under the future emperor Pertinax, who was at this time governor of Syria. It was there, of course, that he met Julia. His duties and leisure time would also have taken him frequently to Antioch, the greatest city in the Eastern Empire after Alexandria. He would have been able personally to learn about the peoples who inhabited this part of the world. The border with Parthia, Rome's perennial enemy whom he would war against as emperor, was only 100 miles away at the Euphrates River. At Apamea, between Antioch and Emesa, his hopes for a grandiose future were encouraged when he consulted the oracle of Zeus Belos. The god's reply (for whatever reason) was a quote from the *Iliad* describing King Agamemnon.

The abortive attempt of Commodus' sister Lucilla to assassinate her brother in 182 A.D. apparently affected Septimius' career. Some of the alleged conspirators had ties with Syria, which had revolted against Commodus' father Marcus Aurelius only seven years before. In the shake-up that followed, Pertinax, who was a friend of Lucilla's husband (also a Syrian), was removed from his post as governor and sent into retirement. A short time later, Septimius was also dismissed. While the reason is not clear, it must have related to his close ties with Pertinax. For the next few years, Septimius spent much of his enforced leisure time at Athens, where he attended lectures, studied religion, and took in the famous sites. As the political climate changed, Septimius was recalled and promoted, and by 187 A.D., he was in Gaul serving his first governorship. In the same year, he married Julia.

The Struggles of a Young Family

Soon after her marriage to Septimius, Julia became pregnant. A son, Bassianus (who would become better known by his nickname, Caracalla, because of the Gallic cloak he liked to wear), was born the following year at Lyons. Septimius' first marriage had left him childless, and already in his early forties, he must have been anxious to be a father. Julia delivered a second son, Geta, in 189 A.D., not long after Septimius returned to Rome with his new family. She had little time to recover since she and her two infant sons would leave within a few months for Sicily, where Septimius was to be proconsul for the year.

While in Sicily, the mounting problems with Commodus in Rome and an uncertain future must have taken their toll on Julia, who had to wonder about her husband's prospects. Her faith in astrology (Septimius is said to have gotten into some minor trouble while in Sicily for consulting astrologers about the imperial position) was a solace for her, but she must have realized all the positive astrological predictions in the world could not stop a crazed emperor's

Figure 8.2   Septimius Severus

wrath. An acquaintance (perhaps a relative) from Emesa had already been eliminated for what appears to have been a frivolous reason. There were other executions.

Severus and Julia weathered the beginning of the storm, and the new father even held the consulship for a month in 190 A.D. But then the appointments ended. For a middle-aged man with a prominent younger wife and infant children whose sole holdings outside of Africa were a house in Rome and a farm in rural Italy, it is doubtful that his inactivity was voluntary—although, as it turned out, it was a good time to keep a low profile. Septimius had no official duties for about a year; then his fortunes revived dramatically when his fellow African, Aemilius Laetus, became Commodus' Praetorian prefect.

In 191 A.D. Laetus arranged Severus' appointment to the governorship of Upper Pannonia, which contained the largest Roman army near Italy. There is no satisfactory administrative explanation for the appointment, since Septimius lacked both the governmental and military experience for such a command. It appears that he and trusted others, mostly Africans (including his brother, who was also named Geta), were being placed in positions of power by Laetus as a prelude to the overthrow of Commodus. He was to be replaced by Severus' former boss in Syria, Pertinax. Septimius was still not a major player at this juncture, but in respect to his advancement, he was now aligned with the right political clique. His future—and Julia's—depended on whether his benefactors could successfully eliminate Commodus.

Pertinax Becomes Emperor

Pertinax, too, had eventually been restored to Commodus' good graces. He was summoned out of retirement in 185 A.D. and made governor of Britain to quell mutinous troops there. In 188 A.D., he served a difficult proconsulship in Africa and, upon his return to Rome in 189 A.D., was made Prefect of the City. Commodus had apparently become so pleased with him that he made Pertinax his colleague in the consulship of 192 A.D.

Pertinax may already have been part of the plot to rid Rome of Commodus at the time of Septimius' appointment in Pannonia. It seems likely because of their service together in Syria. If not, Pertinax had certainly joined Laetus early in 192 A.D. Whether Septimius and the others who owed their positions to Laetus initially

Figure 8.3 *Commodus*

knew about the plot is another story, but they must have had their suspicions. They knew right before it happened because they all had a crucial role to play if something went wrong. When Commodus was assassinated, Pertinax was raised as emperor by the Praetorians before midnight on December 31 and confirmed by the Senate before daybreak.

Upon receiving and verifying the news of Commodus' death, Septimius sacrificed and administered to his troops an oath of allegiance to the new emperor. Certainly, his own future could not have looked brighter. The fact that Julia's brother-in-law (who would later serve Septimius) held a key position in ensuring the safe arrival of Rome's grain supply at Ostia under Pertinax is another indication of the African-Syrian connection at work in the political events of this time. Septimius was left in command of the Danube legions, and it would be from this position that he would make his own successful bid for the throne.

Pertinax, despite his distinguished military and political career, proved unequal to all the difficulties confronting him after Commodus' death. He lost the support of Laetus, who did not prevent mutinous Praetorians from murdering him on March 28, 193 A.D. In his late sixties, he was killed after a rule of only eighty-seven days. Apparently, Septimius had realized the potential for problems and was prepared to step in and take over. According to the historian Herodian, he had a convenient dream right after he had proclaimed Pertinax emperor to his troops that indicated he would soon replace him. Six months later Severus *was* emperor. Even his own astrologers must have been surprised at his rapid rise to the purple.

The Military Dynasty— Severus Proclaimed Emperor

Immediately after Pertinax's murder, another sixty-year-old senator, Didius Julianus, disgraced his long and noteworthy public career by actually purchasing the Empire at a mock auction held by the Praetorians, made dizzy by their apparent ability to control the throne. The act also set a dangerous precedent, for their lesson of power brokering was not lost on subsequent "emperor makers." Rome's Augusti could now be elevated anywhere in the Empire— provided the price and the stakes were right. Public indignation over Julianus' elevation, however, was immediate, and his downfall was ensured by the army, whose leading generals now quarreled over the throne. Septimius was closest to Rome. After guaranteeing the safety of Julia and his children, the avenger of Pertinax (as he now styled

himself) allowed his troops to hail him as emperor at Carnuntum on April 9, 193 A.D. and began the almost 700- (Roman) mile march to the capital. Julia Domna, daughter of the high priest of Elagabal at Emesa, was about to become empress of Rome.

As Septimius neared Rome, Julianus was condemned by the Senate, Septimius was proclaimed emperor, and Julianus was killed in the palace by a soldier on June 1—sixty-six days after he had purchased the Empire. His monies, it appears, could have been better spent. Rome belonged to Septimius without his ever fighting a major battle.

After punishing the murderers of Pertinax and disbanding the untrustworthy Praetorians—ending their 200-year history as an elite, mostly Italian corps—Septimius recruited a new Guard, doubled in size, from his own veterans and entered Rome peacefully on June 9 in civilian garb with his army. According to the historian Dio (74.1.4), who witnessed the accompanying celebration, it was "the most brilliant [spectacle] of any that I have witnessed," but another source, probably more realistic in this instance, says the new emperor's entry into the city inspired only hatred and fear (*Augustan History: Severus* 7.1–3). Although Septimius would not finish eliminating his competition for the throne until 197 A.D., the foundation for Rome's last major dynasty, the Severan, had been laid.

Difficult Beginnings

The stars had indeed been kind to Julia Domna. Marrying a minor king would have been the most someone of her status might expect—but she had married an emperor. She had little time to reflect on her good fortune. Three previous emperors had been murdered in half a year, and Septimius was less experienced than any of them. If ever there was need for new, encouraging horoscopes, it was now.

Certainly, with their faith in astrology, the royal couple had surrounded themselves with practitioners who gave them daily advice; and they must have, like Tiberius, become expert themselves. But Pertinax and Didius Julianus had probably been able, at one time, to point to positive horoscopes about their futures. They had both been killed—and their horoscopes forgotten. Septimius had to avoid their mistakes.

The new emperor differed from his immediate predecessors in two ways. He was a much younger man, in his late forties (with a young wife and family), and he commanded a significant part of the Roman army. The first of these differences had some impact; the second was crucial. Neither Pertinax nor Julianus had the military support necessary to survive. They also could not control the Praetorian Guard. Septimius had proceeded to Rome as if he were moving through enemy lines and was constantly surrounded by armed men. When he abolished the old Guard, he not only ended their ability to influence events at Rome but also removed the former membership permanently from the city. The reconstituted Guard, excluding Italians, was dependent on and loyal to him. He also understood the political realities of the day. An emperor who did not keep his army happy—and that meant frequent cash bonuses—was an emperor who would not last long. Septimius always kept the interests of his troops first and foremost in his mind; in return, they supported him and his successors.

Whether Septimius could now win the entire army's confidence was another question. There were still other generals, with their own troops, who were competitors for the throne. Severus had earlier been able to mollify one of

Figure 8.4 *Praetorian Guardsmen*

them, Clodius Albinus, a fellow African, who controlled Britain. Before he reached Rome to take the throne from Didius Julianus, Severus offered Albinus the title of Caesar, implying that he would succeed him. Albinus accepted the offer and remained in Britain. Later, after Septimius had been proclaimed emperor at Rome, coins were struck in the names of both Septimius and Albinus, and the two were designated consuls for 194 A.D.

Coins were also struck for Julia Domna, celebrating the goddess Venus. Venus, of course, was the divine ancestor of the Julian clan, and her image reinforced the link between the new ruling family and Julius Caesar and Augustus. Perhaps as Caesar had earlier placed a statue of Cleopatra in the Temple of Venus in his Forum to symbolize in some way that she would "mother" a new Rome, Julia Domna, also from the East, was now being groomed to fulfill that role. Certainly, titles that were later applied to her would suggest such.

The most serious threat to Septimius was Pescennius Niger. Niger had been hailed as emperor at Antioch after Pertinax's death, and most of the East backed him. His military strength was not equal to Septimius', but Niger, an Italian, had a great deal of support in Rome from the old aristocracy and also the plebs. Septimius did what he could to undermine Niger's position and strengthen his own. He presented himself to the Romans as the legitimate successor of Pertinax, giving his murdered predecessor a formal funeral, deifying him, and calling himself "Imperator Caesar L. Septimius Severus *Pertinax* Augustus." To keep the Senate happy, he promised that no senator would be put to death. Restive soldiers, as usual, were plied with donatives. Within a month's time, things had been secured to the point that Septimius felt confident enough to leave the capital to settle accounts with Niger.

Julia as Empress

What Julia was doing during this tensive period is not recorded. She and her children must have taken up residence in the Imperial Palace in Rome soon after her husband had secured the city and formally been declared emperor. That in itself was a positive step toward creating an impression of normality—and stability. Other members of Julia's family, most notably her sister Julia Maesa, resided with her, and her brother-in-law now became one of Severus' right-hand men.

We can be sure that other Syrians, either related to Julia or associated with her family, played key roles in ensuring that the new regime

Figure 8.5   *Coin representing Julia Maesa, sister of Julia Domna*

survived. Never before had Syria been in such a position to benefit from Rome, and there must have been forces working, most of all at Emesa, to undermine Pescennius Niger's influence in the East. Certainly, those forces contributed to Septimius' final victory. It would have been impossible for him to leave Rome and his family (part of his own strategy was to seize the children of Niger) so quickly if he did not feel confident about his position. Julia's family connections contributed to that confidence—that and Septimius' belief in her horoscope.

Not surprisingly, Septimius had previously received an omen that foretold Pescennius Niger's fall. A priest of Jupiter had a dream that a "black man" had forced his way into the emperor's camp and had been put to death. Since *niger* in Latin means "black," Pescennius Niger must have been the "black man" in the dream, which portended his ultimate defeat. (Interestingly, the "Domna" part of Julia's name may have been related to Arab names meaning "black." If so, then those who found meaning in such coincidences must have had a time trying to figure out why the emperor's wife and worst enemy shared the same color in their names.) Considering the superstitious mentality of the times, there can be little doubt about the positive impression this omen would have made on Septimius' troops—Niger's defeat was a foregone conclusion.

With the death of Pescennius Niger near Antioch in 194 A.D., Septimius gained control of the entire Eastern Empire. As was his practice, he filled important governmental posts with personal appointees, whose loyalties had been proven. Julia Domna, who would have been anxiously following her husband's progress, now joined him for a triumphal tour of Syria. The fact that both emperor and empress could be far away from Rome in the East for an extended period demonstrates how securely Septimius now held the throne. Returning to Syria as emperor must have given him a large measure of satisfaction, but his purpose was not just to give the East a chance to view its new ruler. The time in Syria allowed him to reestablish ties with important people, now his subjects, that he had made while serving there twelve years earlier. Those ties were important in consolidating his power in a region still shaky from the civil war with Niger.

The visit was also Julia's first since she had left to marry Septimius, and her reception at Emesa must have been spectacular. It was her most important political function to date. Since her family was from a royal line, there is no telling how many Eastern monarchies had become linked with it over the years. Her presence in Syria could do nothing but rally support for the new regime and help check some of the more restive elements still at work. Stories about her imperial horoscope appeared confirmed—and were propagated. Many would have been convinced that destiny had indeed brought her to the throne. The Syrian empress provided the East with a symbol of unity—and of hope. The Western Empire also would have observed her as a beneficial Eastern partner to their African emperor.

Julia accompanied her husband on his campaign across the Euphrates that extended the Empire's Eastern frontier, for which she was given the title *mater castrorum,* or "Mother of the Camp." Obviously, Septimius wanted the army—and Rome—to view her as an active participant in all that he did. Perhaps more important politically, the last respected emperor, Marcus Aurelius, had honored his wife with the same title. Septimius had further legitimized his own claim to the throne by relating himself to Marcus Aurelius as "Son of the deified Marcus Pius." In addition, Bassianus (Caracalla), the seven-year-old son of Julia and Septimius, was renamed "M[arcus] Aurelius Antoninus" and designated "Caesar." Septimius and Julia were preparing to remove the last obstacle to a family dynasty—the now expendable Clodius Albinus.

The End of Clodius Albinus

Septimius' victories beyond the Euphrates in 195 A.D. earned him the triumphal arch named after him in Rome. They also helped him integrate Niger's former soldiers with his own by directing them all against a common enemy. His invasion and success in Mesopotamia did secure and extend the Eastern Roman border, but glory was also a motivation. His victories linked the new emperor to Trajan's Eastern campaign—and even the exploits of the legendary Alexander the Great.

After bringing his Eastern operations to a successful conclusion, Septimius now turned his attention to eliminating Clodius Albinus. For some time, he had been planning on how best to rid himself of his Western partner, who was no longer necessary and was acting—not

Figure 8.6   Clodius Albinus

without encouragement from some in Rome—as though he were emperor. One tradition asserts that Septimius sent couriers to Britain to either assassinate or poison Albinus, but stories of such cloak-and-dagger antics were probably the result of negative propaganda. In this case, as in all others, Septimius and Julia would have consulted the stars. They would also have known Albinus' horoscope, and astrology would have largely directed their actions against him. There was no reason to chance an assassination when Septimius' military superiority appeared overwhelming. And Albinus would have been on guard. He could see how events were shaping up, made clear by the fact that Albinus extended his authority into Gaul in 195 A.D. and officially proclaimed himself emperor.

The renewal of civil war had its negative impact on the citizenry of Rome. The passage from Dio that is cited in Chapter 10 (page 281), in which the Circus crowd expressed its displeasure at the prospect of another prolonged war between Romans, relates to Septimius' campaign against Clodius Albinus. That incident took place in mid-December, 195 A.D. Romans would have to wait until 197 A.D. for the civil war to end, with Albinus' death. Ironically, Albinus was defeated and killed at Lyons in Gaul, where Septimius had earlier been governor and had married Julia and where Caracalla had been born. It is no wonder that the Severan tradition includes the dreams that the future emperor supposedly had while governing at Lyons that indicated he would become emperor and rule the world. Septimius had his former Caesar's head sent to Rome, where it was displayed on a pole.

The Firm-Handed Emperor

Septimius' campaign against Albinus took him through the European provinces of Pannonia, Noricum, Raetia, Germany, and Gaul. After Albinus' defeat, loyal administrators were placed in the erstwhile troubled areas, and Septimius ultimately returned to an anxious Rome. Presumably, Julia had spent this time in the city, her presence acting as a check to subversive elements, her agents gathering information (and horoscopes) on those considered untrustworthy. Now completely secure in his power, the emperor punished supporters of Albinus and others he apparently mistrusted. Brushing away his earlier promise not to execute members of the Senate (he proscribed the senator who had proposed the decree), Septimius put twenty-nine senators to death and confiscated their property. One was the father-in-law of Pertinax! Many of the dead had connections with Africa, a clear sign that an African background would not guarantee safety—or favor. While astrology was critical to Septimius and Julia, it was not in their interests to allow inquiry into their futures by outsiders. Just as Augustus and Tiberius had taken strong measures to discourage private consultations, the imperial couple did also and were continually on guard against "dangerous inquisitiveness."

Septimius surprised many in Rome by connecting himself more closely with Commodus. Since he, like Commodus, was now the "son" of Marcus Aurelius, it was politically wise for Severus to follow this tack. He demanded Commodus' deification, even justifying some of the aberrant emperor's disgraceful behavior. For obvious reasons, the tarnished image of his "brother" could not be allowed to continue. Septimius had already learned that he could do this and whatever else he wanted as long as the army was satisfied. To that end, the prudent emperor gave the army its first major pay increase in over a century and allowed soldiers to marry (or cohabit) while in service, something forbidden since the time of Augustus. With his military dynasty firmly established, Severus once again turned his attention eastward, where the Parthians had renewed their hostilities.

Julia and Septimius— In the East Again

Septimius was again accompanied to the East by Julia and their sons. Even though war was the immediate reason for going, Julia must have looked forward to the expedition. It is doubtful that she ever felt comfortable in Rome, as foreign to her as she was to it. Her language, her life-style, her religion—everything about her was Eastern. It had been only thirteen years since she was hastily uprooted from Emesa and sent directly to Gaul to marry Septimius. With the exception of her last visit East, she had to accommodate herself to a "European" way of life. Her most intimate companions and attendants were fellow Syrians. Her religion, among the most important things in her life, was centered on the god Elagabal, still alien to most Western Romans. The center of the cult remained a thousand miles from Rome; and Julia, her sister, and other members of her family required whatever and whoever were necessary to carry out the proper rites.

Julia's familiarity with that part of the world—family connections and friends, linguistic background, and religious knowledge—was as useful to her husband on this expedition as it had been on the previous Eastern campaign. In many nonmilitary ways, Julia was Septimius' most expert advisor. Also, as empress, mother of the future emperors, and "Mother of the Camp," her presence gave the soldiers, always in need of morale boosters, added incentive to perform well. No empress had ever been as close to the army as Julia; and no empress had ever been in a position to so influence it. Septimius wanted it that way.

Septimius probably also felt that it was safer for the royal family to be together for the duration of the campaign. His prolonged absence could prove dangerous for Julia and their sons, especially since intrigue was always a part of royal life. It apparently did not bother the African emperor otherwise to be away from Rome for extended periods. People at Rome, too, had become used to their emperors controlling affairs from abroad through their experiences with Trajan, Hadrian, and Marcus Aurelius. For Septimius, the royal court was—and conducted its business from—wherever he and his family happened to be. For the next five years, it was in the East.

From Parthia to Egypt

Septimius' campaign against the Parthians was a complete success. There was surprisingly little resistance as the army passed into Mesopotamia from Syria, ferried down the Euphrates to Babylon, and crossed the Tigris River to sack Ctesiphon, the Parthian capital. It was a memorable occasion for Septimius and Julia, for it further affirmed their credentials to rule and added credibility to their regime. Reminiscent of the great Parthian victory of Trajan (whom Septimius was now claiming as his great-great-grandfather) in 115 A.D., Severus had equaled the immortalized achievement of one of Rome's greatest emperors. It was no coincidence that he announced his own Parthian victory in 198 A.D. on the exact date, January 28, that Trajan had become emperor one hundred years earlier. Septimius also took for himself, as if the rightful heir, the title first held by Trajan, "Parthicus Maximus." He further utilized the momentous occasion (using the model of his "father" Marcus Aurelius, who made Commodus co-emperor when he was only fifteen) to confer the titles of "Augustus" on his nine-year-old son, Caracalla, and "Caesar" on Geta.

Like Trajan, Septimius also discovered the impossibility of holding Ctesiphon. It was too far east to be maintained. Northern Mesopotamia was annexed as a province (which had previously existed briefly under Trajan). Most of the rest of Mesopotamia could be controlled but not permanently occupied. Severus ultimately had to withdraw north along the Tigris River. On the way, he tried to take the formidable desert city of Hatra, which had supported Pescennius Niger and would continue to pose a considerable threat to Roman troops in Mesopotamia. Trajan had tried to take the city, and perhaps Septimius' main reason in attacking it was prestige—he saw a chance of succeeding where Trajan had failed. It

is not clear whether he captured the city, but the fact that a Roman garrison was later stationed there may be an indication that Septimius was the first to impose it. Whatever the case, the Eastern provinces had never been more firmly held.

For most of the next year, Septimius appears to have been occupied reorganizing Syria, now divided into two provinces, and the frontiers. Much time must also have been spent in Julia's hometown of Emesa; and not surprisingly, her kinfolk turn up in various administrative posts—one the husband of Julia's sister's daughter, Julia Soaemias, at Apamea. That was also where the oracle of Zeus previously consulted by Septimius was located, and now as emperor, he consulted it again. On this occasion, unlike the first, he received a line from Euripides forecasting a gloomy future for his heirs. Apparently, the oracle was more liberal when dealing with inquirers of less status! Also at this time, the great desert city of Palmyra, long a Roman ally, may have formally become a part of the Empire.

The royal family next moved on to Palestine, the land of the Jews, to whom, reputedly, Septimius was well disposed, and then into Egypt, a land that bordered on the emperor's own African home and whose antiquity and religion had always fascinated him. A man who was apparently never able to get as much education as he desired, Septimius was always the student. Julia, too, was interested in many subjects, particularly philosophy and religion. Seldom, it seems, have a ruler and his wife shared so many interests, political and otherwise, and participated in them equally. In Egypt, both Septimius and Julia could indulge themselves in a scholar's and tourist's paradise. And they did. Even though Septimius was apparently already suffering from gout or arthritis, it did not dampen his appetite to see everything.

An Irate Student Writes Home

ABOUT THE TIME THAT Septimius and Julia visited Egypt, a father living there named Arion received this letter from his neglected son, who had left home to further his education (it is not clear exactly where). Those studies, it seems, had come to a halt (or not begun) for financial reasons, since the youth's teacher would not have been so interested in Arion's arrival if he were not bringing with him his son's tuition. This is the fifth time the son has written, and he is now desperate (apparently, his teacher is ready to leave). He chides his father for not even caring about his welfare. It is clear from what he says that he is also a little homesick. Letters such as this one demonstrate how little family life has changed over the millennia:

> To my lord and father Arion from Thonis greeting. Before all else I make supplication for you every day, praying also before the ancestral gods of my present abode that I may find you and all our folk thriving. Look you, this is my fifth letter to you, and you have not written to me except only once, not even a word about your welfare, nor come to see me; though you promised me saying "I am coming," you have not come to find out whether the teacher is looking after me or not. He himself is inquiring about you almost every day, saying "Is he not coming yet?" And I just say "Yes." Endeavor then to come to me quickly in order that he may teach me as he is eager to do. If you had come up with me, I should have been taught long ago. And when you come, remember what I have often written you about. Come to us quickly then before he goes up country. I send many salutations to all our folk, each by name, together with those who love us. Salutations also to my teachers. Goodbye, my lord and father, and may you prosper, as I pray, for many years along with my brothers whom may the evil eye harm not. Remember our pigeons.
> (*Select Papyri*, Vol. 1, No. 133; *Sammelbuch* 6262)

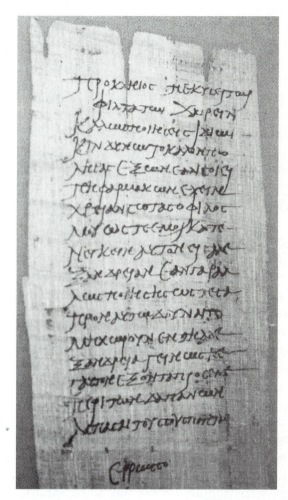

Figure 8.7   *The letter Arion received from his student son would have closely resembled this fine example written in Greek on papyrus, from Alexandria, Egypt.*

As a devotee of the god Serapis, whose cult had originated in Ptolemaic Egypt, Septimius had his first opportunity to visit the god's great temple in Alexandria. Just as Mark Antony had been identified by the Egyptians with Dionysus, many now would have viewed their emperor as the embodiment of Serapis. He was often portrayed with the god's features. His interest—and Julia's—in astrology, superstition, and arcane lore made the Egyptians appear to him as mystifying and as magical (and even fearful) as they do to many neophytes today, and he wanted to inquire into all their "secrets." While there, Septimius sealed the tomb of Alexander the Great in Alexandria. Whether this was done for symbolic reasons or out of superstitious fear (or both) is not clear. Alexander had provided a potent fetish for pretenders and emperors alike. Pescennius Niger was the last to claim he was the new Alexander, and Septimius himself certainly welcomed comparisons, as had Trajan, because of his conquest of Mesopotamia. It was time either to fulfill the identification completely or to take measures to prevent anyone else from doing it. Alexander was now to be regarded as finally dead. (Ironically, it would be Caracalla, present with his parents on this occasion, who would revive the memory and compare himself with the fabled king.) Just as revealing was Septimius' sacrifice at Pompey's tomb at Pelusium on the way to Alexandria. Hadrian had done likewise when he visited Egypt and rebuilt the tomb, but there was more to it for Septimius. The man who had first driven his sword into Pompey was named *Septimius*. It is doubtful that Septimius Severus was related to the assassin, but there was a tradition that this man's descendants would be cursed for what he had done. As superstitious as the emperor was, a reconciliation with the dead was necessary. Also, Pompey was a remote ancestor of Marcus Aurelius, Septimius' "father," and thereby, his ancestor too.

Back to Rome

After settling affairs in Egypt and exploring the sites, the royal family left sometime after August 200 A.D. and sailed back to Syria, staying at Antioch for about a year. Early in 202 A.D., they returned to Rome to celebrate Septimius' *decennalia* on April 9, the beginning of his tenth year of rule.

The celebration was spectacular. It was also a thanksgiving for the safe return of Septimius, Julia, and their sons after a five-year absence. In addition, the date of the *decennalia* was only two days before the emperor's fifty-seventh birthday and five days after the royal couple's elder son, Caracalla, turned fourteen.

To add to the festivities, Caracalla was married to the daughter of Septimius' Praetorian prefect, Plautianus, a native of Leptis Magna and kinsman of the emperor's mother, who had become so powerful that his influence extended into every aspect of the imperial administration. The historian Dio, who was present at all the proceedings, observed:

> On the occasion of the tenth anniversary of his coming to power Severus presented to the entire populace that received the grain dole and to the soldiers of the pretorian guard gold pieces equal in number to the years of his reign. He prided himself especially on this largess, and, in fact, no emperor had ever before given so much to the whole population at once; the total amount spent for the purpose was two hundred million sesterces. The nuptials of Antoninus [Caracalla], the son of Severus, and Plautilla, Plautianus' daughter, were also celebrated at this time; and Plautianus gave as much for his daughter's dowry as would have sufficed for fifty women of royal rank. We saw

the gifts as they were being carried through the Forum to the palace. And we were all entertained together at a banquet, partly in royal and partly in barbaric style. . . . At this time there occurred, too, all sorts of spectacles in honor of Septimius' return, the completion of his first ten years of power, and his victories. At these spectacles sixty wild boars of Plautianus fought together at a signal, and . . . many other wild beasts . . . were slain. . . . For to correspond with the duration of the festival, which lasted seven days, the number of animals was also seven times one hundred.

(*Roman History* 76.1.1–5)

Africa—Septimius and Julia Triumphant

Even before the seven days of the great celebrations in Rome were over, Septimius (always partial to the number 7 since "Septimius" derives from *septimus,* meaning "seventh" in Latin) was probably already planning his next move, a triumphal return to the land of his birth—Africa. Characteristically, he was soon on his way with Julia, Caracalla and his new wife, his younger son, Geta, and Plautianus. Septimius' brother Geta, who had been serving him faithfully for years (one wonders how he felt about being left out of the succession), was probably also part of the company, as were other relatives holding important posts in the Severan administration. No emperor save Hadrian had ever visited Africa. Now its most famous son, at least since Hannibal, was returning as Augustus.

The highlight of the tour was, of course, the royal couple's visit to Leptis Magna, which Septimius had not seen for almost thirty years. The proud city went overboard with statues and dedications celebrating Severus' roots and the city's special relation to him, honoring him, his family (those honoring his parents must have caused

some official embarrassment since Septimius now claimed to be the son of Marcus Aurelius!), and practically everyone else closely associated with him—including his first wife, another hometown product. The people of Leptis even called themselves "Septimiani." In return, the emperor granted the city *ius Italicum,* giving it the status of an Italian city and exempting it from taxation. He also began plans for a new forum and basilica, which were not completed until after his death, and perhaps a large temple to Bacchus and Hercules. Other building and reconstruction projects were initiated.

The winter of 202 A.D. was most likely spent in Leptis Magna. What Julia thought of all this we can only imagine. Few in the Roman world had seen so much of it, and now after fifteen years of marriage, she had finally come to her husband's home in North Africa. The visit must have been long anticipated. Student that she was, she could not have helped but be impressed with visits to Carthage and other sites that had become part of popular Roman history and literature.

Back at Rome

The royal party returned to Rome from Africa to a festive reception about midyear in 203 A.D., certainly in time for the dedication of Septimius' great triumphal arch in the Forum. What was to prove their last stay in the capital turned out to be the longest that Julia and her husband would ever spend, a total of about five years.

When they arrived at the capital, preparations were probably already underway for the Secular Games, which had been celebrated only six times before in Roman history. The seventh (and, as it turned out, the last) was to take place in June of 204 A.D. Held at 110-year intervals (see Chapter 7), their occurrence certainly

Figure 8.8   *The Arch of Septimius Severus in the Forum at Rome (dedicated in 203 A.D.)*

pleased Septimius, who may have been a member of the priesthood that oversaw the ceremonies. Because of his affinity with the number 7, he would also have attached significance to the fact that this seventh celebration fell during his reign. The Games had come to represent the end of one era and the beginning of a new and better age—an idea heartily embraced by the emperor. He and his sons performed their official duties over the three days of prayer and ritual (followed by seven days of games), while Julia, as empress, also played her part. She and 109 other wives honored the goddesses Juno and Diana with sacred banquets. The majority of these women were senators' wives; Julia's niece, Julia Soaemias, also took part.

Symbolically, the first year of the new era, 205 A.D., began with Septimius' and Julia's sons sharing the consulship. It would also be the last year that Julia's dreaded enemy, Plautianus, was alive.

Julia and Plautianus

For many years now, Julia had suffered the abuse of Plautianus. The kinsman and boyhood friend of Septimius, he had been continually at his side through thick and thin since 193 A.D. His power increased dramatically after he became Prefect of the Guard in 197 A.D., and he rose to a position of power that rivaled that of the emperor. Even the authority Sejanus had wielded under Tiberius (see Chapter 5) paled when compared with that of Plautianus, who often treated Septimius contemptuously and frequently slandered and demeaned Julia—even to her husband's face. She hated but feared him. Dio describes his machinations against the hapless empress:

> So greatly did Plautianus have the mastery in every way over the emperor, that he often treated Julia Augusta in an outrageous manner; for he cordially detested her and was always abusing her violently to Severus. He used to conduct investigations into her conduct as well as gather evidence against her by torturing women of the nobility. For this reason she began to study philosophy and passed her days in company with sophists.
> (*Roman History* 75.15.6–7)

A "circle" of literary friends and intellectuals grew up around Julia, probably nothing formal, but simply a group of frequent visitors to her fashionable salon in Rome. There is no question about her own curiosity and intellectual capacity, and it is clear that when she could not be with her husband, she enjoyed the company of talented people. She encouraged the sophist Philostratus, who referred to her as the "philosopher" (and addressed one of his extant letters to her), to write a biography about the wizard Apollonius of Tyana, with whose legendary exploits (mostly concocted) she probably became familiar while she was with her husband at Tyana (in Asia Minor) some years earlier.

Charges that Julia was promiscuous probably also stem mostly from Plautianus' slanders. How intimate her relations now were with her husband, in his late fifties and suffering from gout or arthritis so badly that he often had to be carried on a litter, is unknown. One of the reasons that Septimius probably stayed in Rome so long this time was his declining health—

although it is clear from Dio that he still remained as energetic as possible. While Julia's age is not known, she would have been considerably younger than her husband. Septimius himself was described as being rather wild as a youth (he was even charged with adultery); but as emperor, he was very hard on adulterers. The fact that he never acted on Plautianus' charges of Julia's improper behavior indicates that he did not believe them. With the ubiquitous prefect watching her every move, Julia would have been unwise to give her husband any reason to doubt her. She may have had lovers after his death, but while he lived, there is absolutely nothing to indicate that Septimius ever mistrusted her—or her Syrian family and friends.

Plautianus was also detested by Caracalla. The young emperor was close to his mother and resented the fact that when he was fourteen he had been forced to marry the disagreeable prefect's daughter, whom he detested (Julia certainly would not have favored the marriage either). No one at court seems to have fully fathomed how Plautianus—variously described (by hostile sources) as pale, overweight, gluttonous, vindictive, sensual, perverted, and obnoxious—got away with his behavior toward them and the emperor. Certainly, the wily prefect knew how to manipulate Septimius' superstitious nature and would not have hesitated to concoct favorable horoscopes, but the real answer to his special relationship with the emperor may be in Herodian's statement (3.10.6) that some said the two had been "boy-lovers" in Africa. If true, it would seem that Plautianus had been the dominant partner in the relationship.

It was on the royal party's recent visit to Africa that Plautianus first got into serious trouble. Septimius apparently did not like seeing so many statues of Plautianus in their hometown,

Leptis Magna, and he seems particularly irritated that the prefect had placed his image among those of the emperor's own family. Septimius, Leptis' greatest son, did not want to share the spotlight with anyone. Plautianus' statues were pulled down. Certainly, Julia would have taken advantage of her husband's displeasure and purposefully overemphasized the enormity of the prefect's transgression.

For the time being, nothing else happened, but everyone who hated Plautianus now sensed, for the first time, a crack in his armor. Most assuredly, they did what they could to widen it without endangering themselves. Septimius' brother Geta had also suffered the abuse of Plautianus, and just before he died in 204 A.D., he told his brother everything he knew about the unscrupulous prefect. From that time on, Septimius' attitude toward Plautianus changed completely. Geta had apparently been afraid to say anything previously—or Septimius was unwilling to listen. Geta's deathbed confession would have had great impact on the superstitious emperor.

The fall of Plautianus came in January of 205 A.D. and was orchestrated by young Caracalla and, most certainly, Julia. Caracalla arranged for Septimius to be informed that a plot had been organized by Plautianus to kill him—and Caracalla. Concocted evidence was produced just as the emperor, Julia, and other members of the imperial family were sitting down to dinner on January 22—following, ironically, a palace festival honoring dead ancestors. Since Septimius had just dreamed that Albinus was alive and meant to kill him, he was all the more ready to believe the story about Plautianus, who was summoned to the palace. Caracalla prevented Plautianus from defending himself, seized the prefect's sword, struck him with his fist, and was

only prevented from killing him himself by his father. Before Septimius could do anything, Caracalla ordered a nearby attendant to slay Plautianus. Dio describes what happened next:

> And somebody plucked out a few hairs from [Plautianus'] beard, carried them to Julia and Plautilla [Plautianus' daughter and wife of Caracalla], who were together, before they had heard a word of the affair, and exclaimed, "Behold your Plautianus," thus causing grief to the one and joy to the other. Thus this man, who had possessed the greatest power of all the men of my time, so that everyone regarded him with greater fear and trembling than the very emperors, and who had been led on to still greater hopes, was slain by his son-in-law and his body thrown down from the palace into a street; for it was only afterwards that, at the command of Severus, he was taken up and buried.
> (*Roman History* 76.4.4–5)

That Julia and Plautilla, who despised one another, happened to be together when they received news of Plautianus' death smacks of pre-arrangement by Julia. It suggests her direct involvement in the plot and her desire to see *both* father and daughter suffer for the miseries they had brought to her and her son. Plautilla would soon be banished and was later executed when Caracalla became sole emperor. The Senate was summoned, and Septimius gave the official version of what had happened. A number of Plautianus' closest associates were executed immediately, but reverberations continued to be felt for some time. For the man about whom Septimius supposedly once wrote in a letter, "I love the man so much that I pray to die before he does," the emperor certainly digested the affair in his typical businesslike fashion.

That the Syrian connection was still intact and providing high-ranking government officials is demonstrated by the appointment of Septimius' friend Papinian, who was related to Julia by marriage, as one of the two new Guard prefects who replaced Plautianus. Papinian was not a military man but a jurist. He had probably been serving Septimius since the early days of his administration and had risen to the higher levels of government. Septimius, although not considering himself bound by the law, was always concerned with order and administering justice properly to the Empire's inhabitants. No ruler had more patience or was more directly involved in seeing that his subjects were treated equitably. Political enemies were, of course, the exception. They had much to fear from the emperor, which is evident from the frequent trials of would-be troublemakers during these years. Septimius needed the legal expertise of Papinian to help him comprehend the existing volumes of Roman law and to formulate new laws for contemporary situations. Certainly, Julia, too, had input into her husband's legal decisions. Assisting Papinian and also adding to the atmosphere of jurisprudence of the early third century A.D. was a younger jurist named Ulpian, another Syrian, who, like Papinian, would later be regarded as among the most highly respected legal minds of antiquity.

For a man who had been on the move his entire life, these years in Rome must have been an unwelcome change to Septimius. Dio (76.17.1–3) describes the daily routine of exercise, business, rest, bathing, and dining that the emperor had established for himself, a quite energetic one considering his age and health. He usually lunched with his sons and dined nightly with them, Julia, and other intimates. There were the meetings of the Senate and the numerous trials. Various construction and restoration projects had been initiated during his reign, and

Figure 8.9 *Remains of a portion of the massive Imperial Palace on the Palatine Hill, just above the Circus Maximus, residence of Septimius and Julia Domna and all previous emperors*

some still may have required his attention. It is likely that he was composing his *Autobiography,* which no longer exists, during this time.

While there is no mention of Julia's activities, those of her sons were reportedly shameful, and their undisciplined behavior distressed their parents. Caracalla and Geta had been rivals since childhood, and now that rivalry turned into hatred. Septimius also had to deal with brigands in Italy (see box, page 228) whose elusiveness demoralized the emperor, who was used to clear-cut victories. It is no wonder that

Baebius Marcellinus—A Terminal Case of Baldness

DEALING WITH THE SOCIAL side effects of baldness is something that men (and some women) have had to do in any society in any age. No matter how a person who is bald or balding feels about the subject, one thing is generally accepted—the experience is not fatal. At least the natural process itself is not. For a Roman senator named Baebius Marcellinus, however, his extreme baldness proved to be his fatal flaw. It identified him (along with his dress) as the alleged guilty party in a supposed plot against Severus. The story is told by the historian Dio, who was a senator and eyewitness to the proceedings. It is incredible for its immediacy and an indication of the fear that Septimius engendered in his own Senate. Parts of the narrative would be humorous—such as Dio's touching the top of his head to make sure his own hair was still there—if it were not so tragic.

In the aftermath of Plautianus' death, many people came under scrutiny; and if their activities were judged treasonable, they were executed. Informers were everywhere, and some, like Baebius, were put to death before Septimius even knew that they had been condemned. Dio thought the charge preposterous and knew the man was innocent—but, like his fellow senators, he knew better than to take the side of Marcellinus. According to Dio's account, a man named Apronianus, who was governor of Asia, was condemned in absentia because his nurse supposedly once dreamed he would become emperor. In the process of gathering evidence (which was taken under torture) against Apronianus, a witness was asked whether anyone else knew about the dream. Dio states:

> . . . the man under examination had said, among other things: "I saw a certain bald-headed senator peeping in." On hearing this we [Dio and his fellow senators] found ourselves in a terrible position; for although neither the man had spoken nor Severus written anyone's name, yet such was the general consternation that even those who had never visited the house of Apronianus, and not alone the bald-headed but even those who were bald on their forehead, grew afraid. And although no one was very cheerful, except those who had unusually heavy hair, yet we all looked round at those who were not so fortunate, and a murmur ran about: "It's So-and-so." "No, it's So-and-so." I will not conceal what happened to me at the time, ridiculous as it is. I was so disconcerted that I actually felt with my hand to see whether I had any hair on my head. And a good many others had the same experience. And we were very careful to direct our gaze upon those who were more or less bald, as if we should thereby divert our own danger upon them; we continued to do this until the further statement was read that the bald-head in question wore a purple-bordered toga. When this detail came out, we turned our eyes upon Baebius Marcellinus; for he had been aedile at the time and was extremely bald. So he rose, and coming forward, said: "He will of course recognize me, if he has seen me." After we had commended this course, the informer was brought in while Marcellinus stood by, and for a considerable time remained silent, looking about for a man he could recognize, but finally, following the direction of an almost imperceptible nod that somebody gave, he said that Marcellinus was the man. Thus was Marcellinus convicted for a bald-head's peeping, and he was led out of the senate-chamber bewailing his fate. When he had passed through the Forum, he refused to proceed farther, but just where he was took leave of his children, four in number, and spoke these most affecting words: "There is only one thing that causes me sorrow, my children, and that is that I leave you behind alive." Then his head was cut off, before Severus even learned that he had been condemned.
>
> (*Roman History* 76.8–9.2)

Figure 8.10 *Structural remains and wall paintings from Septimius' headquarters at York, where he died in 211 A.D. They rest in the undercroft of the Medieval Cathedral at York. At the right is a model depicting the headquarters during Septimius' day.*

he began to turn his eye to Britain. Recent rebellions justified his presence there—a way out of his political and personal problems at Rome. As in the past, Septimius left trusted men in key positions. Others, like Papinian, went with him. In 208 A.D., the sixty-three-year-old emperor departed with reinforcements for Britain, intending (unrealistically) to conquer it all. Julia once more accompanied her husband and sons on the campaign.

Septimius' Death in Britain

The expedition to Britain would be the emperor's last. Septimius, who had previously had ceilings in the palace painted with the stars as they appeared when he was born (but arranged so that

no one could use the information to do him harm), would have ensured that the requisite astrological forecasts for the expedition's outcome had been made. But neither Septimius nor Julia needed a horoscope to know his death was fast approaching. And there were the expected omens.

It seems clear that Septimius went, with his family, to Britain to die there while on campaign—thus precluding an ordinary death from his infirmities at Rome. He supposedly spurned initial attempts by the Britons to make peace with him so that he could win a victory over them. He also hoped that war and military discipline would sober up his sons and make them act more responsibly. It did not. Caracalla even tried to hasten his father's death in Britain by killing him—in front of the troops! Septimius chastised him, particularly for his stupidity, but did nothing (his horoscope had probably not forecast his death by his son's hand). What Julia thought about Caracalla's behavior can only be guessed. However, it was clear to both parents that the succession was in trouble, and they must have been reminded of Commodus' outrageous escapades when he succeeded his father, Marcus Aurelius.

Septimius spent the remainder of his life on the Scottish frontier. Julia appears to have passed most of her time at the Roman headquarters at York. Dio preserves an anecdote about her meeting with the wife of a Caledon-

ian leader after a treaty had temporarily stopped the fighting. Apparently intrigued by stories she had heard about the sexual freedom (an indication of her own faithfulness to her husband?) of women in Britain, she asked her companion about it and received this Spartan-like reply:

> . . . a very witty remark is reported to have been made by the wife of Argentocoxus, a Caledonian, to Julia Augusta. When the empress was jesting with her, after the treaty, about the free intercourse of her sex with men in Britain, she replied: "We fulfill the demands of nature in a much better way than do you Roman women; for we consort openly with

Bulla the Bandit—A Not-So-Common Thief

As ironfisted as Septimius was against personal and political enemies, he had his share of problems with outlaws. By disbanding the traditional Praetorian Guard, which was recruited largely from Italy, Severus apparently made other problems for himself. Many of those discharged (and disgraced) now turned to crime as a way of life and terrorized the Italian countryside. Elsewhere, while he was still in the East following his defeat of Pescennius Niger, Septimius was approached by a group of horsemen led by a man who appeared to be a military tribune. The man saluted him, kissed him, and then departed. It was later learned that this was Claudius, a robber who was active in Judaea and Syria. Apparently, he wanted a firsthand look at the emperor—or was demonstrating his boldness. He was never caught.

For Septimius, the most troublesome of these brigands was a fellow named Bulla, who was apparently becoming something of a folk hero before he was caught and executed. Some imperial freedmen even ran off and joined him.

Septimius was rather contemptuous of freedmen in his personal service, but it is doubtful they would have given up their comfortable lives and become thieves. The ones who joined Bulla probably worked the imperial estates in rural Italy. The following account provides details of the bandit's activities:

> At this period one Bulla, an Italian, got together a robber band of about six hundred men, and for two years continued to plunder Italy under the very noses of the emperors and of a multitude of soldiers. For though he was pursued by many men, and though Severus eagerly followed his trail, he was never really seen when seen, never found when found, never caught when caught, thanks to his great bribes and his cleverness. For he learned of everybody that was setting out from Rome and everybody that was putting into port at Brundisium, and he knew both who and how many there were, and what and how much they had with them. In the case of most persons he would take a part of what they had and let

the best men, whereas you let yourselves be debauched in secret by the vilest." Such was the retort of the British woman.

(*Roman History* 76.16.5)

On February 4, 211 A.D., Septimius Severus died of illness at York in Britain. He was two months short of his sixty-sixth birthday. Julia would have been with him during the final days, if for no other reason than to prevent Caracalla from poisoning him. Before he died, Septimius gave these last words of advice to his sons: "Be harmonious, enrich the soldiers, and scorn all other men." He was cremated and his remains brought back to Rome in a purple urn by Julia and her sons. It was placed in the Mausoleum of Hadrian.

Julia and Caracalla

Caracalla certainly heeded his father's final words about "scorn," for he began a systematic "scorn" of people he did not like who had served his father. The prefect Papinian was dismissed. Caracalla reserved most of his scorn, however, for his brother Geta, whom he attempted to have eliminated before leaving Britain. Julia tried to reconcile her sons while at York, but her success was temporary. Caracalla wanted to be

---

them go at once, but he detained artisans for a time and made use of their skill, then dismissed them with a present. Once, when two of his men had been captured and were about to be given to wild beasts, he paid a visit to the keeper of the prison, pretending that he was the governor of his native district and needed some men of such and such a description, and in this way he secured and saved the men. And he approached the centurion who was trying to exterminate the band and accused himself, pretending to be someone else, and promised, if the centurion would accompany him, to deliver the robber to him. So, on the pretext that he was leading him to Felix ["Lucky"] (this was another name by which he was called), he led him into a defile beset with thickets, and easily seized him. Later, he assumed the dress of a magistrate, ascended the tribunal, and having summoned the centurion, caused part of his head to be shaved, and then said: "Carry this message to your master: 'Feed your slaves, so that they may not turn to brigandage.'" Bulla had with him, in fact, a very large

number of imperial freedmen, some of whom had been poorly paid, while others had received absolutely no pay at all. Severus, informed of these various occurrences, was angry at the thought that though he was winning the wars in Britain, through others, yet he himself had proved no match for a robber in Italy; and finally he sent a tribune from his bodyguard with many horsemen, after threatening him with dire punishment if he should fail to bring back the robber alive. So this tribune, having learned that the brigand was intimate with another man's wife, persuaded her through her husband to assist them on promise of immunity. As a result, the robber was arrested while asleep in a cave. Papinian, the prefect, asked him, "Why did you become a robber?" And he replied: "Why are you a prefect?" Later, after due proclamation, he was given to wild beasts, and his band was broken up—to such an extent did the strength of the whole six hundred lie in him.

(Dio, *Roman History* 76.10.1–7)

York
BRITANNIA
Londinium

1 Cologne
BELGICA Bonn
CHATTI
MARCOMANNI
LUGDUNENSIS
Rhine R.
2
Danube River
QUADI
Carnuntum
NORICUM
RAETIA
Lyons
ALPES
3
SARMATAE JAZYGES
TRES
DACIA
Aquileia
4
Sari
Sirmium
Po River
AQUITANIA
Legio
NARBONENSIS
Nimes
DALMATIA
Salonae
MOESIA
SUPERIOR
LUSITANIA
TARRACONENSIS
Tarraco
CORSICA
Rome
MACEDON
SARDINIA
Brundisium
BAETICA
EPIRUS
Iol-Caesarea
Cirta
SICILY
ACHAEA
TINGITANA
CAESARIENSIS
Carthage
MAURETANIA
Lambaesis
NUMIDIA
Leptis Magna
Cyrene
AFRICA
GARAMANTES

1. GERMANIA INFERIOR
2. GERMANIA SUPERIOR
3. PANNONIA SUPERIOR
4. PANNONIA INFERIOR
5. MOESIA INFERIOR
6. OSRHOENE
7. MESOPOTAMIA
8. SYRIA COELE

——————— Frontier
— — — — — Provincial boundary

0   100 200 300 400 500
Miles

Map 19   The Roman Empire in 211 A.D.

GOTHI

Phasis
River

HIBERI

Artaxata

ARMENIA

nizegetusa

5

Sardica

THRACIA

PONTUS ET
BITHYNIA

Byzantium · Chalcedon

· Nicaea

· Cyzicus

CAPPADOCIA

6

Nisibis

GALATIA

ASIA

· Edessa

7

Smyrna

Tigris River

thens

· Ephesus

CILICIA

· Antioch

8

PARTHIA

LYCIA ET PAMPHYLIA

· Emesa

· Palmyra

Seleucia · Ctesiphon

Euphrates River

CYPRUS

Tyre ·

SYRIA PHOENICE

CRETE

SYRIA PALAESTINA

· Alexandria

CYRENAICA

· Petra

ARABIA

AEGYPTUS

Nile River

· Philae

sole emperor, and the fight between the brothers and their supporters continued at Rome. At one point, in the presence of their father's advisors and their distraught mother, they tried to divide the Empire between themselves. Herodian used this occasion to place the following speech in Julia's mouth:

> "My sons, you have found a method of partitioning the land and the sea; between the continents you say lies the barrier of the Pontic sea. But what about your mother? How do you propose to partition her? How am I supposed to divide and carve up this unhappy body of mine? Very well, kill me first and each of you take a part of my torn body to your territory and bury it there. In this way I can be shared out between you along with the land and the sea." With these words she began weeping and crying out. Then she threw her arms around them both and drew them into an embrace, trying to reconcile them. Everyone was overcome with pity and the council broke up. The scheme was rejected and the two brothers returned, each to his own palace quarters. (*History* 3.3.8–9)

Finally, on December 26, Caracalla took matters into his own hand and had Geta killed. Dio dramatically recounts the scene:

> Antoninus [Caracalla] induced his mother to summon them both, unattended, to her apartment, with a view to reconciling them. Thus Geta was persuaded, and went in with him; but when they were inside, some centurions, previously instructed by Antoninus, rushed in in a body and struck down Geta, who at sight of them had run to his mother, hung about her neck and clung to her bosom and breasts, lamenting and crying: "Mother that didst bear me, mother that didst bear me, help! I am being murdered." And so she, tricked in this way, saw her son perishing in most impious fashion in her arms, and received him at his

Figure 8.11   *Geta, the younger son of Septimius and Julia, who was murdered in his mother's lap by order of Caracalla*

death into the very womb, as it were, whence he had been born; for she was all covered with his blood, so that she took no note of the wound she had received on her hand. But she was not permitted to mourn or weep for her son, though he had met so miserable an end before his time (he was only twenty-two years and nine months old), but, on the contrary, she was compelled to rejoice and laugh as though at some great good fortune; so closely were all her words, gestures, and change of color observed. Thus she alone, the Augusta, wife of the emperor and mother of the emperors, was not permitted to shed tears even in private over so great a sorrow. (*Roman History* 77.2.2–6)

Figure 8.12 *Large bronze coin bearing the likeness of Caracalla. The scowl is characteristic of most representations of him.*

It was said that Septimius tolerated Caracalla's outrageous behavior because his love for him outweighed that for his country. The same must be said of Julia. To have her younger son murdered in her arms at the order of the older was a nightmare few mothers have suffered. Yet, despite Dio's account that she lived in fear of Caracalla, the opposite appears true. It was her motherly hand that helped steady the short reign of the mediocre Caracalla. Perhaps she realized he was mentally ill and needed her help. Perhaps she had seen in the stars what was going to happen and accepted it. What is clear is that she did not desert her son, apparently loved him no less (he was all she had left), and advised him as best she could. The closeness of the two is undoubtedly what prompted the vicious rumors of an incestuous relationship. Dio, perhaps unfairly, suggests that the only reason Julia honored her son at all was to retain some of her former power and prevent being relegated to private life. He gives this description of her relationship with Caracalla while he was emperor:

> For the rest, he was staining himself with blood, doing lawless deeds, and squandering money. Neither in these matters nor in any others did he heed his mother, who gave him much excellent advice. And yet he had appointed her to receive petitions and to have charge of his correspondence in both languages, except in very important cases, and used to include her name, in terms of high praise, together with his own and that of the legions, in his letters to the senate, stating that she was well. Need I add that she held public receptions for all the most prominent men, precisely as did the emperor? But, while she devoted herself more and more to the study of philosophy with these men, he kept declaring that he needed nothing beyond the necessaries of life and plumed himself over his pretended ability to live on the cheapest kind of fare; yet there was nothing on land or sea or in the air that we did not regularly supply to him both by private gifts and by public grants.
> (*Roman History* 77.18.2–3)

Julia's title was expanded to "Mother of our Augustus and the Camp and the Senate and the Country." No Augusta had been so honored before. Still, she was not emperor and could do nothing about the reputed twenty thousand men and women, including Papinian, who were killed at Caracalla's order following Geta's murder—or the attempts to erase all traces of Geta's memory. Caracalla also allegedly put to death an elderly daughter of Marcus Aurelius because she had wept with Julia after the death of Geta.

There was little positive to distinguish the rule of Caracalla, which lasted until April of 217 A.D. Dio, who was not a fan, left this interesting assessment:

> Antoninus [Caracalla] belonged to three races; and he possessed none of their virtues at all, but combined in himself all their vices; the fickleness, cowardice, and recklessness of Gaul [where he was born] were his, the harshness and cruelty of Africa [his father's home], and the craftiness of Syria, whence he was sprung on his mother's side.
> (*Roman History* 77.6.1a)

The most notable occurrence during Caracalla's administration was his grant of citizenship to all free inhabitants of the Roman Empire in 212 A.D. The actual impact of the measure has been hotly debated among modern scholars and variously interpreted as weakening or strengthening the Empire. Legal privileges of Roman citizens had already been greatly reduced over the years, but presumably, for those many who had never experienced any such privileges, this was a meaningful act. Symbolically, bestowing citizenship would also have given its recipients more of a sense of "belonging" and thereby enhanced unity within the Empire. However, Dio refers to Caracalla's grant as little more than a fund-raising device. In practical terms, it increased revenue dramatically since some taxes were paid *only* by citizens, allowing Caracalla to keep the military, on whom he was dependent, happy with bonuses. Caracalla's spending on the army was excessive, as the following anecdote from Dio (77.10.4) would suggest. Supposedly, Julia scolded him for squandering too much money on the soldiers and said, "There is no longer any source of revenue, either just or unjust left us. . . ." To which Caracalla replied, showing his sword, "Be of good cheer, mother: for as long as we have this, we shall not run short of money."

The Assassination of Caracalla

Caracalla was assassinated while campaigning in the East against the Parthians. Julia had accompanied him as far as Antioch, where she stayed in order to sort through correspondences and pass on only the most important to her son. In this capacity, she is said to have received a letter from Rome denouncing Caracalla's Praetorian prefect, Macrinus. According to the story, an African seer had proclaimed that

Macrinus, who was with the emperor on the campaign, and his son were plotting to seize the throne. The communiqué's delay in reaching Caracalla was crucial, because in the meantime Macrinus received word that his life was in danger (a less dramatic version of the story simply states that Macrinus intercepted a letter to Caracalla denouncing him). He decided, for self-preservation—there is nothing to indicate that Macrinus was really guilty of anything—that he must strike first and secretly arrange the emperor's death. On April 8, 217 A.D., his agent murdered Caracalla while he was relieving himself by the roadside from the effects of a stomachache. The assassin was killed immediately, and since the army did not know Macrinus was responsible, he was hailed as emperor.

The Death of Julia

Julia did not long survive her son. She had received news of his death while at Antioch. Distressed and fearful of Macrinus, she apparently contemplated suicide, but when the new emperor treated her with respect, her plan changed, and she began to speak abusively about her son's successor:

> Then, as no change was made in her royal retinue or in the guard of Pretorians in attendance upon her, and the new emperor sent her a kindly message, although he had heard what she had said, she took courage, put aside her desire for death, and without writing him any reply, began intriguing with the soldiers she had about her. . . .
>
> (Dio, *Roman History,* 78.23.2–3)

Because of her intrigues, Macrinus ultimately ordered her out of Antioch. She soon died from starvation and complications caused by cancer of the breast. She was probably in her fifties at the time of her death. Dio notes:

. . . he ordered her to leave Antioch as soon as possible and go whithersoever she wished, and she heard, moreover, what was said in Rome about her son, she no longer cared to live, but hastened her death by refusing food, though one might say that she was already in a dying condition by reason of the cancer of the breast that she had had for a very long time.

(*Roman History* 78.23.6)

Finally, Dio took a moment to reflect and moralize upon the unusual life of Julia (who was later deified)—which in itself is interesting, since such commentaries were usually reserved for the passing of famous men:

And so this woman, sprung from the people and raised to a high station, who had lived during her husband's reign in great unhappiness because of Plautianus, who had beheld her younger son slain in her own bosom and had always from first to last borne ill will toward her elder son while he lived [her actions do not support Dio's charge], and finally had received such tidings of his assassination, fell from power during her lifetime and thereupon destroyed herself. Hence no one could in the light of her career, regard as happy each and all who attain great power, unless some genuine and unalloyed pleasure in life and unmixed and lasting good fortune is theirs. This, then, was the fate of Julia. Her body was brought to Rome and placed in the tomb of Gaius and Lucius. Later, however, both her bones and those of Geta were transferred by her sister Maesa to the precinct of Antoninus.

(78.24.1–3)

After Julia: Severan Revival— Julia Maesa and Her Daughters

This was not the end of the influence of strong Severan women nor of the dynasty. Macrinus, an African Moor and the first emperor who was not a senator, never received the support he needed, and his lack of ability (and funds) eventually lost him the army's loyalty. Julia Maesa, Julia Domna's sister, orchestrated his downfall.

Maesa's husband had served Septimius and Caracalla long and well, and she, as sister of the empress, was a familiar figure at court (she lived at the palace) and on campaign. Judging from later evidence of her domineering personality, her influence with the royal family over a twenty-five-year period must have been significant. Now her husband, her sister, and Caracalla were dead, and she had returned to Emesa in Syria. However, she had no intention of sitting by idly. It was her turn to take charge.

Maesa presented her fourteen-year-old grandson Varius Avitus, son of her widowed daughter Julia Soaemias, to Macrinus' disgruntled troops as the illegitimate son of Caracalla—and rightful heir to the throne. The youth, already a priest of the Sun-God Elagabal at Emesa, would soon change his name to one more closely identified with his deity—Elagabalus. He was proclaimed emperor by the soldiers (who received cash incentives), and Macrinus was defeated and executed at Antioch in June of 218 A.D. He had ruled for fourteen months. Once more the Severans held the throne.

Even Rome was unprepared for Elagabalus. The bizarre lad—the first transvestite, homosexual emperor—was so deviant in behavior, feminine in appearance, and exotic in dress that the public abhorred him. His fanaticism for Elagabal added to his unpopularity when he brought the god, in the form of the conical black stone worshipped at Emesa, to Rome and proclaimed him official deity of the Empire. Elagabalus' mother, Soaemias, encouraged the boy's extravagances, hoping to control him and become the power behind the throne; but her

Figure 8.13   *Elagabalus*

Figure 8.14   *Julia Mamaea*

mother, Julia Maesa, soon demonstrated who really was running the Empire.

Concerned that the soldiers would soon react against the aberrant emperor, Maesa persuaded (or forced) him to adopt his thirteen-year-old cousin Severus Alexander, the son of her other daughter, Julia Mamaea. The popularity of Severus Alexander, said to be virtually free of vices, posed so great a threat to Elagabalus that he and his mother decided to have him killed. Their efforts were thwarted by Julia Maesa and Mamaea, who ultimately gave the Praetorians their blessing (and money) to murder Elagabalus and Soaemias in March of 222 A.D.

The End of Severan Rule

The elderly Julia Maesa probably died the following year. Her daughter Mamaea quickly took her place and continued the "rule" of the Severan women. She tolerated no rivals. Under her careful guidance, her son, a pleasant young man but unequal to the tasks set before him, was emperor for thirteen years. On March 21, 235 A.D., the army, weary of domineering Severan females and weak male emperors, murdered Mamaea and her son while they were with the troops near Mainz in Germany. The rule of the African-Syrian emperors was over. Few women in history had exercised power and authority as great as had the Severan Julias of Emesa.

With the end of the Severan Dynasty, the most hectic and chaotic period in Roman history began, that of the "Barracks Emperors" (235–284 A.D.). The favor shown to the military by the Severi inevitably led to the army's selection of the majority of emperors during this era. In a fifty-year period, there were over twenty Augusti, many literally raised out of the barracks (hence the name for the period) by their troops. It would be left to Diocletian, the last of this unlikely group of emperors, to restore order to the Empire.

Figure 8.15
Severus Alexander

Aurelian Draws a Queen—Zenobia of Palmyra

DURING THE PERIOD OF the "Barracks Emperors," a cavalry officer named Aurelian became Augustus and ruled from 270 to 275 A.D. If he had not been assassinated, he might have spared Rome from further chaos and disorder. As it was, he earned the title "Restorer of the Roman World." Aurelian settled rebellions within the Empire, expelled barbarians from Italy and the Danube region, secured the East, and restored his authority over the West. In the process, he encountered and defeated Queen Zenobia of Palmyra in Syria. The most celebrated woman of her time, wrapped in legend and Eastern mystique, Zenobia claimed (incorrectly) to be the descendant and successor of Cleopatra. She and her husband had been valuable allies of Rome against the Persians. After her husband's murder in 267 A.D., she broke with

Rome and occupied Egypt and much of Asia Minor. Aurelian defeated and captured her in 272 A.D. and destroyed Palmyra the next year.

What follows is the most extensive passage we have about Zenobia's personal characteristics. Unfortunately, it comes from the *Augustan History (Scriptores Historiae Augustae),* which is a very uncritical source. Letters, dialogue, matters of personal appearance, and the like should be read with caution. Still, it contains much of the information we have about her. Despite its inaccuracies, the passage conveys an image of what people wanted to think about Zenobia and is indicative of the impact she had on her times:

> . . . Zenobia . . . boasting herself to be of the family of the Cleopatras and the Ptolemies,

(continued)

Aurelian Draws a Queen (continued)

proceeded upon the death of her husband Odaenathus to cast about her shoulders the imperial mantle; and . . . assuming the diadem, she held the imperial power in the name of her sons . . . ruling longer than could be endured from one of the female sex. For this proud woman performed the functions of a monarch . . . and in the end could scarcely be conquered by Aurelian himself, under whom she was led in triumph and submitted to the sway of Rome.

There is still in existence a letter of Aurelian's which bears testimony concerning this woman, then in captivity. For when some found fault with him, because he, the bravest of men, had led a woman in triumph, as though she were a general, he sent a letter to the senate and the Roman people, defending himself by the following justification: "I have heard . . . that men are reproaching me for having performed an unmanly deed in leading Zenobia in triumph. But in truth those very persons who find fault with me now would accord me praise in abundance, did they but know what manner of woman she is, how wise in counsels, how steadfast in plans, how firm toward the soldiers, how generous when necessity calls, and how stern when discipline demands. I might even say that it was her doing that Odaenathus defeated the Persians. . . . I might add thereto that such was the fear that this woman inspired in the peoples of the East and also the Egyptians that neither Arabs nor Saracens nor Armenians ever moved against her. Nor would I have spared her life, had I not known that she did a great service to the Roman state when she preserved the imperial power in the East for herself, or for her children. Therefore let those whom nothing pleases keep the venom of their own tongues to themselves. For if it is not meet to vanquish a woman and lead her in triumph, what are they saying of Gallienus [emperor from 263 to 268 A.D.], in contempt of whom she ruled the empire well? What of the Deified Claudius [Claudius II, who was emperor from 268 to 270 A.D.], that revered and honored leader? For he, because he was busied with his campaigns against the Goths, suffered her, or so it is said, to hold imperial power, doing it of purpose and wisely, in order that he himself, while she kept guard over the eastern frontier of the empire, might the more safely complete what he had taken in hand." This speech shows what opinion Aurelian held concerning Zenobia.

Such was her continence, it is said, that she would not know even her own husband save for the purpose of conception. . . . She lived in regal pomp. It was rather in the manner of the Persians that she received worship and in the manner of the Persian kings that she banqueted; but it was in the manner of a Roman emperor that she came forth to public assemblies, wearing a helmet and girt with a purple fillet, which had gems hanging from the lower edge, while its center was fastened with [a] jewel, used instead of the brooch worn by women, and her arms were frequently bare. Her face was dark and of a swarthy hue, her eyes were black and powerful beyond the usual wont, her spirit divinely great, and her beauty incredible. So white were her teeth that many thought that she had pearls in place of teeth. Her voice was clear and like that of a man. Her sternness, when necessity demanded, was that of a tyrant, her clemency, when her sense of right called for it, that of a good emperor. Generous with prudence, she conserved her treasures beyond the wont of women. She made use of a carriage, and rarely of a woman's coach, but more often she rode a horse; it is said, moreover, that frequently she walked with her foot-soldiers for three or four miles. She hunted with the eagerness of a Spaniard. She often drank with her generals, though at other times she refrained, and she drank, too, with the Persians and the Armenians, but only for the purpose of getting the better of them. At her banquets she used vessels of gold and jewels, and she even used those that had been Cleopatra's. As servants she had eunuchs of advanced age and but very few maidens. She ordered her sons to talk Latin, so that, in fact, they spoke Greek but rarely and with difficulty. She herself was not wholly conversant with the Latin tongue, but nevertheless, mastering her timidity she would speak it; Egyptian, on the other hand, she spoke very well. In the history of Alexandria and the Orient she was so well versed that she even composed an epitome, so it is said; Roman history, however, she read in Greek.

When Aurelian had taken her prisoner, he caused her to be led into his presence and then addressed her thus: "Why is it, Zenobia, that you dared to show insolence to the emperors of Rome?" To this she replied, it is said: "You, I know, are an emperor indeed, for you win victories, but Gallienus and . . . the others I never regarded as emperors. . . . I desired to become a partner in the royal power, should the supply of lands permit." And so she was led in triumph with such magnificence that the Ro-

Figure 8.16   *A rare coin image of Zenobia*

man people had never seen a more splendid parade. For, in the first place, she was adorned with gems so huge that she labored under the weight of her ornaments. . . . Furthermore, her feet were bound with shackles of gold and her hands with golden fetters, and even on her neck she wore a chain of gold, the weight of which was borne by a Persian buffoon. Her life was granted her by Aurelian, and they say that thereafter she lived with her children in the manner of a Roman matron on an estate that had been presented to her . . . which even to this day is still called Zenobia. . . .

(*Augustan History, Thirty Tyrants* [Zenobia] 30.1–27)

Suggestions for Further Reading

Dio's *Roman History* (primarily Books 74–80), Herodian's *History* (primarily Books 2–6), and the *Augustan History,* or *Scriptores Historiae Augustae* (primarily *Severus, Caracalla, Geta, Elagabalus,* and *Severus Alexander*), are the major sources for this chapter. They are available in the Loeb Classical Library editions, and the Penguin edition of the *Augustan History* contains all the above emperors save Severus Alexander. Both Dio and Herodian were contemporaries of the Severi, but Dio, a Roman

senator and close to much of the action, is generally more dependable. He also contains more material about Julia Domna and the other Julias. The *Augustan History* is a scandalous source and must be read with caution. Additional information about the Julias comes from coins and inscriptions and is not readily available. Aside from general histories, recent work on the period is remarkably scarce. By far the best investigation is A. R. Birley's excellent survey *Septimius Severus: The African Emperor,* rev. ed. (New Haven, Conn.: Yale University Press, 1989), which has been very useful in the present study. M.

Grant, *The Severans: The Changed Roman Empire* (New York: Routledge, 1996) is also now available. New material on the Severan women is of mixed quality. The only extensive work is G. Turton, *The Syrian Princesses: The Women Who Ruled Rome A.D. 193–235* (London: Cassell, 1974), who admits that his main purpose is not to carefully examine the sources but to stimulate interest. Other books that contain sections on the women are J. P. V. D. Balsdon's *Roman Women: Their History and Habits* (London: Bodley Head, reprint, 1963), 150–164; and S. Perowne's *The Caesars' Wives* (London: Hodder & Stoughton, 1974), Part 3. See also head-ings on women in Chapters 1, 4, and 8. Other works relevant to this chapter include M. Grant, *The Antonines: The Roman Empire in Transition* (New York: Routledge, 1993); T. Honoré, *Emperors and Lawyers: With a Palingenesia of Third Century Imperial Rescripts 193–305 A.D.,* 2nd ed. (New York: Oxford University Press, 1994); S. Raven, *Rome in Africa,* rev. ed. (New York: Routledge, 1993); and P. Salway, *The Oxford Illustrated History of Roman Britain* (New York: Oxford University Press, 1993) and *A History of Roman Britain* (New York: Oxford University Press, 1997).

9

Crisis and Christians

The Empire under Stress
Vibia Perpetua the Martyr

*I found nothing but a degenerate sort of cult carried
to extravagant lengths.*
(Pliny the Younger on Christianity, *Letters* 10.96)

The period of the "Barracks Emperors" ended when Diocletian, a former Dalmatian peasant who had risen through the military ranks, took control in 284 A.D. He would give the troubled Empire new direction, replacing the long-defunct Principate begun by Augustus with the Dominate; and he, as Dominus (Lord), would turn Rome into a corporate state with totalitarian tendencies. His creation of the Tetrarchy (a system of four rulers) allowed him, as senior Augustus, to oversee the administration of the Eastern half of the Empire, while a co-Augustus did the same in the West. Each Augustus was aided by a Caesar, or junior emperor, who helped ensure regional stability and provide for an orderly succession. At the appropriate time, the Augusti would be replaced by their Caesars, who would then select Caesars of their own.

Already restricted under the Severans, the Tetrarchy's citizens would come to feel more and more that their sole purpose for existence was to pay taxes and to offer their sons as cannon fodder to protect the Empire against the seemingly endless siege of its frontiers. The difficulties of the times also encouraged religious hysteria against Christians. For over two hundred years, Christians were an unfavored sect and had been persecuted sporadically. The first Empirewide persecution had occurred during the rule of the "Barracks Emperors," and there would be further persecutions in the East under Diocletian. They would not subside until

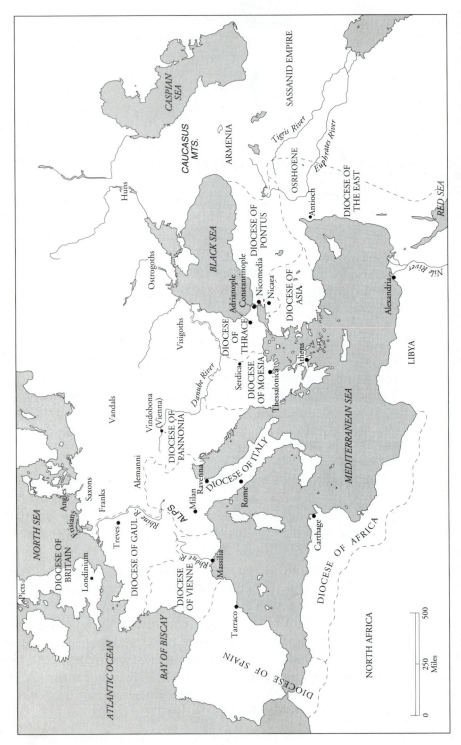

Map 20   The Later Roman Empire (fourth century A.D.). Diocletian's reforms divided the Empire into twelve large administrative districts called dioceses, each governed by a vicar. This reorganization allowed the Tetrarchs to have greater control over the areas they ruled. Tetrarch capitals in the West were at Milan and Treves; in the East, at Thessalonica and Nicomedia, where Diocletian resided. Constantine would later establish the Empire's capital at Constantinople in 330 A.D.

during the reign of Claudius, the emperor expelled "Jews" from Rome supposedly because of the disturbances they were causing over the name of Christ. Apparently, official Rome was already viewing Christians as troublemakers.

By the time of Nero, the majority of Romans probably still knew little about Christianity. However, Nero did try to pin the blame for the Great Fire of 64 A.D. (see pages 149–151) on members of the sect. There is no compelling evidence that Nero started the fire, as popular tradition holds; but because of his publicized plans for large-scale urban renewal at Rome, many pointed their fingers at him. To avoid the heat, Nero unleashed a calculated display of vengeful fury against Christians. At the capital, he rounded up as many as he could find and "punished" them in gruesome fashion. He may have convinced a few Romans that the fire, both a destructive and purifying agent, was in some way preparatory for the coming of the New Kingdom that Christians were always proclaiming. It is clear, however, that the general population did not believe that Christians were responsible and, as this passage from Tacitus reveals, took pity on Nero's victims:

But neither human resources, nor imperial munificence, nor appeasement of the gods, eliminated sinister suspicions that the fire had been instigated. To suppress this rumor, Nero fabricated scapegoats—and punished with every refinement the notoriously depraved Christians (as they were popularly called). Their originator, Christ, had been executed in Tiberius' reign by the governor of Judaea, Pontius Pilatus. But in spite of this temporary setback the deadly superstition had broken out afresh, not only in Judaea (where the mischief had started) but even in Rome. All degraded and shameful practices collect and flourish in the capital.

First, Nero had self-acknowledged Christians arrested. Then, on their information, large

Figure 9.1 *This sculpture group, now at St. Mark's in Venice, is thought to represent Diocletian (second from right?) and his fellow Tetrarchs.*

the Edict of Milan, embraced by Constantine in 313 A.D., proclaimed universal religious freedom. Christianity then became the official state religion. Many had given their lives to ensure its triumph. Vibia Perpetua was one of them. Much had happened before her death.

Christianity and Rome

In the beginning, most Romans discerned little difference between Christians and Jews, and

Toil and Trouble: A Case of Matricide— Nero Disposes of Agrippina

CHRISTIANS WERE NOT THE first to feel the effects of Nero's wrath. His efforts against them were enough, it appears, to earn him the infamous number "666" in the Apocalypse of John (13:18) as well as his representation as "the beast" (17:8); but earlier, in 59 A.D., he was already displaying some of the disagreeable tendencies for which he is best known—as his mother, Agrippina, would soon find out. Usually held in check by the watchful eyes of his tutor and major advisor, Seneca, and Burrus, head of the Praetorian Guard, much of what Nero had done up to this point that was objectionable appears to have been devised in large part to counter or check the influence of his meddlesome mother, Agrippina. She constantly tried to manipulate him, and Nero came more and more to regard her as intolerable—and dangerous.

Matricide has always been viewed by society as perhaps the most heinous crime one can commit. That apparently did not bother Nero, at least initially, but the problem of how to do it—without raising suspicion or public indignation—did. Suetonius (*Nero* 34) says that Nero first tried to poison her three times but that Agrippina, ever mindful of her son's machinations, had taken antidotes in advance. When that did not work, Nero devised a plan to cause the ceiling of her bedroom to fall down on her bed and kill her as she slept, but someone tipped her off. The next reported project, after Nero feigned reconciliation with his mother, was a collapsible boat that would sink and drown her (or she would be crushed in her cabin). Nero's morbid objective almost becomes lost in what begins to resemble a sketch from a comedy about a bumbling, emasculated son trying to rid himself of his overbearing mother. Suetonius frequently provides scandalous and irresponsible anecdotes in his biographies, and our

inclination would probably be to dismiss his comments about Nero's endeavors as colorful fiction if it were not for the fact that Tacitus, greatest of imperial historians, provides some of the same information, especially about the collapsible boat. Tacitus—who was born during Nero's reign and must have grown up hearing all kinds of stories about the emperor, including his execution of Agrippina—was no admirer and could himself turn on Nero with an unflattering phrase or story (as he could most emperors); but the main features of his version of the story (*Annals* 14.3–9), ridiculous as parts might seem, must be close to what actually happened.

Finally, however, he concluded that wherever Agrippina was, she was intolerable. He decided to kill her. His only doubt was whether to employ poison, or the dagger, or violence of some other kind. Poison was the first choice. But a death at the emperor's table would not look fortuitous after Britannicus [the former emperor Claudius' son and Nero's stepbrother] had died there. Yet her criminal conscience kept her so alert for plots that it seemed impracticable to corrupt her household. Moreover, she had strengthened her physical resistance by a preventive course of antidotes. No one could think of a way of stabbing her without detection. And there was another danger: that the selected assassin might shrink from carrying out his dreadful orders.

However, a scheme was put forward by Anicetus, an ex-slave who commanded the fleet at Misenum. In Nero's boyhood Anicetus had been his tutor; he and Agrippina hated each other. A ship could be made, he now said, with a section which would come loose at sea and hurl Agrippina into the water without warning. Nothing is so productive of surprises as the sea, remarked Anicetus; if a shipwreck did away with her, who could be so unreasonable as to blame a human agency instead of wind and water? Besides, when she was dead the emperor could allot her a temple and altars and the other public tokens of filial duty.

This ingenious plan found favor. The time of year, too, was suitable, since Nero habitually attended the festival of Minerva at Baiae. Now he enticed his mother there. "Parents' tempers must be borne!" he kept announcing. "One must humor their feelings." This was to create the general impression that they were friends again, and to produce the same effect on Agrippina. For women are naturally inclined to believe welcome news [Tacitus remarks].

As she arrived from Antium, Nero met her at the shore. After welcoming her with outstretched hands and embraces, he conducted her to Bauli, a mansion on the bay between Cape Misenum and the waters of Baiae. Some ships were standing there. One, more sumptuous than the rest, was evidently another compliment to his mother, who had formerly been accustomed to travel in warships manned by the imperial navy. Then she was invited out to dinner. The crime was to take place on the ship under cover of darkness. But an informer, it was said, gave the plot away; Agrippina could not decide whether to believe the story, and preferred a sedan-chair as her conveyance to Baiae.

There her alarm was relieved by Nero's attentions. He received her kindly, and gave her the place of honor next to himself. The party went on for a long time. They talked about various things; Nero was boyish and intimate—or confidentially serious. When she left, he saw her off, gazing into her eyes and clinging to her. This may have been a final piece of shamming, or perhaps even Nero's brutal heart was affected by his last sight of his mother, going to her death.

But heaven seemed determined to reveal the crime. For it was a quiet, starlit night and the sea was calm. The ship began to go on its way. Agrippina was attended by two of her friends. One of them, Crepereius Gallus, stood near the tiller. The other, Acerronia, leant over the feet of her resting mistress, happily talking about Nero's remorseful behavior and his mother's reestablished influence. Then came the signal. Under the pressure of heavy lead weight, the roof fell in. Crepereius was crushed, and died instantly. Agrippina and Acerronia were saved by the raised sides of their couch, which happened to be strong enough to resist the pressure. Moreover, the ship held together.

In the general confusion, those in the conspiracy were hampered by the many who were not. But then some of the oarsmen had the idea of throwing their weight on one side, to capsize the ship. However, they took too long to concert this improvised plan, and meanwhile others brought weight to bear in the opposite direction. This provided the opportunity to make a gentler descent into the water. Acerronia ill-advisedly started crying out, "I am Agrippina! Help, help the emperor's mother!" She was struck dead by blows from poles and oars and whatever ship's gear happened to be available. Agrippina herself kept quiet and avoided recognition. Though she was hurt—she had a wound in the shoulder—she swam until she came to some sailing-boats. They brought her to the Lucrine lake, from which she was taken home.

There she realized that the invitation and special compliment had been treacherous and

(continued)

Toil and Trouble: A Case of Matricide (continued)

the collapse of her ship planned. The collapse had started at the top, like a stage-contrivance. The shore was close by, there had been no wind, nor rock to collide with. Acerronia's death and her own wound also invited reflection. Agrippina decided that the only escape from the plot was to profess ignorance of it. She sent an ex-slave, Agerinus, to tell her son that by divine mercy and his lucky star she had survived a serious accident. The messenger was to add, however, that despite anxiety about his mother's dangerous experience Nero must not yet trouble to visit her—at present rest was what she needed. Meanwhile, pretending unconcern, she cared for her wound and physical condition generally. . . .

To Nero, awaiting news that the crime was done, came word that she had escaped with a slight wound—after hazards which left no doubt of their instigator's identity. Half-dead with fear, he insisted she might arrive at any moment. "She may arm her slaves! She may whip up the army, or gain access to the senate or Assembly, and incriminate me for wrecking and wounding her and killing her friends! What can I do to save myself?" Could Burrus [the Praetorian Prefect] or Seneca [the philosopher and Nero's tutor] help? Whether they were in the plot is uncertain. But they were immediately awakened and summoned.

For a long time neither spoke. They did not want to dissuade and be rejected. They may have felt matters had gone so far that Nero had to strike before Agrippina, or die. Finally, Seneca ventured so far as to turn to Burrus and ask if the troops should be ordered to kill her. He replied that the Guard were devoted to the whole imperial house and to Germanicus' [Agrippina was Germanicus' daughter: see Chart 2, page 126] memory; they would commit no violence against his offspring. Anicetus, he said, must make good his promise. Anice-

tus unhesitatingly claimed the direction of the crime. Hearing him, Nero cried that this was first day of his reign—and the magnificent gift came from a former slave! "Go quickly!" he said. "And take men who obey orders scrupulously!"

Agrippina's messenger arrived. When Nero was told, he took the initiative and staged a fictitious incrimination. While Agerinus delivered his message, Nero dropped a sword at the man's feet and had him arrested as if caught red-handed. Then he could pretend that his mother had plotted against the emperor's life, been detected, and—in shame—committed suicide.

Meanwhile Agrippina's perilous adventure had become known. It was believed to be accidental. As soon as people heard of it they ran to the beach and climbed onto the embankment or fishing-boats nearby. Others waded out as far as they could, or waved their arms. The whole shore echoed with wails and prayers and the din of all manner of inquiries and ignorant answers. Huge crowds gathered with lights. When she was known to be safe, they prepared to make a show of rejoicing.

But a menacing armed column arrived and dispersed them. Anicetus surrounded her house and broke in. Arresting every slave in his path, he came to her bedroom door. Here stood a few servants—the rest had been frightened away by the invasion. In her dimly lit room a single maid waited with her. Agrippina's alarm had increased as nobody, not even Agerinus, came from her son. If things had been well there would not be this terribly ominous isolation, then this sudden uproar. Her maid vanished. "Are you leaving me, too?" called Agrippina. Then she saw Anicetus. Behind him was a naval captain and lieutenant. . . . "If you have come to visit me," she said, "you can report that I am better. But if you are assassins, I know my son is not responsible. He did not order his mother's death." The murderers closed 'round her bed. First the captain hit her on the head with a truncheon. Then as the lieutenant was drawing his sword to finish her off, she cried out: "Strike here!"—pointing to her womb. Blow after blow fell, and she died.

So far accounts agree. Some add that Nero inspected his mother's corpse and praised her figure; but that is contested. She was cremated that night, on a dining coach, with meager ceremony. While Nero reigned, her grave was not covered with earth or enclosed, though later her household gave her a modest tomb beside the road to Misenum, on the heights where Julius Caesar's mansion overlooks the bay beneath. . . .

In the end, Nero found that he could not hold up to the horrendous deed as well as he had thought. Many scholars would agree that the execution of his mother was a turning point in his life—and that the familiar image of Nero as cruel, unkempt, corpulent, and excessive can be related directly to it.

Figure 9.2   The Emperor Nero, who, before his suicide at age 32 in 68 A.D., had instigated the first persecution of Christians at Rome in 64 A.D.

numbers of others were condemned—not so much for incendiarism as for their anti-social tendencies. Their deaths were made farcical. Dressed in wild animals' skins, they were torn to pieces by dogs, or crucified, or made into torches to be ignited after dark as substitutes for daylight. Nero provided his Gardens for the spectacle, and exhibited displays in the Circus, at which he mingled with the crowd—or stood in a chariot, dressed as a charioteer. Despite their guilt as Christians, and the ruthless punishment it deserved, the victims were pitied. For it was felt that they were being sacrificed to one man's brutality rather than to the national interest. (*Annals* 15.44)

Nero's persecution of 64 A.D. was a minor, though tragic, affair and generally limited to Rome. Unfortunately, because it was the first official act of violence against Christians—and traditionally, the deaths of Peter and Paul were linked to it—it is the persecution that is most remembered today. Ironically, it is better known than the more devastating persecutions that came later, some under emperors much more enlightened and capable than Nero.

Figure 9.3 *Christianity began as a Jewish sect in Judaea. Pictured here is the Jordan River near the traditional site of John's baptism of Jesus.*

Attitudes toward Christians— Official and Otherwise

What appears to be a Christian chapel in the House of the Bicentenary at Herculaneum (see Figure 9.6) with the imprint of a cross on the wall (if so, this is one of the earliest examples of its use as a Christian symbol) suggests that by 79 A.D. Christians had little to fear from their neighbors—or the government. Obviously, the person who owned the house could not have kept his chapel secret. We can only conclude that he was unconcerned about harassment.

Despite today's stereotypical image of Romans seeking Christians under every stone and lions licking their chops waiting for them, the Romans were probably more tolerant of alternative religious practices than most of today's societies. It would appear that under normal circumstances, Christians did not have to fear for their safety. Still, it was probably wise to keep a low profile. Official Rome was always suspicious of movements that could potentially disturb the status quo, especially ones that stirred the masses and were messianic. As monotheists, Christians did not show the same

Figure 9.4 *Grove in Jerusalem identified by the faithful today as the "Garden of Gethsemane," where Jesus was betrayed and arrested (*Matthew *26:36–57)*

tolerance for the polytheism inherent in Roman religion. They denied the traditional gods and refused to participate in the imperial cult. Their behavior was viewed as defiant, antisocial, secretive, and dangerous. They attracted negative attention by purposefully setting themselves apart, causing uneasy administrators to view them as seditious and a threat to the state. On occasion, the most resolute were punished.

Imperial peacetime policy toward Christians in the early second century A.D. is no better illustrated than in an exchange of letters between Pliny the Younger, who by this time was governor (111–113 A.D.) of Bithynia-Pontus on the Black Sea, and the Emperor Trajan. Pliny wrote Trajan frequently about matters in his province, never proceeding into a questionable area without the emperor's approval. Troubled over how he should deal with Christians, he wrote:

> It is my custom to refer all my difficulties to you, Sir, for no one is better able to resolve my doubts and to inform my ignorance.
>
> I have never been present at an examination of Christians. Consequently, I do not know the nature of the extent of the punishments usually

meted out to them, nor the grounds for starting an investigation and how far it should be pressed. Nor am I at all sure whether any distinction should be made between them on the grounds of age, or if young people and adults should be treated alike; whether a pardon ought to be granted to anyone retracting his beliefs, or if he has once professed Christianity, he shall gain nothing by renouncing it; and whether it is the mere name of Christian which is punishable, even if innocent of crime, or rather the crimes associated with the name.

For the moment this is the line I have taken with all persons brought before me on the charge of being Christians. I have asked them in person if they are Christians, and if they admit it, I repeat the question a second and third time, with a warning of the punishment awaiting them. If they persist, I order them to be led away for execution; for, whatever the nature of their admission, I am convinced that their stubbornness and unshakeable obstinacy ought not to go unpunished. There have been others similarly fanatical who are Roman citizens. I have entered them on the list of persons to be sent to Rome for trial.

Now that I have begun to deal with this problem, as so often happens, the charges are becoming more widespread and increasing in variety. An anonymous pamphlet has been circulated which contains the names of a number of accused persons. Amongst these I considered that I should dismiss any who denied that they were or ever had been Christians when they had repeated after me a formula of invocation to the gods and had made offerings of wine and incense to your statue (which I had ordered to be brought into court for this purpose along with the images of the gods), and furthermore had reviled the name of Christ: none of which things, I understand, any genuine Christian can be induced to do.

Others, whose names were given to me by an informer, first admitted the charge and then denied it; they said that they had ceased to be Christians two or more years previously, and some of them even twenty years ago. They all did reverence to your statue and the images of the gods in the same way as the others, and reviled the name of Christ. They also declared that the sum total of their guilt or error amounted to no more than this: they had met regularly before dawn on a fixed day to chant verses alternately amongst themselves in honor of Christ as if to a god, and also to bind themselves by oath, not for any criminal purpose, but to abstain from theft, robbery, and adultery, to commit no breach of trust and not to deny a deposit when called upon to restore it. After this ceremony it had been their custom to disperse and reassemble later to take food of an ordinary, harmless kind; but they had in fact given up this practice since my edict, issued on your instructions, which banned all political societies. This made me decide it was all the more necessary to extract the truth by torture from two slavewomen, whom they call deaconesses. I found nothing but a degenerate sort of cult carried to extravagant lengths.

I have therefore postponed any further examination and hastened to consult you. The question seems to me to be worthy of your consideration, especially in view of the number of persons endangered; for a great many individuals of every age and class, both men and women, are being brought to trial, and this is likely to continue. It is not only the towns, but villages and rural districts too which are infected through contact with this wretched cult. I think though that it is still possible for it to be checked and directed to better ends, for there is no doubt that people have begun to throng the temples which had been almost entirely deserted for a long time; the sacred rites which had been allowed to lapse are being performed again, and flesh of sacrificial victims is on sale everywhere, though up till recently scarcely anyone could be found to buy it. It is easy to infer from this that a great many people could be reformed if they were given an opportunity to repent.

(*Letters* 10.96)

Figure 9.5 *The excavated entrance to the "Tomb of St. Peter" in the Vatican necropolis at Rome*

Figure 9.6 *"Christian chapel" in the Bicentenary House at Herculaneum*

Pliny's comments are revealing for a number of reasons. His unfamiliarity with how to deal with members of the sect would indicate that heretofore the state (Nero excepted) had not paid much attention to singling out Christians for punishment. It is also clear that someone accused of being a Christian was given every opportunity to deny it (and, obviously, many did when faced with punishment). In fact, Pliny almost seems to indicate that those punished were punished more for their obstinacy than their beliefs. Christianity was viewed as being political in nature since Pliny links it with Trajan's ban on political societies. Accusing some-

one of being a Christian was becoming a stock charge, and persons hoping to benefit personally, politically, or financially (or who were genuinely fearful) were lodging it irresponsibly against Christians and non-Christians alike.

Pliny has also provided us with the description of actual Christian practices and beliefs at this time, particularly their ethical values. While he feels the "degenerate cult" can be checked, so many people's lives are endangered that he seeks his emperor's advice. His comments about the

Buried Alive: Cornelia—A Vestal Virgin Goes Astray

THE ROMAN RELIGIOUS TRADITION that Christians were challenging was centuries old, and it seems remarkable that the new faith could ultimately succeed. However, Christianity thrived and grew in an atmosphere created by wars and by social and economic woes that had been developing since the Hellenistic period. The failure of the old religions to alleviate the suffering threw many into a spiritual void. Experimentation with alternative cults and philosophies became widespread and had been going on for some time. Christianity offered so much—immortality—for so little, required neither money nor literacy, cut across all strata of society, and had as its central figure one who had lived and died in recent memory. With the calculated incorporation of familiar elements from the old religion it was replacing, the new faith became irresistible to large numbers within the Empire. The fact that Christians were willing to die for their beliefs made it appear all the more compelling to others.

One venerable Roman religious institution that would succumb to Christianity was that of the Vestal Virgins. They were the priestesses of Vesta, goddess of the hearth, who performed her sacred rites and kept lit the eternal flame of Rome. Among their other functions, they safeguarded wills deposited with them by prominent Romans (such as Caesar and Antony). During the early Empire, Domitian's Chief Vestal was Cornelia. It appears that she and some of her fellow priestesses had wearied of their vows of celibacy. Unfortunately, they had not been discreet enough in their illicit activities. Domitian condemned three of them to death in 83 A.D. and finally caught up with Cornelia in 90 A.D.:

> Taking a far more serious view than his father and brother had done of unchastity among the Vestals, [Domitian] began by sentencing of-

fenders to execution, and afterwards resorted to the traditional form of punishment. Thus, though he allowed the Oculata sisters, and Varronilla, to choose how they should die, and sent their lovers into exile, he later ordered Cornelia, a Chief-Vestal—acquitted at her first trial, but rearrested much later and convicted—to be buried alive, and had her lovers clubbed to death in the Comitium.
> (Suetonius, *Domitian* 8.3–4)

Although nothing more is said about Cornelia, we know something about her life—and death—from general descriptions about Vestal Virgins given by ancient writers. For Cornelia to be chosen to serve the goddess, she

> . . . must, according to the law, be no less than six and no more than ten years old. Both her father and her mother must be alive. She must not be handicapped by a speech or hearing problem or disfigured by some physical defect. . . . Neither one nor both of her parents may have been slaves or may engage in demeaning occupations. . . .
> As soon as a Vestal Virgin has been chosen, escorted to the House of Vesta, and handed over to the *pontifices* [priests], she immediately leaves the control of her father, without a ceremony of manumission or a loss of civil rights, and she acquires the right to make a will. . . .
> (Aulus Gellius, *Attic Nights* 12.1–3, 5, 9)

Cornelia and her colleagues, as indicated above, lived during their years as priestesses in the House of the Vestal Virgins in the Roman Forum. What was expected of them was made perfectly clear:

> These priestesses must remain pure and unmarried for thirty years, offering sacrifices and performing other religious rites in accordance with the law. During the first ten years they must learn these rites; during the second ten

they perform them; and during the remaining ten they must teach others. When the thirty years have been completed, there is no law which prohibits those who so wish from putting aside the headbands and other insignia of the priestly service and marrying. Only a few, however, do so, and they have, during their remaining years, lives which are neither enviable nor very happy. And therefore, taking the unhappy fates of these few as a warning, the rest of the virgins remain in service to the goddess until their deaths, at which time another virgin is appointed by the *pontifices* to take the place of the deceased.

(Dionysius of Halicarnassus, *Roman Antiquities* 2.67)

The Vestal Virgins were highly honored. They were carried about in a litter, and everyone, at risk of great penalty, made room for them to pass. If a Vestal accidentally met a criminal on his way to execution, the condemned man would be spared. Despite such status and prestige, if a priestess strayed, particularly a Chief Vestal (Cornelia, it appears, was caught more than once), the following was the traditional procedure:

For their minor offenses the virgins are punished with stripes, the Pontifex Maximus [Chief Priest] sometimes scourging the culprit on her bare flesh, in a dark place, with a curtain interposed. But she that has broken her vow of chastity is buried alive near the Colline gate. Here a little ridge of earth extends for some distance along the inside of the city-wall. . . . Under it a small chamber is constructed, with steps leading down from above. In this are placed a couch with its coverings, a lighted lamp, and very small portions of the necessaries of life, such as bread, a bowl of water, milk, and oil, as though they would thereby absolve themselves from the charge of destroying by hunger a life which had been consecrated to the highest services of religion. Then

Figure 9.7 *Statue of a Chief Vestal from the House of the Vestal Virgins in the Forum at Rome*

(continued)

Buried Alive: Cornelia   (continued)

the culprit herself is placed on a litter, over which coverings are thrown and fastened down with cords so that not even a cry can be heard from within, and carried through the forum. All the people there silently make way for the litter, and follow it without uttering a sound, in a terrible depression of soul. No other spectacle is more appalling, nor does any other day bring more gloom to the city than this. When the litter reaches its destination, the attendants unfasten the cords of the coverings. Then the high-priest, after stretching his hands toward heaven and uttering certain mysterious prayers before the fatal act, brings forth the culprit, who is closely veiled, and places her on the steps leading down into the chamber. After this he turns away his face, as do the rest of the priests, and when she has gone down, the steps are taken up, and great quantities of earth are thrown into the entrance to the chamber, hiding it away, and making the place level with the rest of the mound. Such is the punishment of those who break their vow of virginity.
(Plutarch, *Numa* 10.4–7)

temples being deserted (a problem that, he says, he is remedying) may be an indication of the spiritual disillusionment that was driving more people to experiment with new faiths like Christianity. Also of interest is his carefulness in obtaining information about Christianity. Pliny cannot legally torture Roman citizens but he can slaves, in this case two women who are deaconesses.

In response to Pliny's questions, Trajan gave this reply:

You have followed the right course of procedure, my dear Pliny, in your examination of the cases of persons charged with being Christians, for it is impossible to lay down a general rule to a fixed formula. These people must not be hunted out; if they are brought before you and the charge against them is proved, they must be punished, but in the case of anyone who denies that he is a Christian, and makes it clear that he is not by offering prayers to our gods, he is to be pardoned as a result of his repentance however suspect his past conduct may be. But pamphlets circulated anonymously must play no part in any accusation. They create the worst sort of precedent and are quite out of keeping with the spirit of our age.
(Pliny, *Letters* 10.97)

Judging from the tone of his letter, Trajan does not seem overly concerned about Christians. He approves of Pliny's actions, but it seems clear he does not want the state's resources spent on tracking them down or his subjects to view him as a persecutor. Unsubstantiated charges are to be given no regard, and he is more than willing to forgive Christians who have recanted. He seems to be saying leave them alone and take action only when unavoidable. Many Romans may have regarded this as enlightened policy—but not Christians. About eighty-five years later, Tertullian probably represented what most of them thought when he wrote this rhetorical and contemptuous response to Trajan's position:

Trajan replied to Pliny that Christians should certainly not be hunted down, but, if they were brought into court, they should be punished.

What a confused and confusing decision! He says that they should not be hunted down, implying that they are innocent, and yet he insists that they should be punished, implying that they are guilty. He pardons them, he persecutes them; he ignores them, he notices them. Why deceive yourself with your decision? If you condemn them, why not also hunt them down? If you don't hunt them down, why not also acquit them? . . . As it is, you condemn a man who is brought into court although no one wanted him hunted down, a man who has not, I think, deserved punishment because he is guilty, but because he was found, although it was forbidden to hunt him down.
(*Apology* 2.7–9)

The Changing World and Religious Hysteria

By the time Tertullian voiced his objections, the general negative feeling toward Christians had hardened. The ongoing, life-threatening problems associated with the reign of Marcus Aurelius incited religious hysteria among the fearful masses, who believed Christians had offended their gods and must be punished. Members of the sect made convenient scapegoats, and Aurelius himself, no friend of Christianity, felt their beliefs and actions were partly responsible for the Empire's disorders. He was encouraged by his former tutor and now close friend, the rhetorician Fronto, a North African who accused Christians of the basest of practices:

These people gather together illiterates from the very dregs of society and credulous women who easily fall prey because of the weakness of their sex. They organize a mob of wicked conspirators who join together at nocturnal assemblies and ritual fasts and inhuman dinners . . . for sacrilegious sacrifice; a secret and light-fearing

Figure 9.8   *Catacombs of the Jordani at Rome. Catacombs were excavated by Christians to bury their dead and provided convenient hiding places during persecutions.*

tribe, silent in public, garrulous in dark corners. They despise temples as if they were tombs, they spit on the gods, they laugh at our sacred rites. . . . They despise political offices and regalia, and wander about half-naked. . . . They scoff at present tortures, but fear those uncertain ones in the future, and they fear a death after death, but do not fear death now! And so for them, a deceptive hope of a comforting after life assuages terror. . . . Everywhere they share a kind of religion of lust, and promiscuously call one another brothers and sisters so that even

Everyday Life for Marcus Aurelius—The Prince Catches a Cold

ALTHOUGH MANY CHRISTIANS TODAY might conclude that everyone who persecuted the sect during its early history was demented, irrational, and unenlightened, this letter of Marcus Aurelius proves otherwise. Aurelius endorsed the notorious persecution at Lyons in 177 A.D. Yet this letter, written to his tutor and lifelong friend, Fronto, when he was twenty-four and visiting his parents, indicates Marcus' studiousness, his sense of humor, his good nature, and his love of family and friends. The letter is also revealing because of its typically human content. However, as emperor, he faced plague, barbarian threats, and public outcry against the Christians. His own sincere religious conviction, as well as the outlandish accusations of Fronto (see pages 256–258), led Marcus to conclude that Christians bore some responsibility for the Empire's ills.

The future ruler of the Roman world writes:

We are all well. Today I worked at my studies from about 3:00 A.M. to about 8:00 A.M., having arranged for some snacks in advance. Between 8:00 and 9:00 A.M., wearing only slippers, I cheerfully paced up and down in front of my bedroom. Then I put on my boots and my short cape (for we had been told to come dressed in that way) and went to say good morning to my lord. We all set off on a hunt, and did daring deeds. We heard by word of mouth that boars had been caught, but we weren't able to see for ourselves. We did, how-

ever, climb quite a steep hill. In the afternoon we returned home.

And I returned to my books. After pulling off my boots and taking off my cape, I stayed on my couch for nearly two hours. I read Cato's speech, "On the Property of Pulchra," and another in which he impeached a tribune. "Hey," you say to your slave, "go as fast as you can and bring me those speeches from the library of Apollo" [on the Palatine Hill with the Imperial Palace]. You will be sending him in vain, for those volumes have followed me here! You must therefore ingratiate yourself with the librarian at the library of Tiberius [also on the Palatine]. You might offer him a tip (which he and I will share equally when I come back to town).

Once I had read these speeches carefully, I wrote a few wretched things, which are only suitable for dedication either to water or to fire. . . .

I seem to have caught a cold; I don't know whether it was from walking in slippers in the morning or from writing badly. I do, it's true, frequently suffer nasal congestion, but today my nose seems to be running much more than usual. And so I will pour oil on my head and go to sleep. I don't think I'll put one drop of the oil in my lamp today, because the riding and sneezing have so tired me out. Farewell, my dearest and sweetest teacher whom I miss (dare I say it!) more than Rome itself.

(Fronto, *Letters* 4.5)

ordinary sexual intercourse becomes incest by the use of a sacred name. . . . Anyone who says that the items they venerate are an ordinary man who was punished by execution for a criminal act and the deadly wood of a cross . . . attributes to these irredeemable and wicked people very appropriate religious objects, so they worship just what they deserve to.

Fronto then proceeds to give a wild account of Christian initiation rites and gatherings:

Tales about their initiation of converts are as disgusting as they are notorious. An infant is wrapped in bread dough so as to deceive the unsuspecting and is placed beside the person being initiated into the rites. The initiate is

required to strike the surface of the bread with blows he presumes are harmless, but he thus kills the infant with wounds not seen by him. And then what an abomination! They voraciously lick up the blood of the infant and greedily tear apart its limbs, and swear alliance over this sacrificial victim and pledge themselves to mutual silence by complicity in this crime. . . . On holy days, they gather for a banquet with all their children, sisters, and mothers, people of both sexes and all ages. There, after much feasting, when the banquet has become heated and intoxication has inflamed the drunken passions of incestuous lust, a dog which has been tied to a lamp is incited to rush and leap forward after a morsel thrown beyond the range of the cord by which it was tied. The telltale light is upset and extinguished, and in the shameless dark they exchange embraces indiscriminately, and all, if not actually, yet by complicity are equally involved in incest. . . .
(Fronto in Minucius Felix, *Octavius* 8.4–9.7 [various passages])

With this kind of venom placed in his ear—by a trusted friend, no less—it is no surprise that the ordinarily rational Marcus Aurelius might be seduced into thinking the worst about Christians. Still, there was no widespread persecution, and the action taken against the sect was mostly local—and inconsistent. A particularly brutal persecution did take place in 177 A.D. at Lyons in Gaul (with or without Marcus' authorization).

The Martyrdom of Vibia Perpetua

One of the most celebrated episodes in early Christianity took place at Carthage on March 7, 203 A.D. A twenty-two-year-old Christian woman named Vibia Perpetua was martyred. Tried and convicted as a Christian, she was condemned to face the beasts in the arena. Her death occurred during the games that were held on the birthday of Geta, the younger son of Septimius Severus. At the time, Septimius and his family were in Africa at Leptis Magna. It may be that the acting governor of Carthage, Hilarianus, hoped to attract the emperor's attention on this day by showing his vigilance against such perceived enemies of the state as Perpetua and her fellow Christians. It does not appear that Septimius noticed—and there is no reason that he should have.

Nothing indicates that Septimius personally harbored any ill will toward Christians. He, a devotee of Serapis, and his wife, Julia, of Elagabal, both must have suffered from some form of prejudice for their religious convictions during their lives. Comments made by the Christian writer Tertullian (*Scapula* 4.5–6)—who, like Septimius, was from Africa—indicate that Septimius did protect high-ranking Christians from an angry mob, and that a therapist in his company (who probably treated his gout or arthritis) was a lifelong Christian. He also states that while Septimius was governing Gaul at Lyons in 188 A.D., Julia employed a Christian wet nurse for Caracalla. The great persecution of Christians had taken place in Lyons only a decade earlier. Consequently, the royal family was very familiar with Christians and knew some extremely well. Subsequent Severan emperors were also sympathetic to Christians.

Septimius, however, was notorious for suppressing any possible danger to the stability of the Empire, and since Trajan's time, there had been an official imperial policy on how to deal with recalcitrant Christians. His personal feelings had nothing to do with how Christians were legally treated. Perpetua's death was a routine matter, and the emperor would have viewed the persecutions that had broken out in Egypt shortly after his visit there in 200 A.D. in similar fashion.

Figure 9.9   A representation of the god Serapis, favorite of Septimius Severus and a major rival of Christianity

Perpetua's Own Story

What makes the martyrdom of Vibia Perpetua stand out from other instances of Christians dying for their beliefs during this period is the fact that we have her own record of her final days. It is contained in a document entitled "The Martyrdom of Saints Perpetua and Felicitas," which is included in the *Acts of the Christian Martyrs*.

Born in the town of Thuburbo in Africa, Perpetua was from good family and, as is apparent from her memoir, was well educated. Her story is said to be as she left it (although we might suspect some later editing for literary purposes), and because of its straightforward and simple style, it is considered genuine.

When Vibia was arrested, she had just converted to Christianity but had given herself over to it completely, for her fervor was certainly more than one might expect from a neophyte. Her father did everything he could to force her to renounce her faith—but one of her two brothers was also a recent convert and her mother seems sympathetic. She was said to have been newly married, but, oddly, she makes no mention of a husband in her account. She was nursing an infant at the time of her imprisonment.

Vibia was arrested with other young Christians like herself. Apparently, they were all members of the same group, which consisted of Perpetua and at least four others: two young men named Saturninus and Secundulus, a slave, Revocatus, and a slave girl (usually identified as Perpetua's personal servant), Felicitas. The tradition holds that the latter was pregnant and gave birth while in prison. The leader of the group was another man, named Saturus, who was not present when the others were seized but later gave himself up voluntarily. How Perpetua and the others were caught is not clear. Perhaps their youthful exuberance displaced caution and attracted the unwanted attention of local authorities. Whatever the case, they were all now to become arena showpieces in the birthday celebration of Geta.

Vibia begins her account by describing her father's efforts after her arrest to make her give

Figure 9.10 *Christian graffiti representing the fish and anchor, familiar symbols for the faithful. Fish in Greek (ἰχθύς) was an acronym for "Jesus Christ, Son of God, Savior." The anchor represented salvation and hope.*

up Christianity. She says he was so "angered by the word 'Christian'" that she thought he was going to "pluck my eyes out." The father, apparently an affectionate and caring parent, sees his headstrong daughter caught in the tentacles of a dangerous religious cult. Vibia revels in her defiance of his pleas, the Devil's arguments, to shake her resolve.

After her father departed without accomplishing anything, Vibia was relieved and thanked the Lord that she did not see him again

for a few days. During that time, she and her friends were baptized and then imprisoned. Perpetua describes what happened:

> A few days later we were lodged in the prison; and I was terrified, as I had never before been in such a dark hole. What a difficult time it was! With the crowd the heat was stifling; then there was the extortion of the soldiers; and to crown all, I was tortured with worry for my baby there.
>
> Then Tertius and Pomponius, those blessed deacons who tried to take care of us, bribed the soldiers to allow us to go to a better part of the prison to refresh ourselves for a few hours. Everyone then left that dungeon and shifted for himself. I nursed my baby, who was faint from hunger. In my anxiety I spoke to my mother about the child, I tried to comfort my brother, and I gave the child in their charge. I was in pain because I saw them suffering out of pity for me. These were the trials I had to endure for many days. Then I got permission for my baby to stay with me in prison. At once I recovered my health, relieved as I was of my worry and anxiety over the child. My prison had suddenly become a palace, so that I wanted to be there rather than anywhere else. (3.4–9)

From the above passage, it appears that Vibia's father showed his disdain for his daughter's behavior by not accompanying his wife and son (Vibia's Christian brother) to visit her in prison. The two deacons of whom Vibia speaks are naturally concerned over the predicament of their young Christian friends and had the wherewithal to bribe the jailors to give them better treatment. Perhaps these same deacons brought Vibia's son to her to nurse, since the child does not appear to have been staying with her family. If he were, there would have been no need for her to commend the boy's care to her mother and brother. Ultimately, she is able to keep the baby with her.

The ministrations of the deacons to Vibia and her friends while they were in prison present a puzzling contradiction. If at this time, as some believe, Roman officials were imprisoning Christians simply because they were Christians, why were the deacons—and Vibia's Christian brother—allowed to come and go as they pleased? To suggest that they kept their Christian identities so secret that none but the initiated knew who they were is unrealistic. And just the interest they showed in imprisoned Christians would have raised official suspicions about who they were. Obviously, nobody cared. The only thing that distinguished Perpetua and her fellow inmates from the other Christians who knew them was their recent conversion to Christianity—and that must be why they were arrested. They were caught—as a group—and they and their leader (who converted them) were executed after refusing to recant.

The official procedure followed in this case was in line with an edict supposedly issued by Septimius Severus forbidding anyone to convert to Christianity. While there is no compelling evidence to confirm that Severus ever issued such an order, no one can deny that local administrators enforced, at their discretion, such a policy to prevent the growth of Christianity. It appears that Hilarianus did at Carthage.

Vibia continues her narrative:

A few days later there was a rumor that we were going to be given a hearing. My father also arrived from the city, worn with worry, and he came to see me with the idea of persuading me.

"Daughter," he said, "have pity on my grey head—have pity on me your father, if I deserve to be called your father, if I have favored you above all your brothers, if I have raised you to reach this prime of your life. Do not abandon me to be the reproach of men.

Think of your brothers, think of your mother and your aunt, think of your child, who will not be able to live once you are gone. Give up your pride! You will destroy all of us! None of us will ever be able to speak freely again if anything happens to you."

This was the way my father spoke out of love for me, kissing my hands and throwing himself down before me. With tears in his eyes he no longer addressed me as his daughter but as a woman. I was sorry for my father's sake, because he alone of all my kin would be unhappy to see me suffer.

I tried to comfort him saying: "It will all happen in the prisoner's dock as God wills; for you may be sure that we are not left to ourselves but are all in his power."

And he left me great sorrow.

(5.1–6)

No daughter, it seems, could have had a more concerned father (although, inevitably, his behavior, too, was motivated partly by selfishness); he says himself that he had favored her over his sons—an unusual position for a father to take in the Ancient World. Clearly, he felt that pride, not religious conviction, was dictating his daughter's behavior. Few contemporaries would have disagreed. Her death as a martyr for a "degenerate cult" would have been viewed as meaningless and disgraceful.

The words of Vibia's father would have moved most to pity. For her, they were the latest attempt by the Devil to dissuade her and had no impact. She continues her story:

One day while we were eating breakfast we were suddenly hurried off for a hearing. We arrived at the forum, and straight away the story went about the neighborhood near the forum and a huge crowd gathered. We walked up to the prisoner's dock. All the others when questioned admitted their guilt. Then, when it came my turn, my father appeared with my son,

Family Matters: Calpurnia—Orphan, Wife, Niece, and Granddaughter

INSIGHTS INTO EVERYDAY FAMILY life during the Roman period are rare, and the relationship shared by Vibia Perpetua and her father is certainly revealing in many ways—although stressful in this particular instance. A young woman named Calpurnia has indirectly provided additional knowledge for us about the interaction of individuals in a Roman family, albeit one of higher status than Perpetua's and living in the second century A.D. Calpurnia was the wife of Pliny the Younger (quoted elsewhere in the text), and through Pliny's correspondence with her, her aunt, and her grandfather, we learn much about the relationship between a husband and a wife, the concerns of her relatives, and the way an in-law deals with his wife's family. Of course, Pliny was familiar with the latter kind of "politic" since Calpurnia was his third wife. He also had known her family since boyhood, and Calpurnia's grandfather, Calpurnius Fabatus, a wealthy individual in his own right, oversaw the management of Pliny's estates in Comum (modern Como in northern Italy), where Pliny was born.

The difference in age between Pliny and Calpurnia is great (from Pliny's description below, she appears to be in her early teens), a situation that was not atypical among Romans—and Pliny indicates that what was originally a marriage of convenience had blossomed into love. Calpurnia was an orphan, and her aunt and grandfather (her father's sister and father) certainly saw their friend Pliny as a desirable partner to provide for and look after her. Not all family relations in Rome may have been as caring as this one seems to have been, but what is striking is that it reflects our own ideals about what a family relationship ought to be.

Unfortunately, Pliny and his young wife were deprived of children because of her miscarriage (see below). Calpurnia would later accompany Pliny to Bithynia-Pontus (in the eastern part of the Empire) when he was posted to govern there by the Emperor Trajan (c. 110 A.D.). However, when her grandfather died unexpectedly, she had to return to Italy to be with her aunt. Calpurnia would never see her husband again, since Pliny died not long after (c. 113 A.D.).

Below are several letters from Pliny's correspondence in the order in which they appear. Note the similarities of the recipients' names and their male and female equivalents, a standard Roman practice within families.

To Calpurnia Hispulla, Pliny's wife's aunt
(Letters 4.19)

You are a model of family affection, and loved your excellent and devoted brother as dearly as he loved you; you love his daughter as if she were your own, and, by filling the place of the father she lost, you are more than an aunt to her. I know then how glad you will be to hear that she has proved herself worthy of her father, her grandfather and you. She is highly intelligent and a careful housewife, and her devotion to me is a sure indication of her virtue. In addition, this love has given her an interest in literature: she keeps copies of my works to read again and again and even learn by heart. She is so anxious when she knows that I am going to plead in court, and so happy when it is all over! (She arranges to be kept informed of the sort of reception and applause I receive, and what verdict I win in the case.) If I am giving a reading she sits behind a curtain near by and greedily drinks in every word of appreciation. She has even set my verses to music and sings them, to the accompaniment of her lyre, with no musician to teach her but the best of masters, love.

(continued)

Family Matters (continued)

All this gives me the highest reason to hope that our mutual happiness will last forever and go on increasing day by day, for she does not love me for my present age nor my person, which will gradually grow old and decay, but for my aspirations to fame; nor would any other feelings be suitable for one brought up by your hands and trained in your precepts, who has seen only what was pure and moral in your company and learned to love me on your recommendation. For you respected my mother like a daughter, and have given me guidance and encouragement since my boyhood; you always foretold that I should become the man I am now in the eyes of my wife. Please accept our united thanks for having given her to me and me to her as if chosen for each other.

To Calpurnia, his wife (6.7)

You say that you are feeling my absence very much, and your only comfort when I am not there is to hold my writings in your hand and often put them in my place by your side. I like to think that you miss me and find relief in this sort of consolation. I, too, am always reading your letters, and returning to them again and again as if they were new to me—but this only fans the fire of my longing for you. If your letters are so dear to me, you can imagine how I delight in your company; do write as often as you can, although you give me pleasure mingled with pain.

To Calpurnia (7.5)

You cannot believe how much I miss you. I love you so much, and we are not used to separations. So I stay awake most of the night thinking of you, and by day I find my feet carrying me (a true word, carrying) to your room at the times I usually visited you; then finding it empty I depart, as sick and sorrowful as a lover locked out. The only time I am free from this misery is when I am in court and wearing

Figure 9.11   Sculpture of a Roman woman contemporary with Calpurnia and her husband Pliny the Younger

myself out with my friends' lawsuits. You can judge then what a life I am leading, when I find my rest in work and distraction in troubles and anxiety.

To Calpurnius Fabatus, his wife's grandfather (8.10)

I know how anxious you are for us to give you a great-grandchild, so you will be all the more sorry to hear that your granddaughter has had a miscarriage. Being young and inexperienced she did not realize she was pregnant, failed to take proper precautions, and did several things which were better left undone. She has had a severe lesson, and paid for her mistake by seriously endangering her life; so that although you must inevitably feel it hard for your old age to be robbed of a descendant already on the way, you should thank the gods for sparing your granddaughter's life even though they denied you the child for the present. They will surely grant us children later on, and we may take hope from this evidence of her fertility though the proof has been unfortunate.

I am giving you the same advice and encouragement as I use on myself, for your desire for great-grandchildren cannot be keener than mine for children. Their descent from both of us should make their road to office easy; I can leave them a well-known name and an established ancestry, if only they may be born and turn our present grief into joy.

To Calpurnia Hispulla (8.11)

Remembering how you love your brother's daughter more tenderly than a mother, I feel that I ought to begin with the second half of my news, so that happiness may come first and leave no room for anxiety. And yet I am afraid your relief will turn to fear again, and your joy at hearing that your niece is out of danger will be tempered by your alarm at her narrow escape. By now her good spirits are returning as she feels herself restored to herself and to me, and she is beginning to measure the danger she has been through by her progress towards recovery. The danger was indeed grave—I hope I may safely say so now—through no fault of her own, but perhaps of her youth. Hence her miscarriage, a sad proof of unsuspected pregnancy. So though you are still without a grandchild of your brother's to comfort you for his loss, you must remember that this consolation is postponed, not denied us. We build our hopes on her, and she has been spared. Meanwhile, explain this accident to your father, as it is the sort women can more easily understand.

dragged me from the step, and said: "Perform the sacrifice—have pity on your baby!"

Hilarianus the governor, who had received his judicial powers as the successor to the late proconsul Minucius Timinianus, said to me: "Have pity on your father's grey head; have pity on your infant son. Offer the sacrifice for the welfare of the emperors" [meaning Septimius, Caracalla, and Geta].

"I will not," I retorted.

"Are you a Christian?" said Hilarianus.

And I said: "Yes, I am."

When my father persisted in trying to dissuade me, Hilarianus ordered him to be thrown to the ground and beaten with a rod. I felt sorry for father, just as if I myself had been beaten. I felt sorry for his pathetic old age.

Then Hilarianus passed sentence on all of us: we were condemned to the beasts, and we returned to prison in high spirits. But my baby had got used to being nursed at the breast and to staying with me in prison. So I sent the deacon Pomponius straight away to my father to ask for the baby. But father refused to give him over. But as God willed, the baby had no further desire for the breast, nor did I suffer any inflammation; and so I was relieved of any anxiety for my child and of any discomfort in my breasts.

(6.1–8)

There was, as Vibia's father indicated, much pride in her resolution to die. In this passage, she seems almost pleased that a "vast crowd" has gathered to watch her and her friends be examined. Again, her father tries to dissuade her, even holding up her baby (it is never explained how he obtained the infant, nor is there ever any mention of Vibia's mother or brother again). Her steadfast refusal causes her father to suffer humiliation and physical abuse. She says she felt sorry—but she does nothing. Even the magistrate, Hilarianus, whose official behavior seems very much in line with Trajan's stated policy toward Christians, gives her every opportunity to change her mind. She is a young woman of status, and he would rather avoid condemning her to death. Instead, she glories in her reply to his question before the gathered throng: "Are you a Christian?" "Yes, I am." In utter frustration, her father takes his grandchild and will not return him to his daughter. She apparently soothes her guilt at being separated

Horrors of the Arena—Seneca Observes the Slaughter

MODERN STEREOTYPICAL IMPRESSIONS ARE that *all* Romans thoroughly enjoyed watching people being slaughtered in the arena, and that in a case like Perpetua's, life stopped while every man, woman, and child in the neighborhood rushed to enjoy the blood being spilled. As in any society, there was a sizable segment attracted to such blood spectacles; but as this passage from Seneca (the Stoic philosopher and tutor of Nero) indicates, many others found them repulsive. In this instance, it is not even gladiators—or Christians—who are involved, but condemned criminals. The arena had many uses, but it oftentimes served as the state's vehicle for executing criminals. What Seneca describes was no show for popular consumption—although from the dialogue he puts in their mouths, those who were present apparently viewed it as such. There was no sport involved. These were simply executions carried out by the criminals themselves—no one survived—and thereby, it was the worst kind of display to witness. Seneca reacts to what he saw and cannot, in this case, restrain his moral indignation:

There is nothing more harmful to one's character than attendance at some spectacle, because vices more easily creep into your soul while you are being entertained. When I return from some spectacle, I am greedier, more aggressive, and more addicted to pleasurable sensations; I am more cruel and inhumane—all because I have been with other humans! Recently I happened to stop at a noon-hour entertainment, expecting humor, wit, and some relaxing intermission when men's eyes could rest from watching men's blood. But it was quite the opposite. The morning matches had been merciful in comparison. Now all niceties were put aside, and it was pure and simple murder. The combatants wore absolutely no protection. Their whole bodies are exposed to one another's blows, and thus each never fails to injure his opponent. Most people in the audience prefer this type of match to the regular gladiators or the request bouts. And why not! There are no helmets or shields to deflect the swords. Who needs armor anyway? Who needs skill? These are all just ways to delay death. In the morning, men are thrown to the lions and the bears; at noon, they are thrown to the spectators. The spectators demand that combatants who have killed their opponents be thrown to combatants who will from the infant by convincing herself that God had willed it so.

Some days later, Vibia was praying and says she surprised herself by suddenly speaking out the name of her long dead brother, Dinocrates. This Dinocrates had apparently died of cancer of the face when he was seven years old, and Vibia had not thought about him (presumably in respect to how he might be suffering spiritually after death) until now. It is unlikely that Dinocrates was ever baptized, and Vibia's own

prayers and thoughts about her salvation now prompted her to pray for him. She says she prayed day and night for Dinocrates until she was convinced that "he had been delivered from his suffering." By that time, she and her friends had been transferred to the military prison: "For we were supposed to fight with the beasts at the military games to be held on the occasion of the Emperor Geta's birthday."

As the final day approached, the behavior of Vibia and her friends evoked the admiration

---

in turn kill them, and they make a victor stay for another slaughter. For every combatant, therefore, the outcome is certain death. They fight with swords and with fire [punishment if they did not fight]. And this goes on while the arena is supposedly empty. "But one of these men is a robber." And so? "But he killed a man." Well, since he killed a man, he deserves capital punishment. But what did you do, you wretch, to deserve the punishment of watching?—"Kill him, whip him, burn him! Why does he approach combat so timidly? Why does he kill so reluctantly? Why does he die so unwillingly? Why must he be driven with whiplashes to face sword wounds? Let them expose their naked chests to one another's weapons. This is the intermission for the gladiators. So let's have some men murdered. Don't just stop the entertainment!" Don't you understand that bad examples recoil upon those who set them?

(*Letters* 7.2–5)

Many animals also died unnecessarily in the arena in the name of entertainment. They were to kill or be killed. Sometimes hundreds died in a single display. Even exotic, rare creatures were

imported from all over the Empire to be dispatched. Vibia Perpetua was ingloriously tossed by a heifer (said to have been matched with her because of its sex), but the tradition maintains that her associates faced a bear, a leopard, or a wild boar—indication, perhaps, of the magistrate's meager budget or the scarcity of beasts available. At any rate, Cicero apparently felt the Roman taste for destroying magnificent animals had become excessive when, as governor of Cilicia in 50 B.C., he penned this satiric response to a friend, who as aedile had asked him to send panthers for the games he was organizing:

Dear Caelius,

About the panthers! The matter is being handled with diligence and according to my orders by men who are skillful hunters. But there is a remarkable scarcity of panthers. And they tell me that the few panthers left are complaining bitterly that they are the only animals in my province for whom traps are set. And therefore they have decided, or so the rumor goes, to leave my province and move to Caria. . . .

(*Letters to His Friends* 2.11)

and pity of even the prison warden (whom later tradition made a Christian), who was impressed by their resolve to die for their faith. Certainly, this was something that drew many to Christianity as the true religion. Again, there does not seem to be any general animosity toward Christians expressed here—merely adherence to the law. Vibia's father, emotionally spent, comes to see her for the last time. She writes:

> Some days later, an adjutant named Pudens, who was in charge of the prison, began to show us great honor, realizing that we possessed some great power within us. And he began to allow many visitors to see us for our mutual comfort.
>
> Now the day of the contest was approaching, and my father came to see me overwhelmed with sorrow. He started tearing the hairs from his beard and threw them on the ground; he then threw himself on the ground and began to curse his old age and to say such words as would move all creation. I felt sorry for his unhappy old age.
>
> (9.1–3)

Perpetua's last entry was on the eve of the games in which she died. She indicates that her coming fight is not to be with beasts but with the Devil and that she will be victorious. We are told that she was tossed and injured by a heifer and later dispatched by a gladiator (see box, pages 266–267).

The Dreams of Perpetua

While Vibia Perpetua was imprisoned, she had a series of elaborate dreams. These dreams, in particular, made the story of her martyrdom special, imbuing it with a spiritualism that has been admired by pious Christians over the centuries. Clearly, Vibia was an intense individual in a desperate situation, but the completeness of her dreams makes one wonder how she could have remembered them so exactly. However, if they were tampered with, the changes appear to have been minor. The dreams are dreamlike, lack the kind of "Christian coloring" found in visions known to be fictional, have a personal element, and contain non-Christian imagery that one would expect from someone only recently converted. Also, modern experts (mostly Freudians and Jungians) who have interpreted Vibia's dreams have found many of the accepted archetypical images in them.

Early Christians, of course, saw Perpetua's dreams as inspirational and related their content directly to Christian theology and her struggle against the Devil. The first dream occurred shortly after she was imprisoned. Her brother asks her to pray for a vision from God to indicate whether she will live or die. The next day, she relates the following dream to him:

> I saw a ladder of tremendous height made of bronze, reaching all the way to the heavens, but it was so narrow that only one person could climb up at a time. To the sides of the ladder were attached all sorts of metal weapons: there were swords, spears, hooks, daggers, and spikes; so that if anyone tried to climb up carelessly or without paying attention, he would be mangled and his flesh would adhere to the weapons.
>
> At the foot of the ladder lay a dragon [serpent?] of enormous size, and it would attack those who tried to climb up and try to terrify them from doing so. And Saturus [the leader of Vibia's group] was the first to go up, he who was later to give himself up of his own accord. He had been the builder of our strength, although he was not present when we were arrested. And he arrived at the top of the staircase and he looked back and said to me: "Perpetua, I am waiting for you. But take care; do not let the dragon bite you."

"He will not harm me," I said, "in the name of Jesus Christ."

Slowly, as though he were afraid of me, the dragon stuck his head out from underneath the ladder. Then, using it as my first step, I trod on his head and went up.

Then I saw an immense garden, and in it a grey-haired man sat in shepherd's garb; tall he was, and milking sheep. And standing around him were many thousands of people clad in white garments. He raised his head, looked at me, and said: "I am glad you have come, my child."

He called me over to him and gave me, as it were, a mouthful of the milk he was drawing; and I took it into my cupped hands and consumed it. And all those who stood around said: "Amen!" At the sound of this word I came to, with the taste of something sweet still in my mouth. I at once told this to my brother, and we realized that we would have to suffer, and that from now on we would no longer have any hope in this life.

(4.3–10)

To the Christian faithful, the meaning of this dream was obvious. Perpetua and Saturus defeated the Devil (represented by a dragon, or serpent) and ascended to heaven, where they are welcomed by Jesus.

In the three visions that follow, Vibia dreams first of the sufferings of her dead brother, Dinocrates, next of his having been spiritually cleansed and healed (as a result of her prayers), and finally of her forthcoming ordeal in the arena. This last dream, in which Perpetua becomes a man and wrestles with an Egyptian, occurs on the eve of her fight with the beasts:

The day before we were to fight with the beasts I saw the following vision. Pomponius the deacon came to the prison gates and began to knock violently. I went out and opened the gate for him. He was dressed in an unbelted white

Figure 9.12 *Perpetua's dream about her combat in the arena does have a basis in fact. Women also participated in gladiatorial combats, as this first–second century* A.D. *relief commemorating the service and release of Amazon and Achilla demonstrates.* *(British Museum)*

tunic, wearing elaborate sandals. And he said to me: "Perpetua, come; we are waiting for you."

Then he took my hand and we began to walk through rough and broken country. At last we came to the amphitheater out of breath, and he led me into the center of the arena.

Then he told me: "Do not be afraid. I am here, struggling with you." Then he left.

I looked at the enormous crowd who watched in astonishment. I was surprised that no beasts were let loose on me; for I knew that I was condemned to die by the beasts. Then out came an Egyptian against me, of vicious appearance, together with his seconds, to fight with me. There also came up to me some handsome young men to be my seconds and assistants.

My clothes were stripped off, and suddenly I was a man. My seconds began to rub me down with oil (as they are wont to do before a contest).

Then I saw the Egyptian on the other side rolling in the dust. Next there came forth a

The Divorce of Zois and Antipater

WE DO NOT KNOW if Perpetua was recently divorced, but if she was, then the procedure may have been close to the one cited below. This divorce took place in Egypt (Vibia, of course, was from an area of Africa near Carthage) in 13 B.C., long before Perpetua lived, but it is so straightforward that most of its terms were probably still applicable in the third century A.D.:

To Protarchus [title of a government official], from Zois daughter of Heraclides, accompanied by her brother and guardian Irenaeus son of Heraclides, and from Antipater son of Zeno:—

Zois and Antipater agree that they have separated from one another and severed their arrangement to live together. . . . And Zois agrees that Antipater has returned to her, handed over from his household, the items he received as her dowry, namely clothing valued at 120 silver drachmas and a pair of gold earrings. Both parties agree henceforth the marriage contract will be null and void . . . and from this day it will be lawful for Zois to marry another man and for Antipater to marry another woman, with neither party being liable to prosecution.

(*Select Papyri* 6 [*BGU* 1103])

man of marvellous stature, such that he rose above the top of the amphitheater. He was clad in a beltless purple tunic with two stripes (one on either side) running down the middle of his chest. He wore sandals that were wondrously made of gold and silver, and he carried a wand like an athletic trainer and a green branch on which there were golden apples.

And he asked for silence and said: "If this Egyptian defeats her he will slay her with the sword. But if she defeats him, she will receive this branch." Then he withdrew.

We drew close to one another and began to let our fists fly. My opponent tried to get hold of my feet, but I kept striking him in the face with the heels of my feet. Then I was raised up into the air and I began to pummel him without as it were touching the ground. Then when I noticed there was a lull, I put my two hands together linking the fingers of one hand with those of the other and thus I got hold of his head. He fell flat on his face and I stepped on his head.

The crowd began to shout and my assistants started to sing psalms. Then I walked up to the trainer and took the branch. He kissed me and said to me: "Peace be with you, my daughter!" I began to walk in triumph towards the Gate of Life. Then I awoke. I realized that it was not with wild animals that I would fight but with the Devil, but I knew that I would win the victory.

(10.1–14)

As in the other dreams, Perpetua (and fellow Christians) would have interpreted her dream only in the context of Christianity. She fights with the Devil, represented as an Egyptian (perhaps because of the recent Christian persecutions in Egypt), while a Christ figure, the wondrously tall trainer of gladiators who awards her the branch, oversees the match. Modern psychoanalysis of Perpetua's dreams, however, has indicated reasons for her martyrdom that go well beyond the simple surface appearance and suggest that she was deeply troubled. Her behavior has been variously interpreted as that of a young woman denying contemporary social life, breaking away from

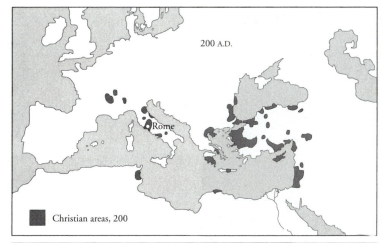

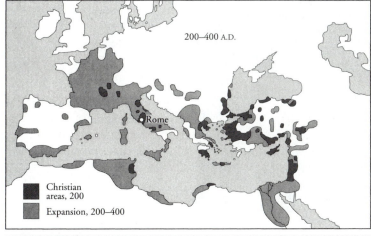

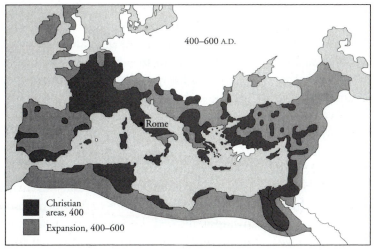

Map 21
The spread of Christianity

Figure 9.13
Constantine

"traditional familial patterns of patriarchal domination," or seeking relations with members of the opposite sex that were fraternal and asexual. Christianity provided the means by which she could accomplish her desires.

It would be nice to know exactly what had initially prompted Vibia Perpetua's conversion to Christianity—apparently, at short notice. The mysterious situation regarding her husband and recently born infant might provide a clue. Perpetua, herself, *never* mentions her husband. Was he dead, had he divorced her, had he run off, did he ever exist (the child may have been illegitimate)? If we knew the answers, we might be able to more fully understand Perpetua's motivations. As it is, all we know is that she found death in Christianity to be the answer to *all* her problems. The faith responded by making her a saint.

Christianity in the Later Roman Empire

The endorsement of Christianity by Constantine and the favoritism he subsequently showed toward it allowed the newly unshackled religion to thrive. Victor in the civil wars that followed the collapse of the Tetrarchy (it failed to survive

Figure 9.14
Central mosaic floor panel from a Roman building at Hinton St. Mary, Dorset, England, which some, because of the Chi-Rho symbol and pomegranates denoting immortality, have identified as the earliest known representation of Christ. (British Museum)

Figure 9.15
Mosaic of a Christian church from the end of the fifth century A.D. *(Louvre, Paris)*

its founder) and sole emperor by 324 A.D., Constantine ensured Christianity's eventual triumph and was a staunch supporter of orthodoxy. Since so many Roman citizens were Christians by this time, the position he chose inevitably had political as well as religious implications. One of his reasons for transferring the Empire's capital to Constantinople in the East in 330 A.D. was designed to appeal to the faithful: The new religion needed a new capital, untainted by the beliefs of the past.

As with any successful movement, the Christian triumph brought the bad with the good. Now part of the establishment, the Church made up for what it had previously lacked in resources and power. The leadership took advantage of its favored position. Those who had looked to Christianity to soothe social ills were sadly disappointed. Heretics and pagans suffered the Christian wrath. Ultimately, Theodosius (379–395 A.D.), the last great Roman emperor of the East and West, closed what remained of the old religious shrines and confiscated their treasures. The oracle at Delphi was shut down after a thousand years of operation, and the Olympic Games were disbanded in 393 A.D. As he was orchestrating the final realization of a Christian Roman Empire, Theodosius' chief religious advisor, Ambrose, the bishop of Milan, Augustine, and Jerome were already setting the foundation for the Medieval Church. The door was fast closing on the Ancient World.

Suggestions for Further Reading

Many of the most pertinent ancient passages related to the rise of Christianity have been cited in the text. Others (including excerpts from later Christian writers) may be found in collections such as the previously mentioned sourcebooks of Lewis and Reinhold and of Shelton. The best place to find the complete story of Vibia Perpetua is in the Oxford edition (1972) of *The Acts of the Christian Martyrs* ("The Martyrdom of Perpetua and Felicitas"), with Introduction and translation by H. Musurillo. For more recent literature, see R. Rousselle, "The Dreams of Vibia Perpetua: Analysis of a Female Christian Martyr," *Journal of Psychohistory* 14 (1987): 193–206; and M. R. Lefkowitz, "The Motivations for St. Perpetua's Martyrdom," *Journal of the American Academy of Religion* 44 (1976): 417–421. E. R. Dodds, *Pagan & Christian in an Age of Anxiety* (New York: Norton, 1970; first published, Cambridge University Press, 1965), also includes a section (47–53) on Vibia in his fundamental study.

For religion in general, see A. Wardman, *Religion and Statecraft Among the Romans* (London: Granada, 1982); and J. Ferguson, *The Religions of the Roman Empire* (Ithaca, N.Y.: Cornell University Press, 1970). There are so many studies of Christianity that only a few can be mentioned. Good introductions are provided by H. Chadwick, *The Early Church*, Vol. 1 (Baltimore: Penguin Books, 1967); H. Mattingly, *Christianity in the Roman Empire* (New York: Norton, 1967); W. H. C. Frend, *The Rise of Christianity* (London: Darton et al., 1984); and R. MacMullen, *Christianizing the Roman Empire A.D. 100–400* (New Haven, Conn.: Yale University Press, 1984). More specific studies include J. Rives, "Human Sacrifice Among Pagans and Christians," *Journal of Roman Studies* 85 (1995): 65–85; G. Anderson, *Sage, Saint and Sophist: Holy Men and Their Associates in the Early Roman Empire* (New York: Routledge, 1994); P. F. Esler, *The First Christians in Their Social World* (New York: Routledge, 1994); G. Clark, *Women in Late Antiquity: Pagan and Christian Lifestyles* (New York: Oxford University Press, 1993); L. Michael White, *Building God's House in the Roman World: Architectural Adaptation Among Pagans, Jews, and Christians* (Baltimore: The Johns Hopkins University Press, 1990); and D. Kyrtatas, *The Social Structure of the Early Christian Communities* (New York: Routledge, 1987).

Work has been done on Diocletian and Constantine by S. Williams, *Diocletian and the Roman Recovery* (London: Batsford, 1985); T. D. Barnes, *The New Empire of Diocletian and Constantine* (Cambridge, Mass.: Harvard University Press, 1982); M. Grant, *Constantine the Great: The Man and His Times* (New York: Scribner, 1993); and R. MacMullen, *Constantine* (London: Croom Helm, 1980). H. M. D. Parker, *History of the Roman World from A.D. 138 to 337*, rev. ed. (London: Methuen, 1969), ends his general history with the death of Constantine.

General Reading

On the Later Empire, see R. MacMullen, *Corruption and the Decline of Rome* (New Haven, Conn.: Yale University Press, 1988), and *Roman Government's Response to Crisis, A.D. 235–337* (Yale, 1976); P. Brown, *The World of Late Antiquity A.D. 150–750* (New York: Norton, 1989), which is also nicely illustrated; and the detailed study (not for the general reader) by A. H. M. Jones, *The Later Roman Empire 284–602*, 2 vols. (Norman: University of Oklahoma Press, 1964). On barbarians, see P. J. Heather, *Goths and Romans, 332–489* (New York:

Oxford University Press, 1992); and W. Goffart, *Barbarians and Romans, A.D. 418–584: The Techniques of Accommodation* (Princeton, N. J.: Princeton University Press, 1987). On women, see K. G. Holum, *Theodosian Empresses: Women and Imperial Domination in Late Antiquity* (Berkeley and Los Angeles: University of California Press, 1982). Other recent works of interest include A. Cameron, *The Mediterranean World in Late Antiquity, A.D. 395–600* (New York: Routledge, 1994); H. Elton, *Warfare in Roman Europe A.D. 350– 425* (New York: Oxford University Press, 1996); M. H. Dodgeon and S. N. C. Lieu, *The Roman Eastern Frontier and the Persian Wars A.D. 226–363: A Documentary History* (New York: Routledge, 1994); J. E. Grubbs, *Law and Family in Late Antiquity: The Emperor Constantine's Marriage Legislation* (New York: Oxford University Press, 1995); J. Matthews, *The Roman Empire of Ammianus* (Baltimore: The Johns Hopkins University Press, 1990); and C. Haas, *Late Roman Alexandria* (Johns Hopkins, 1996).

Recent Additions

P. Brown, *Authority and the Sacred: Aspects of the Christianisation of the Roman World* (Cambridge: Cambridge University Press, 1997); R. MacMullen, *Christianity & Paganism in the Fourth to Eighth Centuries* (New Haven: Yale University Press, 1997); J. E. Salisbury, *Perpetua's Passion* (New York: Routledge, 1997), now the major work on Vibia Perpetua; and S. N. C. Lieu and D. Montserrat (eds.), *Constantine: History, Historiography, and Legend* (New York: Routledge, 1998).

Recent General Additions

S. Williams and G. Friell, *Theodosius: the Empire at Bay* (New Haven: Yale University Press, 1995); N. P. Milner (trans.), *Vegetius: Epitome of Military Science* (Philadelphia: University of Pennsylvania Press, 1996), is a late source (end of the fourth century A.D.?) but our only Roman military handbook to survive intact; J. Rich (ed.), *The City of Late Antiquity* (New York: Routledge, 1996); R. Southern and K. R. Dixon, *The Late Roman Army* (New Haven: Yale University Press, 1996); H. Wolfram, *The Roman Empire and Its Germanic Peoples* (Berkeley and Los Angeles: University of California Press, 1997); M. Grant, *From Rome to Byzantium: The Fifth Century A.D.* (New York: Routledge, 1998); G. W. Bowersock, et al., *Late Antiquity; A Guide to the Postclassical World* (Cambridge, Mass.: Harvard University Press, 1999); G. Friell and S. Williams, *The Rome that Did Not Fall* (New York: Routledge, 1999); M. Grant, *The Collapse and Recovery of the Roman Empire* (New York: Routledge, 1999; and R. Miles (ed.), *Constructing Identities in Late Antiquity* (New York: Routledge, 1999).

IO

Emperors and Entertainment

Crowds, Cheers, and the Circus Maximus
Diocles the Charioteer

All Rome is in the Circus today.
(Juvenal, *Satire,* 11.197)

For a thousand years and more, through the administrations of countless magistrates and almost a hundred emperors—whether Italian, provincial, barbarian, traditional in religious belief or Christian—despite change, upheaval, and transformation, one thing remained constant for the Roman people throughout the generations: their love of circuses and the chariot races that took place in them. The people who gathered to watch the races during the Republic, the Empire, and even into the Byzantine world were at any given moment a microcosm of the Roman world. It is only fitting, therefore, that the final chapter be reserved for the greatest circus, the Circus Maximus at Rome, and for the drivers whose reputations endured the centuries. One of the most famous charioteers of them all was Gaius Appuleius Diocles.

The Circus Maximus

Circuses in Rome were not, as in recent times, assortments of clowns, trapeze artists, acrobats, trained animals, and other specialty acts collected under a "Big Top" and directed by a "Ringmaster" (although our word *circus* comes from the Latin *circus* ["circle"] and one could, at various times, find the equivalent of most of the above in a Roman circus). Originally, circuses were multipurpose facilities that functioned foremost as chariot racetracks—mostly for two- and four-horse teams—and as Pliny the Younger contemptuously observed, the races were popular to the extreme:

> I have been spending all the last few days amongst my notes and papers in most welcome peace. How could I—in the city? The

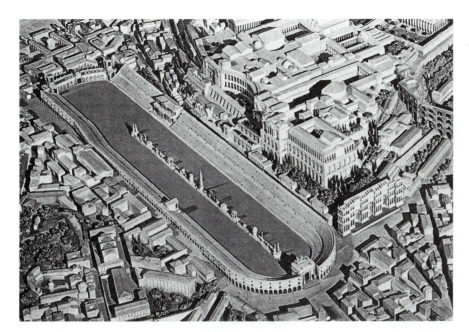

Figure 10.1
A reconstruction of the Circus Maximus as it appeared during the Late Empire. Above and right, on the Palatine Hill, is the sprawling Imperial Palace.

Races were on, a type of spectacle which has never had the slightest attraction for me. I can find nothing new or different in them: once seen is enough, so it surprises me all the more that so many thousands of adult men should have such a childish passion for watching galloping horses and drivers standing in chariots, over and over again. . . . When I think how this futile, tedious, monotonous business can keep them sitting endlessly in their seats, I take pleasure in the fact that their pleasure is not mine. And I have been very glad to fill my idle hours with literary work during these days which others have wasted in the idlest of occupations.

(*Letters* 9.6)

Pliny's disdain for the mindless masses who frequented the races was apparently more the result of snobbery than any real conviction. His true feelings are more accurately gauged by the fact that his own signet ring had a chariot team represented on it! Even Pliny, despite his protes-

tations, had succumbed to the lure of the Circus. Few could remain immune:

The truth is that the Roman crowd revelled in these spectacles where everything combined to quicken their curiosity and arouse their excitement: the swarming crowd in which each was carried off his feet by all, the almost incredible grandeur of the setting, the perfumes and gaily-colored toilets, the sanctity of the ancient religious ceremonies, the presence of the august emperor, the obstacles to be overcome, the perils to be avoided, the prowess needed to win, the unforeseen vicissitudes of each of the contests which brought out the powerful beauty of the stallions, the richness of their accoutrements, the perfection of their training, and above all the agility and gallantry of drivers and riders.

(Carcopino, *Daily Life* 215)

There were dozens of circuses throughout the Empire, and the city of Rome had four

Figure 10.2
The modern site of
the Circus Maximus

major tracks: the Circus Flaminius, laid out in 221 B.C.; the Circus of Caligula and Nero, built in the first century A.D.; the Circus of Maxentius from the early fourth century A.D.; and the oldest and grandest of them all (probably the largest spectator facility ever built), the Circus Maximus. Located in a depression between the Aventine and Palatine Hills, the Circus Maximus sat directly below the Imperial Palace. Its history traditionally went back to the time of the kings—but it did not approach the monumental proportions that would characterize it during the Empire until Julius Caesar established its canonical shape of two long sides ending in a semicircle. Augustus completed Caesar's work, and succeeding emperors continued to improve and rebuild the structure. By 103 A.D., it had reached its most impressive stage with Trajan's massive reconstruction.

The Circus was immense by any standard. Externally, its length was about 680 yards (over

a third of a mile), while its width was 150 yards. The most recent estimates place its seating capacity at about 150,000, although some ancient sources make it 250,000 and more. It is difficult to reconcile this discrepancy. Modern figures are based on the best available physical evidence, but the Romans were notorious for overcrowding, and we can never know how many people they actually packed into the Circus. Still, it is not easy to account for an additional 100,000 spectators, and the ancient figures may have included those who watched from the hills overlooking the track. In the earliest days, everyone viewed the races in this manner because there were no seats. Whatever the explanation, officials at the Circus had to accommodate the mass of Rome's racing fans. Disruptions and minor violence characterized every circus day. Turning away tens of thousands of disgruntled spectators who had come, sometimes from great distances, to view (and wager) on the contests and catch a glimpse of the emperor would not have been wise policy!

The arena of the Circus measured about 635 by 85 yards, or roughly twelve times that of the Colosseum, another of Rome's great spectator facilities. Its floor was a bed of compacted earth covered with a layer of sand, designed to allow the chariots to hold the track (especially on the turns), to save the horses from injury, and to drain off water. Attendants carefully maintained the surface before, during, and after a race, and probably wetted it down between contests to limit the dust.

At one end of the Circus were twelve starting gates (*carceres*). Running down the middle of the arena, closer to the rounded end of the facility (see Figure 10.3), was a long, narrow barrier (frequently identified as the *spina* but more accurately called the *euripus*). Approximately 365 yards in length, it was covered with an assortment of shrines, altars, and other monuments, including two large obelisks brought from Egypt. It was around this barrier, which had turning posts (*metae*) at each end, that the chariots whirled seven death-defying times (about 3 miles), always to the driver's left. Seven large bronze dolphins at one end of the barrier and seven "eggs" at the other were used to indicate the lap number. The dolphin became a racing symbol because it was fast and sacred to Neptune, the god of the sea and of horses. Since a bronze dolphin was part of the starting mechanism at the Hippodrome in Olympia, where the Olympic Games were held, the Circus's dolphins may also have provided a link with the older tradition of horse racing in Greece. The eggs evoked memories of Castor and Pollux, patron gods of horses and horsemen, who were traditionally sprung from an egg. As lap counters, however, the dolphins and eggs probably benefited the crowd more than the charioteers,

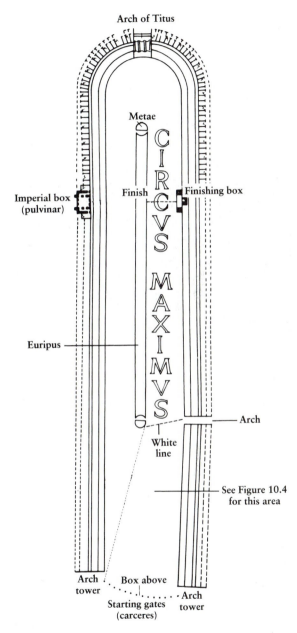

Figure 10.3   *Plan of the Circus Maximus by the early third century A.D.*

who were totally involved in the race. They must have depended on personal lap counters who were stationed closer to the track.

As the Circus evolved from a temporary facility (modeled, like the events that took place in it, on Greek and Etruscan precedents) into a massive complex, the Romans learned by experience how to guarantee fair play. The Circus was designed so that every competitor had an equal chance to win. The twelve marble-faced starting gates, each about 10 feet wide, were arranged on a line so that every chariot would travel an equal distance to a "break line" on the right side of the central barrier (see Figure 10.4). The barrier was about 165 yards, or one-third the length of the arena floor, from the gates and was angled slightly to the left. This was done to eliminate any disadvantage to drivers in the top lanes. Otherwise, they would approach the barrier at too extreme an angle and probably crash into it or the other teams. When the gate doors were opened simultaneously by a mechanism, the chariots were required to stay within marked lanes until they reached the break line. Then they could jockey for the best position. Obviously, they wanted to keep as close to the barrier as possible, while staying clear of, or crowding out, their competitors. The turns, not surprisingly, were where most accidents (and deaths) took place.

Officials watched the entire race to make sure that no fouls were committed and that there was no question about the winner. Since the prestige of the racing factions and the wagers of a large betting public were on the line, the contests were very carefully judged. Reruns were not uncommon.

Immediately before each race, the presiding magistrate drew lots in front of the crowd to determine which driver's team would occupy each

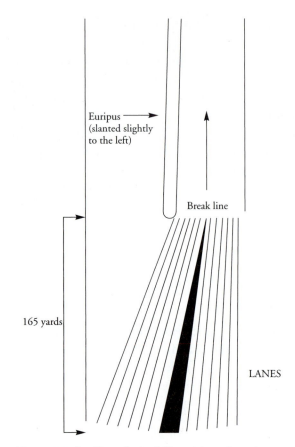

Figure 10.4 *Hypothetical disposition of starting gates and lanes to give all drivers equal access to the break line*

starting gate. Lots did not automatically assign a gate but allowed a charioteer to select the one he wanted. The driver who chose first did not necessarily have an advantage over his competition, for depending on the rest of the draw, what seemed a good choice at the beginning may not have turned out that way in the end. Consequently, it was the skill of the driver and his team that determined the outcome. No one could complain that he had not had an equal opportunity to win at the start.

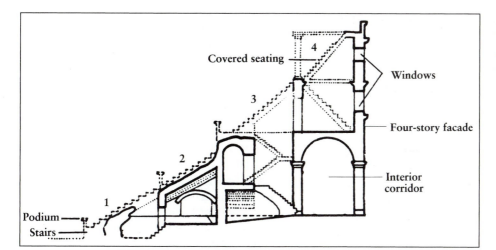

Figure 10.5
*Simplified cross
section of southeast
end of the Circus*

Once closed behind their gates, the charioteers and their teams waited impatiently for the magistrate to drop a white napkin from a stand above them. The signal activated a mechanism that threw open the doors and released them from their stalls. A modern scholar re-creates the final seconds:

> The signal for the trumpet to sound the start was given by the presiding consul, praetor, or aedile, who threw a white napkin from the height of his tribune into the arena. The gesture was critical and the great personage in himself was a sight worth seeing. Over a tunic, scarlet like Jupiter's, he had draped an embroidered Tyrian toga. Like a living statue, he held in his hand an ivory baton surmounted by an eagle on the point of flight, and on his head he wore a wreath of golden leaves so heavy that a "slave or player at his side had to help him to hold it up."
>
> At the president's feet, the chariots [were in the gates] which the draw had allotted to them for the start. . . . Each upheld the honor of the party or *factio* [see the section on factions following]. . . . While the horses pawed the ground, branches on their heads, tail held in air by a tight knot, mane starred with pearls,

breast-plate studded with plaques and amulets, necks bearing a flexible collar and a ribbon dyed with the colors of their party, the *auriga* [driver] . . . stood upright in his chariot, helmet on head, whip in hand, leggings swathed round calf and thigh, clad in a tunic the color of his *factio*, his reins bound round his body, and by his side the dagger that would sever them in case of accident.

(Carcopino, *Daily Life* 216–217)

During the reign of Augustus, this scene was typically repeated twelve times each racing day. Caligula doubled that number, and twenty-four races daily remained fairly standard, although Domitian once ran a hundred (the number of laps was reduced); and on an afternoon in 192 A.D., Commodus is said to have staged thirty races in two hours! At the end of each race, the winner was awarded a palm or crown of victory and prize money.

More Than a Racetrack

It would be a mistake to view the Circus as nothing more than a glorified horse-racing facility.

Ovid's Racetrack Romance

NOT EVERYONE WENT TO the Circus to see the races. In the following passage from the *Amores,* the poet Ovid, who wrote during the time of Augustus, pictures himself seated next to an alluring young lady. She has come to see her favorite win, but Ovid's interest in the race went only as far as it pleased the lady—his main objective was to impress her. The episode appears to have occurred during a single visit to the Circus, but it is more likely a composite, based on several of Ovid's grandstand flirtations. The poet knew the Circus well, and he also mentions it in his *Art of Love* (1.135–164) as an ideal place to pick up women. Advice on such subjects may have been appreciated in some circles, but it is doubtful that Augustus approved. The contents of Ovid's poems were probably a bit more racy than the moral standards of the day allowed—perhaps a contributing factor to the poet's exile in 8 A.D. to the Black Sea area. He was never allowed to return.

Many Circus seats were free, and spectators had to come early to get them. All seats were made of stone by Trajan's day, but a cushion had already become required gear for Circus-goers many years before. The sun could make spectators uncomfortable, especially since hot, heavy togas were the only acceptable dress for the privileged class. There were covered seats in the uppermost tier of the Circus that must have demanded the highest prices, but even someone seated there could have problems. During the second century A.D., in the reign of Antoninus Pius, a section of the preferred seating collapsed and 1,112 people were killed.

In his poem, Ovid contributes to our knowledge about what went on in the stands—and on the track—at the Circus. He adds a human element that we would not otherwise have:

> I'm not sitting here because of my enthusiasm for race horses; but I pray that the chariot driver you favor may win. I came here, in fact, so that I might sit beside you and talk to you. I didn't want the love which you stir in me to be concealed from you. So, you watch the races, and I'll watch you. Let's each watch the things we love most, and let's feast our eyes on them.

> Oh, how lucky is the chariot driver you favor! Does he have the good fortune to attract your attention? Let me, please, have that good fortune. Carried out of the starting gate by galloping horses, I will drive aggressively, sometimes giving the horses their heads, sometimes whipping their backs. Then I will graze the turning post with my inside wheel. But if I catch sight of you as I race along, I will stop and let the reins slacken and fall from my hands. . . . . .

> Why are you edging away from it? It's no use. The seat marker forces us to touch. Yes, the Circus does offer some advantages in its seating rules.

> Hey, you, on the right, whoever you are, be more considerate of the lady! You're hurting her by pressing up against her. And you, too, behind us. Draw in your legs, if you have any sense of decency, and don't stick your bony knees in her back.

> Oh dear, your skirt is trailing a bit on the ground. Lift it up, or here, I will do it. . . . (But what will happen when I see her ankles? Even when they were hidden I burned with passion. Now I am adding flames to a fire, water to a flood. From the sight of her ankles I can well imagine the other delights which lie carefully hidden under her clothing.) Would you like me to stir a light breeze by using my program as a fan? . . .

> But look, the procession has arrived. Quiet, everyone! Pay attention! It's time for applause. The golden procession has arrived. Victory is riding in front, her wings outstretched. Be with me, Victory, and make me victorious in love.

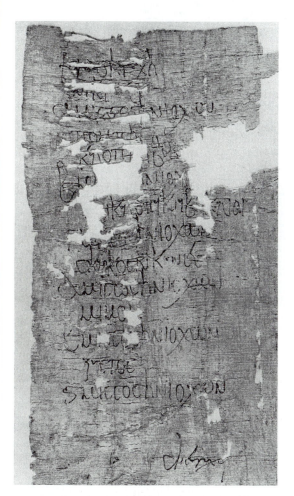

Figure 10.6 *A circus program from the sixth century* A.D.

You who trust yourselves to the sea can clap for Neptune. I have no interest in seafaring; I'm a landlubber. And you, there, soldier, clap for Mars, your patron god. I hate warfare. It's peace I like, and it's in peace that you find love. Let Phoebus help the augurs, and Phoebe the hunters. Minerva, seek applause from the craftsmen. Farmers, stand up! Here comes Ceres and delicate Bacchus. Boxers should show reverence to Pollux and horsemen to Castor. Now it's my turn to applaud, sweet Venus, for you and your archer cupids. Nod in support of my plans, oh goddess. Make my new girlfriend receptive to my advances and willing to be loved. Look, she nodded and gave me a favorable reply. Well, then, I'm only asking you to agree to what the goddess has already promised. . . . I swear, in front of all these witnesses and by this procession of the gods, that I will cherish you as my girlfriend forever.

Oh, but your legs are dangling. You can, if you wish, rest your toes on the railing.

Good, the track is clear and ready for the first big race. The praetor gives the signal and the four-horse chariots break from the starting gates. I can see the driver you're cheering for. I'm sure he'll win. Even his horses seem to know what you want.

Oh no, he's swinging wide around the turning post. What are you doing? The driver in second position is coming up from behind. Pull on the left rein with your strong hand! Oh, we're cheering for an idiot and a coward.

Come on, call them back, citizens. Wave your togas and give them the message. Good, they're calling them back. Oh dear, don't let the waving togas mess your hair. Here, you may hide under the folds of my toga.

The starting gates are opening again, the horses break, and the different-colored teams fly onto the track. Now, gallop ahead and take a clear lead! Fulfill my girlfriend's hopes, and my own. (Good! Her wishes have been granted, mine remain to be granted. He has won the palm, I am still reaching for mine. Ah, she smiled, and promised me something with her sly eyes.) Enough for this place. Satisfy the rest of my desires elsewhere.

(*Amores* 3.2)

Figure 10.7   Remains of shops and entrances that opened up into the Circus Maximus'
interior corridor

Astrologers considered it a microcosm not only of the Roman world but also of the universe, and they based predictions on its configurations and the races. The twelve starting gates, for example, represented the twelve signs of the zodiac; the seven laps, the days of the week; the twenty-four races, the hours of the day; and the turning posts—around which four-horse (the sun) and two-horse (the moon) chariots raced, as heavenly bodies race around the heavens—were representations of East and West.

In the stands, merchants, tradesmen, farmers, soldiers, cooks, bureaucrats, the unemployed, and even slaves shared the same sun with senators, the royal family, and often the emperor himself. Only the Circus's restricted seating prevented social distinctions from dissolving alto-

gether in a moment of frenzy when all cheered their favorites, more demigods than men.

Inside its four-story facade, the Circus was a maze of shops, rooms, stairways, and arcades. Throngs of people moved about the great interior corridor that provided access to any part of the structure. Vendors hawked their wares and sold refreshments and souvenirs; and, of course, there were always prostitutes, gamblers, pickpockets, girl watchers, and drunks.

Since there was some time between races and the races themselves did not last long (certainly less than ten minutes), many spectators probably came outside to watch only for the start of a contest. They stood on the stairs or any place they could find while the race was on, and when it was over, they went back inside. It is doubtful that anyone remained seated during a race, and thousands of transient spectators would have swelled the grandstands considerably past the 150,000 seating capacity during a race.

The Circus, then, was literally a meeting place for the Roman world. During the Empire, it was also the one place where the emperor could communicate with a large segment of the population. It was difficult for the emperor to gauge the needs and sentiments of the people he ruled. In an authoritarian regime, it was almost impossible for the populace to express itself about taxes, high prices, injustices, war, and peace. Both sides could make their feelings known at the Circus. The incident that Dio witnessed in 196 A.D. (see Chapter 8), when the Circus crowd indicated its displeasure over the civil war between Septimius Severus and Clodius Albinus, is a good example:

> While . . . the entire world was disturbed by this situation, we senators remained quiet, at least as many of us as did not, by openly inclining to the one or the other, share their dangers and their hopes. The populace, however, could not restrain itself, but indulged in the most open lamentations. It was at the last horse-race before the Saturnalia, a countless throng of people flocked to it. I, too, was present . . . and I heard distinctly everything that was said. . . . They had watched the chariots racing . . . without applauding, as was their custom, any of the contestants at all. But when these races were over and the charioteers were about to begin another event, they first enjoined silence upon one another and then suddenly all clapped their hands at the same moment and also joined in a shout, praying for good fortune for the public welfare. . . . Then, applying the terms "Queen" and "Immortal" to Rome, they shouted: "How long are we to suffer such things?" and "How long are we to be waging war?" And after making some other remarks of this kind, they final-

ly shouted, "So much for that," and turned their attention to the horse race.
> (*Roman History* 75.4.2–5)

There were always intermittent protest and riot in the Circus, but from examples like this one, it is difficult to accept wholesale the usual characterization of the racing crowd as an undisciplined rabble, always on the verge of eruption. Juvenal's oft-quoted remark that the population of his day was only interested in "bread and circus games" is an obvious overstatement, made by a man who knew better but was overly concerned with the social ills and morality of his day. The same probably holds true for the historian Tacitus' observation that plebeians had nothing better to do than to hang around places like the Circus. The behavior of the typical Roman fan who attended the Circus was, within the standards of the day, probably no better or worse than that of his or her modern counterpart.

The image of the hapless emperor under constant siege by restless mobs who used the Circus and other spectator facilities as spawning grounds for dissent is unrealistic for most of Roman history. "Riots" took place within recognized boundaries of behavior. The ruler was to provide for his people and, as long as he did, he received their enthusiastic support. If he did not, the people reacted. Both sides knew how far they could go. Rome was an authoritarian regime and had a large police and military force. An example from Caligula's reign clearly indicates who really wielded the power:

> At this time occurred chariot races. This is a kind of sport to which the Romans are fanatically devoted. They gather enthusiastically in the circus and there the assembled throngs make requests of the emperors according to their own pleasure. Emperors who rule that

such petitions are to be granted automatically are highly popular. So in this case they desperately entreated Gaius [Caligula] to cut down imposts and grant some relief from the burden of taxes. But he had no patience with them, and when they shouted louder and louder, he dispatched agents among them in all directions with orders to arrest any who shouted, to bring them forward at once and to put them to death. The order was given and those whose duty it was carried it out. The number of those executed in such summary fashion was very large. The people, when they saw what happened, stopped their shouting and controlled themselves, for they could see with their own eyes that the request for fiscal concessions resulted quickly in their own death.

(Josephus, *Jewish Antiquities* 19.24.7)

Like any intelligent ruler (excluding Caligula—his behavior on this day convinced those who were planning to assassinate him to do so), most of Rome's emperors recognized human nature. They needed to give their subjects diversions that would distract them from daily problems and divert their attention away from politics. Political dissent during the Empire was channeled from the polling place to the racing window. Without public entertainment, general restlessness could ensue, causing possible destabilization of the state and other problems—all more serious than any disturbances that might arise in the stands of the Circus:

> It was the height of political wisdom for the emperor not to neglect even actors and other performers of the stage, the circus, and the arena, since he knew that the Roman people is held fast by two things above all, the grain supply and the shows, that the success of the government depends on amusements as much as on serious things. Neglect of serious matters entails the greater detriment, of amusements the greater unpopularity. The money largesses are less eagerly desired than the shows; the largesses appease only the grain-doled plebs singly and individually, while the shows keep the whole population happy.

(Fronto, *Elements of History* 17)

As an additional crowd-pleasing tactic, emperors often offered prizes, money, and other treats, including a banquet at the end of the day, to help soothe any aggressions built up over a particularly devastating racing day. It was also good public relations for the emperor to make a personal appearance at the Circus, albeit in his imperial box (*pulvinar*), to make the people feel that he shared their simple pleasures. Emperors who overindulged in the racing scene, however, learned that they had to restrain their enthusiasm, since their favoritism toward a certain driver or horse could cause fans with similar dispositions to become overconfident and more inclined to violence. Even if an emperor did not care for the races, it was still wise to put in an occasional appearance.

In the days of the Later Empire when authority was sometimes shared by several rulers, it is no surprise to find the circuses in their capitals, as at Rome, situated directly next to their palaces. It was an architectural arrangement that had become much too important, politically, for any emperor to disregard.

Drivers, Fans, and Factions

While the Circus was many things to many people, the central interest was, of course, the charioteers and their teams. The latter were carefully bred; the former usually lacked any kind of respectable pedigree. Most drivers started as slaves or low in the social order, a fact that probably enhanced their image, since they seemed to be free from conventional moral and

social restraints. Those from similar back-
grounds could identify with their heroes and
hope to emulate their success. The status that
accrued to these "sand-splattered daredevils"
was not unlike—yet still surpasses—that given
to modern-day sports superstars.

Prominent charioteers were chums of some
emperors; gilded busts and portraits of the most
famous were set up all over town; they were
consulted as magicians, since their winning
ways could be explained only in terms of magical power. Their wealth was proverbial. Juvenal
laments that a driver could net a hundred times
the wages of a lawyer (*Satire* 7.112–114), and
the poet Martial speaks of fifteen bags of gold
won in an hour (10.74). Charioteers' criminal
antics—which included "doping" and poisoning rivals' horses (and sometimes the rivals
themselves) and "doctoring" races—often
spilled over into the public. Nero, himself a professional rowdy and avid fan of the races, was
prompted to crack down on charioteers because
they molested, robbed, or beat up passersby in
the streets. Generally, charioteers were "above
the law." The outlandish emperor Elagabalus
offered his solution to the problem by making a
charioteer his police chief! By the Late Empire,
the Prefect of Rome was actually forbidden to
punish them.

The reason authorities were so cautious in
dealing with charioteers is obvious. Their fans
were fanatics and, as with many modern sports
enthusiasts, were easily aroused. One loyal supporter supposedly threw himself on the funeral
pyre of his deceased hero, while others went so
far as to decorate their tombs with images of
chariots and the Circus. To help their favorites
win, zealous fans often resorted to magic and
even "curse tablets." The following curse was
designed to ruin the chances of a charioteer
named Eucherius:

Figure 10.8　Statue of a charioteer

I conjure you up, holy beings and holy names;
join in aiding this spell, and bind, enchant,
thwart, strike, overturn, conspire against,
destroy, kill, break Eucherius, the charioteer,
and all his horses tomorrow in the circus at
Rome. May he not leave the barriers well; may
he not be quick in contest; may he not outstrip
anyone; may he not make the turns well; may
he not win any prizes; and if he has pressed
someone from behind, may he not overtake

him; but may he meet with an accident; may he be bound; may he be broken; may he be dragged along by your power, in the morning and afternoon races. Now! Now! Quickly! Quickly!

(*Inscriptiones Graecae ad Res Romanas Pertinentes*, Vol. 1, No. 117)

Even horse dung was in high demand among enthusiasts, who ran about dissecting recent droppings to determine the diet and health of their favorites and rivals.

Each charioteer drove for one of four circus factions (*factiones*), identified by the colors green, blue, red, and white (Domitian added two more, gold and purple, but they were short-lived). Fans were devoted more to the faction color than they were to individual drivers, although everyone had their favorite to cheer. When a driver changed factions, he did not take his fans with him, no more than would a modern player if he moved from a team in New York to one in Chicago.

Factions began as little more than professional stables run for profit by private individuals. Magistrates responsible for conducting the races would contract with them to provide horses, drivers, equipment, and other personnel and paraphernalia necessary to stage a competition. Each stable had fans, or partisans, who supported its drivers at the races. Initially, everything needed for a successful day of racing had to be assembled from the ground up each time a meet was held. This was expensive and confusing, and there was little consistency in quality. The rise of professional stables gradually helped to ensure quality and held costs down. However, the popularity of the circuses continued to grow, as did the demand for more races. Costs began to escalate—for which faction heads (*domini*), holding a virtual track monopoly, were mostly responsible. By the Late

Empire, the emperors had assumed control over the faction stables, not only because of the financial drain but also because of the increasing political influence and power of the factions.

Even though their main interest was profit, faction heads were as vulnerable to racetrack mania as everyone else. One innovative owner even sent race results to his hometown by carrier pigeon, whose legs were dyed with the winning color! Pliny, in the same letter in which he expressed contempt for the racing scene, also described the frenzy evoked by the faction colors:

> . . . If they were attracted by the speed of the horses or the driver's skill one could account for it, but in fact it is the racing-colors they really support and care about, and if the colors were to be exchanged in mid-course during a race, they would transfer their favor and enthusiasm and rapidly desert the famous drivers and horses whose names they shout as they recognize them from afar. Such is the popularity and importance of a worthless shirt. . . .
> (*Letters* 9.6)

Few practices of modern fans can equal those of Roman racing partisans. They even intermixed granules dyed the same color as their faction's with the sand on the track!

Of the four factions, the Greens and Blues were by far the most important and, predictably, had the greatest number of fans. Each of the minor factions, the Reds and Whites, appear to have become linked with a major faction, although the nature of their precise relationship is unclear. What is known is that the Greens were the most prominent of all factions. Juvenal indicates their popularity in this passage:

> . . . The roar that assails my eardrums
> Means, I am pretty sure, that the Greens
>   have won—otherwise
> You'd see such gloomy faces, such sheer
>   astonishment

(a)

Figure 10.9a and b
These two remarkable fragments fully capture the excitement of the Circus— detailing the action, the drivers, and the chariots and horse teams. Physical aspects include the euripus, *the* metae, *and the bronze dolphin lap counters. (Louvre, Paris)*

(b)

As greeted the Cannae disaster, after our
  consuls
Had bitten the dust.
(*Satire* 11.197–201)

The Greens were also the favorite of Caligula, who often dined and slept at their great stable house (replete with social staff, stewards, cooks, and clerks). He supposedly once gave 20,000 gold pieces to a Green driver he admired.

Races were always between factions—three teams from each if all twelve stalls were filled. Should a foul be committed against one color by another or if a favored driver suffered some humiliation in or outside the Circus, fan reaction could be immediate and violent. Besides emotion, money was involved.

By the fourth century A.D., political instability and declining police supervision led to a dramatic rise in violent circus-related incidents. Riots broke out in Rome in 355 A.D. when the charioteer Filoromus was arrested. In 390 A.D., seven thousand people were massacred at Thessalonica in Greece, reputedly as a result of rioting over the arrest of a favorite for making homosexual advances toward a general. The general was lynched by the mob! Charioteers became ringleaders for so many kinds of public disturbances that in 394 A.D. the Emperor Theodosius banned the display of their pictures everywhere except at the entrance to circuses. Ammianus Marcellinus, the last great historian of antiquity, disgusted at riotous circus crowds, characterized them as follows:

These spend all their life with wine and dice, in low haunts, pleasures, and the games. Their temple, their dwelling, their assembly, and height of all their hopes is the Circus Maximus. You may see many groups of them gathered in the fora, the cross-roads, the streets, and their other meeting-places, engaged in quarrelsome arguments with one another, some (as usual) defending this, others that. Among them those who have enjoyed a surfeit of life, influential through long experience, often swear by their hoary hair and wrinkles that the state cannot exist if in the coming race the charioteer whom each favors is not first to rush forth from the barrier and fails to round the turning-point closely with his ill-omened horses. And when there is such a dry rot of thoughtlessness, as soon as the longed-for day of the chariot-races begins to dawn, before the sun is yet shining clearly they all hasten in crowds to the spot at top speed, as if they would outstrip the very chariots that are to take part in the contest; and torn by their conflicting hopes about the result of the race, the greater number of them in their anxiety pass sleepless nights.
(*Roman History* 28.4.29–31)

Christian writers had already become convinced that the circuses were the Devil's playground. Tertullian warned members of his flock to stay clear of them or risk endangering their immortal souls. Even faced with such a prospect, Christians did not let their seats in the Circus get cold, for the races continued well into the Christian era, the last recorded contest at Rome occurring in 549 A.D.

The Career of Diocles

Of the great charioteers adored by Roman crowds and made immortal by their antics, few rivaled Gaius Appuleius Diocles, a Lusitanian from Spain. His career is the best documented of any driver we know. During the reigns of Hadrian and Antoninus Pius, Diocles completed a twenty-four-year career that brought him fabulous wealth, prestige, and recognition throughout the Empire. Only a handful of charioteers over the centuries could boast of similar achievements. In his day, Diocles practically owned the Circus Maximus.

Diocles competed in 4,257 races and was victorious on 1,462 occasions. (He is also credited with three victories and three ties in the two-horse chariot race, but for some reason, while included in his start total, they have been omitted from his win total.) He began his career with the Whites in 122 A.D. when he was eighteen, and it was two long years before his first victory. In 128 A.D., he transferred to the Greens, but he had joined the Reds by 131 A.D. This was a bold move because of the popularity of the Greens, but Diocles suffered no apparent damage. He racked up hundreds of victories for the Reds before his retirement fifteen years later at age forty-two. Obviously, he could have driven for any stable he pleased, but he stuck with the Reds for the major part of his career. He would not have done so if it were not to his advantage.

Diocles' races were almost exclusively in the four-horse chariot, or *quadrigae,* and, in addition to his numerous triumphs, he also placed 1,438 times (most of them seconds). Even the best, however, sometimes come up empty, and Diocles failed to place in 1,351 races. He was no less a "superstar," for 1,064 of his victories came in single-entry races that pitted the best driver from each stable against one another. The prestige of winning such races is clear. Diocles' admirers, comparing his victories with those of a Blue driver named Epaphroditus, pointed out that while the latter had more wins, only 911 were in the single-entry races—153 short of Diocles' impressive total!

Diocles also captured 110 crowns in opening races, which attracted great attention. These races followed a splendid street parade, and the charioteers participating in the races were part of the procession. Consequently, this initial contest was something like a "feature race" with special significance attached to it.

In almost a third of his victories, Diocles won in the final stretch. More often than not, he held the lead from start to finish. In team-entry races that pitted two or even three chariots (we know of only one case of four) from one stable against the same number from the other stables, Diocles won 398 victories. In these races, success depended less on individual skill than it did on team effort. The stable's "number one" driver was assisted by secondary drivers, whose main function was to interfere with the opposition and help him win. There was little to be gained by competing in such races, and the money could not have been as good as in the single-entry races. This is probably the reason for the small number of victories Diocles garnered in this category.

Although Diocles broke the records of several famous predecessors, he was not even close to the 3,559 victories of Pompeius Musclosus or the 2,048 of Flavius Scorpus, both drivers for the Greens. However, Diocles was selective in his choice of races. He literally "went for the gold," and when his purses were compared with those of his greatest competitors, he was in a class by himself. By the time he was finished, his prize money totaled almost 36,000,000 sesterces, a sum that would have made him a multimillionaire today. Even so, his earnings did not come easily. From the statistics given for his career, Diocles must have competed in an average of 177 races per year—which means he raced three or four times each circus day. Such a grueling schedule makes the record of Scorpus, who compiled his incredible 2,048 victories before he was twenty-seven years old, all the more remarkable.

Diocles may not have been any better than some of Rome's other celebrated charioteers, but he did have one advantage over most of them: He lived to enjoy his wealth and fame.

The racetrack was a frequent scene of tragedy, and many drivers met their deaths there. A driver could be crushed against the barrier or lose a wheel; wrapping the ends of the long horse reins around his waist could be fatal if he could not reach the knife in his belt to cut himself free in an emergency; fouling and interfering with his opponents during a race could have dangerous consequences, as could risky displays of showmanship. A brief life was often abruptly ended on a sunny Roman afternoon, and the premature demise of a luminary such as Scorpus brought the pens of even Rome's greatest poets to life. Martial sorrowfully noted the lat-

A Circus Race—Consentius Tests His Skills

THE FULLEST ACCOUNT WE possess of a Roman chariot race comes from a romanticized poem by Sidonius Apollinaris, bishop of Auvergne, addressed to Consentius, a young friend and competitor in the race. It is the first day of January (and cold) sometime around 450 A.D. According to Sidonius, the emperor's custom was to stage a special private racing session on this day for amateur charioteers, chosen from among the young men at court. In the race, there are two teams of two drivers (a principal and his second) manning four-horse chariots. Even though they are not professionals, they wear the faction colors—in this case green and red are teamed with blue and white. The poet wishes us to believe that the contest is taking place in Rome, but it actually occurred in Ravenna, which, by this time, was the capital of the Western Empire. Despite taking such liberties, Sidonius' account accurately reflects most of the details of a professional race—including a devastating accident.

The race is ready to begin: Consentius has drawn his lot; the crowd is cheering; and Sidonius describes the action:

> Thereupon . . . you chose one of the four chariots by lot and mounted it, laying a tight grip on the hanging reins. Your partner did the same, so did the opposing side. Brightly gleam the colors, white and blue, green and red. . . .

> Servants' hands hold mouth and reins and with knotted cords force the twisted manes to hide themselves, and all the while they incite the steeds, eagerly cheering them with encouraging pats, and instilling a rapturous frenzy. There behind the barriers chafe those beasts, pressing against the fastenings, while a vapory blast comes forth between the wooden bars and even before the race the field . . . is filled with their panting breath. They push, they bustle, they drag, they struggle, they rage, they jump, they fear and are feared; never are their feet still, but restlessly they lash the hardened timber. At last the herald with loud blare of trumpet calls forth the impatient teams and launches the fleet of chariots into the field. . . . The ground gives way under the wheels and the air is smirched with the dust that rises in their track. The drivers, while they wield the reins, ply the lash; now they stretch forward over the chariots . . . and so they sweep along, striking the horses' withers and leaving their backs untouched.

> The charioteers reach the break line, and the track narrows as they race along the central barrier, jockeying for position. Coming off the first turn, Consentius is dead last but his partner has taken the lead. The opposition hopes that he will swing out too far on the turn so that they may move inside and pass him. They have no regard for Consentius and have already dismissed him

ter's passing at the end of the first century A.D. and spoke of him in the most glowing terms:

> Let grieving Victory tear to pieces her Idumaean palms, and you, Adoration, beat your naked breast with cruel hands. Let Honor put on mourning, and sad Glory cut her hair once crowned with victory, and throw it as an offering on the wanton flames of the pyre. Alas, foul trick of Fortune! Cheated of the flower of your youth, Scorpus, you are fallen, and all too soon you harness the dark horses of Death. Why did the finishing post to which you did so often hasten with speedy course in your chariot become the finish of your own life?
> (*Epigrams* 10.50)

---

as a contender. But he is lying low, waiting for the right moment:

> As for you, bending double with the very force of the effort you keep a tight rein on your team and with consummate skill wisely reserve them for the seventh lap. The others are busy with hand and voice, and everywhere the sweat of drivers and flying steeds falls in drops on to the field. The hoarse roar from applauding partisans stirs the heart, and the contestants, both horses and men, are warmed by the race and chilled by fear. Thus they go once round, then a second time; thus goes the third lap, thus the fourth; but in the fifth turn the foremost man, unable to bear the pressure of his pursuers, swerved his car aside, for he had found, as he gave command to his fleet team, that their strength was exhausted. Now the return half of the sixth course was completed and the crowd was already clamoring for the award of the prizes; your adversaries, with no fear of any effort from you, were scouring the track in front with never a care, when suddenly you tautened the curbs all together, tautened your chest, planted your feet firmly in front, and chafed the mouths of your swift steeds . . . fiercely. . . . Hereupon one of the others, clinging to the shortest route round the turning-post, was hustled by you, and his team, carried away beyond control by their onward rush, could no more be wheeled round in a harmonious course. As you saw him pass before you in disorder, you got ahead of him by remaining where you were, cunningly reining up. The other adversary, exulting in the public plaudits, ran too far to the right, close to the spectators; then as he turned aslant and all too late after long indifference urged his horses with the whip, you sped straight past your swerving rival. Then the enemy in reckless haste overtook you and, fondly thinking that the first man had already gone ahead, shamelessly made for your wheel with a sidelong dash. His horses were brought down, a multitude of intruding legs entered the wheels, and the twelve spokes were crowded, until a crackle came from those crammed spaces and the revolving rim shattered the entangled feet; then he, a fifth victim, flung from his chariot, which fell upon him, caused a mountain of manifold havoc, and blood disfigured his prostrate brow. Thereupon arose a riot of renewed shouting [Consentius had won!]. . . . Next the just emperor ordered silken ribbons to be added to the victors' palms and crowns to the necklets of gold, and true merit to have its reward; while to the vanquished in their sore disgrace he bade rugs of many-colored hair to be awarded.
> (*Carmina* 23.307–427)

Figure 10.10
A representation of the charioteer Scorpus on a funeral monument from the reign of Domitian (81–96 A.D.)

Martial also composed an epitaph for Scorpus:

> I am Scorpus, the glory of the roaring Circus, the object of Rome's cheers, and her short-lived darling. The Fates, counting not my years but the number of my victories, judged me to be an old man.
> (*Epigrams* 10.53)

Others did not receive such a distinguished send-off, but their careers ended just as suddenly. Fuscus, a driver for the Greens, had the remarkable distinction of winning his first time out, but his luck only held for 57 more victories; he died at age 24. Crescens had 686 starts and over a million sesterces in his pocket; he was dead at 22. Aurelius Mollicius had already racked up 125 victories by the time his 20 years ran out. His brother made it to 29 and won 739 times. M. Nutius Aquilius lived to be 35, but he started late and had only been driving for 12

years. Some novices were little more than children when they took their fatal spills.

Although life was a fragile commodity for charioteers, some remained competitive to age fifty and even sixty. The latter were exceptional and viewed as oddities. Since skill—not age—dictated when a driver began (Crescens' first victory at thirteen makes Diocles appear aged when he recorded his first start at eighteen) and when he retired, a career could span several decades. Avillius Teres, for example, was racing under Domitian, yet he competed against Diocles in the latter's first victory in 124 A.D. To survive so long, there was little room for mistakes. As if the normal dangers of the track were not enough, drivers pandered to the crowd with novelty races and trick riding that increased their chances for a fatal accident. Diocles was well known for such antics, so it is clear he did not survive by "playing it safe." It was he, for instance, who first raced a team of seven un-yoked horses to victory, netting a nice purse of 50,000 sesterces for his trouble. His skill was also demonstrated by the fact that he reached the hundred-victory mark in a single year, an accomplishment few other drivers could boast.

The ancients observed that it was not strength or fast horses that won victories, but the brain of the charioteer. Certainly, this applies to Diocles, who, unlike many of his colleagues, also had the good sense to know when to quit. Still, he must have left the Circus with numerous scars, since no one was immune to the frequent accidents that characterized the racing scene. Being hurt was bad enough, but the true test of courage may have been surviving the treatment Pliny the Elder describes for curing charioteers' wounds:

> Sprains and injuries caused by a blow they treat with the dung of wild boars, collected in the spring and dried. The same remedy is applied to charioteers who have been dragged or injured by a wheel, or severely bruised in any other way; in an emergency it can be used fresh. Some think that it is more efficacious if it is boiled in vinegar. More cautious doctors burn it to ash and mix it with water; the Emperor Nero is said to have refreshed himself regularly with this cordial, trying even by this method to prove himself a real charioteer. If you cannot get wild boar's dung, the next best is that of the domestic pig.
> (*Natural History* 28.237)

Whatever the real or imagined benefits of boar dung, there must have been other, less odious methods of treatment discovered over the centuries and passed on among the brotherhood. Stable doctors had to know every possible remedy to return a charioteer to the track as quickly as possible. Extended absences benefited neither driver nor stable. Also, a drug problem must have characterized the racing scene, since opiates had been in widespread use as painkillers for centuries. The abuse of such substances needs no formal documentation to be believed.

The Horses

Like all good drivers, Diocles had to be an excellent judge of horses and learned quickly

---

Tigellinus—Breeder of Mares and Nightmare for Rome

WE ARE FORTUNATE TO HAVE the name of one horse breeder—Ofonius Tigellinus—although breeding horses is not why he is best remembered. He was the Praetorian prefect and notorious sidekick of Nero, who probably came to know him through their shared interest in racehorses. Ancient opinions of Tigellinus are universally negative. He was reputed to have come from a poor background, and because of his handsome looks, he was able to ingratiate himself in high circles. However, an attractive face by itself could not have gained him access to the royal family and other important aristocrats, so his family (he received an inheritance) must have

(continued)

Tigellinus—Breeder of Mares and Nightmare for Rome (continued)

had some connections. He is said to have had adulterous relationships with two of Caligula's sisters and, in 39 A.D., was banished to Greece, where he supposedly took up fishing. Claudius allowed him to return on condition that Tigellinus keep permanently out of his sight, so he purchased land in Apulia and Calabria and started raising racehorses. Eventually, he met the young Nero and indulged the latter's appetite for the racing scene (and other things!). As emperor, Nero enhanced the fortune and status of his friend, and after 65 A.D., Tigellinus' role at court was a decisive and destructive one. Not surprisingly, he would ultimately betray Nero and survive his downfall in 68 A.D.; but the following year, after living through the short months of Galba's reign, Otho forced him to commit suicide.

The historian Tacitus sketches a portrait of the end of a man he thoroughly despised—an end in which the Circus played a part:

> Ofonius Tigellinus was of obscure parentage; his youth had been infamous and in his old age he was profligate. Command of the city watch and of the praetorians and other prizes which belong to virtue he had obtained by vices as the quicker course; then, afterwards, he practiced cruelty and later greed, offenses which belong to maturity. He also corrupted Nero so that he was ready for any wickedness; he dared certain acts without Nero's knowledge and finally deserted and betrayed him. So no one was more persistently demanded for punishment from different motives, both by those who hated Nero and by those who regretted him. Under Galba, Tigellinus had been protected by the influence of Titus Vinius, who claimed that Tigellinus had saved his daughter. He undoubtedly had saved her, not, however, prompted by mercy (he had killed so many victims!) but to secure a refuge for the future, since the worst of rascals in their distrust of the present and fear of a change always try to secure private gratitude as an offset to public detestation, having no regard for innocence, but wishing to obtain mutual impunity in wrong-doing. These facts made the people more hostile towards him, and their old hatred was increased by their recent dislike for Titus Vinius. They rushed from every part of the city to the Palatine and the fora, and, pouring into the circus and theaters where the common people have the greatest license, they broke out into seditious cries, until finally Tigellinus, at the baths of Sinuessa, receiving the message that the hour of his supreme necessity had come, amid the embraces and kisses of his mistresses, shamefully delaying his end, finally cut his throat with a razor, still further defiling a notorious life by a tardy and ignominious death. (*Histories* 1.72)

which were the most dependable. The best became "captains" and were positioned as the right-yoke horse, which Romans believed was the decisive position on a team. Over his 24-year career, Diocles drove dozens of horses. Nine of them he led to their 100th victory; one to its 200th. He never forgot to credit his favorites, and we know that 5 of them—Abigeius, Lucidus, Pompeianus, Cotynus, and Galata—contributed to 445 of his victories. In the year Diocles won 127 times, Abigeius, Lucidus, and Pompeianus participated in 103 of the races. Other charioteers had even greater success with individual horses, but Diocles is credited as the best driver of African horses. African and Spanish horses appear to have been the most likely

Sport and Defection: An Early Example—Thomas the Charioteer

THE DEFECTION OF SPORTS and entertainment figures from East to West is something we have usually associated with more recent days. However, the following letter indicates that a prominent charioteer named Thomas "defected" to the West, where he apparently expected to be well rewarded for the reputation he brought with him. The letter, sent by Theodoric, the Ostrogothic king of Italy (493–526 A.D.), to the Prefect of Rome, is very complimentary to Thomas, whose name reveals him to be a Christian (or perhaps a Jew). Theodoric wishes to subsidize the famous charioteer largely because Thomas has come of his own free will to perform in the Western part of the old Roman Empire. This was a definite slight to the more sophisticated East and its capital, Constantinople, and Theodoric was not going to let such a propaganda coup slip by. The letter was penned by the king's secretary Cassiodorus, a prominent Christian writer and career administrator, who, ironically, loathed chariot racing. The letter's contents show how important the circuses and drivers continued to be as morale boosters and distractions during a period in Italy that is generally regarded as depressed. Theodoric's rational view of the charges of witchcraft lodged against Thomas is quite revealing and atypical of what one might expect from a barbarian king. Only the letter's first two paragraphs are reproduced here:

> Since reliability and honesty are rare in public performers, it is all the more admirable when one of these men exhibits a good character; everyone likes to find something praiseworthy in an unexpected quarter. When the charioteer Thomas came recently from the East, We after due consideration bestowed on him a reasonable allowance, until We could prove his skill and character. Since he is acknowledged to have achieved the highest position in this sport, and since of his own free will he has left his country and chosen the seat of Our empire as his sphere of activity, We have adjudged him worthy of a monthly grant, so that We might leave no doubt of our opinion of a man who has recognized the primacy of Italy in the world.
>
> His success on the track has made him famous, and he has been carried to victory even more by the enthusiasm of his admirers than by his chariots. He transferred his services to the faction which had been going downhill and which was the despair of its supporters; having himself been responsible for this by his efforts for their rivals he now proceeded to gladden their hearts, sometimes overcoming his opponents by his own skill, sometimes defeating them by the speed of his horses. His frequent success caused him to be accused of witchcraft; a reputation for this appears to be a recommendation in racing circles. For when victory cannot be attributed to the merits of a driver, it must necessarily be put down to magic.
> (Cassiodorus, *Variae* 3.51)

to win, but the Romans also raced horses from Italy, Greece, Gaul, Mauretania, and Cyrenaica.

The names of numerous horses have come down to us, often with their color and sire noted. Few mares are mentioned, so it appears they were not used in great number. Names were not much different from those applied to modern equines. A white horse was likely to be called Snowy; a fast horse, Flier; an unusually large or powerful horse, Ajax. There were many horses, and names were often repeated. Crescens, Scorpus, and Diocles, for instance, all had a horse named Cotynus.

Stables were equipped with veterinarians, trainers, groomers, harnessmen, and others necessary to maintain horses at peak condition. The animals were brought along slowly and usually started racing when they were about age five—although it could be earlier. Part of the delay was probably due to the difficulty of teaching the animals to run effectively as a team. Also, horses sent out prematurely were more likely to be injured. Successful stallions were in demand, as they are today, for breeding, but they had to do their duty without furlough, since it was unprofitable to remove a winning horse from the track.

Crowds could become as anxious about a horse as a driver, and the most successful equines were known by sight. Their genealogies were required knowledge among the faithful, and they were pictured in art. Tuscus, for example, had won 386 victories; Victor, 429. Martial complained that he was not as well known as a certain racehorse. Caligula's favorite, Incitatus— who, we are told, was the proud owner of a marble stable, an ivory stall, purple blankets, a jeweled collar, a house, a team of slaves, and furniture—was so successful the story spread that the emperor wished to make him a Roman consul!

Equine careers could be long, and there is at least one example of a horse having his own offspring as a running mate. Generally Romans let their racehorses retire gracefully, and some were even honored with gravestones after an old age of rest and grazing:

> Sired on Gaetulian sands by a Gaetulian stallion, speedy as the wind, in your life unmated, now, Hasty, you dwell in Lethe.
> (*Corpus Inscriptionum Latinarum* 6.10082)

Diocles' end was apparently as restful as some of his horses. When he gave up racing, he retired to the small Italian hill town of Praeneste (modern Palestrina). There, he evidently lived out the remainder of his life with his family in the quietude of rural Italy. A dedication in his name was erected at this place by his son and daughter.

The Later Years of the Circus

Remarkably, the greatest days of chariot racing and of the factions were yet to come. Circuses would last another thousand years after Diocles and would reach their pinnacle under the Byzantine emperors in the East at Constantinople. They increased in popularity after Rome became Christian. Tertullian certainly would have been disappointed that his warnings had gone unheeded, and moderns who cite the races as a sign of Rome's "moral decay" must look elsewhere. Among Byzantine Christians, saints had to compete with charioteers for the peoples' affections.

When the races finally did decline in the twelfth century A.D., it was largely because they were no longer affordable—more a case of economics than morality. Those who had always viewed them as evil were glad to see them go, for, as a comment made centuries earlier indicated, "It is not exactly a congregation of Catos that comes together at the circus."

Figure 10.11   *The remains of the Circus of Maxentius (early fourth century A.D.). Located outside Rome on the Appian Way, it is among the best preserved of Roman circuses.*

Figure 10.12   *This relief on the base of the obelisk shown in Figure 10.13 depicts the Emperor Theodosius the Great watching the games from his box with members of the royal family (c. 390 A.D.) at Constantinople.*

Figure 10.13   *Site of the Great Circus at Constantinople, successor to the Circus Maximus at Rome. This obelisk from Egypt once decorated the racetrack's* euripus. *Today, it is over-shadowed by the minarets of the Blue Mosque, built on the spot formerly occupied by the Byzantine Imperial Palace.*

Suggestions for Further Reading

The best starting place is H. A. Harris, *Sport in Greece and Rome* (Ithaca, N.Y.: Cornell University Press, 1972), who devotes Chapters 10–15 to the circus and chariot racing. Diocles' career (*CIL* 6.10048; *ILS* 5287) can be found translated in J. Shelton, *As the Romans Did* (New York: Oxford University Press, 1988), 356, No. 349; and N. Lewis and M. Reinhold, *Roman Civilization,* Vol. 2 (New

York: Harper & Row, 1966), 230. J. P. V. D. Balsdon, *Life and Leisure in Ancient Rome* (New York: McGraw-Hill, 1969), 314–324; and J. Carcopino, *Daily Life in Ancient Rome* (New Haven, Conn.: Yale University Press, 1940), 212–221, are easily accessible works with short sections on the races. The latter, in particular, must be read with some caution, for it contains outdated information. All previous surveys of the physical and technical aspects of circuses are now subservient to the massive and thorough study of J. Humphrey, *Roman Circuses: Arenas for Chariot Racing* (Berkeley and Los Angeles: University of California Press, 1986), which is more oriented toward specialists. A. Cameron's *Circus Factions* (Oxford: Clarendon Press, 1976), the most extensive work on the history and development of the factions, and *Porphyrius the Charioteer* (Oxford: Clarendon Press, 1973) are also required reading, although the latter is more concerned with Byzantine racing and much too technical to keep the nonacademician's interest. See also R. Syme, "Scorpus the Charioteer," *American Journal of Ancient History* 2 (1977): 86–94. A brief but revealing look at Roman behavior at the Circus may be found in T. W. Africa's "Urban Violence in Imperial Rome," *Journal of Inter-disciplinary History* 2 (1971): 3–21. E. J. Brill has published R. L. Sturzebecker's *Athletic-Cultural Archaeological Sites in the Greco-Roman World* (Leiden, 1985), a useful photo atlas that describes and illustrates remaining circuses, hippodromes, and other ancient athletic-cultural facilities. There is no definitive ancient source on circuses, but those authorities who preserve much of our knowledge have been identified in the text. On horses, see A. Hyland, *Equus: The Horse in the Roman World* (London: Batsford, 1990). See also the section on Roman spectacles and entertainment in "Recent General Additions" at the end of Chapter 5.

Epilogue

*An event is something that happens at a particular
point in space and at a particular time.*
(S. Hawking, *A Brief History of Time*)

In 476 A.D., the last Roman emperor of the West was overthrown by the German Odoacer. Historians today use that date to mark the end of Roman rule in Western Europe, although contemporaries probably noticed little difference at the time. Since the late third century A.D., Roman influence in the West had been steadily declining, and barbarians, mostly Germanic, were filling administrative posts, staffing the army, and constituting an ever-increasing segment of the population.

Odoacer's seizure of power in the West was probably not as dramatic an event as it seems to us. The Roman Empire had not "fallen"; there was no great "bang" or "thud" to signal the end of one era and the beginning of another. In fact, Odoacer "legitimized" his own rule by accepting the nominal authority of the emperor of the East. All that really changed was that the process of "barbarization" that had been going on for at least three centuries was now complete. The Eastern half of the Empire was not similarly affected and continued to flourish as the Byzantine Empire for another thousand years. When we speak of the "fall of Rome," 1453 A.D. is perhaps the more appropriate date, the year that the Ottoman Turks captured Constantinople and Islamized what had been the Byzantine Empire.

The reasons for the survival of the Eastern half of the Roman Empire are not difficult to determine. The East had always been more stable than the West. Civilization was older there and more deeply rooted; most of the major cities were in the East, and it was the economic and population center of the Empire. People in crucial positions were more dependable, literacy remained more or less constant, and collecting taxes and raising armies were not the chores they had become in the West. Most later emperors were from the East, and interest in Rome and the West had been declining. As senior Augustus, Diocletian had established his residence at Nicomedia in Asia Minor and never even visited Rome until the end of his reign. Constantine formalized the importance of the Eastern Empire by establishing Constantinople as the new capital. Constantinople was an impregnable city—a fact that ultimately encouraged barbarians coming into the Empire from the East to move on to easier "pickings" in the West. Constantine drew on whatever was left of the West's talent and resources, a process that continued well into the early Byzantine Empire. At the end, Rome was not even the capital of the West, having been replaced by Ravenna. Christianity also gave strength to the East as Christians were willing to defend their emperors and the holy city of Constantinople.

With the de-emphasis of the West, barbarians inevitably replaced Romans in important posts. Many had been Romanized and some were extremely capable, but the mass of the "new Romans" were uneducated, primitive, and disunified. It is no mystery why, by the beginning of the period popularly referred to as the "Dark Ages" (500–700 A.D.), the Roman administrative, legal, and fiscal systems had completely broken down and municipal life had all but disappeared in most parts of Europe. The common traditions and customs that had constituted for centuries the bonding cement of Roman society meant little to the majority of the Germanic population who now inhabited the West. The beliefs, customs, and manners of the society had changed: Rome had changed.

The only organized institution of authority that might have restored some order in the West was the Church, but it was ill equipped to do so. Over the centuries, barbarians were converted to Christianity, and the Church provided some cultural and civilizing influence. The efforts of the Church, however, proved to be a "mixed blessing." The early Church in the West bears large responsibility for the purposeful destruction of much of the Latin classical literary tradition, and it helped hasten the final "collapse" of the West by drawing much-needed funds and capable administrators from the secular world into the Church. The Church administered spiritual consolation, but a crumbling society needed more tangible kinds of

support. Peasants often feared the Church, an acquisitive landlord, as much as their Roman-German barbarian overlords. Many high Church officials were corrupt and far more worldly than their Christian frocks allowed. Those who maintained their integrity were confronted with many problems. Often, the popes in Rome were weak, intimidated by the Eastern monarchs who continued to claim authority over them. They looked for champions to protect them from the threats of barbarian chieftains. Stronger popes, like Leo I who confronted Attila the Hun, found themselves not only defenders of the faith but also defenders of the city of Rome itself. In the Byzantine East, things were different.

The Byzantine Empire was the inheritor and continuator of the old Roman Empire. The administration, the legal system, and the bureaucracy were Roman. The cultural orientation, language, and philosophical inspiration were Greek (tempered by oriental influences and Christianity). Constantinople, the capital of the Later Roman Empire, now became the Byzantine capital. Just as the Roman West changed drastically, the East also changed until a definite and recognizable Byzantine culture, distinct from anything that had existed previously, emerged. The Byzantines maintained a remarkably high level of culture and continued to assert their nominal control over the barbarian West, a compelling sign that they, at least, did not consider themselves an entity separate from the old Roman Empire. When Constantinople finally fell to the Ottoman Turks in 1453 A.D., many of the scholars, teachers, artists, legal experts, and others who had been instrumental in preserving and perpetuating the language and culture they had inherited from the Eastern Roman Empire took their knowledge westward. There they

E.1
The walls of Constantinople

helped sow the seeds for the Italian Renaissance and the final recovery of Medieval Europe.

The ways in which the Romans have influenced Western society are almost too numerous to mention. For centuries, the Romans' erroneous belief that they were descended from the Trojans continued to influence Europe. As late as the thirteenth century, the British thought they were descended through the Romans from Brute the Trojan; the Franks claimed Francus, son of the Trojan prince Hector, as their ancestor. More realistically, the European political and legal tradition was built squarely on the tradition inherited from Rome. As for the United States, more than one modern scholar has noted that there is probably no government in the world more like the Roman. The Founding Fathers had not forgotten the explanations provided by Polybius and Cicero about how the checks and balances in the Roman Republican constitution worked. Political nomenclature also reflects a Roman heritage. The word *candidate,* for example, comes from *candidatus,* the "chalked-white toga" a Roman would wear at election time to make himself conspicuous to the voting public. *Election, nominate,* and *vote* are Latin derivatives. Portions of Washington, D.C., resemble a Roman city; and the eagle and fasces, Roman symbols of authority, are represented in many buildings.

The Romans have also influenced our names. Abraham Lincoln is a perfect example.

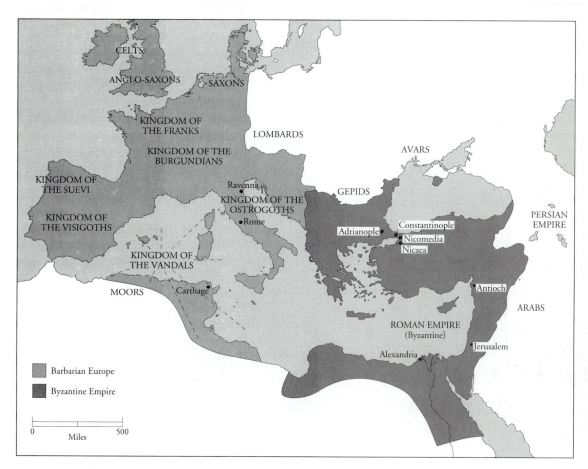

Map 22 *Barbarian Europe and the Byzantine Empire c. 500* A.D.

Everyone knows that Abraham is a biblical name, but few would guess that "Lincoln" comes from a corruption of the name of the Roman town of Lindum (*Lin*) Colonia (*Coln*) in Britain. The names of Roman gods identify planets, spacecraft, and cars. Our months have Roman names, and our calendar is based ultimately on one introduced by Julius Caesar. Saturday was originally Saturn's day. Among our cities, there are Romes, Senecas, Ciceros, and Londons, and countless street and business names reflect our Roman heritage. Sports facilities are called "Colosseum (Coliseum)" and

"Forum," and we buy "Mars" candy bars and "Magnavox" appliances.

The Latin language has provided over half our English vocabulary, and scientific terminology depends on it. In our schools, *curriculum* subject names such as *literature, religion, linguistics,* and *science* are Latin derivatives. All U.S. coins bear the Latin inscription *e pluribus unum* ("out of many one"), and dollar bills include a line from Vergil's *Aeneid,* "Novus Ordo Seclorum" ("New Order of the Ages"). We still use *patrician* and *plebeian* to denote the wealthy and the poor, the high and the low. Expressions

E.2
Remains of the later
Byzantine palace at
Constantinople

such as "He isn't worth his salt" (Roman troops were often paid in salt) remain current.

Many religious practices that preceded Christianity (or were contemporary with it) helped to form Christian tradition. The custom of giving gifts at Christmas originated in the practice of masters and slaves exchanging gifts during the Saturnalia, the Roman festival celebrated at the same time as the Christian holiday. Ambrose, Augustine, and Jerome were all products of the Roman Empire, and it was during the Later Empire that Christianity triumphed and became the major religion of the West.

The Romans cast a long shadow that touches daily our routines, our traditions, and our language. Despite serious interruptions and periods of confusion, we continue to be affected by these people. When barbarians destroyed Rome in 410 A.D., Augustine insisted that the "spiritual city" of Rome still stood. In ways he never could have imagined, Augustine was right. The "spiritual city" of Rome does still stand today.

Whose Millennium Is It, Anyway?—Passing Time: "Little Dennis" (Dionysius Exiguus) Leaves a Big Impression

THE WORLD RECENTLY CELEBRATED the end of the second millennium—but should it have? It is the second millennium only according to the calendar that Western society depends upon to keep track of time—one that has a Christian foundation. It is based, ultimately, on a calculation for the birth of Jesus. Hence, it is more accurately the Western, Christian second millennium rather than any significant turning point for *all* the world's peoples. There were at least three millennia of civilization before the birth of Christ and numerous dating systems before and after him, which are founded on entirely different criteria. The year 2000 is (of course, the parallels are not exact because not everyone began the year at the same time), according to the earliest Egyptian calendar, 6236; by the old Roman calendar, the year is 2753, calculated from the founding of the city of Rome (A.U.C.— *Ab Urbe Condita*). This is the year 5760 according to the Jewish idea about the Creation; for Moslems, it is the year 1420, because their calendar began with the flight of Mohammed from

E.3 *The observatory (tower) of the Caracol at the Maya center of Chichén Itzá in Yucatan, which was used from at least 800–1200 A.D. Its windows and shafts were oriented to indicate the azimuths for south and west, the equinoxes, and the summer solstice. The Maya were master astronomers, and according to the current Maya great cycle, the year 2000 is actually 5119.*

(continued)

Whose Millennium Is It, Anyway? *(continued)*

Mecca; it is 2544 according to the Buddhist calendar, 1378 for the Persians, and in the current Maya great cycle, 5119. The list goes on.

There are many systems for calculating the year that are different from our own. Unfortunately, the one we use is badly flawed. Few in modern society even know who is ultimately responsible for devising the dating system by which the new millennium's arrival was calculated—nor did they realize that, technically, the celebration was premature. The actual start of the new millennium is more correctly January 1, 2001. Many would attribute this to the fact that Europe was not yet familiar with the concept of zero when a sixth-century Christian monk named Dionysius Exiguus (c. 510–560 A.D.) created the dating system (Hindu-Arabic numbers would not be introduced until centuries later, and there appears to be no significant appearance of zero before the eleventh century). Consequently, when Dionysius devised his system of dating, he began his count with the year "1"—not "0"—and 2000 becomes only the last year of the second millennium, not the beginning of the third. Still, with or without zero, no one can be "0" years of age, and even today, some societies consider an infant to be "1" at birth. (We, too, often say a baby is in its "first year".) Perhaps a more correct understanding comes from Dionysius' placement of Jesus' birth on 25 December A.U.C. 753 by the Roman calendar—but not starting his actual count of years until the New Year, 1 January A.U.C. 754 (1 A.D.), coincidentally, when Jesus should have been circumcised (January 1 is still the feast of the circumcision). Whatever the case, one cannot have a decade before completing ten full years or a second millennium without completing a full two thousand years. 2001 begins the next millennium.

When Dionysius first devised his system (originally, he had been asked by the Pope to cal-culate future dates for Easter, a "floating" holy day), he had no idea when Christ was born. He did not wish to base any of his new calculations on a calendar already widely in use which began with the first year of the Emperor Diocletian's reign (which we now date, using Dionysius' system, to 284 A.D.). According to that calendar, Dionysius was living in *Anno Diocletiani,* the year of Diocletian, 247—or, by our current system of dating, 531 A.D. Because Diocletian had persecuted Christians, Dionysius found it distasteful that some of his Christian brothers had been calculating the date for Easter using this calendar. (Despite Dionysius' reservations, it continued to be used by many Christians—including Copts in Egypt today, for whom the year 2000 is actually 1716 *Anno Diocletiani.* They preferred to view this period not as one stained by an anti-Christian emperor but, conversely, as the "Era of the Martyrs.") He believed that years should be counted, instead, from the "incarnation of our Lord." However, there was no way to determine the birth of Christ precisely. The Gospels offered little help. Matthew indicates that Christ was born during the reign of Herod the Great. By the system we use today—based ultimately on the one devised by Dionysius—this would place Christ's birth in or before 4 B.C., when Herod died. Luke states that Jesus was born during the census of Quirinius, which, by the same modern calculations (also based on Dionysius' system), took place in 6 A.D. Historically, however, Quirinius was legate of Syria—not Judaea, so any census he ordered would not have applied to Mary and Joseph. There is also no evidence that Romans required people to return to the place of their birth to be counted. Hence, the story in Luke appears designed more to attach Jesus' birth to Bethlehem (thus fulfilling the Old Testament prophecy) than reality. Dionysius, of course, as most Christians today, would have had no reason to doubt the tradition. Ultimately, we do not know how Dionysius arrived at the date that he finally selected for Jesus' birth and designated "year 1," but he may have based his calculations on a statement in Luke (3:1 and 3:23). Luke says that Jesus was about thirty in the fifteenth year of the reign of the Emperor Tiberius. Using this as a starting point, Dionysius may have then reassured himself about the correctness of his conclusion about the year by associating it with certain astrological events that he believed also occurred in the same year. When he had convinced himself of the correctness of his calculations and that he indeed had discovered the precise year of Jesus' birth, he began his count. However, the fact is that neither Dionysius nor any of us today know the date of Jesus' birth, and the one he selected has as much to recommend it as the diverse and unconfirmed dates given by Matthew and Luke. In respect to the latter, those who follow Matthew in calculating the millennium should have celebrated it back in 1997, while those who accept Luke will have to contain themselves until 2006! Those who celebrated in 2000 were, unfortunately, either four years late—or six years early. Whatever the case, Dionysius' incorrect system and his designation of each year as *Anno Domini,* "the year of our Lord"—ironically abbreviated with the same two letters, A.D., that had distinguished the calendar of *Anno Diocletiani*—ultimately became the way that the Christian world—and, today, because of a need for uniform schedule, most of the world—keeps track of time. Its acceptance, however, was long in coming.

It was not Dionysius but his more famous friend and fellow monk, Cassiodorus, who first used the new system of *Anno Domini* in a published work. The English monk, Bede, the most famous churchman of his day, gave the system further credibility in the eighth century, using it

E.4 *Witness to Bede. Saxon Chancel (681 A.D.) of St. Paul's Church, Jarrow, England. While it has undergone many changes over the centuries, the basic stone structure and some windows actually date to the time when Bede lived at Jarrow and wrote the* Ecclesiastical History of England, *the first significant work to incorporate Dionysius' system of* Anno Domini.

in his *Ecclesiastical History of England,* the most prominent and influential work of its time. In the ninth century, Charlemagne brought Dionysius' work into the mainstream when he incorporated the *Anno Domini* system into the business of the Carolingian Empire. Still, most Christians continued to regard time as God's own affair, and

(continued)

Whose Millennium Is It, Anyway? (continued)

as long as they knew the dates for saints' days and feast days, they were satisfied. Natural signs people had always depended upon guided their activities. Besides, many Christians believed that the world would end soon, anyway. Who needed a precise system to keep track of time?

It was not until 1300 A.D. that Dionysius' system became a way of life for most of Christian Europe and firmly entrenched within the church hierarchy. In that year, Pope Boniface declared that it was the beginning of a new century, *Anno Domini* 1300, and celebrated a jubilee to commemorate thirteen centuries of Christianity. This gave final sanction to Dionysius' calculations. Subsequently, in the fifteenth century, Johannes Gutenberg invented the printing press, which allowed for the spread of Dionysius' system through the mass production of calendars, schedules, and anything else related to time. In 1582, Pope Gregory made the necessary adjustments to the Julian calendar that had been devised by Julius Caesar to bring it back in line with the solar year, thereby creating the Gregorian Calendar we use today (although it was only adopted in England and the American colonies in 1752; the Greek and Russian Orthodox Churches still use the Julian calendar).

The *Anno Domini* (A.D.) system of Dionysius now became almost inseparable from the identification of calendar years, but it was not until the seventeenth century, some eleven hundred years after Dionysius, that B.C. ("Before Christ"), a system that identifies and calculates the years before Christ's birth, first appears. The man who

E.5
Calendars have always been based on the sun, the moon, or a combination of both. The position of stars and constellations has also been important in time reckoning. Ancient people in England, for example, used structures like Stonehenge (shown here) on the Salisbury Plain to track heavenly bodies and log the passage of time.

seems responsible is a French astronomer named Denis Petau, who, while teaching at the Collège de Clermont in Paris in 1627, first incorporated it into his work. Hence, it was not until the seventeenth century that the current system of identifying dates as A.D. or B.C. finally fell into place.

Today, some wish to eschew the use of A.D. and B.C. designations for dates because of the Christian implications of these abbreviations. Instead of A.D., *Anno Domini,* the "Year of our Lord," and B.C., "Before Christ," they use a secularized system consisting of C.E., for the "Common Era," and B.C.E., for "Before the Common Era." The current text uses the centuries-old system of B.C. and A.D. but not for any religious reason—today, their religious connotations have been all but forgotten by most or never explained (indeed, "After Death" is a more common response to the meaning of A.D. than *Anno Domini)*—but because they are the more established and familiar way of denoting time. Furthermore, most modern scholarship continues to adhere to this system, and last but not least, C.E. and B.C.E. are still based on the same periods of time designated by A.D. and B.C. and Christ's life—ultimately, the same confused system devised by Dionysius Exiguus almost fifteen centuries ago.

Reading: D. E. Duncan's *Calendar: Humanity's Epic Struggle to Determine a True and Accurate Year* is an excellent introduction for the general reader interested in the calendar, and it includes more than enough supplemental bibliography.

S. J. Gould, *Questioning the Millennium* (New York: Harmony Books, 1997)

Glossary and Pronunciation Guide

Included here are brief descriptions of major historical figures, sites, and other terms mentioned in the text. The pronunciation is indicated for most entries, although it should be noted that consistency is not always possible and pronunciation will inevitably vary among instructors.

Actium (ak´-ti-um), site on the northwestern coast of Greece where the forces of Octavian defeated Antony and Cleopatra in 31 B.C. and determined the fate of the Roman world

aedile (ē´-dīl), one of four yearly elected officers in charge of entertainment in Rome and city management (see Chart 1)

Aeneid (ē-nē´-id), the epic story of the Trojan prince Aeneas, who fled the destruction of Troy and came to Italy, where he married a Latin princess and became the ancestor of the Roman people

Agrippa (a-grip´-a), Octavian's admiral who engineered the victory at Actium in 31 B.C.; married to Octavian's daughter Julia in 21 B.C.; received proconsular *imperium* and tribunician powers from Augustus; died in 12 B.C.

Agrippina (a-grip-ēn´-a) "the Elder," daughter of Julia and Agrippa (above); wife of Germanicus; mother of Caligula; arrested on charges of plotting against Tiberius; died in 33 A.D.

Agrippina "the Younger," daughter of above; mother of Nero; last wife of Claudius (below); executed by her son in 59 A.D. for meddling in his affairs

Alexandria, in Egypt; greatest city in the Hellenistic world; capital of the Ptolemies; site of the great Library; home of Cleopatra

Antigonids (an-tig´-o-nids), dynastic name of the successors of Alexander's general Antigonus, whose family ruled Macedonia during much of the Hellenistic period

Antioch (an´-tē-ok), once capital of Seleucid and Roman Syria; third city of the East after Alexandria and Seleucia on the Tigris

Antoninus Pius (an-tō-nīn´-us pī´-us), Roman emperor from 137 to 161 A.D.

Antony, Mark (Marcus Antonius), c. 82–30 B.C., one of the leading figures at the end of the Roman Republic; Caesarian; triumvir with Octavian and Lepidus in 43 B.C.; defeated with Cleopatra at Actium in 31 B.C.; committed suicide in 30 B.C.; grandfather of Claudius; great-grandfather of Caligula; great-great-grandfather of Nero

Archimedes (ar-ki-mē´-dēz), technological wizard, mathematician, and inventor whose engines defended Syracuse during the Roman siege of 213–212 B.C.

Attila (a-til´-a), leader of the Huns, who ravaged much of the Roman Empire in the mid-fifth century A.D.; traditionally, turned away from sacking Rome by Pope Leo I

Augustine (o´-gus-tēn), one of the "Fathers" and chief theologian of the early Latin Christian Church; author of the *Confessions* and *City of God*

Augustus (o-gus´-tus), 63 B.C.–14 A.D., first Roman emperor; established the Principate and laid the foundation for the imperial system at Rome; see Octavian

Aurelian (o-rē′-li-an), Roman emperor 270–275 A.D.; briefly restored unity to the Empire during the period of the "Barracks Emperors"

Bithynia-Pontus (bi-thin′-i-a), Roman province on the Black Sea where Pliny the Younger governed (111–113 A.D.) and dealt with Christians

Brundisium (brun-diz′-i-um), city on the eastern side of the heel of Italy; departure port for all points East; Treaty of Brundisium negotiated here in 40 B.C.

Brutus (brōō′-tus), 85–42 B.C., the most famous of Caesar's assassins; died with his fellow conspirators at Philippi in 42 B.C.

Byzantine (bi′-zan-tīn), name applied to the Eastern half of the old Roman Empire after the barbarization and collapse of the West; the Byzantine Empire ended when Constantinople was captured by the Ottoman Turks in 1453 A.D.

Caesar, Gaius Julius, 100–44 B.C., triumvir with Crassus and Pompey; conqueror of Gaul; led first invasion of Britain; victor in the civil war with Pompey; consul and dictator; paramour of Cleopatra; assassinated in 44 B.C. by Brutus and his fellow conspirators

Caesarion (sē-zar′-i-on), or Ptolemy XV, reputed son of Caesar by Cleopatra; disposed of by Octavian

Caligula (ka-lig′-ū-la), or Gaius, third emperor of Rome from 37 to 41 A.D.

Camillus (ka-mil′-us), traditional hero who humbled the Etruscan city of Veii and rescued Rome after the Gallic sack in 387 B.C.

Campania (kam-pān′-ya), district of Italy where Naples (Neapolis), Pompeii, Herculaneum, Misenum, and Capua are located

Cannae (kan′-ē), in southeastern Italy; site of Rome's disastrous defeat by Hannibal in 216 B.C.

Capitoline (ka′-pi-tō-līn), hill overlooking the Forum that served as a natural fortress during the early days of Rome and on whose summit were the major temples to Jupiter and Juno

Capri (kap′-rē), island south of the Bay of Naples; favorite retreat of Tiberius

Capua (kap′-u-a), city in western Italy (Campania); Spartacus' slave revolt began here

Caracalla (ka-ra-kal′-a), son of Septimius Severus and Julia Domna; emperor from 211 to 217 A.D.; conferred citizenship on all free residents within the Empire in 212 A.D.

Carrhae (kar′-ē), site in Mesopotamia where Crassus was defeated in 53 B.C. and killed by the Parthians

Carthage, African city of Phoenician origin that created an empire in North Africa and Spain; greatest rival of Rome in the western Mediterranean; fought and lost three Punic wars with the Romans; home of Hannibal

Cassius (ka′-si-us), one of the main conspirators who assassinated Caesar; died with Brutus at Philippi in 42 B.C.

Catiline (ka′-ti-līn), led a conspiracy to overthrow the Roman government in 63–62 B.C.

Cato the Elder (kā′-tō), one of the major conservative Roman politicians of the second century B.C.; Cicero held him up as a model of old age

Cato the Younger, 95–46 B.C, leading conservative politician and major opponent of Caesar; uncle and father-in-law of Brutus; committed suicide in Africa in 46 B.C. after Pompey's defeat

censor (sen′-sōr), highest office in the *cursus honorum;* two were elected every five years to take the census and "censor" the citizen rolls (see Chart 1)

Centuriate assembly, one of the two Republican assemblies consisting of all adult male citizens; voting reflected the interests of the wealthy; elected higher magistrates of Rome and had legislative functions (see Chart 1)

Cicero (si′-se-rō), 106–43 B.C., leading conservative politician of the Late Republic; consul in 63 B.C.; author of numerous orations, philosophical and rhetorical works, and letters; proscribed by Antony in 43 B.C. and executed

Circus Maximus, at Rome; the greatest chariot racetrack in the Roman world

Claudius, fourth emperor of Rome, 41–54 A.D.

Cleopatra (klē-ō-pa´-tra), 69–30 B.C., queen of Egypt and last of the Ptolemies; paramour of Caesar and "wife" of Antony, with whom she was defeated at Actium in 31 B.C. by Octavian; committed suicide in 30 B.C.

Clodius (klō´-di-us), tribune in 58 B.C.; notorious political thug who ostensibly represented the popular cause but used his unsavory tactics mostly for personal gain; murdered by his rival Milo in 52 B.C.

Clodius Albinus (al-bīn´-us), rival of Septimius Severus; Caesar of the latter until he became expendable and was killed in battle in 197 A.D.

Colosseum, the Flavian Amphitheater at Rome; begun by Vespasian and dedicated under Titus in 80 A.D.; the most famous gladiatorial arena in the Roman world; seating capacity was about 50,000

Commodus (kom´-o-dus), son of Marcus Aurelius; emperor from 180 to 192 A.D.

concilium plebis (kon-sil´-i-um ple´-bis), the plebeian assembly (often identified with the Tribal Assembly); see Chart 1

Constantine (kon´-stan-tīn), sole emperor of East and West from 324 to 337 A.D.; made Christianity a legal religion and helped ensure its eventual triumph; established Constantinople

Constantinople (kon-stan-tin-ō´-pul), the new, Christian capital of the Later Roman Empire established on the Bosphorus by Constantine in 330 A.D.

consul (kon´-sul), highest yearly office in the *cursus honorum;* the two consuls were the chief civil and military officers at Rome (see Chart 1)

Cornelia (kor-nē´-li-a), mother of Tiberius and Gaius Gracchus; daughter of Scipio Africanus; one of the most prominent women in Republican history

Crassus (kra´-sus), c. 115–53 B.C., one of the leading figures of the Late Republic; member of the "First Triumvirate" with Caesar and Pompey; defeated and killed by Parthians at Carrhae in 53 B.C.

cursus honorum, the mandatory sequence of elected offices during the Roman Republic that included quaestor, praetor, consul, and censor

Decius (de´-si-us), ruled during the period of the "Barracks Emperors" from 249 to 251 B.C.; launched first Empirewide persecution of the Christians

denarius (de-nar´-i-us), a silver coin worth 4 sestertii or 16 (bronze) asses; the equivalent in modern currency is impossible to calculate, but, for example, a baker was paid 60 denarii a day in 300 A.D.

dictator, official chosen to take charge of the state during an emergency for a six-month period; by the first century B.C., the dictatorship was used as a political tool (e.g., by Caesar)

Didius Julianus (di´-di-us jū-li-an´-us), Roman emperor from March to June 193 A.D.

Dio Cassius (dī´-o ka´-si-us), wrote a *Roman History* from the beginnings to 229 A.D.; contemporary source for the rule of Commodus and the Severan emperors

Diocles (dī´-o-klēs), one of Rome's greatest charioteers; performed in the Circus Maximus during the second century A.D.

Diocletian (dī-o-klē´-shan), 245–313 A.D., "founder" of the Later Roman Empire; emperor from 284 to 305 A.D.; replaced the defunct Principate with the Dominate and turned Rome into a corporate state with totalitarian tendencies; created the Tetrarchy (a system of four rulers) to administer the Empire

Dionysus (dī-o-nī´-sus), the Greek god of fertility, the vine, wine, and drunkenness; a dying god; identified as Bacchus among the Romans

Dionysius Exiguus (dī-ō-nīsh´-i-us eg-zig´yōo-us), c. 510–560 A.D., Christian monk who established the A.D. (*Anno Domini*) dating system

Domitian (do-mish´-an), son of Vespasian; brother of Titus; emperor from 81 to 96 A.D.; last Flavian ruler

Drusus (drū´-sus), (1) brother of Tiberius; (2) son of Tiberius; (3) brother of Caligula

Elagabalus (e-la-ga´-ba-lus), emperor 218–222 A.D.; grandson of Julia Maesa; grandnephew of Julia Domna; son of Julia Soaemias; (Varius Avitus) took the name Elagabalus from the Syrian Sun-God of Emesa, Elagabal

Emesa (e-mā´-sa), city in Syria; center of worship of the Sun-God Elagabal; home of Julia Domna and her family

Enna (en´-a), city in Sicily where the First Sicilian Slave War (135–132 B.C.) began

equites (e´-qui-tās), members of the equestrian order (*Equester Ordo*); nonnoble, nonsenatorial, nonpolitical order of wealthy men during the Late Republic who formed a small middle group of bankers, moneylenders, entrepreneurs, tax collectors, tradesmen, plantation owners, contractors, and other businessmen

Etruscans (ē-trus´-kans), advanced, powerful people living in Etruria north of Rome, who exerted the strongest early cultural influence upon the developing Romans; they lived in city-states and reached their peak while Rome was still struggling; eventually they were absorbed and became part of the Roman fabric

Eunus (yōō´-nus), Syrian slave who led the First Sicilian Slave War (135–132 B.C.)

Forum, the political, social, and religious center of Rome (the temples of Jupiter and Juno on the Capitoline Hill and the Imperial Palace on the Palatine overlooked it)

Fronto (fron´-tō), distinguished orator, teacher, and friend and tutor of Marcus Aurelius; his unflattering opinion of Christians undoubtedly affected Marcus' views toward the sect

Gaul, Roman province (largely what is today France, the lowland countries, and western Germany); Cae-sar completed the Roman conquest of the Gauls; the Emperor Claudius was born at Lyons in Gaul, and Septimius Severus and Julia Domna married there

Germanicus (jer-ma´-ni-kus), nephew of Tiberius; husband of Agrippina the Elder; father of Caligula; he was to be Tiberius' successor, and his unexpected death in 19 A.D. brought suspicion upon Tiberius and strained relations with the dead prince's family

Geta (ge´-ta), younger son of Septimius Severus and Julia Domna; murdered by his brother, Caracalla, in 212 A.D.

Gracchus, Gaius (grak´-us, gī-yus), younger brother of Tiberius Gracchus (below); turned the popular cause into a viable political movement for the first time in Roman history; tribune in 123 and 122 B.C.; took his own life in 121 B.C. when political riots erupted in Rome and his enemies in the Senate invoked the *senatus consultum ultimum* to eliminate him legally

Gracchus, Tiberius (tī-bē´-ri-us), son of Tiberius Sempronius Gracchus the Censor and Cornelia (see above); tribune in 133 B.C.; resentment over his land reform bill and his support for the popular cause resulted in his assassination when he ran for reelection as tribune, initiating the civil bloodshed that would characterize the Late Republic

Hadrian (hā´-dri-an), Roman emperor 117–138 A.D.

Hannibal (han´-i-bal), Carthaginian general who brought Rome to the brink of defeat in the Second Punic War; defeated at Zama in 202 B.C.; committed suicide in 183 B.C.

Hellenistic, term meaning "Greek-like" and applied to the eastern Mediterranean world following the death of Alexander in 323 B.C.

Herculaneum (her-kū-lā´-nē-um), one of the cities destroyed during the eruption of Mt. Vesuvius on August 24, 79 A.D.

Herod (he´-rod), the Idumaean who was made king of Judaea by Antony and Octavian in 40 B.C.

Hiero (hī´-e-ro), tyrant of Syracuse and ally of Rome during the First Punic War; employed Archimedes' talents to strengthen the defenses of Syracuse

Horace (ho´-rus), Latin poet; friend of Augustus, Maecenas, and Vergil; author of odes and satires

Horatius Cocles (ho-rā´-shus kok´-lēs), traditional hero of Rome who turned back single-handedly an Etruscan assault at the bridge across the Tiber River

Isis (ī´-sis), Egyptian goddess; wife of Osiris and mother of Horus; during the Hellenistic period the cult of Isis spread over the Mediterranean world; Ptolemaic queens, including Cleopatra, often identified with her

Josephus (jō-sē´-fus), born 37/8 A.D., Jewish priest and political leader turned historian, who allied himself with the Flavians and produced *The Jewish War* and *Antiquities of the Jews*

Julia (jūl´-ya), the daughter of Julius Caesar; married to Pompey until she died in childbirth in 54 B.C.

Julia, the daughter of Augustus; wife, successively, of Marcellus, Agrippa, and Tiberius; banished for her adulteries; died in 14 A.D. not long after her father

Julia Domna (dom´-na), empress and wife of Septimius Severus; mother of Caracalla and Geta (above); first Syrian empress; honored as no Augusta before her

Julia Maesa (mā´-sa), sister of Julia Domna; mother of Julia Soaemias and Mamaea (below); exerted major influence on the rule of the Empire

Julia Mamaea (ma-mā´-a), younger daughter of Julia Maesa; mother of Severus Alexander, whom she dominated as emperor; murdered with her son in Germany by the army in 235 A.D.

Julia Soaemias (sō-ām´-i-as), daughter of Julia Maesa; mother of Elagabalus; murdered with her son by Praetorians in 222 A.D.

Juno (jū´-nō), wife of Jupiter; Hera to the Greeks

Jupiter (jū-pi-ter), head of the Roman pantheon; Zeus to the Greeks

Juvenal (jū´-ve-nal), Roman satirist of the early second century A.D.; author of the *Sixteen Satires*

latifundia (la-ti-fun´-di-a), the large agricultural estates of Roman senatorial and equestrian landowners; those in southern Italy and Sicily were largely responsible for spawning major slave revolts in the Late Republic

Latin League, league of Latin cities (including Rome) in Latium defeated by Rome in 338 B.C.: became the foundation of Rome's Italian empire

Latium (lā´-shum), area in west central Italy inhabited by the Latin people; where Rome is located

legate (leg´-it), provincial governor during the Empire; or subordinate of a proconsul (e.g., Septimius Severus in Africa); or commander of a legion

Leptis (or Lepcis) Magna (lep´-tis mag´-na), major city in Tripolitania in Roman Africa; home of Septimius Severus

Livia (li´-vi-a), 58 B.C.–29 A.D., wife and empress of Augustus for over fifty years; mother of Tiberius; began the tradition of powerful imperial women at Rome

Livy (li´-vē), greatest historian of the Roman Republic; during the reign of Augustus, he wrote a history from the beginnings of Rome to almost the end of the first century B.C.

Macedonia (ma-se-dōn´-i-a), geographically, the area to the north of the Greek peninsula; home of Alexander; one of the three great Hellenistic kingdoms; ruled by the Antigonid dynasty

Macrinus (ma-krī´-nus), Praetorian prefect who had Caracalla assassinated; succeeded him and ruled briefly from April 217 to June 218 A.D.

Macro (ma´-krō), helped in the overthrow of Sejanus and succeeded him as Praetorian prefect; grandson-in-law of Thrasyllus (below), court astrologer of Tiberius; he and his wife, Ennia, influenced Caligula but ultimately were forced by him to commit suicide

Maecenas (mi-sēn´-as), diplomat, friend, and literary advisor to Augustus; helped orchestrate the Treaty of Brundisium in 40 B.C.; friend and patron to Vergil, Horace, and other literary luminaries

Marcellus (mar-sel´-us), the "Sword of Rome"; first Roman general to enjoy success against Hannibal in the Second Punic War; directed the siege and capture of Syracuse (213–211 B.C.)

Marcellus, nephew and heir apparent of Augustus; married Julia; died in 23 B.C.

Marcus Aurelius (mar´-kus o-rē´-li-us), last of the five "Good" or "Adopted" emperors; ruled from 161 to 180 A.D.; father of Commodus

Marius (ma´-ri-us), one of Rome's greatest generals; reorganized the army at the end of the second century B.C.; held a record seven consulships; died in 86 B.C. during the civil war with Sulla

Milo (mī´-lo), tribune in 57 B.C.; praetor in 55 B.C.; led the gang of hoodlums and ruffians who opposed Clodius (see above) and his thugs; their antics brought political violence at Rome to a peak during the 50s B.C.; represented the *optimates'* interests

Misenum (mi-sēn´-um), city across the Bay of Naples from Mt. Vesuvius; the major Western naval station; where Pliny the Younger and his mother and uncle were when Vesuvius erupted

Nero (nē´-rō), fifth emperor of Rome and last of the Julio-Claudian Dynasty; ruled from 54 to 68 A.D.; first emperor to persecute the Christians

Nerva (ner´-va), first of the five "Good" or "Adopted" emperors; ruled from 96 to 98 A.D.

Octavia (ok-tā´-vi-a), sister of Octavian; married to Antony 40–32 B.C. and produced two daughters by him; grandmother of Claudius; great-grandmother of Caligula; also mother of her niece Julia's first husband, Marcellus

Octavian, *see* **Augustus**; legal heir of Caesar; member of the "Second Triumvirate" with Antony and Lepidus; completed "Roman Revolution" with defeat of Antony and Cleopatra at Actium; became Rome's first emperor in 27 B.C.

Odoacer (ō-dō-ā´-ser), German who overthrew the last Roman emperor of the West in 476 A.D.

optimates (op-ti-ma´-tās), "the best"; name loosely applied to members of that faction in the Senate during the Later Republic that upheld the old traditional ideas of government and resisted change; conservatives (e.g., Cicero and Cato the Younger)

Ostrogoths (os´-trō-goths), literally "eastern Goths"; Germanic barbarians who settled in Italy in the late fifth century A.D.; Theodoric was their greatest king

Ovid (o´-vid), prominent poet during the time of Augustus, who exiled him to the Black Sea area for life; wrote the *Art of Love,* the *Metamorphoses,* and numerous other poetic works

Palatine (pa´-la-tīn), hill between the Forum and the Circus Maximus where the Imperial Palace was located; site of the earliest settlement of Rome

Papinian (pa-pi´-ni-an), Syrian lawyer who served under Septimius Severus and would later be regarded among the most respected legal minds of antiquity; Praetorian prefect after death of Plautianus (below); executed by Caracalla in 212 A.D.

Parthia (par´-thi-a), kingdom centered in Mesopotamia and Iran on the Eastern borders of the Roman Empire; long-standing foe of Rome; warred with Crassus, Antony, and a number of emperors

patricians (pa-tri´shans), the small, elite privileged class of the early Roman Republic that controlled all important matters; those citizens who were not plebeians

Pertinax (per´-ti-naks), Roman emperor from January to March of 193 A.D.

Pescennius Niger (pe-sen´-i-us nī´-jer), rival of Septimius Severus; raised as emperor by his legions in Syria after the murder of Pertinax (above), he was defeated in battle and later executed in 195 A.D.

Petronius (pe-trō´-ni-us), authored the *Satyricon* during the reign of Nero

Pharsalus (far-sā´-lus), site in northern Greece; Pompey was defeated here by Caesar in 48 B.C.

Philippi (fi-lip´-ī), site in northern Greece; Brutus, Cassius, and their fellow conspirators were defeated here by Antony and Octavian in 42 B.C.

Plautianus (plo-te-a´-nus), fellow African, friend, and Praetorian prefect of Septimius Severus; exerted tremendous influence upon the emperor until his reputed treachery was exposed and he was put to death in 205 B.C.

plebeians (ple-bē´-ans), all Roman citizens who were not patricians; the lower classes

plebiscite (ple´-bi-sīt), decision made in the *concilium plebis* that had the effect of law and was binding on all Romans after 287 B.C.

Pliny the Elder (pli´-nē), uncle of Pliny the Younger (below); author of an extensive *Natural History;* was fleet commander at Misenum when Mt. Vesuvius erupted and perished in the disaster

Pliny the Younger, c. 61–113 A.D., Roman author and governor of Bithynia-Pontus (above); major source for the description of the eruption of Mt. Vesuvius and the treatment of Christians in the second century A.D.

Plutarch (plū´-tark), Greek biographer and moralist of the first–second centuries A.D.; author of the lives of many important Romans

Polybius (po-li´-bi-us), Greek historian of the second century B.C. who chronicled Rome's conquest of the Mediterranean

Pompeii (pom-pā´-yē), one of the cities on the Bay of Naples destroyed by the eruption of Mt. Vesuvius on August 24, 79 A.D.

Pompeius, Sextus, troublesome son of Pompey (below) who, with his fleet, continued to push the Republican cause after his father's death and harass Octavian and Antony; killed by agents of the latter in 36 B.C.

Pompey (pom´-pē), **(Gnaeus Pompeius Magnus),** 106–48 B.C., one of the leading figures of the Late Republic; member of the "First Triumvirate" with Caesar and Crassus; during the civil war with Caesar, he was defeated at Pharsalus in 48 B.C. and later assassinated in Egypt

Pontifex Maximus (pon´-ti-feks mak´-si-mus), the chief priest at Rome; head of the college of pontifices who presided over the state cult

populares (pop-ū-lār´-ās), name loosely applied to members of the faction in the Senate during the Late Republic that believed that change in government was necessary and that change could best be brought about by appealing to the people and supporting the popular cause (e.g., Caesar)

Porcia (pōr´-sha), daughter of Cato the Younger; wife of Brutus

praetor (prē´-tor), next to the consuls, the highest yearly elected magistrate at Rome; oversaw the judiciary system; praetors also were provincial governors and had military duties (see Chart 1)

Praetorian Guard, the emperor's bodyguard, established by Augustus; stationed in and around Rome; the original body may have numbered no more than 4,500; its size varied under different emperors

Princeps (prin´-keps), title adopted by Augustus and his successors, meaning "first citizen"; the Principate gets its name from this position

proconsul, Roman provincial governor, usually of consular rank

Ptolemy (to´-le-mē), general of Alexander; founder of the Hellenistic kingdom of the Ptolemies in Egypt in the fourth century B.C.

Ptolemy XII (Auletes), Cleopatra's father

Ptolemy XIII, Cleopatra's husband-brother with whom she struggled for control of Egypt; defeated by Caesar and drowned in the Nile in 47 B.C.

Pyrrhus (peer´-us), king of Epirus who invaded Italy in 280 B.C. and was driven out in 275 B.C.; Rome's first significant international foe; his defeat allowed Rome to exercise its authority over southern (Greek) Italy

quaestor (kwēs´-tor), first office in the *cursus honorum;* duties were primarily financial (see Chart 1)

Rhodes (rōdz), a large Greek island off the coast of southern Asia Minor; known as an intellectual center in antiquity; refuge of Tiberius where he met the Greek astrologer Thrasyllus (below)

Romulus (rō´-mū-lus), the traditional founder of the city of Rome in 753 B.C.; twin brother of Remus

Rubicon (rū´-bi-kon), river that legally formed the northern border of Roman Italy with Cisalpine Gaul; Caesar crossed the Rubicon in January 49 B.C. to begin the civil war with Pompey

Samnites (sam´-nīts), fierce hill people in south central Italy who warred with Rome in the fourth–third centuries B.C.

Scipio Aemilianus (skip´-i-ō ē-mi-li-a´-nus), adopted grandson of Scipio Africanus (below); destroyed Carthage in 146 B.C.; reduced Numantia in Spain in 133 B.C.; brother-in-law of the Gracchi brothers

Scipio Africanus, brought the Second Punic War to a close with his defeat of Hannibal at Zama in 202 B.C.

Scorpus (skōr´-pus), one of Rome's most famous charioteers; killed in the Circus at the end of the first century A.D. at age twenty-seven

Sejanus (se-jā´-nus), Tiberius' Praetorian prefect, the "partner of his labors" who betrayed him; executed in 31 A.D.

Seleucids (se-lū´-sids), dynastic name of the successors of Alexander's general, Seleucus, who ruled Syria and Mesopotamia during the Hellenistic period

Senate, the guiding body of the Roman Republic (see Chart 1)

senatus consultum ultimum (se-na´-tus con-sul´-tum ul´-ti-mum), the "final decree of the Senate," or formal declaration of a state of emergency by the Roman Senate

Seneca (se´-ne-ka), Stoic philosopher, writer, and tutor to Nero; exerted influence on Nero's administration until his suicide (at Nero's order) in 65 A.D.

Servilia (ser-vil´-i-a), mother of Brutus; mistress of Caesar; half sister of Cato

Severus, Septimius (se-ve´-rus, sep-ti´-mi-us), founder of the Severan Dynasty (193–235 A.D.); emperor from 193 to 211 A.D.; husband of Julia Domna; first emperor from Africa

Sicily, large island at the toe of Italy; colonized by Greeks; became Rome's first province in 241 B.C. as a result of the First Punic War

sophist (so´-fist), teacher who taught for a fee and emphasized rhetoric and oratory

Spartacus (spar´-ta-kus), Thracian gladiator who led a great slave revolt in Italy from 73 to 71 B.C.

Spurinna (spu-ri´-na), distinguished elderly friend of Pliny the Younger who, while in his seventies, held his third and last consulship under Trajan

Stoicism (stō´-i-sizm), Hellenistic philosophy begun by Zeno; Stoics believed that a divine Providence ordered all things and that one should bear one's burden in life without emotion; Stoics also accepted rational suicide (e.g., Cato the Younger)

Suetonius (swē-tō´-ni-us), author of the *Twelve Caesars;* secretary of Hadrian

Sulla (sul´-a), victor in the Roman civil wars of the eighties against Marius (d. 86 B.C.) and his supporters; ambitious and self-serving, Sulla was also a staunch conservative, and, as dictator, he reaffirmed the Senate's control of the Republican government; he effectively curbed progress made by the popular movement and eliminated most of its leadership; in 79 B.C., he resigned (and died in 78 B.C.), but his example of what could be achieved through force practically guaranteed future political upheaval and doomed the Republic

Syracuse, in Sicily; greatest city in the Greek West; Archimedes' weapons defended it during the Roman siege (213–211 B.C.)

Tacitus (ta´-si-tus), greatest historian of the Early Empire; wrote the *Annals* and *Histories;* consul under Domitian; friend of Pliny the Younger

Tertullian (ter-tul´-i-an), influential Christian writer from North Africa; active largely during the Severan Dynasty

Tetrarchy (tet´-rar-kē), system of four rulers devised by Diocletian to maintain order and control of the Roman Empire

Theodoric (thē-od´-ō-rik) "the Great," king of the Ostrogoths in Italy from 493 to 526 A.D.

Theodosius (the-o-dō´-si-us), orthodox Christian and last great emperor of the entire Roman Empire; ruled from 379 to 395 A.D.; closed the final door on paganism

Thrasyllus (thra-si´-lus), Greek court astrologer and lifelong friend of Tiberius

Tiber (tī´-ber), river in west central Italy on whose banks Rome was founded

Tiberius (tī-bē´-ri-us), son of Livia; succeeded his stepfather Augustus to become Rome's second emperor; ruled 14–37 A.D.

Tigellinus (ti-jel-ī´-nus), Nero's notorious Praetorian prefect; he gained influence with the emperor during the latter part of his reign, encouraging his excesses; outlived Nero but was forced to commit suicide by Otho in 69 A.D.

Titus (tī´-tus), son of Vespasian; captured Jerusalem in 70 A.D. and brought the Jewish War to an end; emperor from 79 to 81 A.D.; Mt. Vesuvius erupted during his reign

Trajan (trā´-jan), Roman emperor from 98 to 117 A.D.; first non-Italian emperor; expanded Empire to its greatest geographical limits

Tribal assembly, the more democratic of the two Republican assemblies in which all adult male citizens participated; elective and legislative functions; often identified with the *concilium plebis* (see Chart 1)

tribunes, officers of the plebeians (see Chart 1)

Triumvirate (First), extralegal coalition of Crassus, Pompey, and Caesar formed in 60 B.C. in an attempt to control Roman politics

Triumvirate (Second), legal coalition of Antony, Octavian, and Lepidus formed in 43 B.C. to control Roman politics

Veii (vē´-yē), nearby Etruscan city with which Rome warred until its defeat by Camillus in 396 B.C.

Venus, Roman goddess of love; mother of Aeneas; family of Julius Caesar and Augustus (Julians) traced its origin to her through Aeneas' son Iulus or Julus

Vergil (vur´-jil), epic poet; author of the *Aeneid* during the reign of Augustus; friend of Maecenas and Horace; died in 19 B.C.; also wrote the *Eclogues* and *Georgics*

Verginius Rufus (ver-ji´-ni-us rū´-fus), consul, statesman, and elderly friend of Pliny the Younger, who mentioned him in his *Letters*

Vespasian (ves-pa´-shan), Roman emperor from 69 to 79 A.D.; founder of the Flavian Dynasty (69–96 A.D.)

Vesuvius (ve-sū´-vi-us), volcano on the Bay of Naples whose eruption on August 24, 79 A.D. destroyed Pompeii and Herculaneum

Vibia Perpetua (vi´-bi-a per-pe´-tu-a), a young Christian woman who was martyred at Carthage during the reign of Septimius Severus

York (Eburacum), Roman administrative headquarters in Britain near the Scottish frontier; Septimius Severus died here in 211 A.D.

Zama (zā´-ma), site of Hannibal's defeat in North Africa by Scipio Africanus in 202 B.C.

Acknowledgments

Chapter 1

Translations in this chapter are by I. Scott-Kilvert, Polybius, *Histories* 1.1.5, in *The Rise of the Roman Empire*, Penguin Classics (London, 1979). Copyright © 1979 by I. Scott-Kilvert. All rights reserved. With permission from the publisher; R. Lattimore, Claudia Inscriptions (*Inscriptiones Latinae Liberae Rei Publicae 973* and *Inscriptiones Latinae Selectae 8403*), No. 134 in M.R. Lefkowitz and M.B. Fant, *Women's Life in Greece & Rome*, The Johns Hopkins University Press (Baltimore, 1982). Reprinted by permission of The Johns Hopkins University and Gerald Duckworth; J. Wilkes, "Soldier's Letter" (*Berliner Griechische Urkunden [Ägyptische Urkunden aus den Königlichen Museen zu Berlin* 13.15.1]), in *The Roman Army*, Cambridge University Press (New York, 1972). With permission from the publisher; S. Levin, Aelius Aris-tides, *To Rome* 11–13 and Pliny, *Natural History* 3.5.66–67, 222, No. 54, from *Roman Civilization* by N. Lewis and M. Reinhold. Copyright © 1990 Columbia University Press. Reprinted by permission of the publisher; J.E. Stambaugh, Cicero, *Contra Rullum, De Lege Agraria*, 2.96 and Livy, *History of Rome* 40.4.7 in *the Ancient City of Rome*, The Johns Hopkins University Press (Baltimore, 1988). Reprinted by permission of The Johns Hopkins University; R. Humphries, Juvenal, *The Satires*, Indiana University Press (Bloomington, 1958). With permission from the publisher; C. Stace, Plautus, *Rudens Curculio, Casina*, 4.1, Cambridge University Press (New York, 1981). With permission from the publisher; Reprinted by permission of the publishers and the Loeb Classical Library from Seneca, *Epistles*, Vol. IV, translated by R.M. Gummere, Cambridge, Mass., Harvard University Press, 1917; B. Radice, Pliny, *The Letters of the Younger Pliny*, 8.17,

Penguin Classics (London, 1969). Copyright © 1969 by B. Radice. All rights reserved; Reprinted by permission of the publishers and the Loeb Classical Library from Livy, *History of Rome,* Vol. V, translated by B. O. Foster, Cambridge, Mass., Harvard University Press, 1953; I. Scott-Kilvert, Polybius, Histories 6.55, in *The Rise of the Roman Empire*, Penguin Classics (London, 1979). Copyright © 1979 by I. Scott-Kilvert. All rights reserved. With permission from the publisher; A. de Sélincourt, *The Early History of Rome*, Penguin Classics (London, 1960). Copyright © 1960 by A. de Sélincourt. With permission from the publisher; A. de Sélincourt, Livy, *The War with Hannibal*, Penguin Classics (London, 1965). Copyright © 1965 by the Estate of A. de Sélincourt; Used with permission; J.E. Stambaugh, Livy, *History of Rome*, 21.4.3–10 in *The Ancient City of Rome*, The Johns Hopkins University Press (Baltimore, 1988). Reprinted by permission of The Johns Hopkins University; Reprinted by permission of the publishers and the Loeb Classical Library from Cornelius Nepos, *Hannibal*, translated by J.C. Rolfe, Cambridge, Mass., Harvard University Press, 1929; S.V. Spryidakis and B.P. Nystrom, Plutarch, *Marcellus* 14–19 in *Ancient Greece, Documentary Perspectives*, Kendall-Hunt (Dubuque, 1985); I. Scott-Kilvert, Polybius, *Histories* 1.1.5, 6.53–54 in *The Rise of the Roman Empire*, Penguin Classics (London, 1979). Copyright © 1979 by I. Scott-Kilvert. All rights reserved. With permission from the publisher; Reprinted by permission of the publishers and the Loeb Classical Library *from* Diodorus Siculus*, Library of History*, Vol. XI, translated by Francis R. Walton, Cambridge, Mass., Harvard University Press, 1957; Reprinted by permission of the publishers and the Loeb Classical Library from Cicero, *Tusculan*

Disputations, Vol. XVIII, translated by J.E. King, Cambridge, Mass., Harvard University Press, 1945.

Chapter 2

Translations in this chapter are by A. de Sélincourt, Livy, *The War with Hannibal,* Penguin Classics (London, 1965). Copyright © 1965 by the Estate of A. de Sélincourt. With permission from the publisher; A.de Sélincourt, Livy, *The Early History of Rome* 3.16.3, Penguin Classics (Baltimore, 1960). Copyright © 1960 by A. de Sélincourt; Reprinted by permission of the publishers and the Loeb Classical Library from Plutarch, *The Parallel Lives,* Vol. X, translated by B. Perrin, Cambridge, Mass., Harvard University Press, 1921. (*Tiberius and Gaius*); Reprinted by permission of the publishers and the Loeb Classical Library from Diodorus Siculus, *Library of History,* Vol. XII, translated by Francis R. Walton, General Index by Russel M. Geer, Cambridge, Mass., Harvard University Press, 1967; B. Radice, Pliny, *The Letters of the Younger Pliny,* 3.14, Penguin Classics (London, 1969). Copyright © 1969 by B. Radice. All rights reserved. With permission from the publisher; R. Warner, Plutarch, *Crassus* 8.1–11.7, in *Fall of the Roman Republic,* Penguin Classics (London, 1958). Copyright © 1958 by R. Warner.With permission from the publisher.

Chapter 3

Translations in this chapter are by I. Scott-Kilvert, Plutarch, *Brutus and Antony,* in *Makers of Rome,* Penguin Classics (London, 1965). Copyright © 1965 by I. Scott-Kilvert. With permission from the publisher; Reprinted by permission of the publishers and the Loeb Classical Library from Appian, *Roman History,* Vol. III, translated by Horace White, Cambridge, Mass., Harvard University Press, 1913; D.R. Shackleton Bailey, Cicero, *Cicero's Letters to His Friends,* Vols. 1 and 2, Penguin Classics (London, 1978). Copyright © 1978 by D. R. Shackleton Bailey. Letters 9.9, 11.1; M.L. Clarke, Plutarch, *Brutus,* in *The Noblest Roman,* Cornell University Press (Ithaca, 1981). Copyright © 1981 by Thames and Hudson Ltd. Used with permission; D.R. Shackleton Bailey, Cicero, *Cicero's Letters to Atticus,* Penguin Classics (London, 1978). Copyright © 1978 by D. R. Shackleton. Used with permission; R. Warner, Plutarch, *Caesar,* in *Fall of the Roman Republic,* Penguin Classics (London, 1958). Copyright © 1958 by R. Warner. With permission from the publisher; S.A. Handford, Caesar, *The Conquest of Gaul,*

Penguin Classics (London, 1982). Copyright © 1951 by the Estate of S.A. Handford. Introduction and revisions copyright © 1982 Jane F. Gardner. All rights reserved. Used with permission.

Chapter 4

Translations in this chapter are by I. Scott-Kilvert, Plutarch, *Brutus and Antony,* in *Makers of Rome,* Penguin Classics (London, 1965). Copyright © 1965 by I. Scott-Kilvert ; R. Warner, Plutarch, *Caesar,* in *Fall of the Roman Republic,* Penguin Classics (London, 1958). Copyright © 1958 by R. Warner; S.A. Handford, Caesar, *The Conquest of Gaul,* 49.12. Penguin Classics (London, 1982). Copyright © 1951 by the Estate of S.A. Handford. Introduction and revisions copyright © 1982 Jane F. Gardner. All rights reserved. Used with permission; D.R. Shackleton Bailey, Cicero, *Cicero's Letters to Atticus,* Penguin Classics (London, 1978). Copyright © 1978 by D. R. Shackleton. With permission from the publisher; Reprinted by permission of the publishers and the Loeb Classical Library from Dio Cassius, *Roman History,* Vol. V, translated by Earnest Cary, Cambridge, Mass., Harvard University Press, 1917; Reprinted by permission of the publishers and the Loeb Classical Library from Appian, *Roman History,* Vol. III, translated by Horace White, Cambridge, Mass., Harvard University Press, 1913; Horace, *Satires* 1.5.1–33, 37–51, 79–97, 104, No. 323 and the Turia Inscription (CIL 6.1527, 31670 [ILS 8393]), No. 288 from *As the Romans Did, A Source Book in Roman Social History, Second Edition* by Jo-Ann R. Shelton. Copyright © 1988, 1998 by Oxford University Press. Used by permission of Oxford University Press, Inc.; Reprinted by permission of the publishers and the Loeb Classical Library from Florus, *Epitome of Roman History,* translated by E.S. Forster, Cambridge, Mass., Harvard University Press, 1929.

Chapter 5

Translations in this chapter are reprinted by permission of the publishers and the Loeb Classical Library from Cicero, *Philosophical Treatises,* Vol. XX, translated by W.A. Falconer, Cambridge, Mass., Harvard University Press, 1923. (*On Divination* 1.2); P. Green, Juvenal, *The Sixteen Satires* 6.553–564, Penguin Classics (London, 1967). Copyright © 1967 by P. Green. Used with permission; Tacitus, *The Annals of Imperial Rome,* translated by Michael Grant (Penguin Classics, 1956, sixth revised edition 1989). Copyright © 1956, 1959, 1971, 1973, 1975, 1977, 1989 Michael Grant Publications, Ltd.; R. MacMullen, Firmicus Maternus, *Mathesis* 2.30.3–4 in *Enemies of the Roman Order*, Harvard University Press (Cambridge, Mass., 1966), 132. With permission from the publisher; J.P. Sullivan, Petronius, *The Satyricon*, Penguin Classics (London, 1977). Copyright © 1977 by J.P. Sullivan. All rights reserved. With permission from the publisher; Reprinted by permission of the publishers and the Loeb Classical Library from Josephus, *Jewish Antiquities,* Vol. XII, translated by L.H. Feldman, Cambridge, Mass., Harvard University Press, 1965; P. V. Davies, Macrobius, *The Saturnalia*, Columbia University Press (New York, 1969). With permission from the publisher; Reprinted by permission of the publishers and the Loeb Classical Library from St. Augustine, *The City of God*, Vol. II, translated by W.M. Green, Cambridge, Mass., Harvard University Press, 1963. (5.1); Reprinted by permission of the publishers and the Loeb Classical Library from *Papyri*, Vol. I, translated by A.S. Hunt and C.C. Edgar, Cambridge, Mass., Harvard University Press, 1932. (No. 199).

Chapter 6

Translations in this chapter are by B. Radice, Pliny, *The Letters of the Younger Pliny*, Penguin Classics (London, 1969). Copyright © 1969 by B. Radice. All rights reserved. With permission from the publisher; Tacitus, *The Annals of Imperial Rome,* translated by Michael Grant (Penguin Classics, © 1956, sixth revised edition 1989). Copyright (1956, 1959, 1971, 1973, 1975, 1977, 1989 Michael Grant Publications, Ltd. (1.61—62, 15.38–41, 2.47); B. Flower and E. Rosenbaum, Apicius, *The Roman Cookery Book*, Harrap (London, 1974). With permission from the publisher; Various Inscriptions from *Roman Civilization* by N. Lewis and M. Reinhold. Copyright © 1990 Columbia University Press. Reprinted by permission of the publisher; M. Grant, *Cities of Vesuvius, Pompeii and Herculaneum*. Copyright © 1971 Weidenfeld and Nicholson. With permission from the publisher; J.C. Fant in M.K. Lefkowitz and M.B. Fant, *Women's Life in Greece & Rome*, No. 210, p. 213, The Johns Hopkins University Press (Baltimore, 1982). Reprinted by permission of The Johns Hopkins University and Gerald Duckworth; Joseph Jay Deiss, *Herculaneum, Italy's Buried Treasure*, pp. 98–100. Copyright © 1966, 1985 by Joseph Jay Deiss. Copyright renewed 1994 by Joseph Jay Deiss. Reprinted by permission of HarperCollins Publishers, Inc.; J. Lindsay, *The Writing on the Wall,* Frederick Muller (London, 1960); Josephus, *The Jewish War,* translated by G.A. Williamson, revised by E. Mary Smallwood (Penguin Classics 1959, revised edition 1981). Copyright © 1959, 1969 G.A. Williamson. Reprinted by permission of Penguin Books, Ltd.; Pliny Describes His Villa from *As the Romans Did, A Source Book in Roman Social History, Second Edition* by Jo-Ann R. Shelton. Copyright © 1988, 1998 by Oxford University Press. Used by permission of Oxford University Press, Inc.; Reprinted by permission of the publishers and the Loeb Classical Library from Martial, *Epigrams,* Vol. I, translated by W.C.A. Ker, Cambridge, Mass., Harvard University Press, 1943.

Chapter 7

Translations in this chapter are by B. Radice, Pliny, *The Letters of the Younger Pliny*, Penguin Classics (London, 1969). Copyright © 1969 by B. Radice. All rights reserved. Used with permission from the publisher; Claudia, Letters from *Women in the Classical World, Image and Text* by Elaine Fantham et al. Copyright © 1995 by Elaine Fantham, Helene Peet Foley, Natalie Boymel Kampen, Sarah B. Pomeroy, and H.A. Shapiro. Used by permission of Oxford University Press, Inc.; L. Casson, Lucian, "A Voyage to the Underworld" in *Selected Satires of Lucian*, The Norton Library (New York, 1968). Copyright © 1962 by L. Casson. All rights reserved; P. Green, Juvenal, *The Sixteen Satires* 10.188–247, Penguin Classics (Baltimore, 1967). Copyright © 1967 by P. Green; M.R. Lefkowitz, Epigraphica II in *Women's Life in Greece & Rome*, The Johns Hopkins University Press (Baltimore, 1982). Copyright © 1982 by M.B. Fant and M.R. Lefkowitz. All rights reserved. Reprinted by permission of The Johns Hopkins University Press and Gerald Duckworth; Lucian, *The Baths*, 5–8, 315, No. 309 from *As the Romans Did, A Source Book in Roman Social History, Second Edition* by Jo-Ann R. Shelton. Copyright © 1988, 1998 by Oxford University Press. Used by permission of Oxford University Press.

Chapter 8

Translations in this chapter are from Herodian, *History of the Empire*, Vol. 1, translated by C.R. Whittaker, Cambridge, Mass., Harvard University Press, 1969. With permission from the publisher and the Loeb

Classical Library; Reprinted by permission of the publisher and the Loeb Classical Library from Dio Cassius, *Roman History,* Vol. IX, translated by Earnest Cary, Cambridge, Mass., Harvard University Press, 1927; Reprinted by permission of the publisher and the Loeb Classical Library from *Papyri,* Vol. I, translated by A.S. Hunt and C.C. Edgar, Cambridge, Mass., Harvard University Press, 1932. (Student Letter, #133); Reprinted by permission of the publisher and the Loeb Classical Library from *Scriptores Historiae Augustae,* Vol. III, translated by D. Magie, Cambridge, Mass., Harvard University Press, 1932.

Chapter 9

Translations in this chapter are from B. Radice, Pliny, *The Letters of the Younger Pliny* 10.96, 10.97, Penguin Classics (London, 1969). Copyright © 1969 by B. Radice. All rights reserved. With permission from the publisher; Tacitus, *The Annals of Imperial Rome,* translated by Michael Grant (Penguin Classics, 1956, sixth revised edition 1989). Copyright © 1956, 1959, 1971, 1973, 1975, 1977, 1989 Michael Grant Publi-cations, Ltd. (15.44); R. Graves, Suetonius, *The Twelve Caesars* (revised with an Introduction by M. Grant), Penguin Classics (London, 1979). Copyright © 1957 by R. Graves, copyright © 1979 by M. Grant Publications Ltd. All rights reserved. With permission from the publisher; Tacitus, *The Annals of Imperial Rome,* translated by Michael Grant (Penguin Classics, 1956, sixth revised edition 1989, pp. 313–317). Copyright © 1956, 1959, 1971, 1973, 1975, 1977, 1989 Michael Grant Publications, Ltd.; Aulus Gellius, *Attic Nights,* 12.1–3, 5, 9, 387–388, No. 379; from *As the Romans Did, A Source Book in Roman Social History, Second Edition* by Jo-Ann R. Shelton. Copyright © 1988, 1998 by Oxford University Press. Used by permission of Oxford University Press, Inc.; Dionysius of Halicarnassus, *Roman Antiquities* 2.67, 388, No. 380 from *As the Romans Did, A Source Book in Roman Social History, Second Edition* by Jo-Ann R. Shelton. Copyright © 1988, 1998 by Oxford University Press. Used by permission of Oxford University Press, Inc.; Reprinted by permission of the publishers and the Loeb Classical Library from Plutarch, *The Parallel Lives,* Vol. I, translated by B. Perrin, Cambridge, Mass., Harvard University Press, 1914. (*Numa*); Tertullian, *Apology,* 2.7–9, 416, No. 400, Seneca, *Letters* 7.2–5, 348–349, Cicero, *Letters to His Friends,* 2.11, 348, No. 343 from *As the Romans Did, A Source*

Book in Roman Social History, Second Edition by Jo-Ann R. Shelton. Copyright © 1988, 1998 by Oxford University Press. Used by permission of Oxford University Press, Inc.; Fronto, *Letters* 4.5, 324, No. 322, Minucius Felix, Octavius 417–418, No. 401 from *As the Romans Did, A Source Book in Roman Social History, Second Edition* by Jo-Ann R. Shelton. Copyright © 1988, 1998 by Oxford University Press. Used by permission of Oxford University Press, Inc.; H. Musurillo, Vibia Perpetua in "The Martyrdom of Perpetua and Felicitas" in *The Acts of The Christian Martyrs,* The Clarendon Press (Oxford, 1972). With permission from Oxford University Press; The Divorce of Zois and Antipater, *Select Papyri* 6 [BGU 1103] 50, N. 61 from *As the Romans Did, A Source Book in Roman Social History, Second Edition* by Jo-Ann R. Shelton. Copyright © 1988, 1998 by Oxford University Press. Used by permission of Oxford University Press, Inc.

Chapter 10

Translations in this chapter are by P. Green, Juvenal, *The Sixteen Satires,* Penguin Classics (London, 1967). Copyright © 1967 by P. Green. With permission from the publisher; B. Radice, Pliny, *The Letters of the Younger Pliny* 9.6, Penguin Classics (London, 1969). Copyright © 1969 by B. Radice. All rights reserved. With permission from the publisher; Reprinted by permission of the publishers and the Loeb Classical Library from Dio Cassius, *Roman History,* Vol. IX, translated by Earnest Cary, Cambridge, Mass., Harvard University Press, 1927; Ovid, *Amores* 3.2 from *As the Romans Did, A Source Book in Roman Social History, Second Edition* by Jo-Ann R. Shelton. Copyright © 1988, 1998 by Oxford University Press. Used by permission of Oxford University Press, Inc.; Reprinted by permission of the publishers and the Loeb Classical Library from Josephus, *Jewish Anti-uities,* Vol. XII, translated by L.H. Feldman, with alterations by A. Cameron (*Circus Factions* [Oxford, 1976], 162–163), Cambridge, Mass., Harvard University Press, 1965; Fronto, *Elements of History,* from *Roman Civilization* by N. Lewis and M. Reinhold, 229–230. Copyright © 1990 Columbia University Press. Reprinted by permission of the publisher; Inscriptions, Graecae ad Res Romanas Pertinetes, Vol. 1, No. 117, No 169, 570, from *Roman Civilization* by N. Lewis and M. Reinhold. Copyright © 1990 Columbia University Press. Reprinted by permission of the publisher;

Reprinted by permission of the publishers and the Loeb Classical Library from Dio Cassius, *Roman History,* Vol. IX, translated by Earnest Cary, Cambridge, Mass., Harvard University Press, 1927; Reprinted by permission of the publishers and the Loeb Classical Library from Ammianus Marcellinus, *Excerpta Valesiana,* Vol. III, translated by J.C. Rolfe, Cambridge, Mass., Harvard University Press, 1939; Reprinted by permission of the publishers and the Loeb Classical Library from Sidonius, *Poems and Letters,* Vol. I, translated by W.B. Anderson, Cambridge, Mass., Harvard University Press, 1936; H.A. Harris, Martial, *Epigrams* 10.50, 10.53, *Sport in Greece and Rome,* 209–210, 212, 230–231, (Ithaca: Cornell University Press, 1972). Copyright © 1972 Thames and Hudson. All rights reserved. With permission from Cornell University Press; Pliny, *Natural History* 28.237, *Sport in Greece and Rome,* 209–210, 212, 230–231, (Ithaca: Cornell University Press, 1972). Copyright © 1972 Thames and Hudson. All rights reserved. With permission from Cornell University Press; Corpus Inscriptonum Latinarum 6.10082, *Sport in Greece and Rome,* 209–210, 212, 230–231, (Ithaca: Cornell University Press, 1972). Copyright © 1972 Thames and Hudson. All rights reserved. With permission from Cornell University Press; Cassiodorus, *Variae,* 3.51 all from *Sport in Greece and Rome,* 209–210, 212, 230–231 (Ithaca, Cornell University Press, 1972), © 1972 Thames and Hudson. All rights reserved; Reprinted by permission of the publishers and the Loeb Classical Library from Tacitus, *Histories,* Vol. II, translated by Clifford H. Moore, Cambridge, Mass., Harvard University Press, 1925.

Illustration Credits

Figures

Chapter opening coin: Karen A. Peters; courtesy of Harlan J. Berk, Ltd.

1.1	Museo della Civilitá Romana, Rome.
1.2	Museo della Civilitá Romana, Rome.
1.3	Photo by author.
1.4	Photo by author.
1.5	Photo by author.
1.6	Photo by author.
1.7	Photo by author.
1.8	Photo by author.
1.9	Staatliche Museum, Berlin.
1.10	Photo by author.
1.11	Photo by author.
1.12	Photo by author.
1.13	From J. G. Landels, *Engineering in the Ancient World* (Berkeley and Los Angeles: University of California Press, 1981). Copyright © 1978 J. G. Landels.
2.1	Soprintendenza Archeologica delle Province de Napoli e Caserta.
2.2	Musée du Petit Palais, Paris.
2.3	Rheinisches Landesmuseum Trier.
2.4	Rheinisches Landesmuseum Trier.
2.5	Paul Zahl, National Geographic Society.
2.6	Photo by author.
3.1	Museo del Prado, Madrid.
3.2	Vatican Museum, Rome.
3.3	Musée Archeologique, Rabat.
3.4	The NY Carlsberg Glypotek, Copenhagen.
3.5	Photo by author.
3.6	The Montreal Museum of Fine Arts.
3.7	Karen A. Peters; courtesy of Harlan J. Berk, Ltd.
3.8	Photo by author.
3.9	Photo by author.

3.10	Photo by author.
3.11	Photo by author.
3.12	Photo by author.
4.1	Photo by author.
4.2	Copyright © The British Museum.
4.3	Deutsches Archaeologisches Institut, Rome.
4.4	Photo by author.
4.5	Deutsches Archaeologisches Institut, Rome.
4.6	Staatliche Museum, Berlin.
4.7	Copyright © The British Museum.
4.8	Photo by author.
5.1	Photo by author.
5.2	Photo by author.
5.3	Photo by author.
5.4	Photo by author.
5.5	Michael F. Miller
5.6	Judith J. Kebric
5.7	The NY Carlsberg Glypotek, Copenhagen.
5.8	Photo by author.
5.9	Photo by author.
5.10	Capitoline Museum, Rome.
5.11	Photo by author.
6.1	Photo by author.
6.2	Photo by author.
6.3	Photo by author.
6.4	Photo by author.
6.5	Photo by author.
6.6	Photo by author.
6.7	Photo by author.
6.8	Photo by author.
6.9	Photo by author.
6.10	Photo by author.
6.11	Photo by author.
6.12	Photo by author.
6.13	Photo by author.

6.14   Photo by author.
6.15   Photo by author.
6.16   Photo by author.
6.17a   Photo by author.
6.17b   Photo by author.
6.18   From J. Shelton, *As the Romans Did: A Sourcebook in Roman Social History* (New York: Oxford University Press, second edition, 1988).
7.1   Photo by author.
7.2   Photo by author.
7.3   Photo by author.
7.4   Museo Nazionale, Naples.
7.5   Vatican Museum, Rome.
7.6   Deutsches Archaeologisches Institut, Rome.
7.7   Museo Nazionale, Naples.
7.8   Photo by author.
7.9   Photo by author.
7.10   Photo by author.
7.11   Photo by author.
7.12   Photo by author.
7.13   Photo by author.
7.14   Photo by author.
7.15   Photo by author.
7.16   Photo by author.
7.17   Photo by author.
8.1   Photo by author.
8.2   Photo by author.
8.3   Photo by author.
8.4   Musée du Louvre, Paris.
8.5   Dennis Korbylo (author's collection).
8.6   Photo by author.
8.7   Photo by author.
8.8   Photo by author.
8.9   Photo by author.
8.10   Photo by author.
8.11   Photo by author.
8.12   Dennis Korbylo (author's collection).
8.13   Deutsches Archaeologisches Institut, Rome.
8.14   Copyright © The British Museum.
8.15   Photo by author.
8.16   Leonard Von Matt.
9.1   Photo by author.
9.2   Photo by author.
9.3   Photo by author.
9.4   Photo by author.
9.5   Scavi Archeologici de S. Pietro, Vatican.
9.6   O. Louis Mazzatenta, National Geographic Society.

9.7   Museo Nazionale, Rome.
9.8   Leonard Von Matt.
9.9   Photo by author.
9.10   Instituto Suore Benedettine de Priscilla, Rome.
9.11   Photo by author.
9.12   Photo by author.
9.13   Photo by author.
9.14   Photo by author.
9.15   Photo by author.
10.1   From L. B. Dal Maso, *Rome of the Caesars* (Florence: Bonechi-Edizioni, "Il Turismo," 1984, reprint).
10.2   Photo by author.
10.3   From J. Humphrey, *Roman Circuses and Arenas for Chariot Racing* (Berkeley and Los Angeles: University of California Press, 1985). Copyright © 1985 John H. Humphrey.
10.4   From J. Humphrey, *Roman Circuses and Arenas for Chariot Racing* (Berkeley and Los Angeles: University of California Press, 1985). Copyright © 1985 John H. Humphrey.
10.5   From J. Humphrey, *Roman Circuses and Arenas for Chariot Racing* (Berkeley and Los Angeles: University of California Press, 1985). Copyright © 1985 John H. Humphrey.
10.6   The Egypt Exploration Society
10.7   From J. Humphrey, *Roman Circuses and Arenas for Chariot Racing* (Berkeley and Los Angeles: University of California Press, 1985). Copyright © 1985 John H. Humphrey.
10.8   Vatican Museum, Rome.
10.9a   Photo by author.
10.9b   Photo by author.
10.10   Superintendancy of Galleries, Urbino: J. C. M. Toynbee and the British School at Rome.
10.11   Photo by author.
10.12   Photo by author.
10.13   Photo by author.
E.1   Photo by author.
E.2   Photo by author.
E.3   Photo by author.
E.4   Photo by author.
E.5   Photo by author.

Maps

18   From J. J. Deiss, *Herculaneum,* rev. ed. (New York: Harper & Row, Publishers), 1985, 17. Copyright © 1985, 1966 Joseph Jay Deiss.

All other maps are by Martha Gilman Roach.

Index